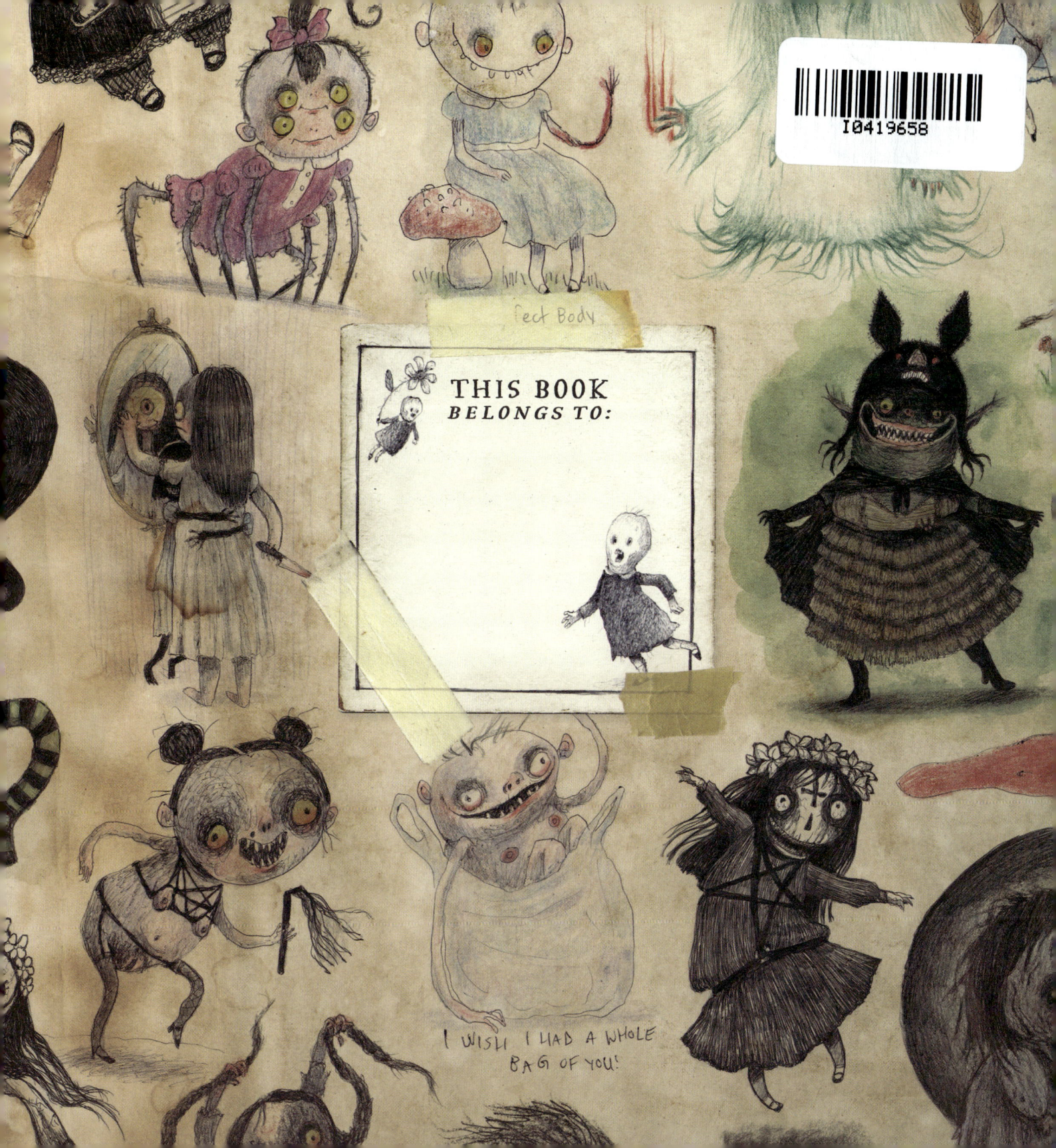

THIS BOOK
BELONGS TO:

fect Body

I WISH I HAD A WHOLE
BAG OF YOU!

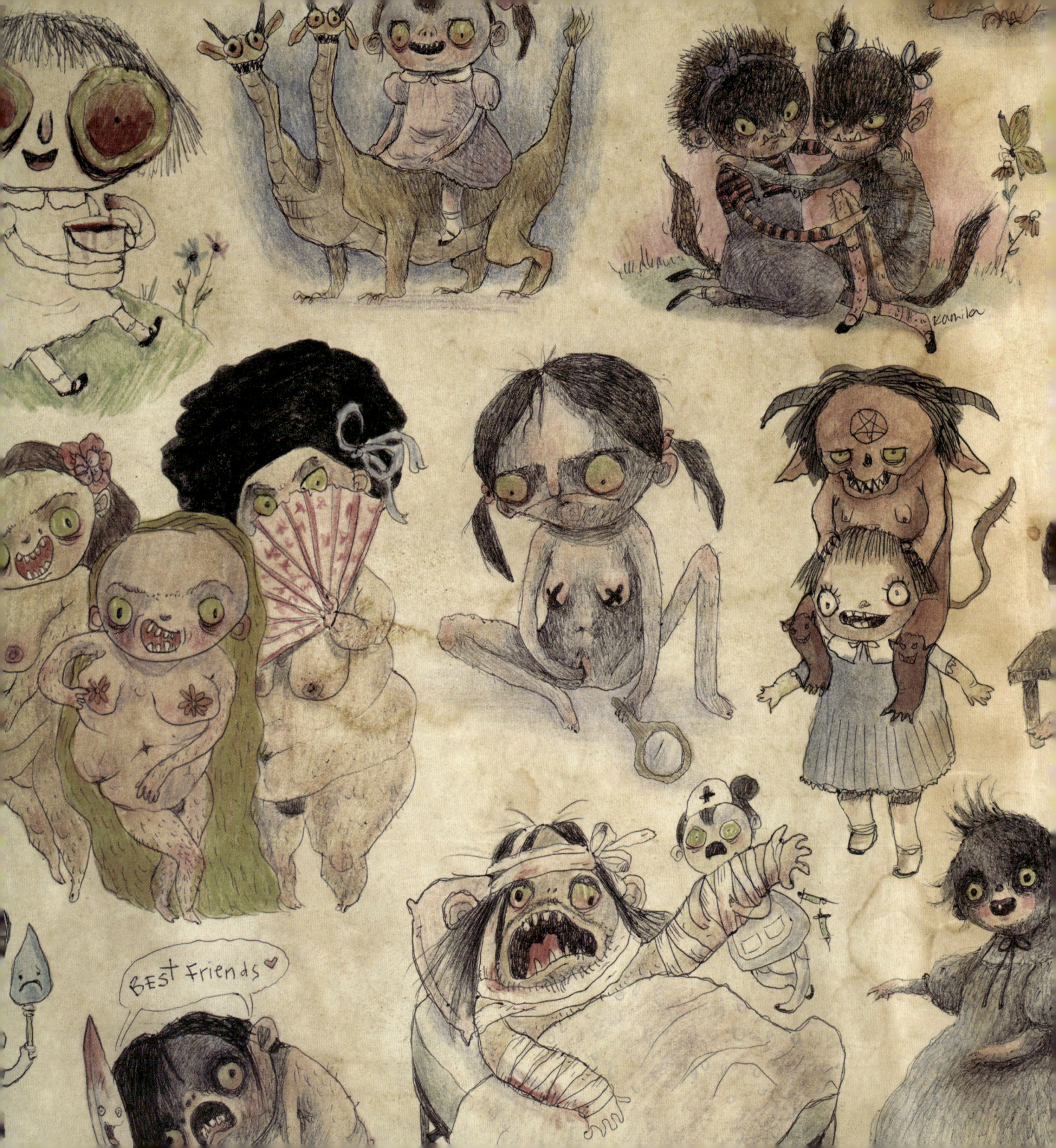

Best Friends ♥

I CAN BE MYSELF WHEN EVERYONE I KNOW IS DEAD...

The delightfully dreadful art of
KAMILA MLYNARCZYK

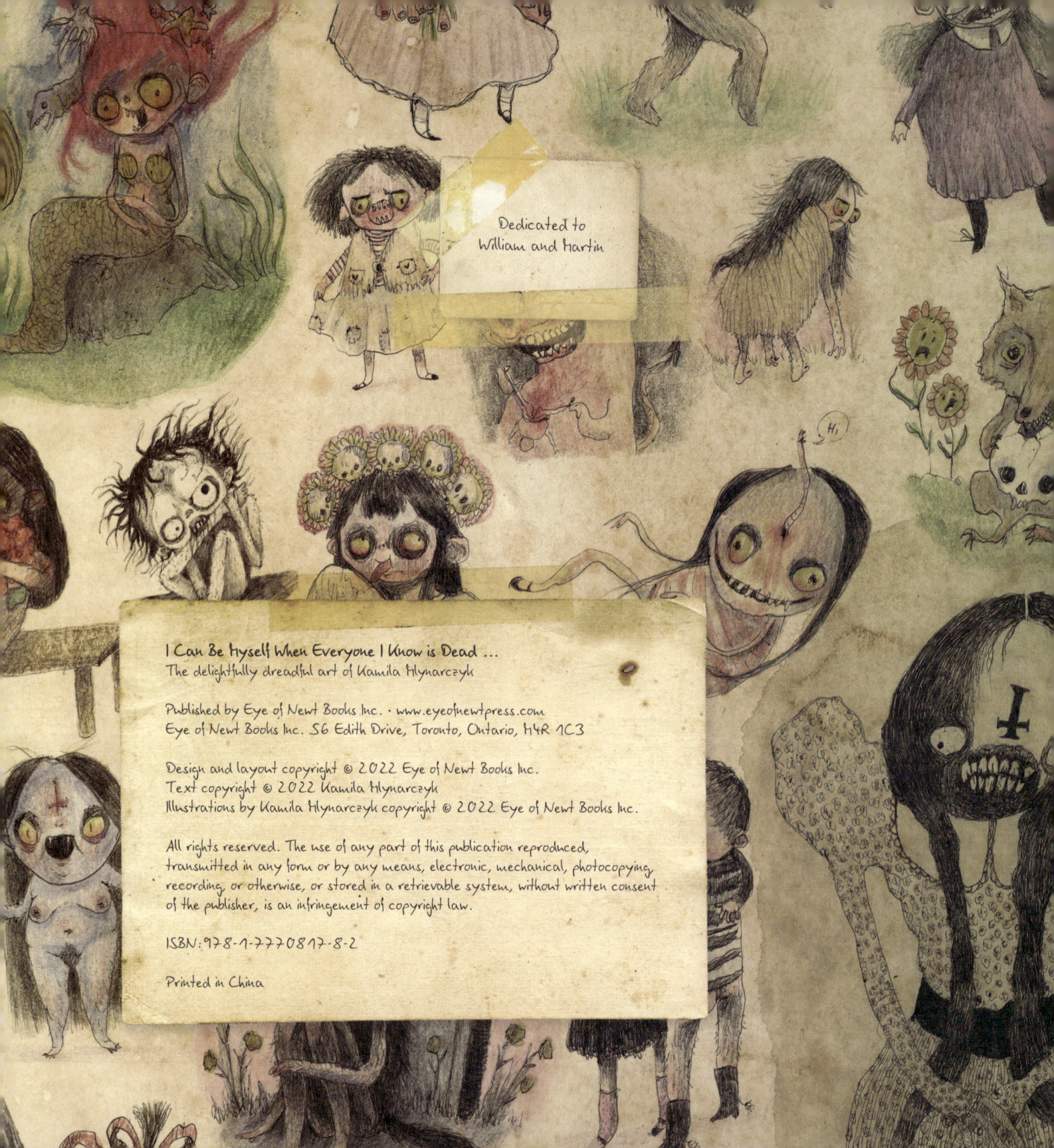

Dedicated to
William and Martin

I Can Be Myself When Everyone I Know is Dead ...
The delightfully dreadful art of Kamila Hlynarczyk

Published by Eye of Newt Books Inc. · www.eyeofnewtpress.com
Eye of Newt Books Inc. 56 Edith Drive, Toronto, Ontario, M4R 1C3

Design and layout copyright © 2022 Eye of Newt Books Inc.
Text copyright © 2022 Kamila Hlynarczyk
Illustrations by Kamila Hlynarczyk copyright © 2022 Eye of Newt Books Inc.

ISBN: 978-1-7770817-8-2

Printed in China

I CAN BE MYSELF WHEN EVERYONE I KNOW IS DEAD...

The delightfully dreadful art of
KAMILA MLYNARCZYK

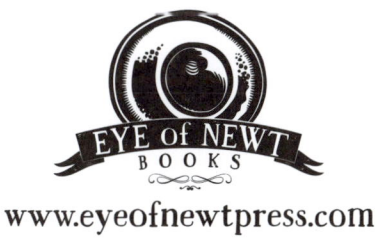

EYE of NEWT
BOOKS

www.eyeofnewtpress.com

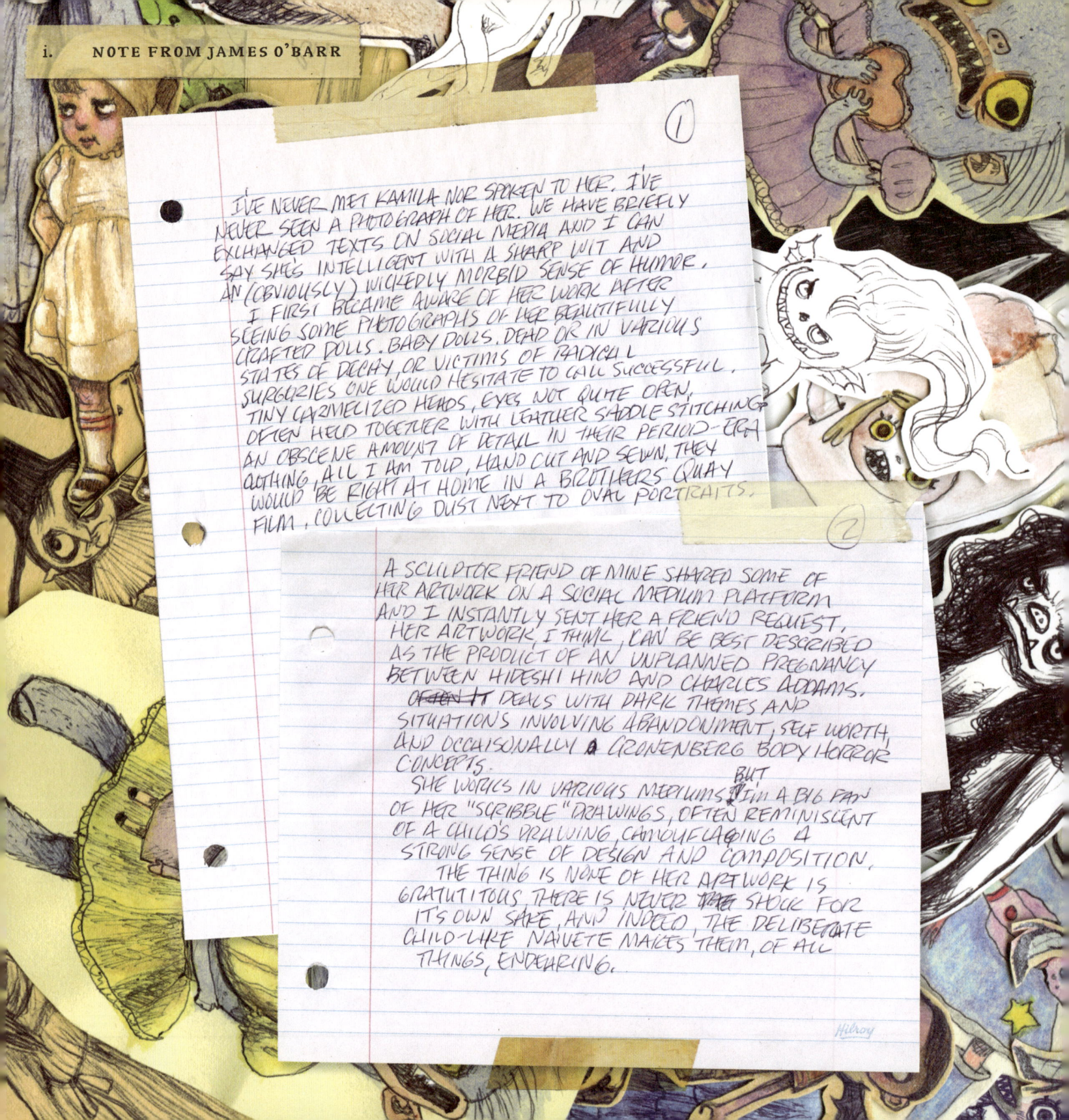

①

I'VE NEVER MET KAMILA NOR SPOKEN TO HER. I'VE NEVER SEEN A PHOTOGRAPH OF HER. WE HAVE BRIEFLY EXCHANGED TEXTS ON SOCIAL MEDIA AND I CAN SAY SHE'S INTELLIGENT WITH A SHARP WIT AND AN (OBVIOUSLY) WICKEDLY MORBID SENSE OF HUMOR.

I FIRST BECAME AWARE OF HER WORK AFTER SEEING SOME PHOTOGRAPHS OF HER BEAUTIFULLY CRAFTED DOLLS. BABY DOLLS. DEAD OR IN VARIOUS STATES OF DECAY, OR VICTIMS OF RADICAL SURGERIES ONE WOULD HESITATE TO CALL SUCCESSFUL. TINY CARMELIZED HEADS, EYES NOT QUITE OPEN, OFTEN HELD TOGETHER WITH LEATHER SADDLE STITCHING, AN OBSCENE AMOUNT OF DETAIL IN THEIR PERIOD-ERA CLOTHING, ALL I AM TOLD, HAND CUT AND SEWN, THEY WOULD BE RIGHT AT HOME IN A BROTHERS QUAY FILM, COLLECTING DUST NEXT TO OVAL PORTRAITS.

②

A SCULPTOR FRIEND OF MINE SHARED SOME OF HER ARTWORK ON A SOCIAL MEDIUM PLATFORM AND I INSTANTLY SENT HER A FRIEND REQUEST. HER ARTWORK, I THINK, CAN BE BEST DESCRIBED AS THE PRODUCT OF AN UNPLANNED PREGNANCY BETWEEN HIDESHI HINO AND CHARLES ADDAMS.

IT DEALS WITH DARK THEMES AND SITUATIONS INVOLVING ABANDONMENT, SELF WORTH, AND OCCAISONALLY A CRONENBERG BODY HORROR CONCEPTS.

SHE WORKS IN VARIOUS MEDIUMS BUT I'M A BIG FAN OF HER "SCRIBBLE" DRAWINGS, OFTEN REMINISCENT OF A CHILD'S DRAWING, CAMOUFLAGING A STRONG SENSE OF DESIGN AND COMPOSITION.

THE THING IS NONE OF HER ARTWORK IS GRATUITITOUS. THERE IS NEVER SHOCK FOR IT'S OWN SAKE, AND INDEED, THE DELIBERATE CHILD-LIKE NAIVETE MAKES THEM, OF ALL THINGS, ENDEARING.

Hilroy

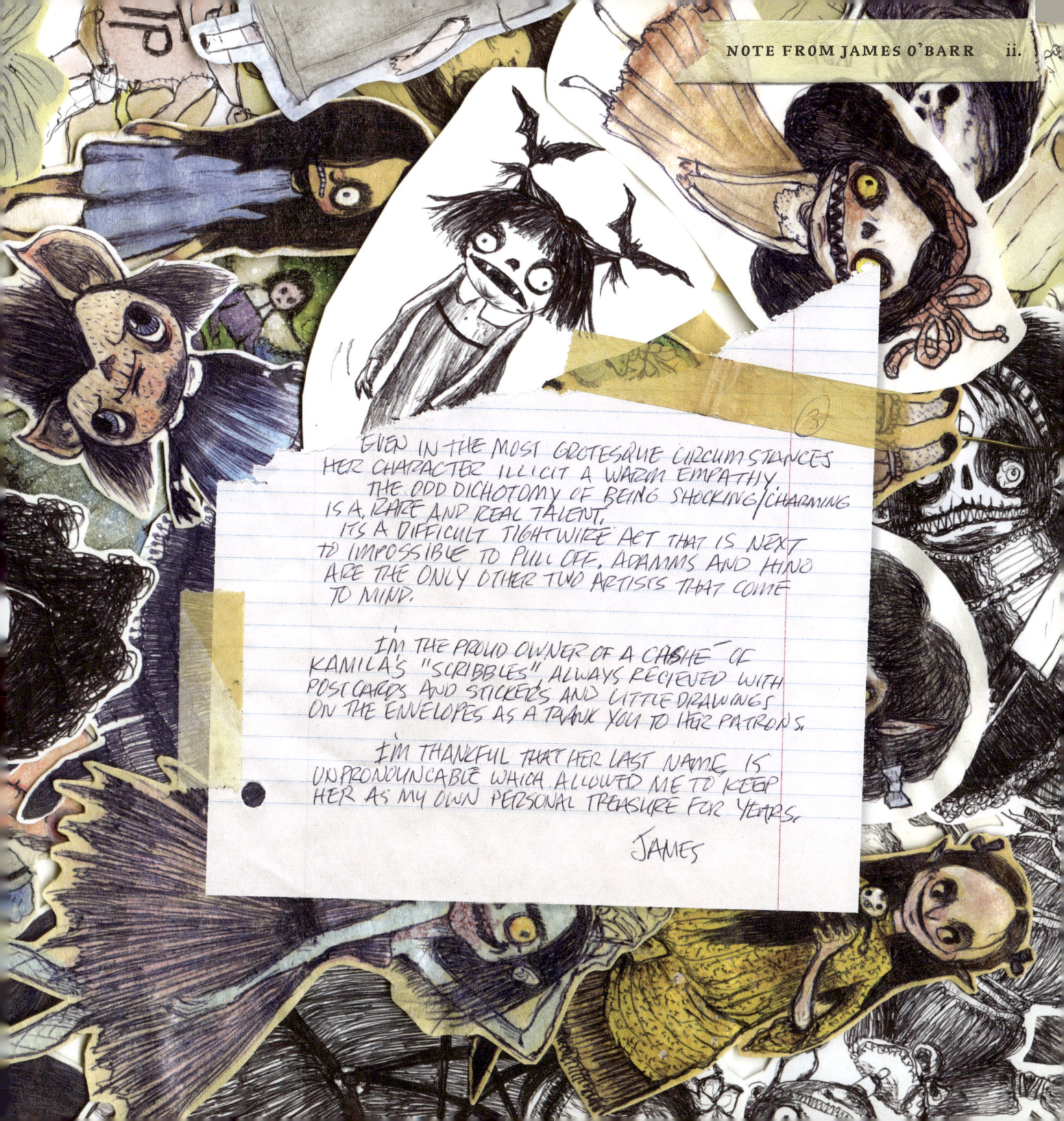

EVEN IN THE MOST GROTESQUE CIRCUMSTANCES
HER CHARACTER ILLICIT A WARM EMPATHY.
   THE ODD DICHOTOMY OF BEING SHOCKING/CHARMING
IS A RARE AND REAL TALENT.
   ITS A DIFFICULT TIGHTWIRE ACT THAT IS NEXT
TO IMPOSSIBLE TO PULL OFF. ADAMMS AND HINO
ARE THE ONLY OTHER TWO ARTISTS THAT COME
TO MIND.

   I'M THE PROUD OWNER OF A CASHÉ OF
KAMILA'S "SCRIBBLES" ALWAYS RECIEVED WITH
POSTCARDS AND STICKERS AND LITTLE DRAWINGS
ON THE ENVELOPES AS A THANK YOU TO HER PATRONS.

   I'M THANKFUL THAT HER LAST NAME IS
UNPRONOUNCABLE WHICH ALLOWED ME TO KEEP
HER AS MY OWN PERSONAL TREASURE FOR YEARS.

                              JAMES

One day I noticed this wonderfully dark and twisted illustration
on social media that was "liked" by many of the artists that
I know and admire. As I scrolled through other images by this
artist, I saw more and more well-known artists commenting on her
work. The more artwork I encountered, the more of a fan I became!
I wondered why I hadn't heard of her before.

So, I did a quick online search and all I found of Kamila was
a link to her Etsy store and this photo ...

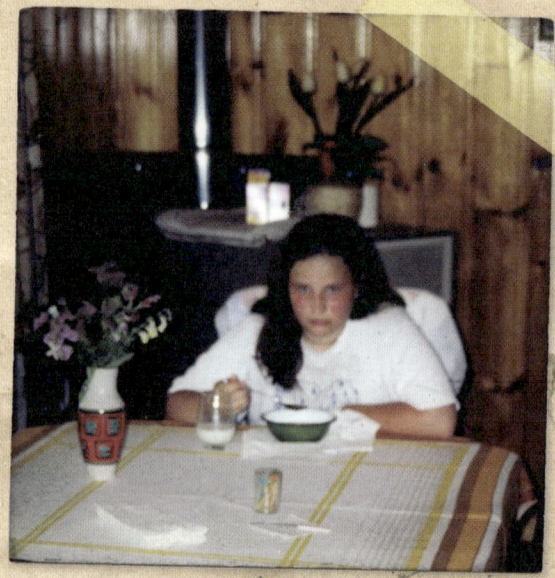

Now I was really intrigued!

The sum of my research up to that point concluded the following:
1. Kamila was either a 9-year-old girl who didn't like soup,
   or she had avoided having her personal life exposed on
   social media for many years.
2. She had a huge following of well-known artist who seemed
   to love and connect with her work.
3. She was an incredibly prolific artist who seemed to
   undercharge for her art (check out her Etsy store
   and you will see what I mean).

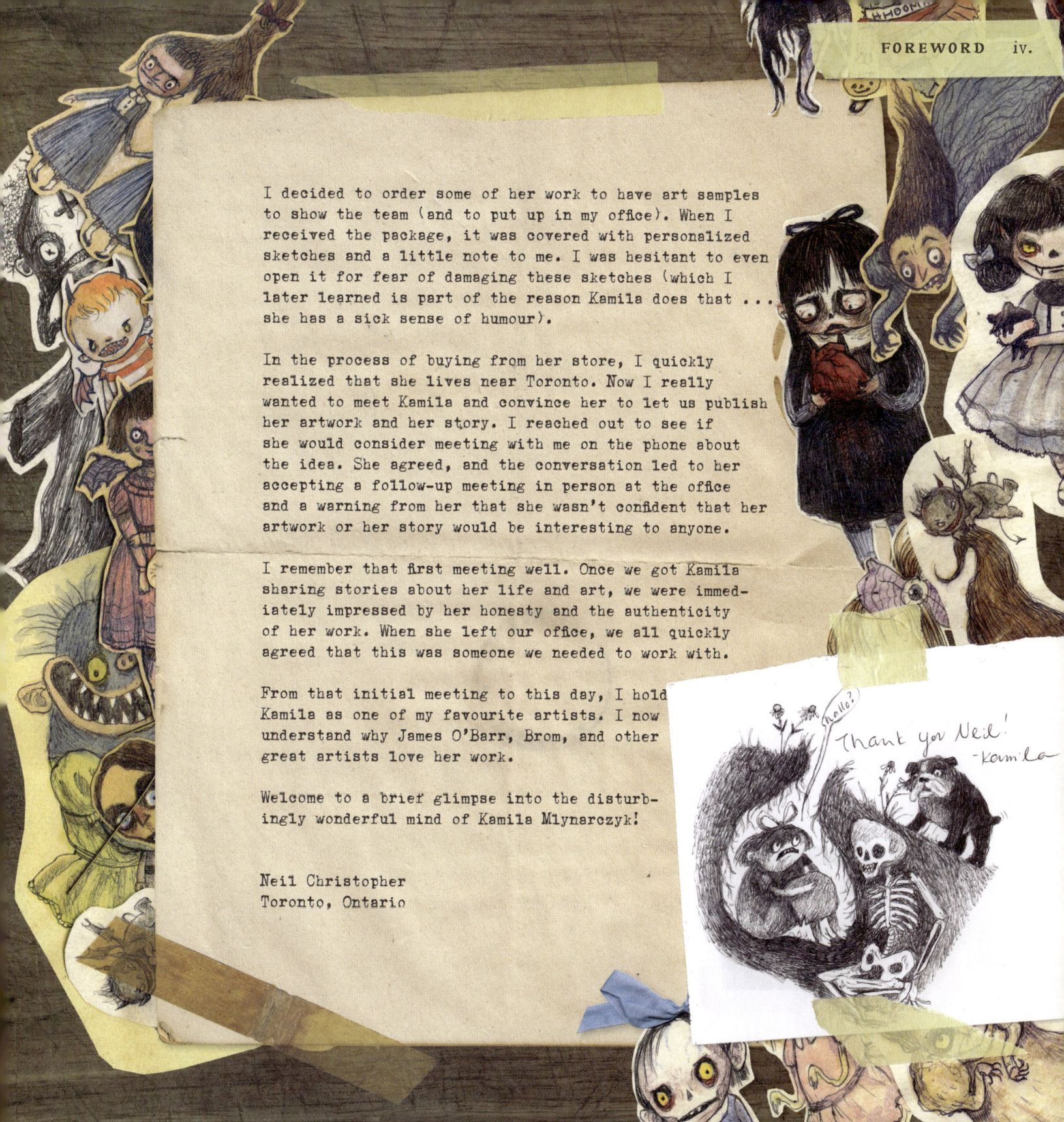

I decided to order some of her work to have art samples
to show the team (and to put up in my office). When I
received the package, it was covered with personalized
sketches and a little note to me. I was hesitant to even
open it for fear of damaging these sketches (which I
later learned is part of the reason Kamila does that ...
she has a sick sense of humour).

In the process of buying from her store, I quickly
realized that she lives near Toronto. Now I really
wanted to meet Kamila and convince her to let us publish
her artwork and her story. I reached out to see if
she would consider meeting with me on the phone about
the idea. She agreed, and the conversation led to her
accepting a follow-up meeting in person at the office
and a warning from her that she wasn't confident that her
artwork or her story would be interesting to anyone.

I remember that first meeting well. Once we got Kamila
sharing stories about her life and art, we were immed-
iately impressed by her honesty and the authenticity
of her work. When she left our office, we all quickly
agreed that this was someone we needed to work with.

From that initial meeting to this day, I hold
Kamila as one of my favourite artists. I now
understand why James O'Barr, Brom, and other
great artists love her work.

Welcome to a brief glimpse into the disturb-
ingly wonderful mind of Kamila Mlynarczyk!

Neil Christopher
Toronto, Ontario

Thank you Neil!
-Kamila

hello?

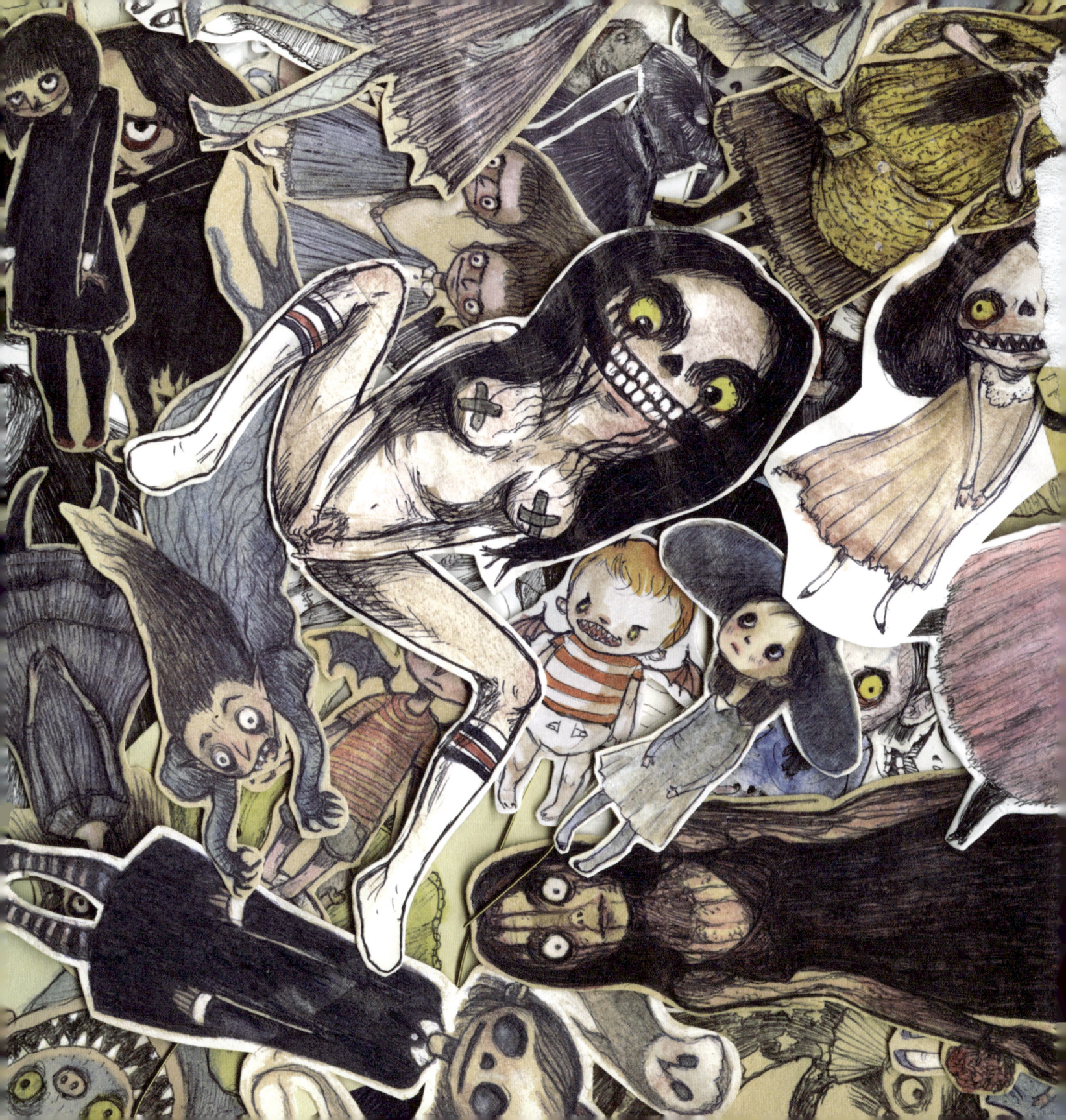

TABLE OF CONTENTS

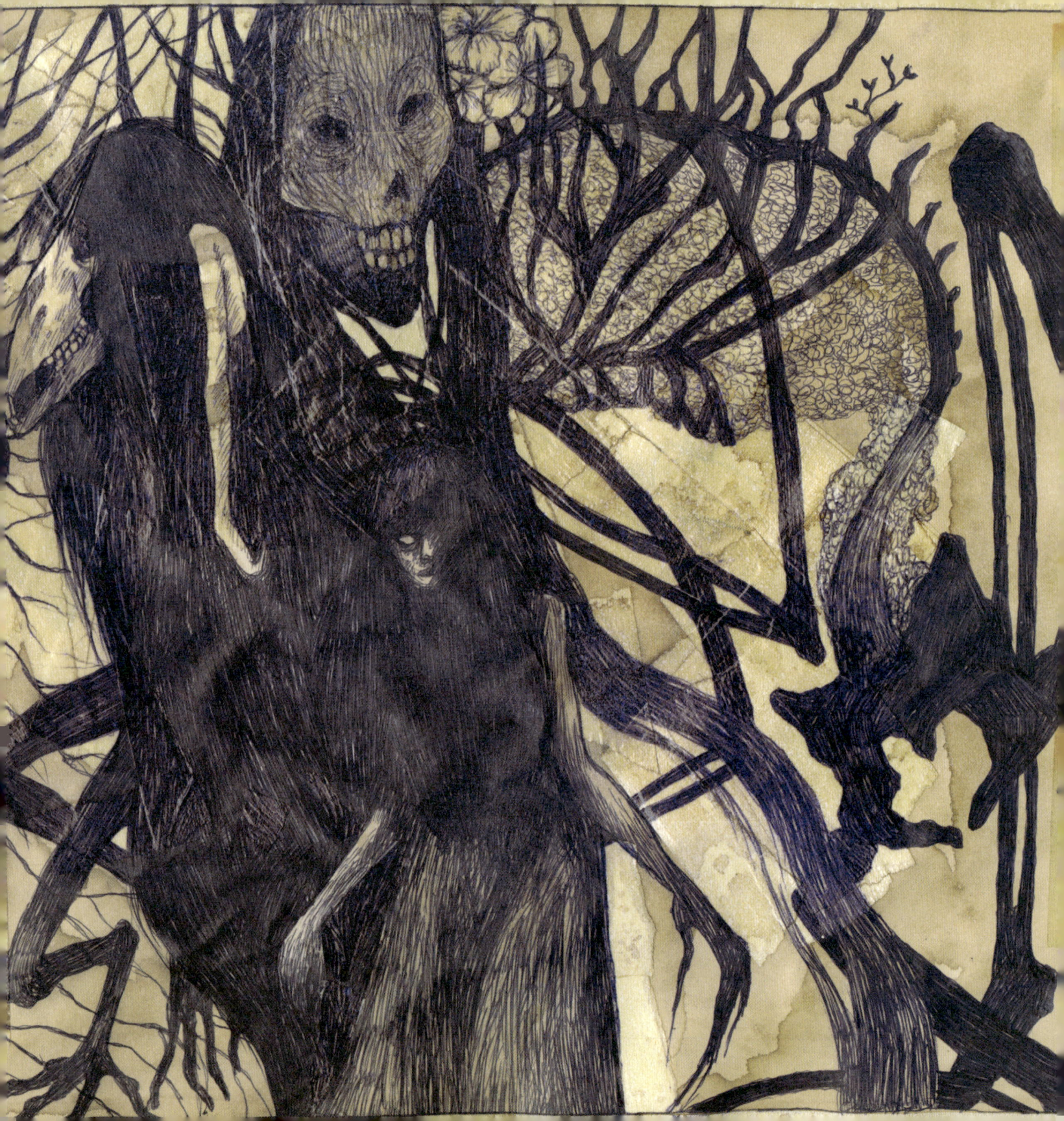

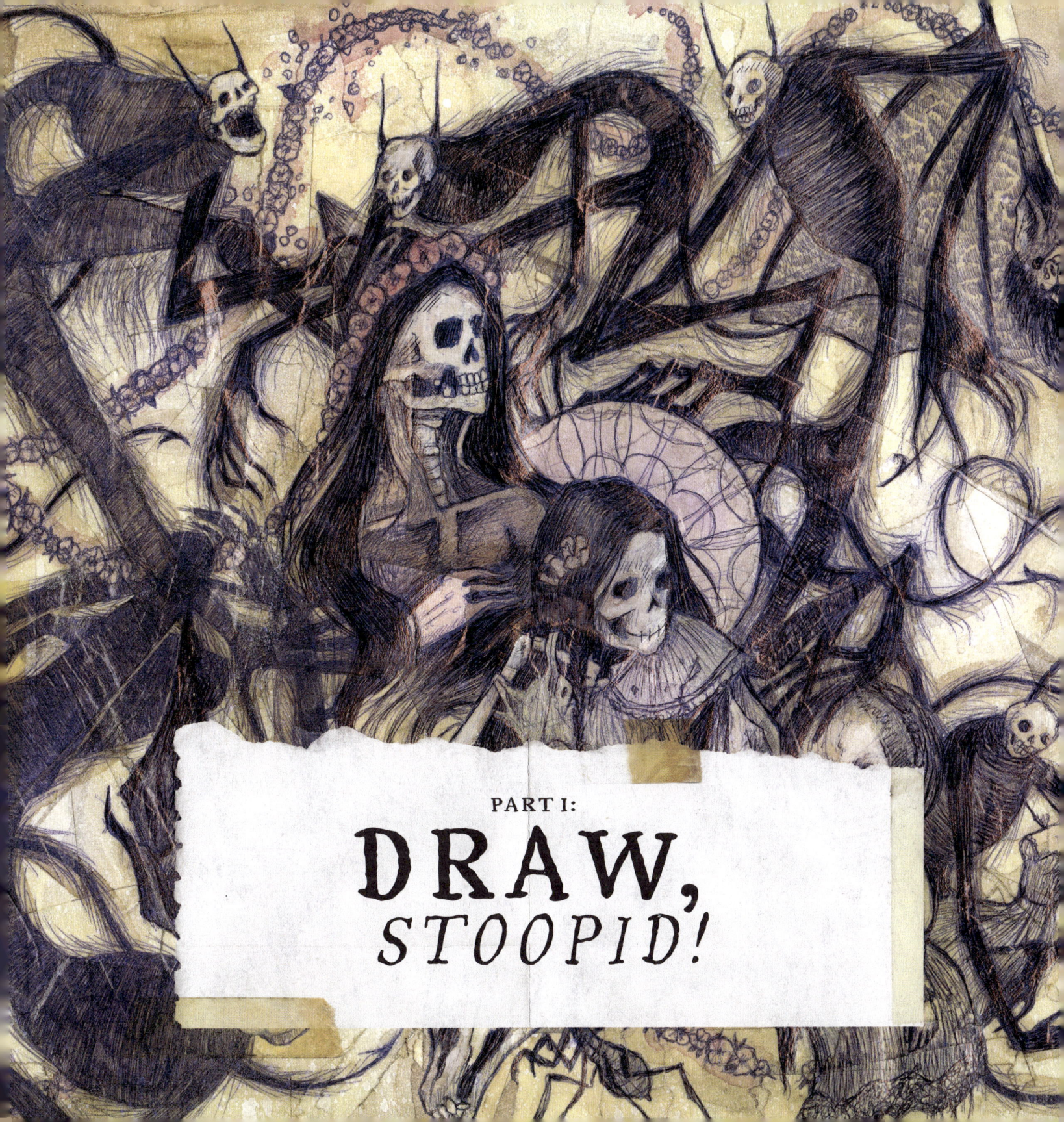

PART I:

DRAW,
STOOPID!

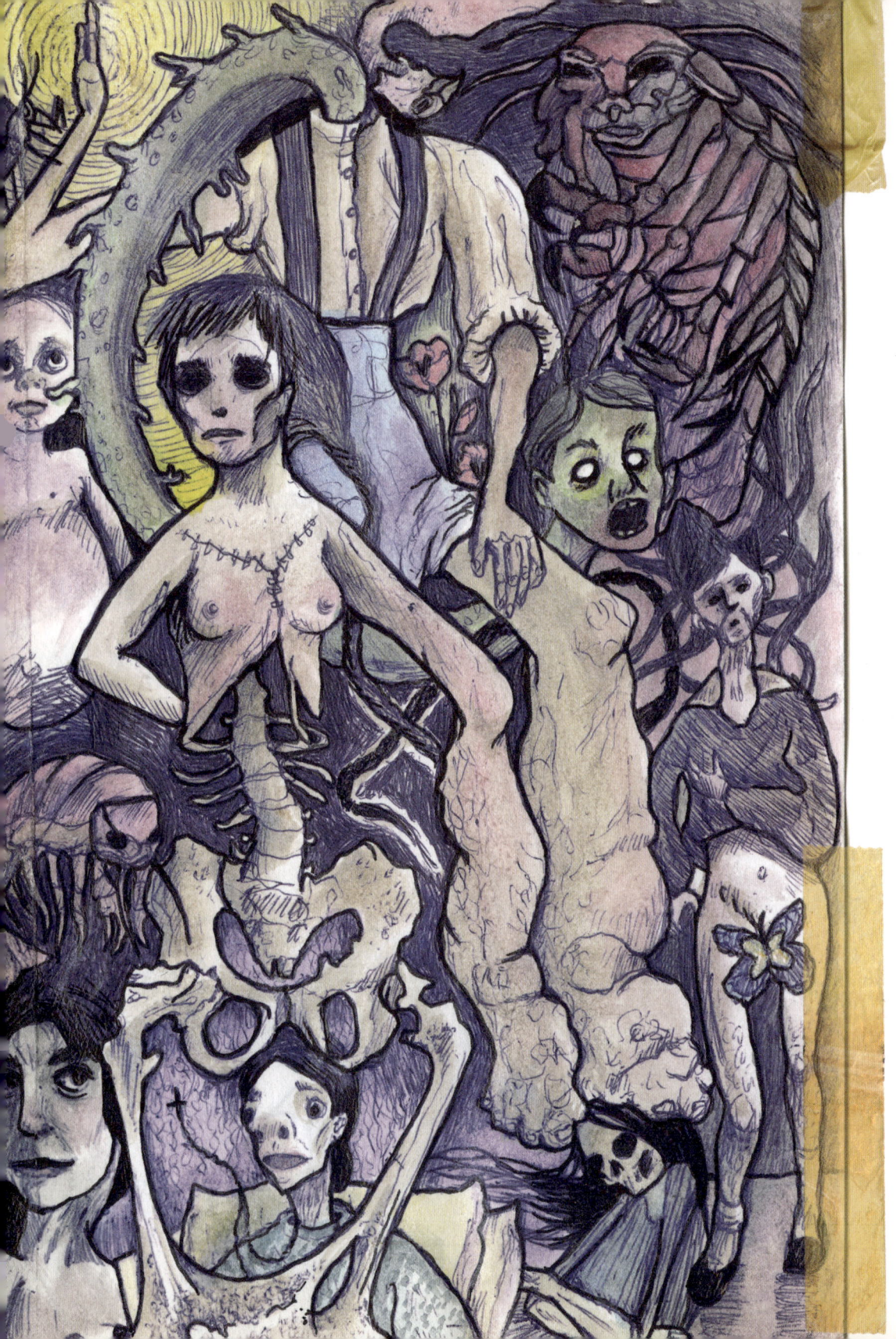

I take what I love and add it in if the inspiration strikes. So these are sketches inspired by medical journals and medical anomalies. I steal it, take it, and I use it. I make it my own. That's ultimately what art is to me. Find visual inspirations and that unique combination becomes an interesting style.

THIS IS WHEN I FORCED MYSELF TO USE MY hand to draw again. I would sit in front of a sketchbook or scrap of paper or napkin until I'd filled it. That's why there are so many references, and a lot of concepts. I had to fill two full sketch pages a day. It was torture; and then it was fun.

When I was a kid I did some horrible, fucked-up pornographic drawing in the back of a library book. I don't know what came over me, I was just skimming a book, and then I think I thought, "If I draw on this library book, no one's even going to know it was me who drew it. It'll be completely anonymous." So, I just drew. I should have run with that feeling. It was that feeling of being incredibly naughty and anonymous that drew me back into drawing as an adult. I use drawing as a coping mechanism for unhappiness. I get into really crazy-bad moods, and then I draw it out. Like, putting it on paper releases it from inside of me. I think it's shocking for most people. I don't think most people look at a drawing of a hanging girl and think it's cathartic. But I do. That's the horror language, it's a story all in one image that is tragic and sweet and, in some ways, comedic—definitely fucked-up—but it's cathartic release. I mean, it's why we even watch horror movies!

Nothing can be as fucked-up as it is in reality, though. I think that's why horror is a huge influence for me. I use horror as a language. Deer skulls; murdered girls in the haunted woods; occult stuff; family dynamics; the un-intelligent, tragic, wild, monster-man; etc. can all be used to show how I'm feeling in a way that

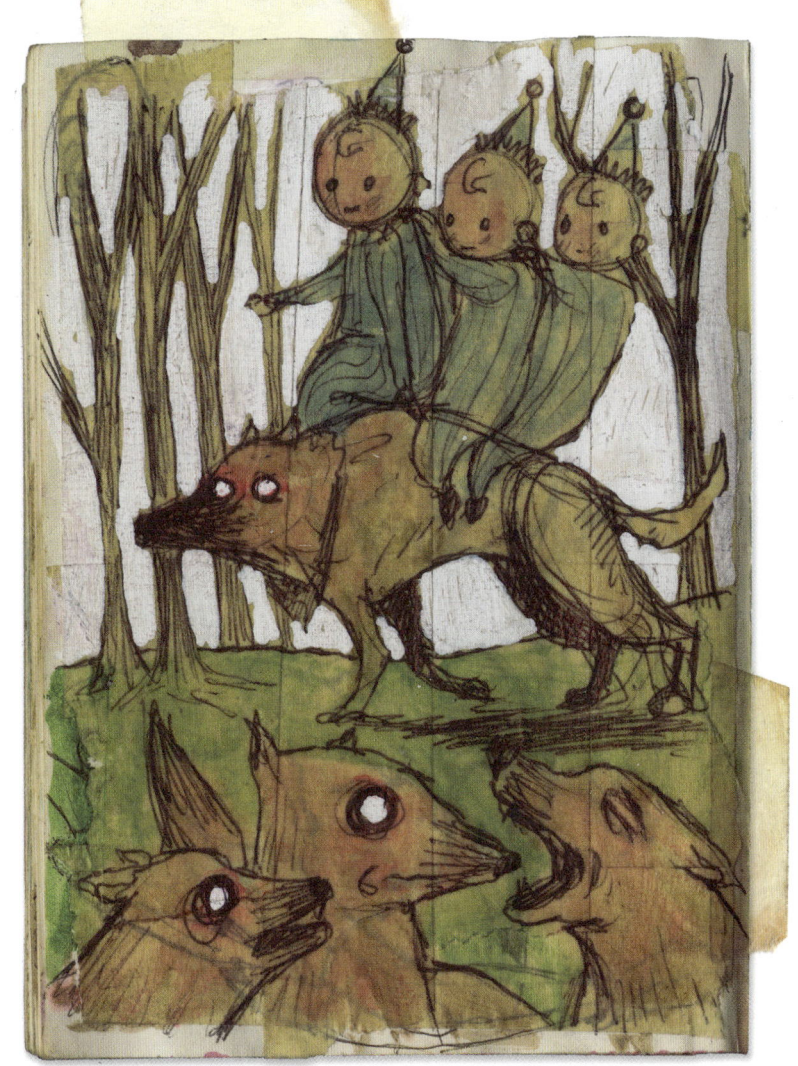

Children mounted on animals is just very aesthetically pleasing to me. I particularly like children paired with wolves. My mum got me a Polish book when I was very little that was filled with drawings and stories of werewolves and wolves that follow that classic medieval plotline of a wolf figure dragging a baby away. What did she hope I would turn into when she gave me that book? It was full of amazing images, and it must have imprinted on me. It became a part of my visual language as a kid. I was influenced a lot by Polish books, cartoons, and of course, the church. I'm not religious at all, I'm totally irreverent, but the church and all of its symbolism is part of my horror language. I love to tease it and get cheeky and playful.

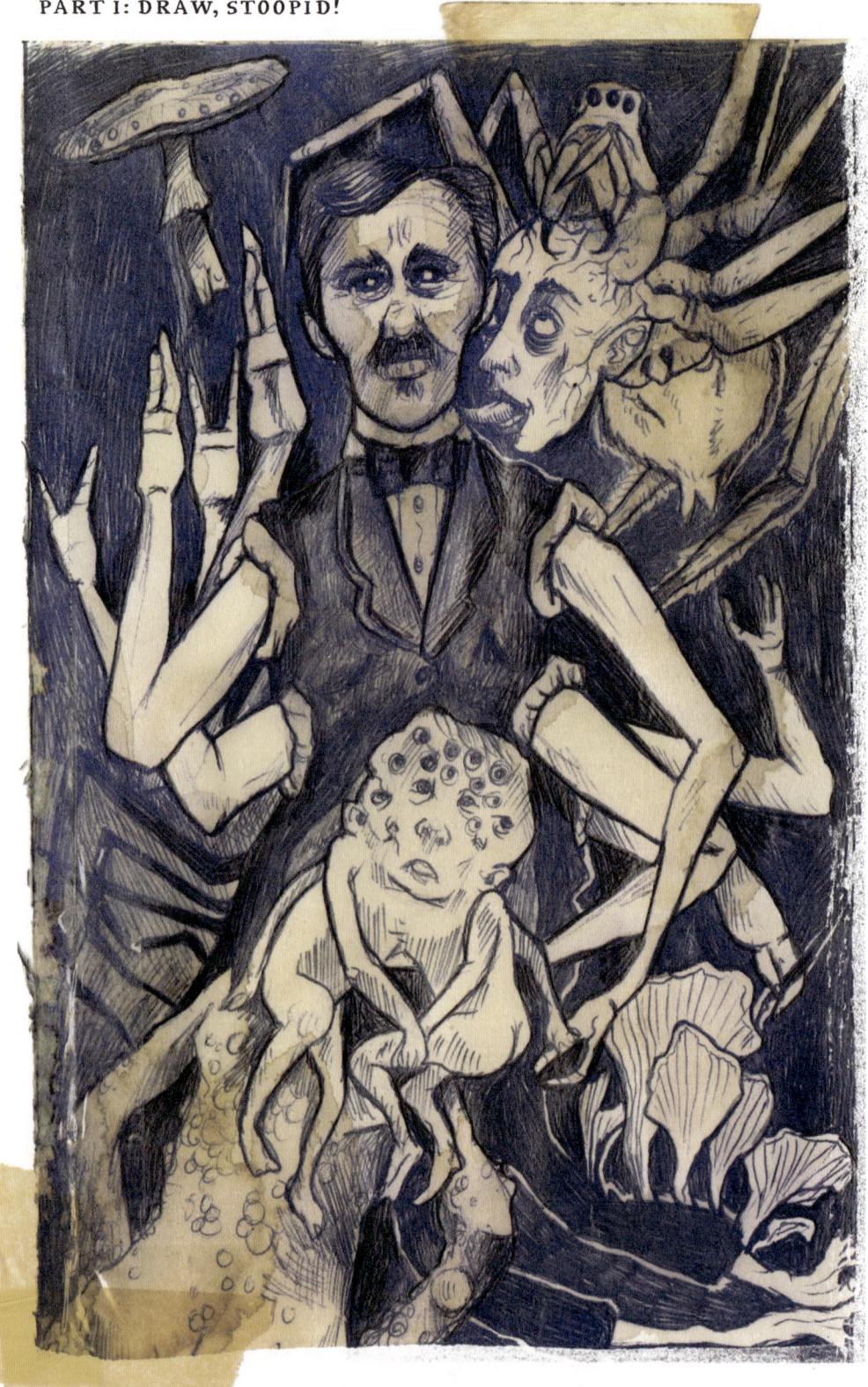

isn't as fucked-up as it is in reality. For instance, I think that true horror can be found within family dynamics and relationships; it's only ever people that act horrific in real life. Horror is personal, it's emotion.

I didn't notice before but once I had all my art collected for this book I realized: I only draw children! Even before I had my son, I drew children and I think it's because everything about children is supposed to be optimistic and cheerful, hopeful, and open—but it can just as easily be the opposite and that truth is terrifying. Maybe it's my

Anatomy is such a good source of strange things. Nothing is as fucked-up as reality, right? Human bodies that are deformed, but in a way that's naturally occurring and makes sense are so interesting to me. If it exists in nature, no matter how weird it is, it looks plausible rather than just made up. In one of my anatomy books that shows medical anomalies I saw a boy who only had two long fingers and afterwards I only drew two-fingered figures.

long lament for lost childhood, or my way of making my feelings more understandable and clear. Children are really allowed to express themselves emotionally, it's sweet and expected, but adults are so restrained. Kids really resonate with me. Books like *Coraline* and films like *The Nightmare Before Christmas* tap into this truth as well. It's more universal than just me, this perverse mixing of children with horror. I love it, and I'm not really scared of anything except family stuff, like ghost girls in closets and little boys getting hurt. And it's always the moms! Mothers can be terrifying; I can see how easy it is to slip into a truly horrific mother role and damage someone. One person can damage another so easily. One person can damage a whole family. It's a real fear of mine.

This girl has had an autopsy performed on her. She has black claws which symbolize the extent of her sins.

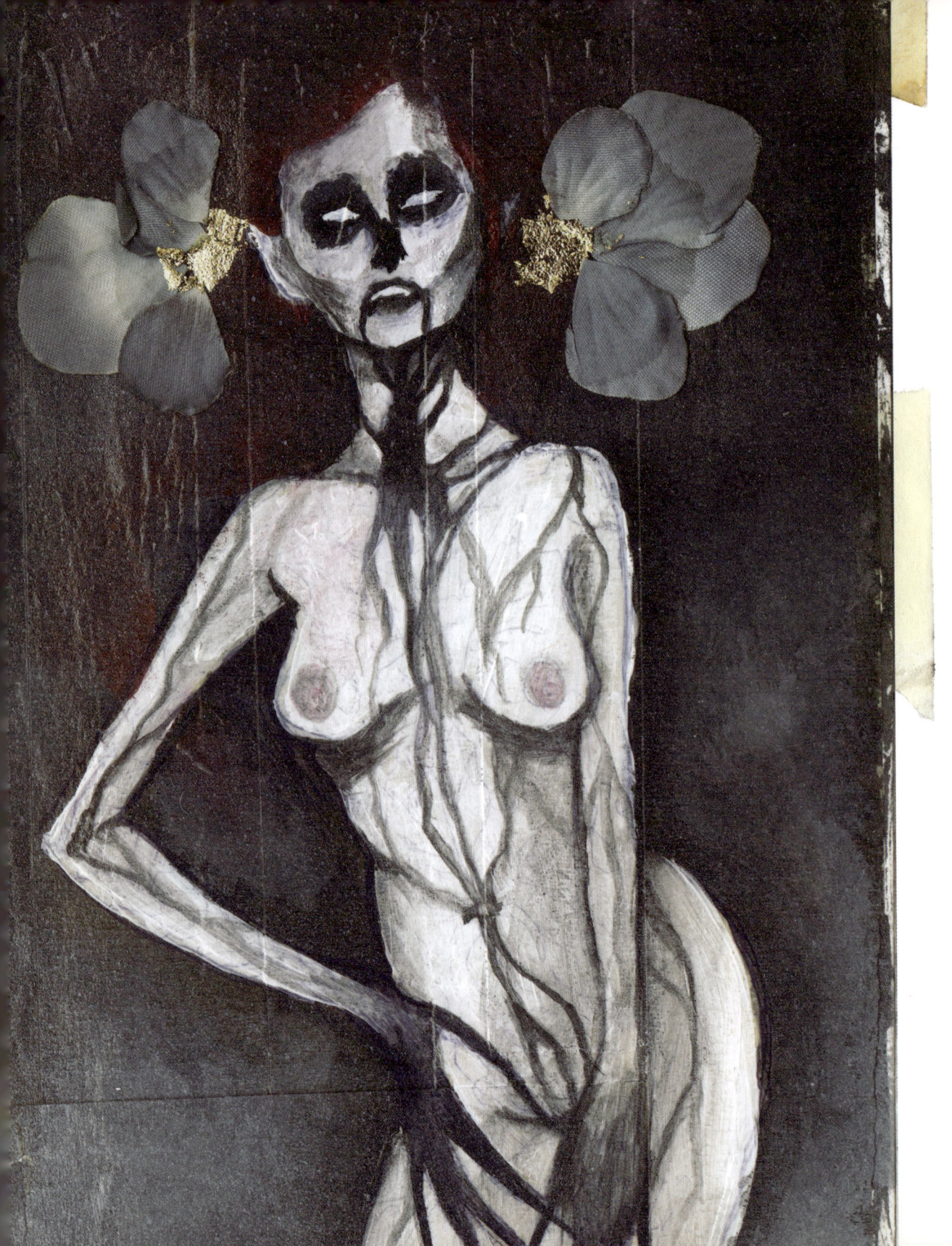

This one's on
masking taped
garbage, and
these are fake
flowers and gold
leaf. Black hands to
symbolize all the sins
committed during
life. I was doing
true, serious horror.

I grew up in a little village in the mountains of Poland. We have a strange accent —we're the "hillbilly" people in Poland. So I don't know proper Polish, I just know Polish slang. My grandma, when she was alive, would always tell me ghost stories. It's funny, my mum and grandma and everyone else would always discourage me from anything spooky or horrific or sadistic. They'd say, "That stuff will poison your brain." But they were the biggest culprits! They were the ones telling me all these awesome, terrifying stories in the first place. Grandma would tell me this horror story of a person who goes to a graveyard and picks a flower off a grave and becomes haunted until the flower is returned. A great classic haunting story. My mum told me she saw a ghost when she was little, maybe five, with her sister, and it was a giant floating mass. They all had ghost stories. My parents were so against horror, but then they would tell me all these really fucked-up, real-life stories. They dragged me to church and taught me about spirits, and ghosts, and satanism. What did they expect?

I started to plan my art dolls. I usually hate planning my art, but it led to sketching, and that led to drawing and my "re-learning how to draw" phase. Initially, I was intimidated by creating something permanent on paper, and I went through a long phase of drawing on masking tape in shitty ballpoint pen. The thing about drawing in pen, though, is that it's in pen. So, I'd take masking tape and mask over anything I didn't like. I'd just cover up the bad stuff and keep working on the same image. I really liked physically

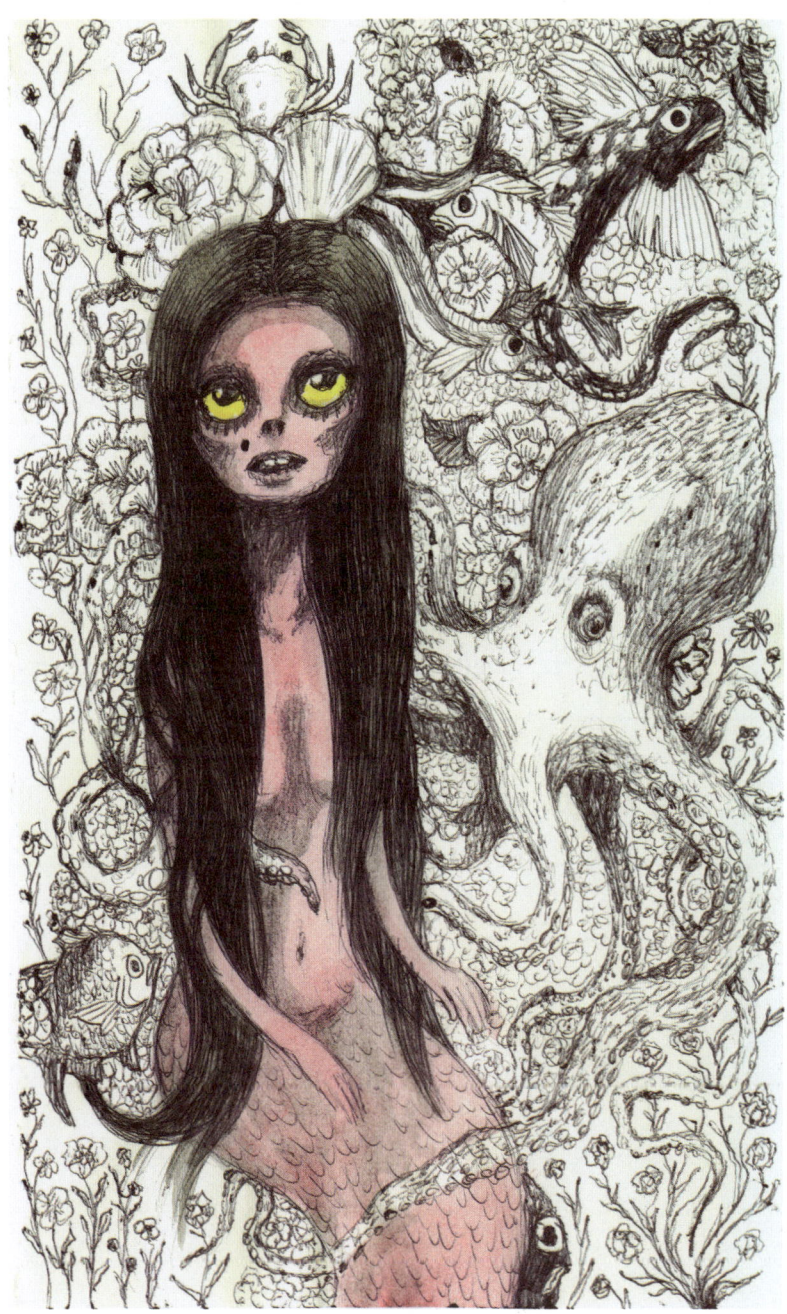

This was probably near the tail end of these old drawings, where I was going with a more simple and clean style. I found beauty and value in a more stylized approach.

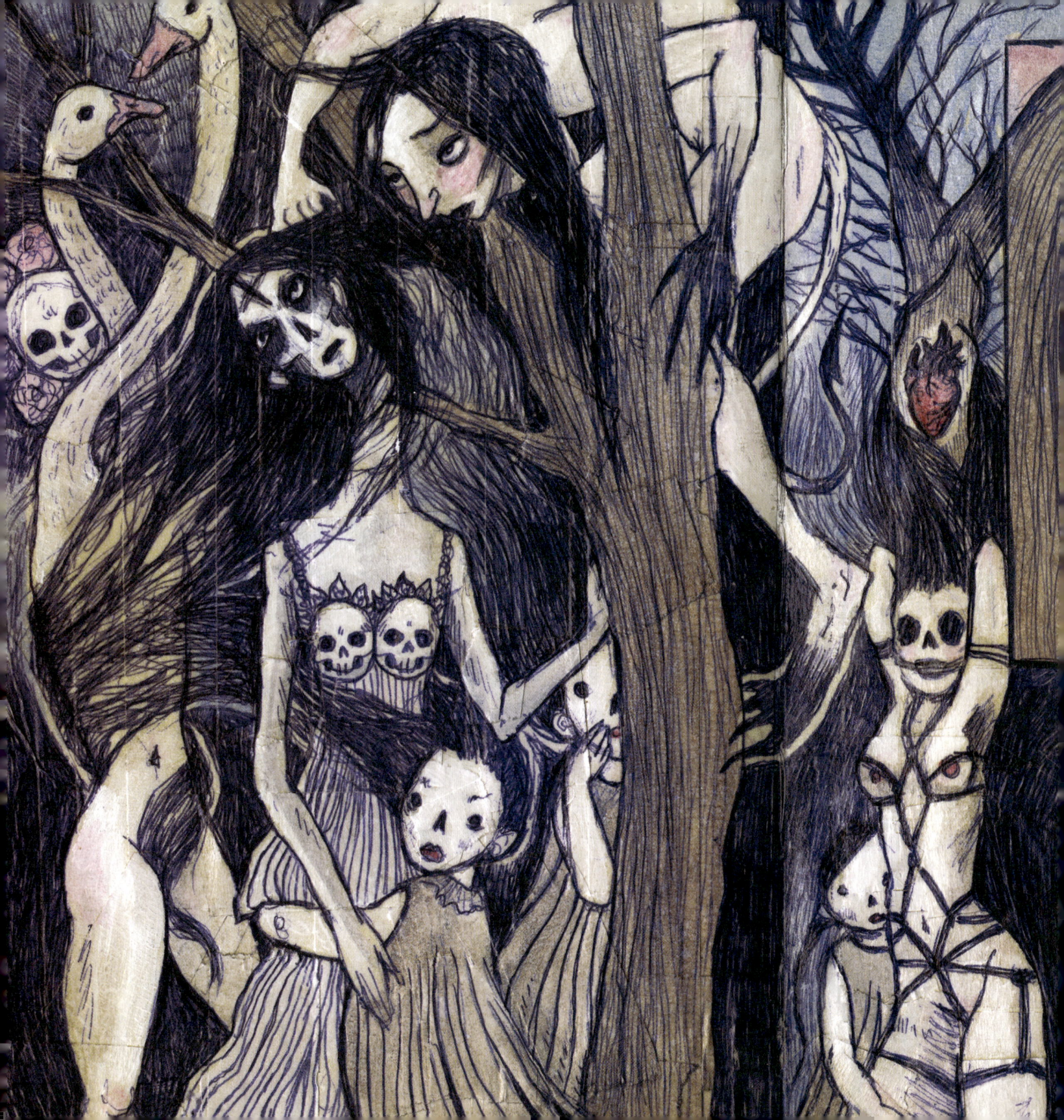

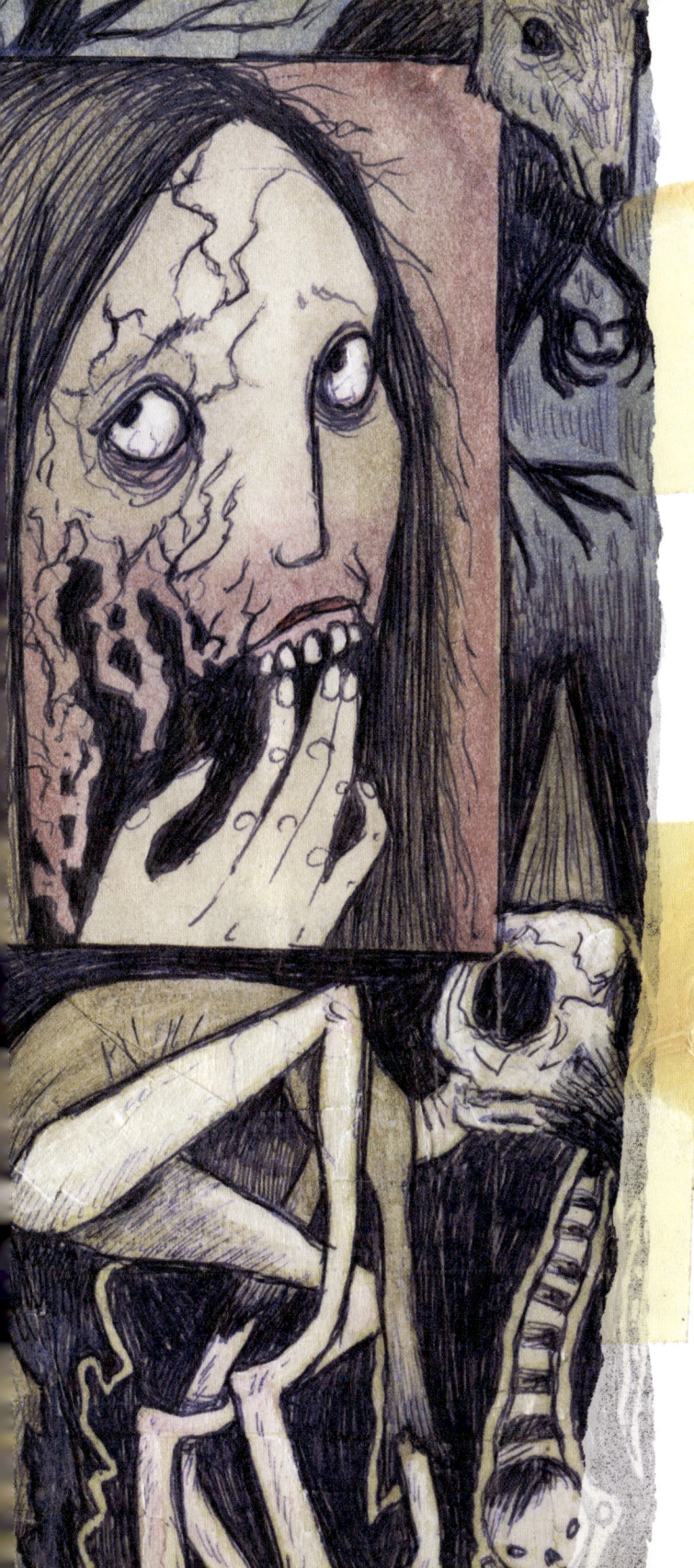

changing what I was working on, maybe a remnant from the art dolls, but I felt it took the pressure off. I was way too serious when I started drawing, I felt a lot of anxiety. This whole re-learning section isn't nearly as personal as the rest. It was truly a struggle to fill paper with drawings. It was making me feel better, though I didn't know how far I could push it or how much better I could feel in my life when I let the absurd shine a little more. As soon as I found that drawing was a coping mechanism, I transformed into a child artist. Like I was back in the library, secretly doodling obscenities.

I also had to re-learn how to paint! I hated the idea of painting but I loved colour. Still do! And what I did to take the pressure off was paint with coffee. I even used the grounds sometimes. Coffee adds a mystery to the image, I never know what it's going to look like. Room for fuck-ups makes Kamila a happy artist. When it dries, the paper crinkles up, which is an interesting experiment with lots of room for weirdness. I would let coffee dry in layers and paint it with a brush on top just to give an image a little bit more shade and dimension.

This one's also on garbage, but it's only
    garbage if you think it's garbage!
  This was when I was moving into my more
cartoony, absurd style. Near the tail end
of re-learning how to draw. I'm opening up a
little more. The evolution from complex style
    to this simpler linework is pretty clear.
      There's emotion here.

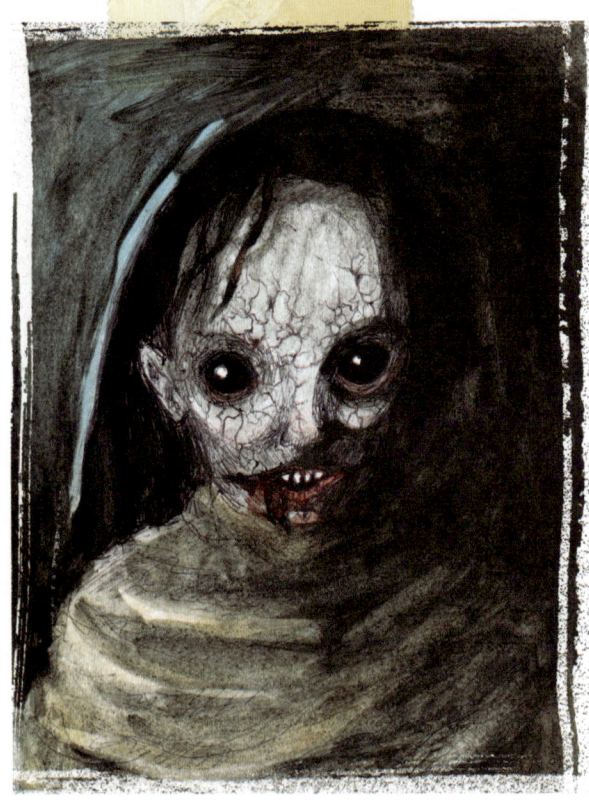

This was inspired by a Hexican anthology that I watched.
It was about a black-eyed ghost that lived in Hayan ruins. It just
appealed to me. It was a female ghost, it's face was cracked, and
it had black eyes. I don't think I'm alone in this as an artist, but
I always feel like some things are technically lazy or overly complex.
For me, all-black or all-white eyes are tricky. I think they look
and feel lazy. I did a sculpture of a zombie once, and I thought she
shouldn't have very piercing eyes, so at first I painted them but they
were too bright and vivid, then I got over myself and I made them
milky and glassy, basically really simple white, and it looked great.
It can work, but I have to convince myself that it'll work.
    Let go of those inclinations and move with the art.

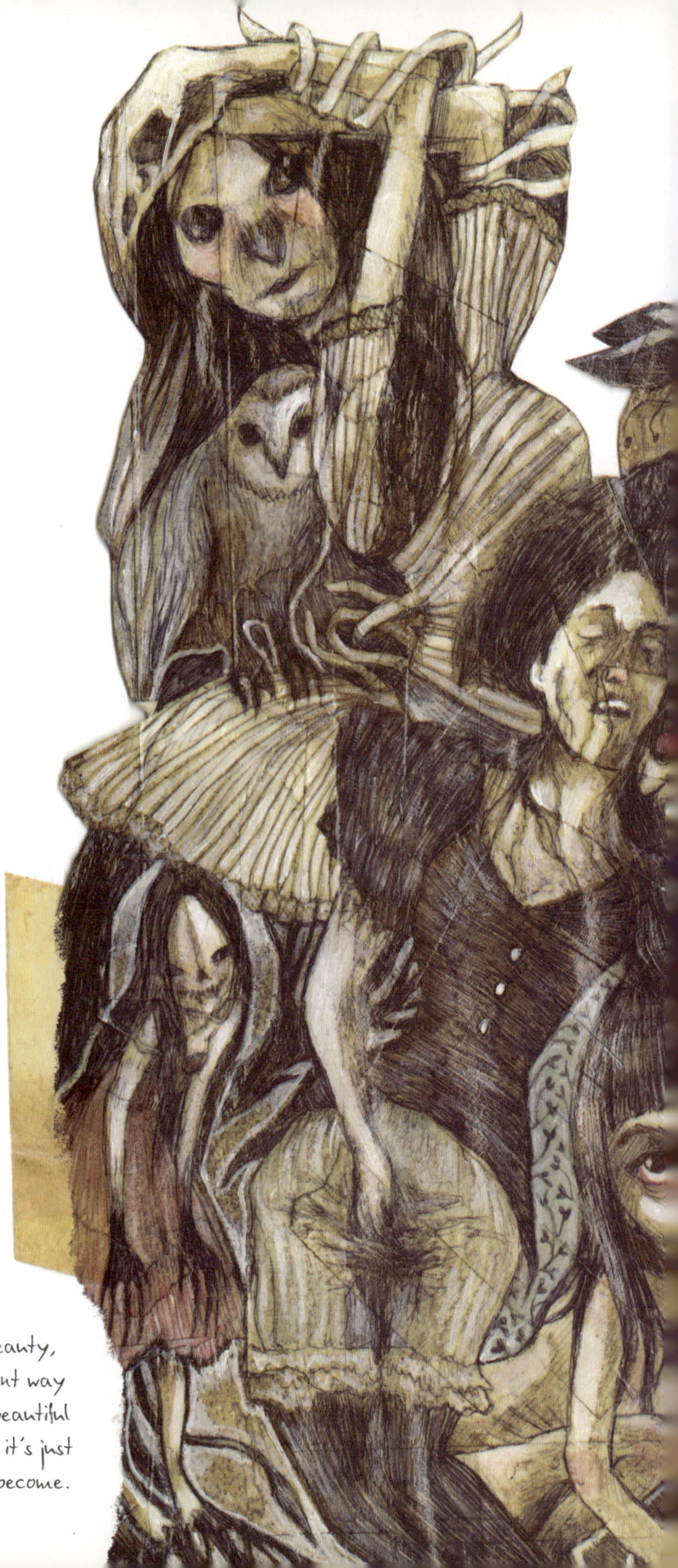

This is my murder collage. Gory is beauty,
decay can be beauty, it's just a different way
of being exquisite and unique. I mean, normal beautiful
things are all over, they're boring. Sometimes it's just
interesting to see what the human body can become.

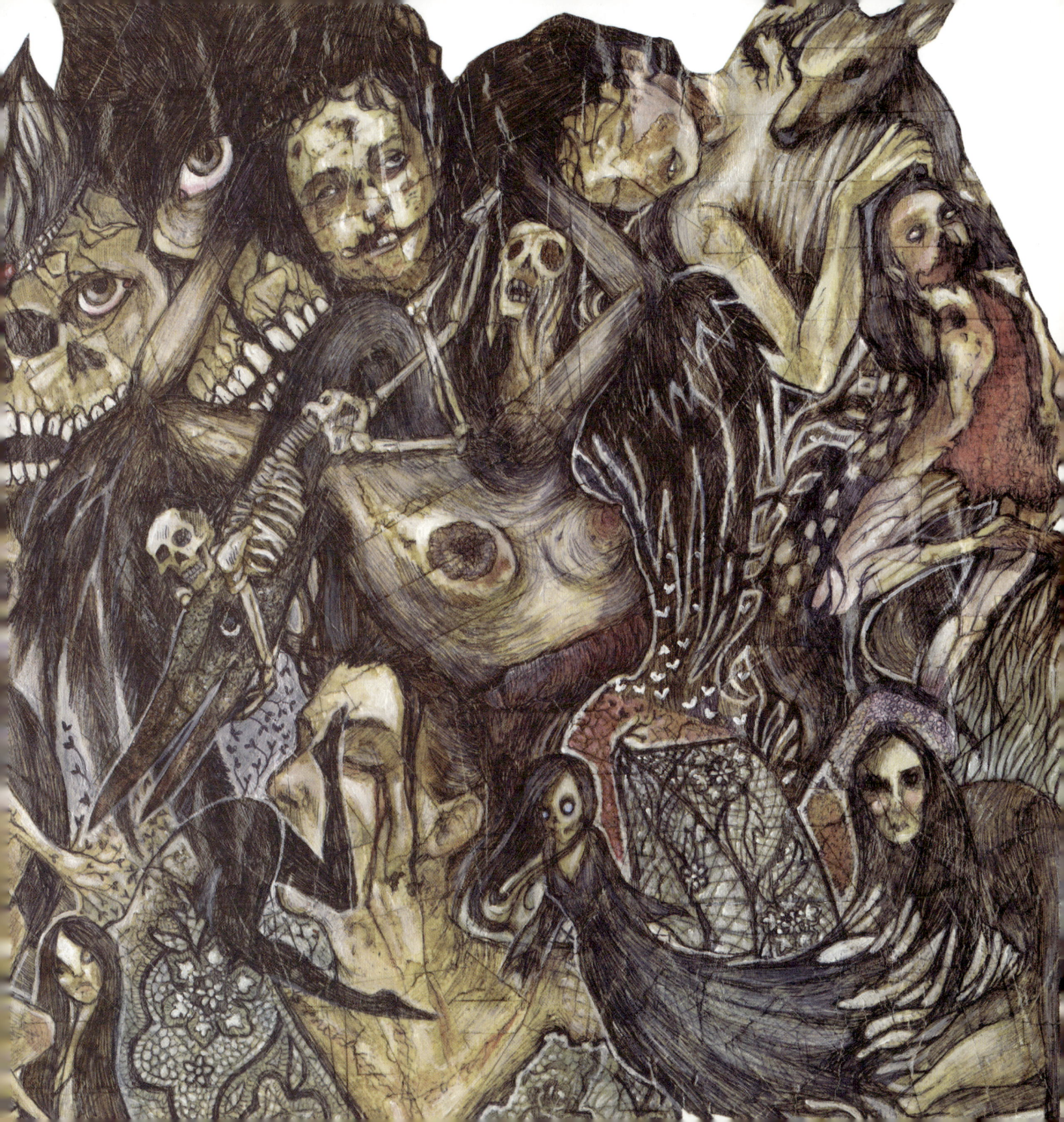

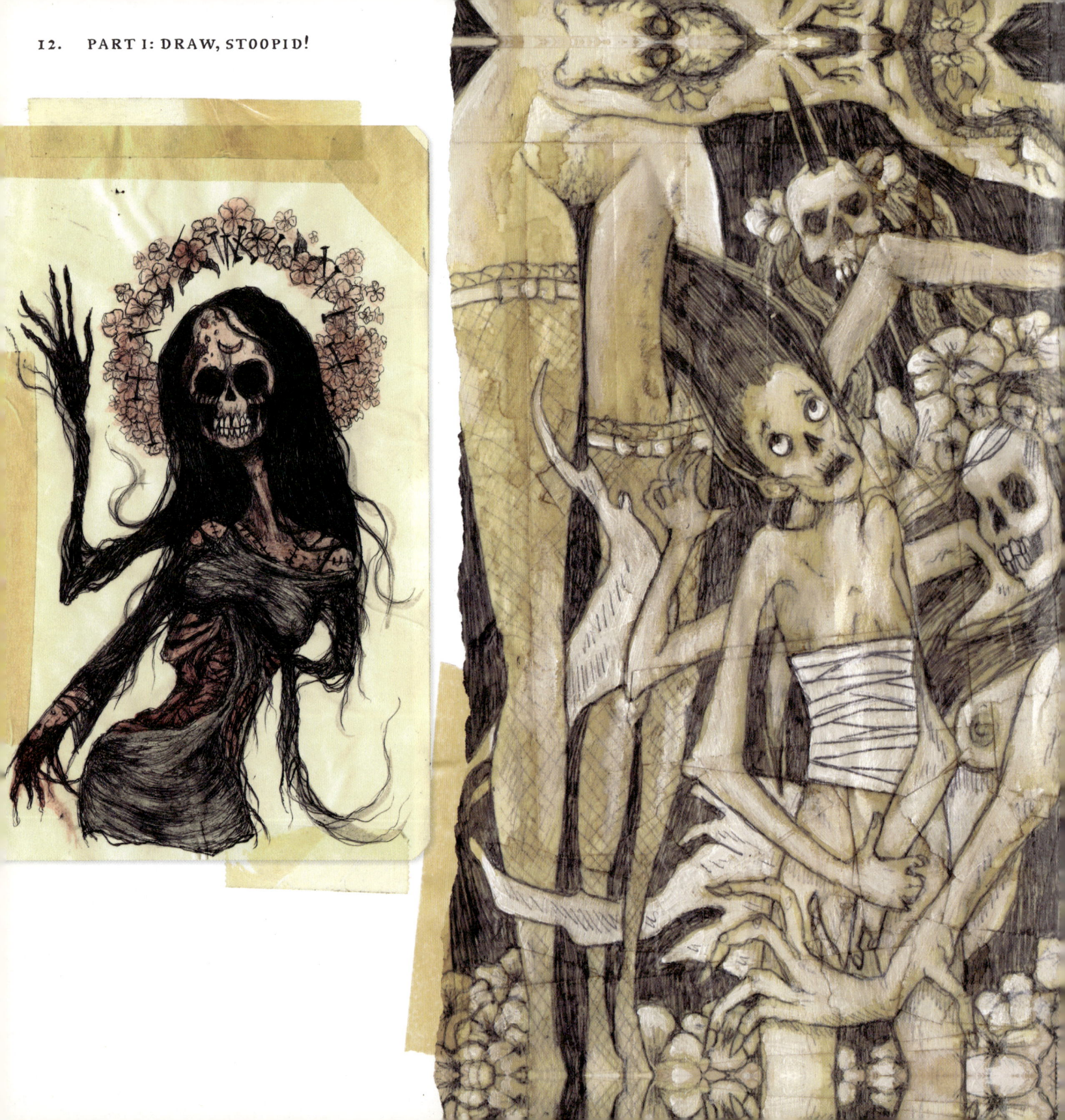

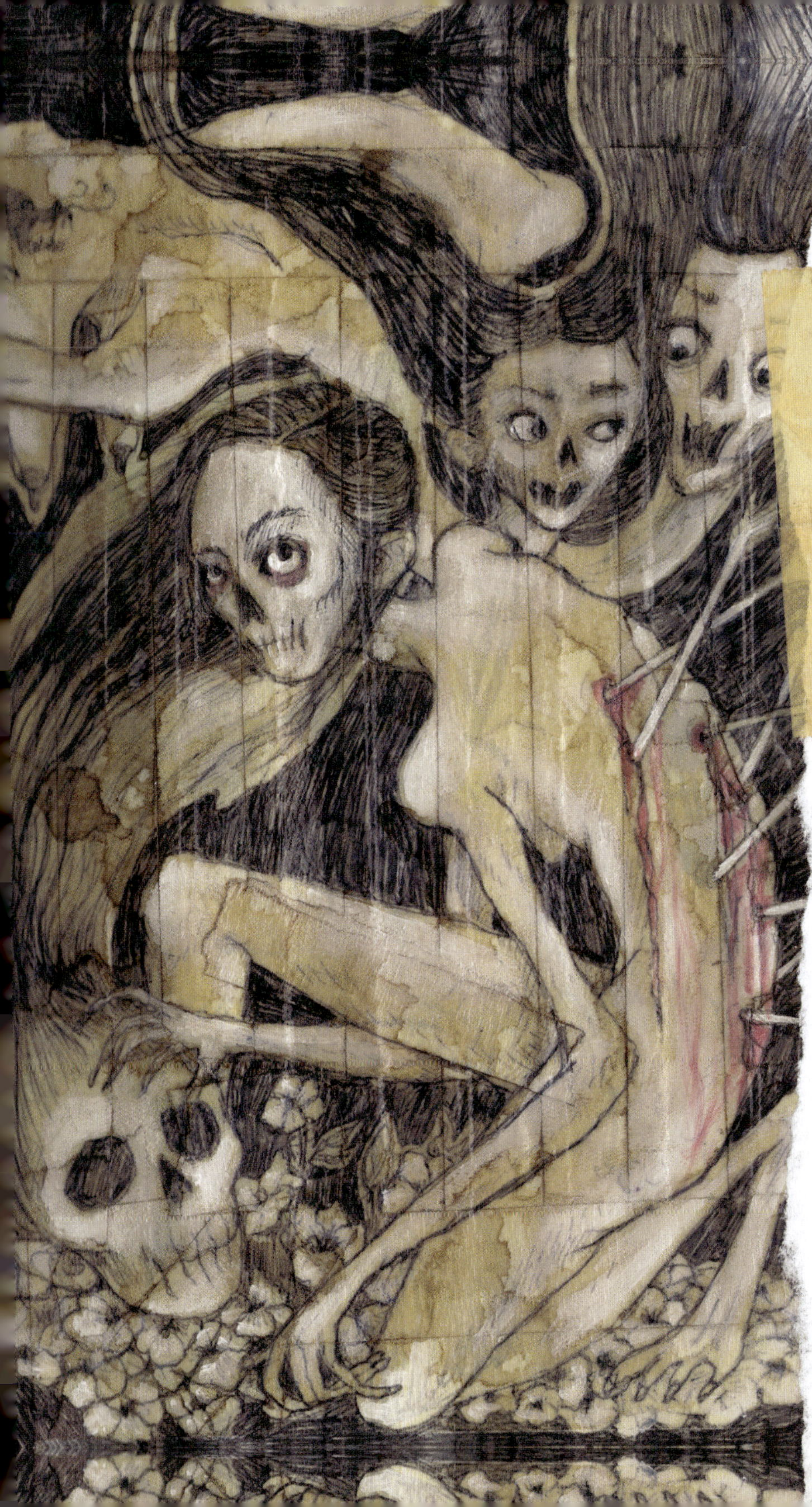

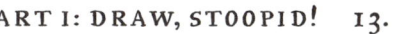

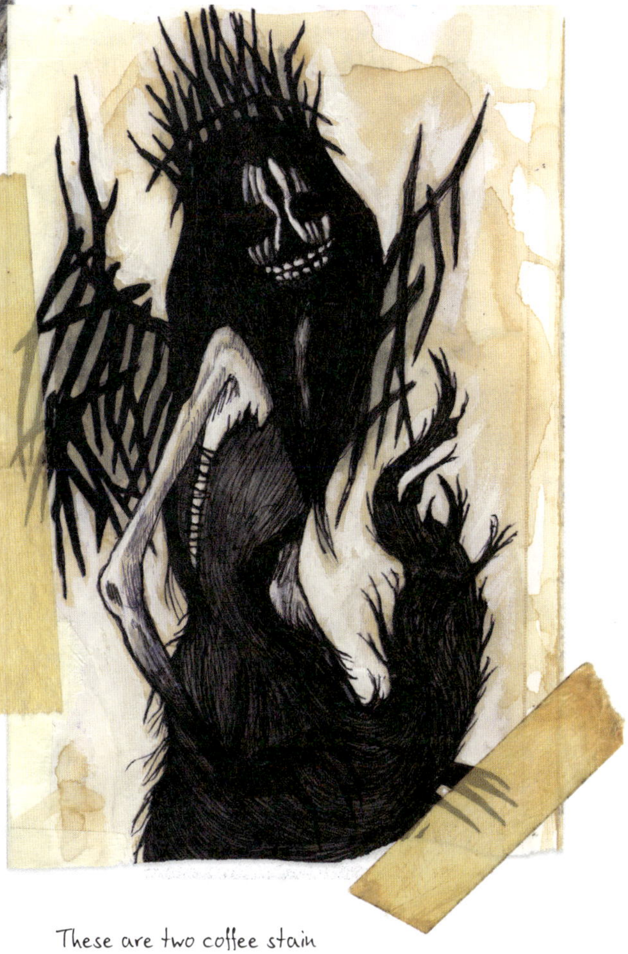

These are two coffee stain pieces. I was embracing the whole "I'm a garbage person" thing. This is my life.

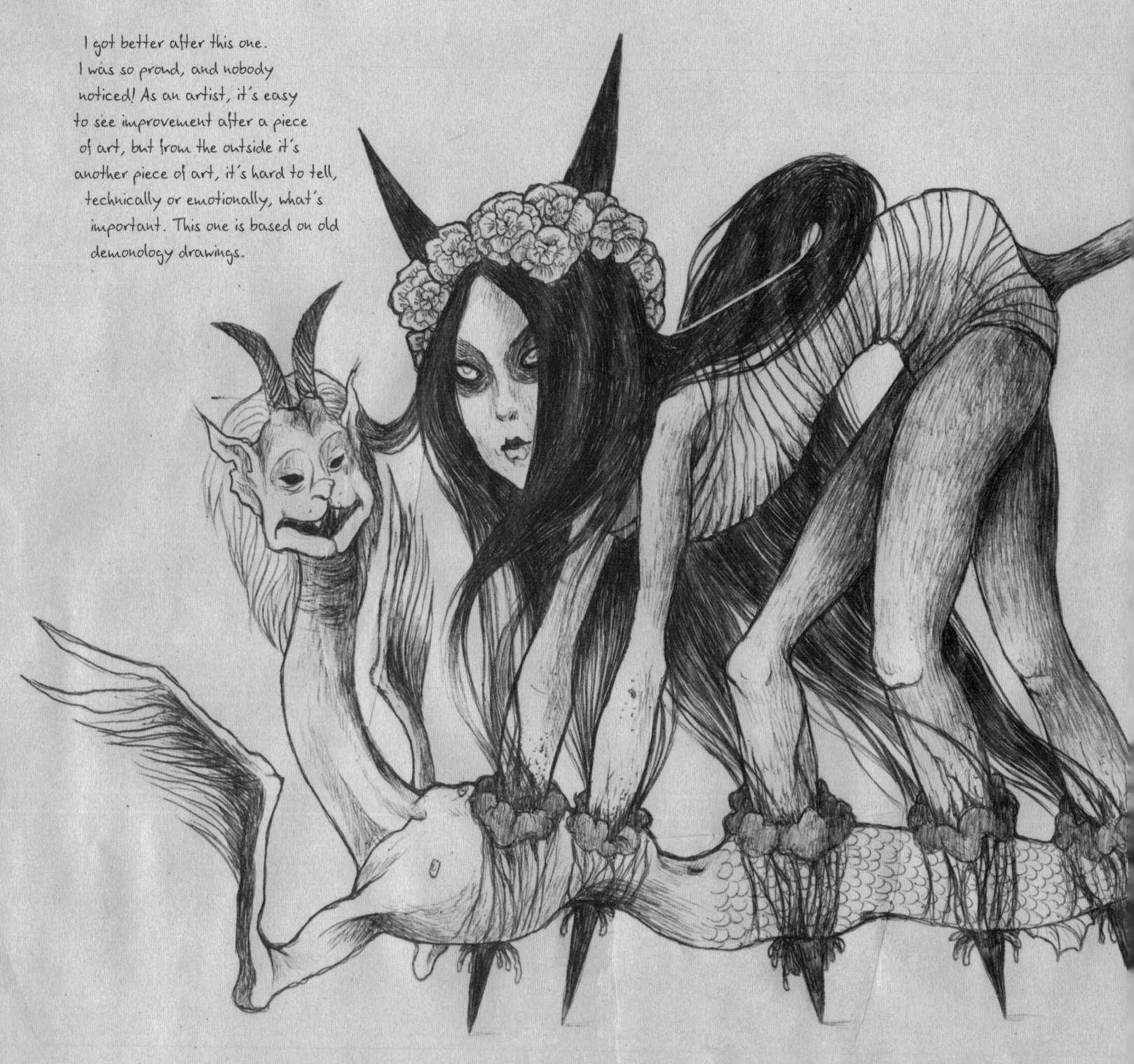

I got better after this one.
I was so proud, and nobody
noticed! As an artist, it's easy
to see improvement after a piece
of art, but from the outside it's
another piece of art, it's hard to tell,
technically or emotionally, what's
important. This one is based on old
demonology drawings.

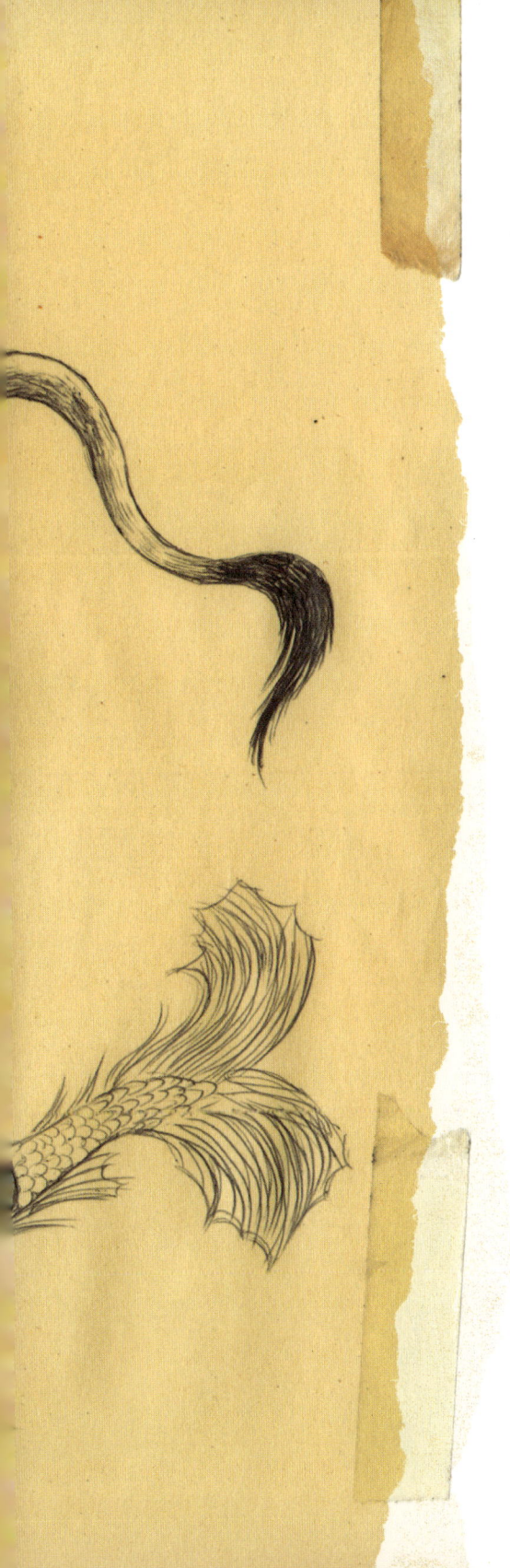

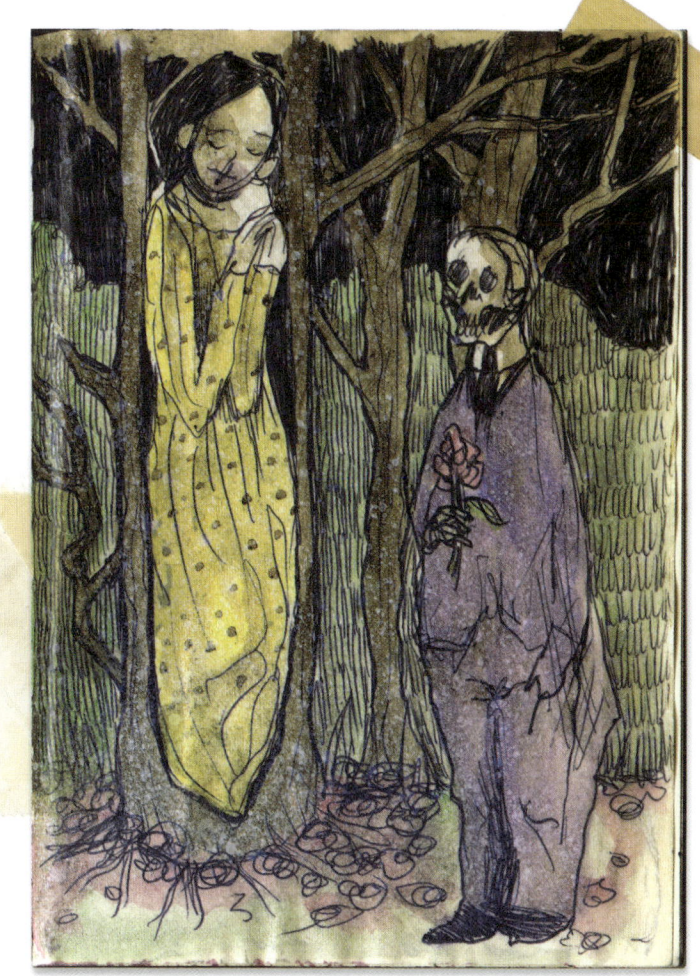

Oh, this is my obsession with women inside trees. Based on "Bella in the Wych Elm" which is a real story from England. I watched a documentary about it. This woman's skeleton was found in the bole of a Wyche elm, and her fingers were spread all around the trunk of the tree. They deduced that she was around thirty-five years-old and that she had been placed inside the tree "while still warm" and that she'd been there for over a year. She had suffocated from taffeta being shoved down her throat. Even before Bella, though, I was putting people in trees. When I found the documentary, I thought, "Oh, this was made for me!" The Bella story was linked to the occult and it was never really solved. Real-life horror. This piece also draws on my affinity for the forest and nature, my love of walks, and terrifying myself with my own imagination. It draws on horror tropes. It tickles me.

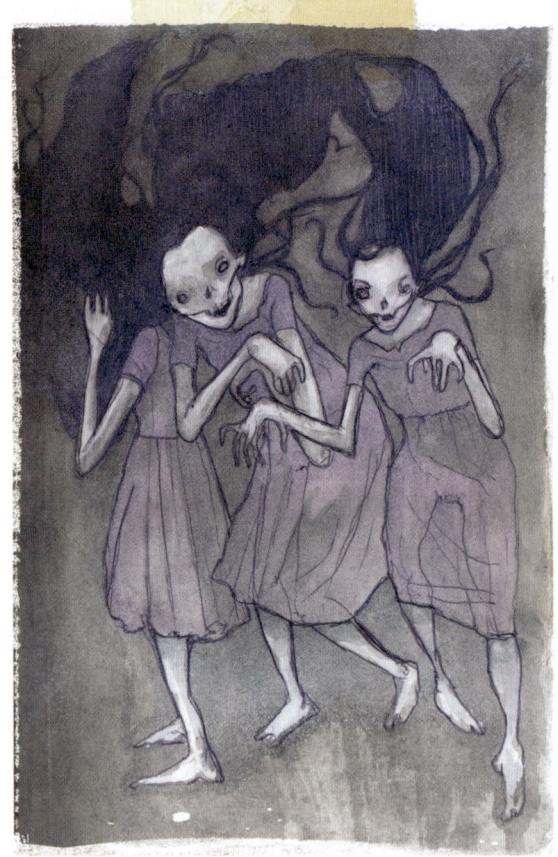

These are my take on Javier Botet's *Mama* test
footage. The video has him on a pulley rig, manipulating
his body and looking like a creepy ghost woman. He was also
wearing a really cool paper mask. Plus, I love the hair.
Hair was a huge part of *Mama*; it was such a creepy,
awesome tool they used.

People get weird with female horror
characters. There are a lot of really badass
male horror characters, but a lot of female
figures, like harpies, have their breasts out
and people don't know what to do with a sexual
female horror figure. It's like male artists don't
want to make it as terrifying as it should be.
It's as though they think, "I can't make the
breasts ugly." It scares them on a penis level.

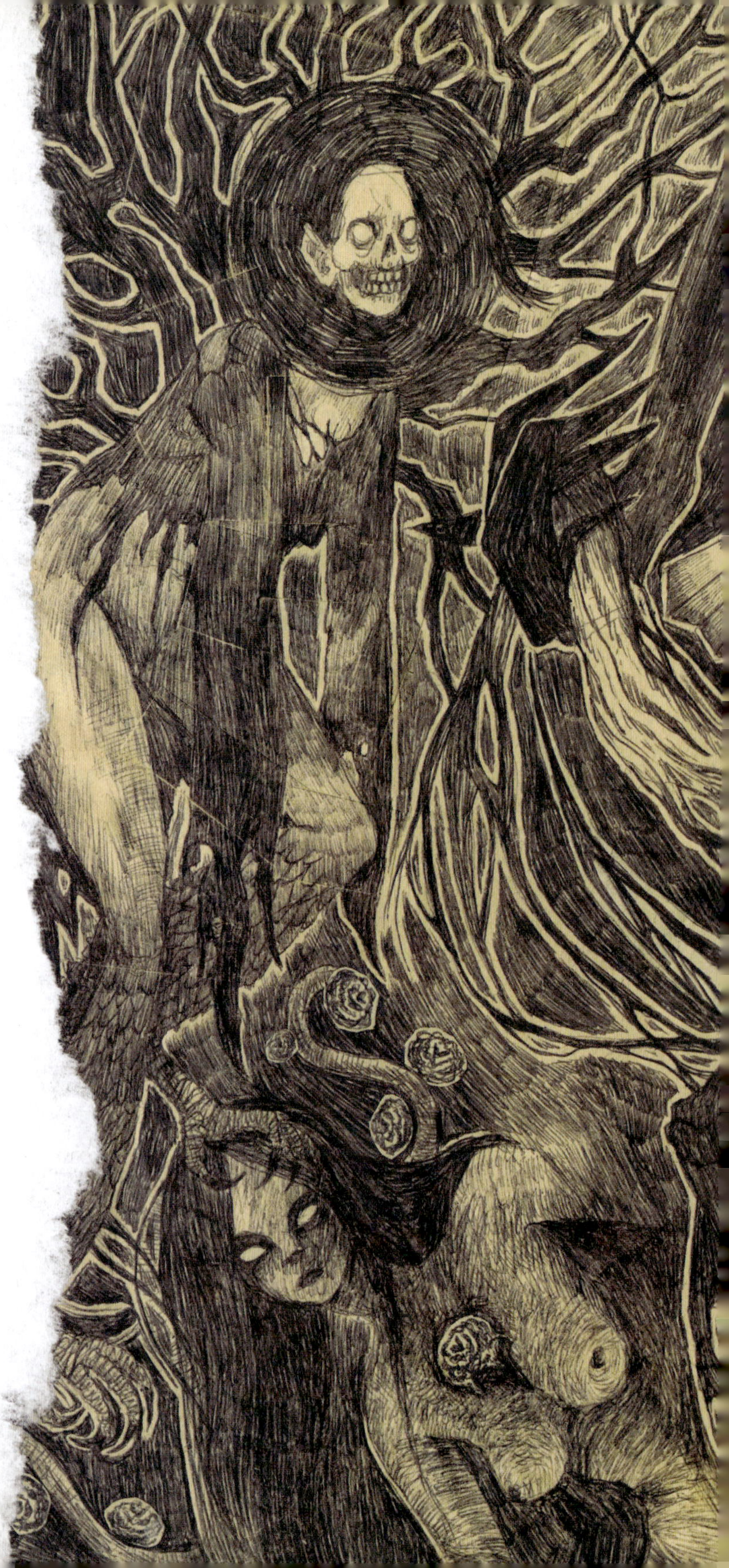

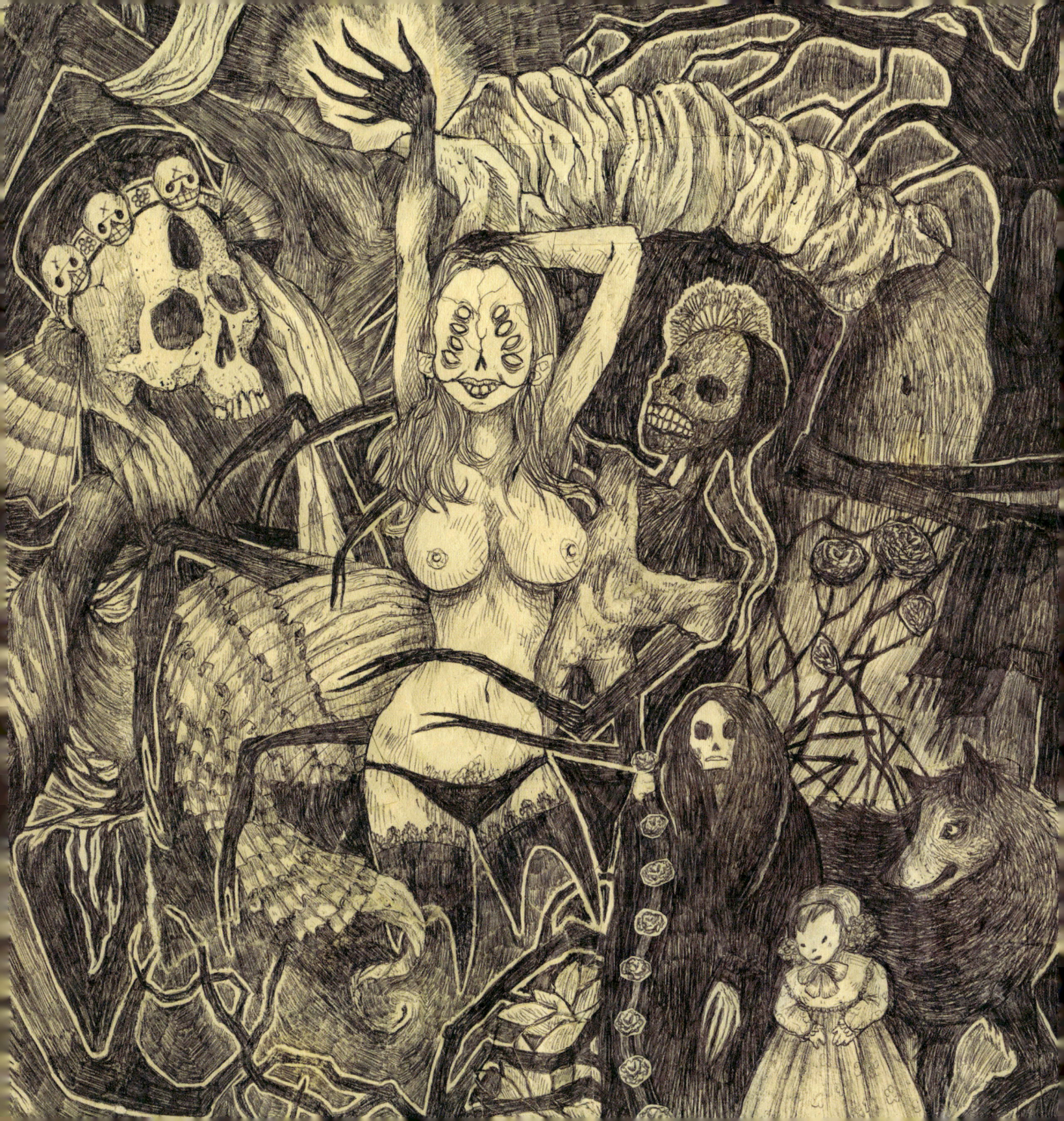

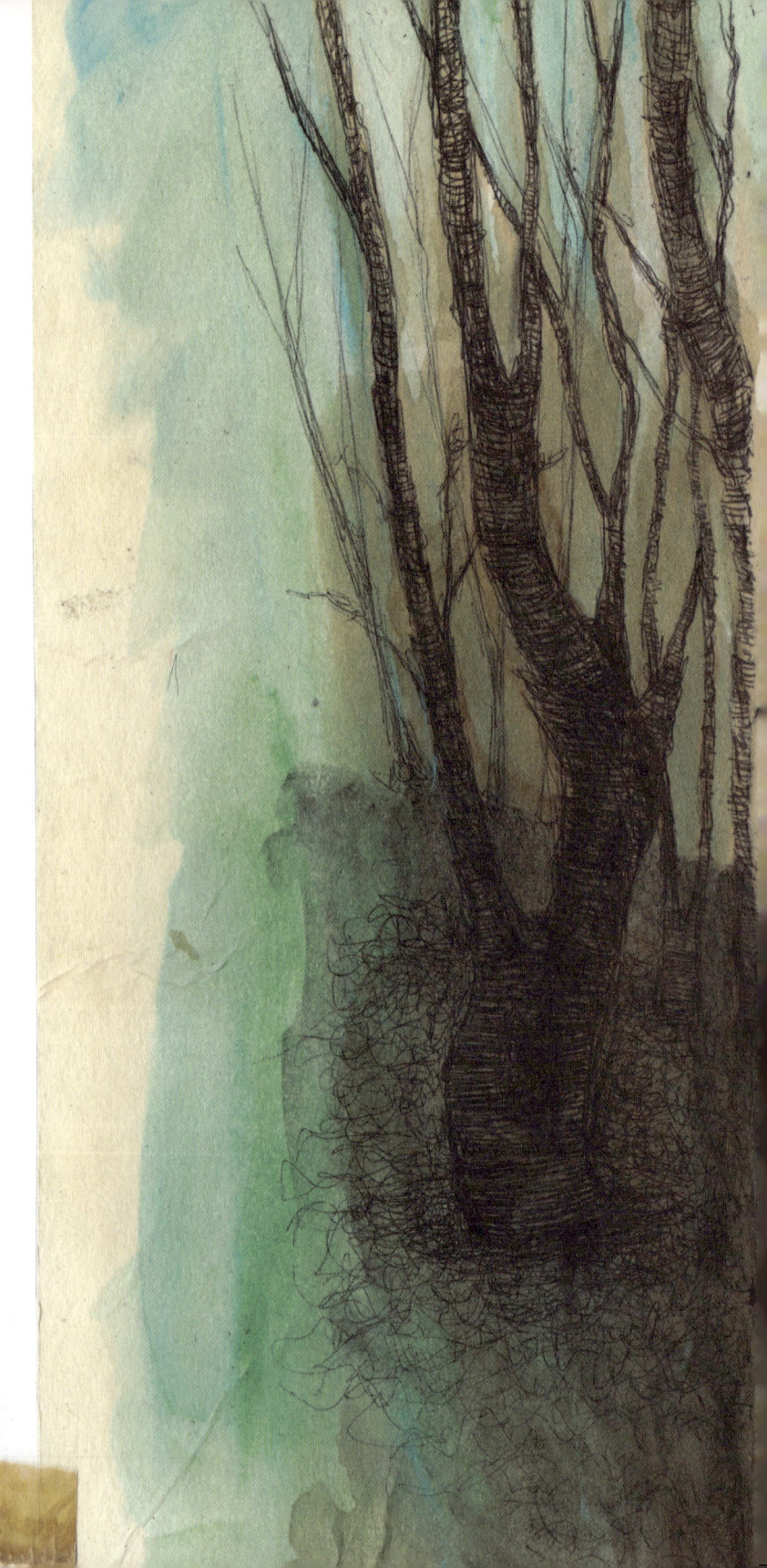

I have always been a walker. Not a zombie, that would be cool. Just someone who goes out into the forest to walk. I don't like walking with other people, I want to walk alone with my thoughts. I don't listen to music either. My walks give my mind a break. My thoughts get to settle in, and then new ideas bubble up. It's fascinating how the mind will continue to work without any effort, so I just let it.

When I walk, I have this recurring fantasy or daydream that happens. It's part of my routine.

I think it stems from my love of mummies. There are so many different types of mummies from different places, and they were all created by the dry air, in different ways, intentionally, accidentally. So, sometimes, when I'm walking, especially in forests, I have this weird fantasy that I'm following this mummy that's stiffly walking ahead of me. Just shuffling ahead, slowly, creekily, shuffling. I'm following her. I love her, my horror walking guide. This is her.

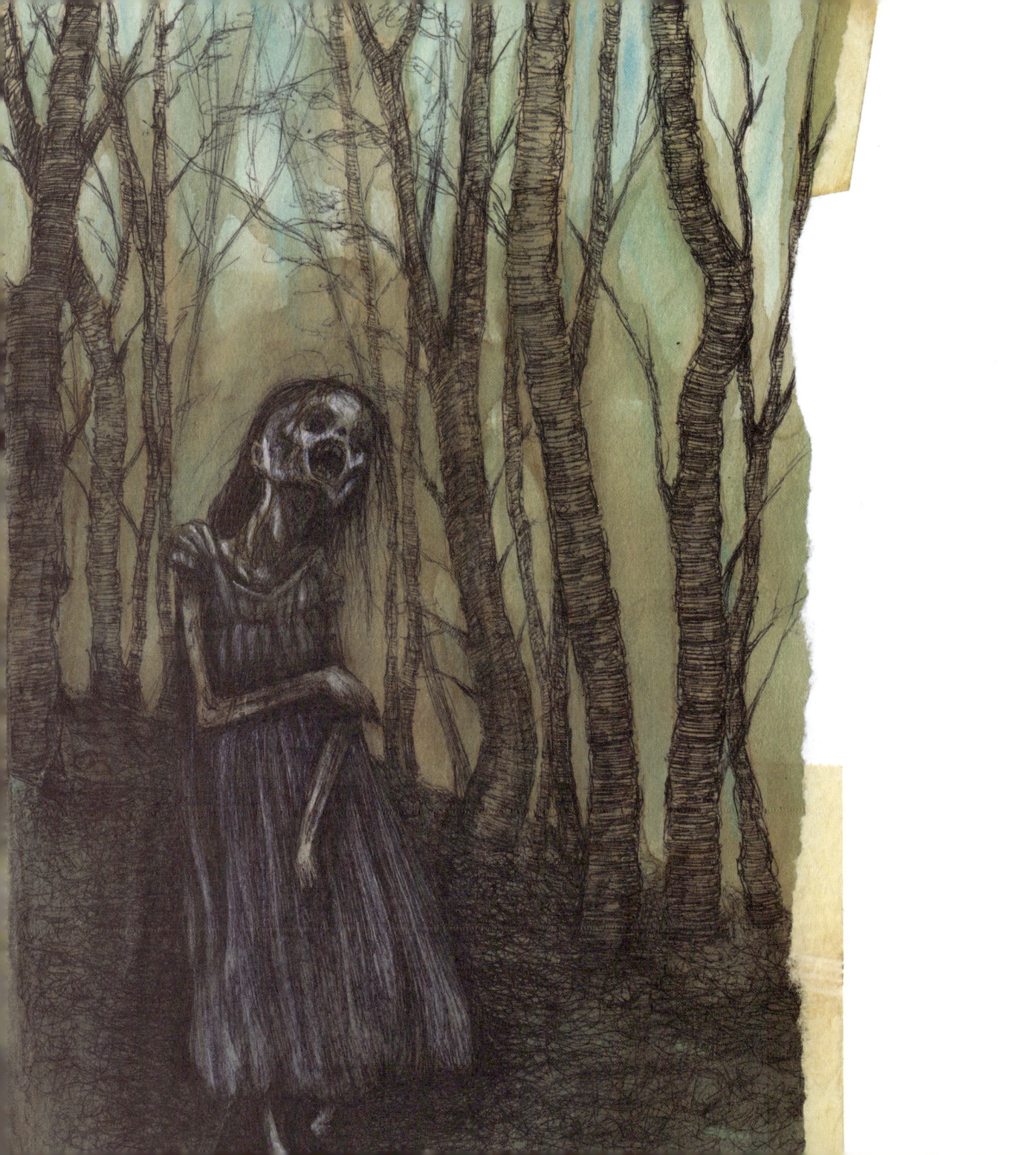

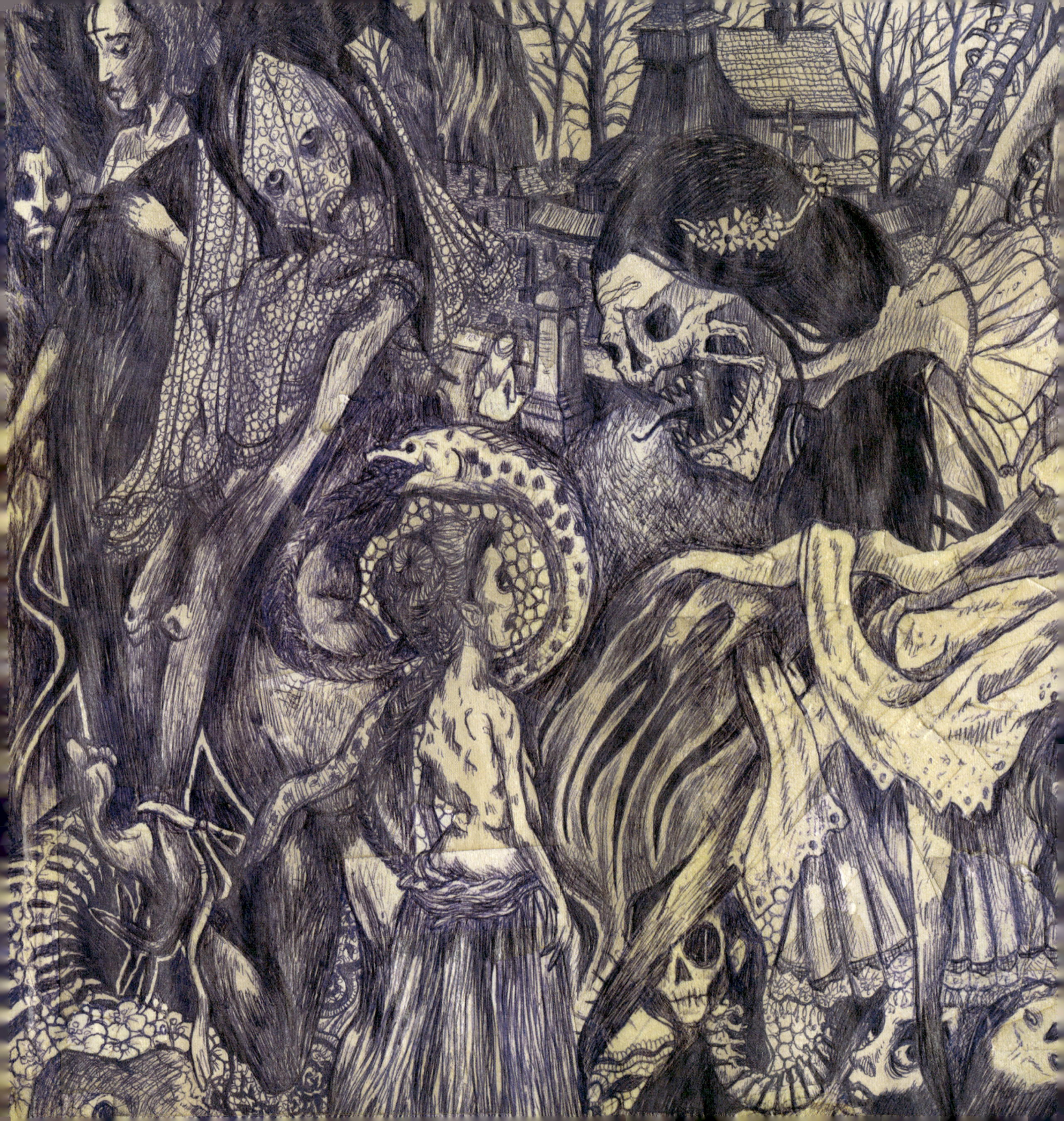

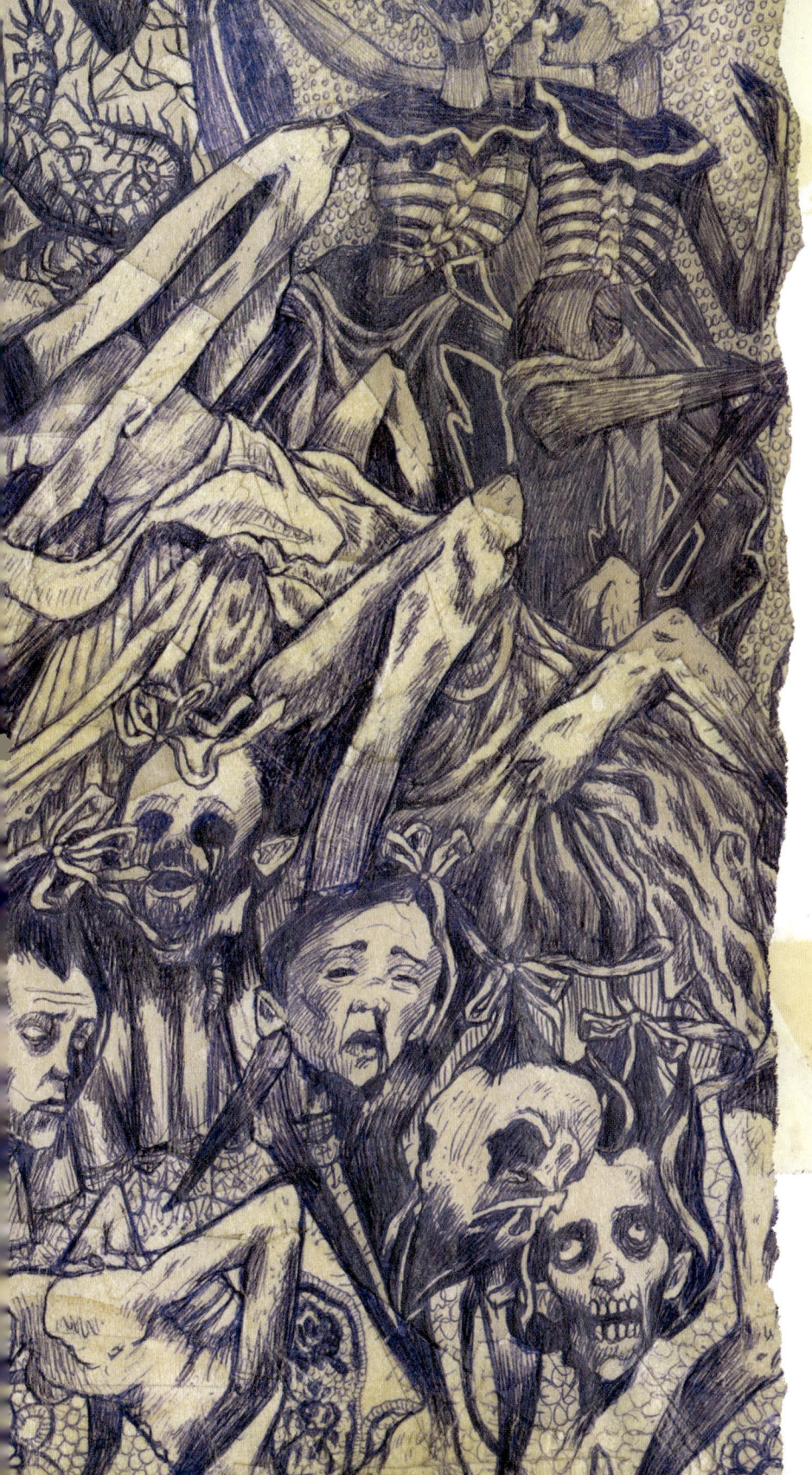

A completely therapeutic collage.
In the top corner is the old church from my
village in Poland [Note: St. Michael Archangel's
Church in Debno, Poland]. It's a twelfth
century church, and it's a historic site in
Poland, and that's the village I grew up in.
I was baptized here, and my grandma would
take me to church there every day. The inside
is all wood, and it's covered in beautiful,
colourful collages. It's part of me, it's my
village, it's where I grew up, and that's where
my parents are from, all my grandparents,
my whole family. A strange little village with
that historic church dead centre. Poland, and
my Polish roots, have such a sway over me.
I left Poland when I was three, but I feel like
I didn't really leave until I was much older.
I lived life in Polish, with Polish tradition,
and Polish food for so long before I came to
school in Canada, and then even in school
I was a bit of an outcast; my only real identity
was Polish for so long. It still is. I remember this
church, vivid memories of my family around the
town, in the rain. When I look at this picture,
I think of that place and being that young child.

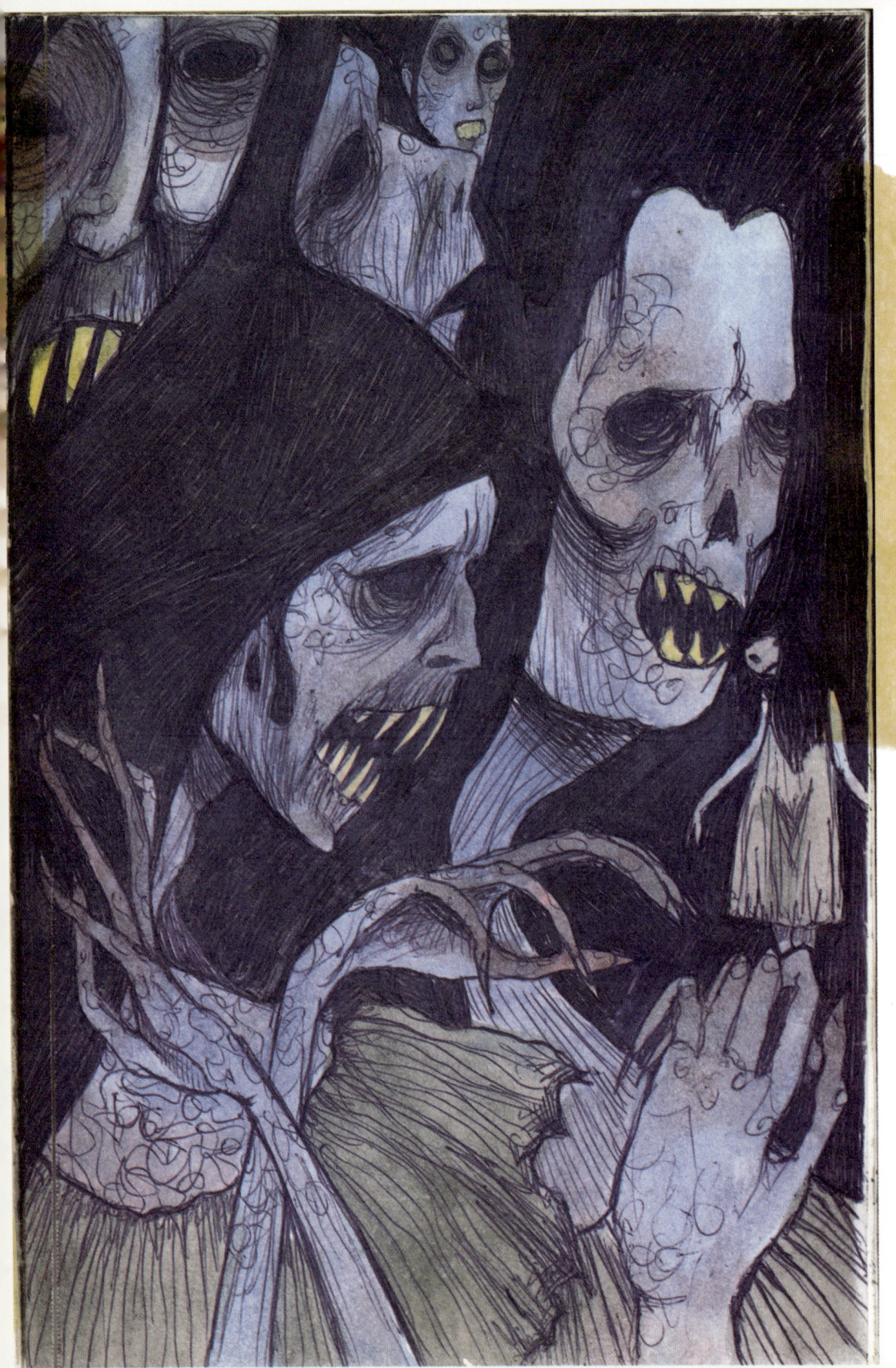

These are a set of distorted creatures like *hama* and the flute woman from *IT*. Their eyes are distorted in death, they aren't aligned, their faces aren't symmetrical. Junji Ito, a Japanese manga artist, has an elongated, tall woman character that's absolutely terrifying, it's so inspiring! There's one story where this boy is looking through a telescope, and he's looking at all the apartment buildings across the street and there's this woman, and she looks right at him, right into his telescope. Then she runs out of her apartment, down the street, and the boy can see that she's running into his apartment building. He stands there and watches her come. She bursts into his room and kills him. Amazing. It blew my mind. I think I'd just stand there too and let her murder me with a knife.

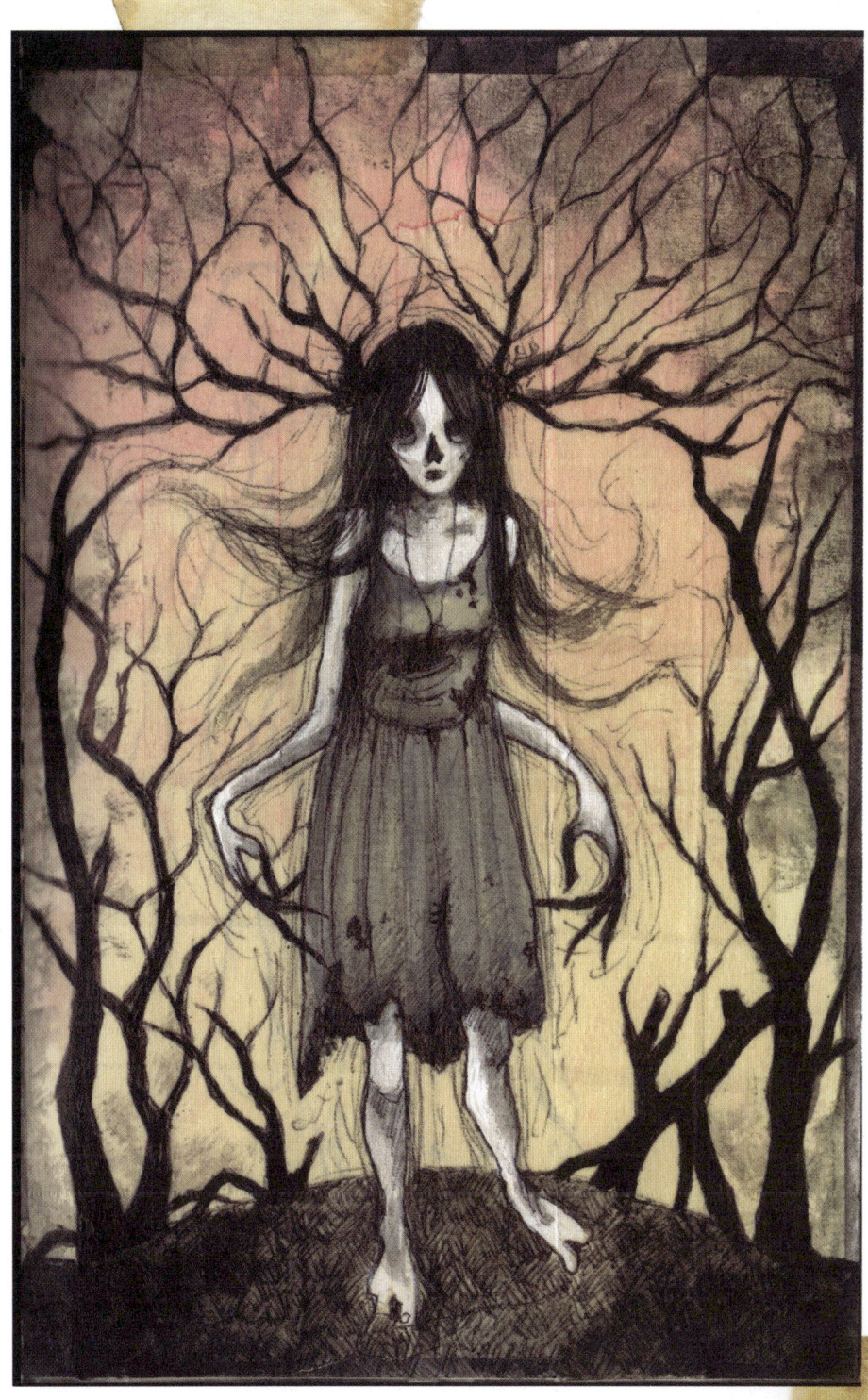

This one's on masking tape with shitty pencil crayons so that the colour isn't too bright. It's also inspired by *hama*, obviously, but also my obsession with dead, murdered girls in the woods, with sisters, and with hair. This is my portrait of obsessions.

hama was released when I was starting to draw again, and it gave me a creative burst. The trailer resonated with me. I was looking forward to the film so much that I skipped a surgery to go watch it. I was just experiencing the most intense pain I've ever felt and I blew it off. I said to myself, "I can't have surgery this weekend because *hama*'s coming out."

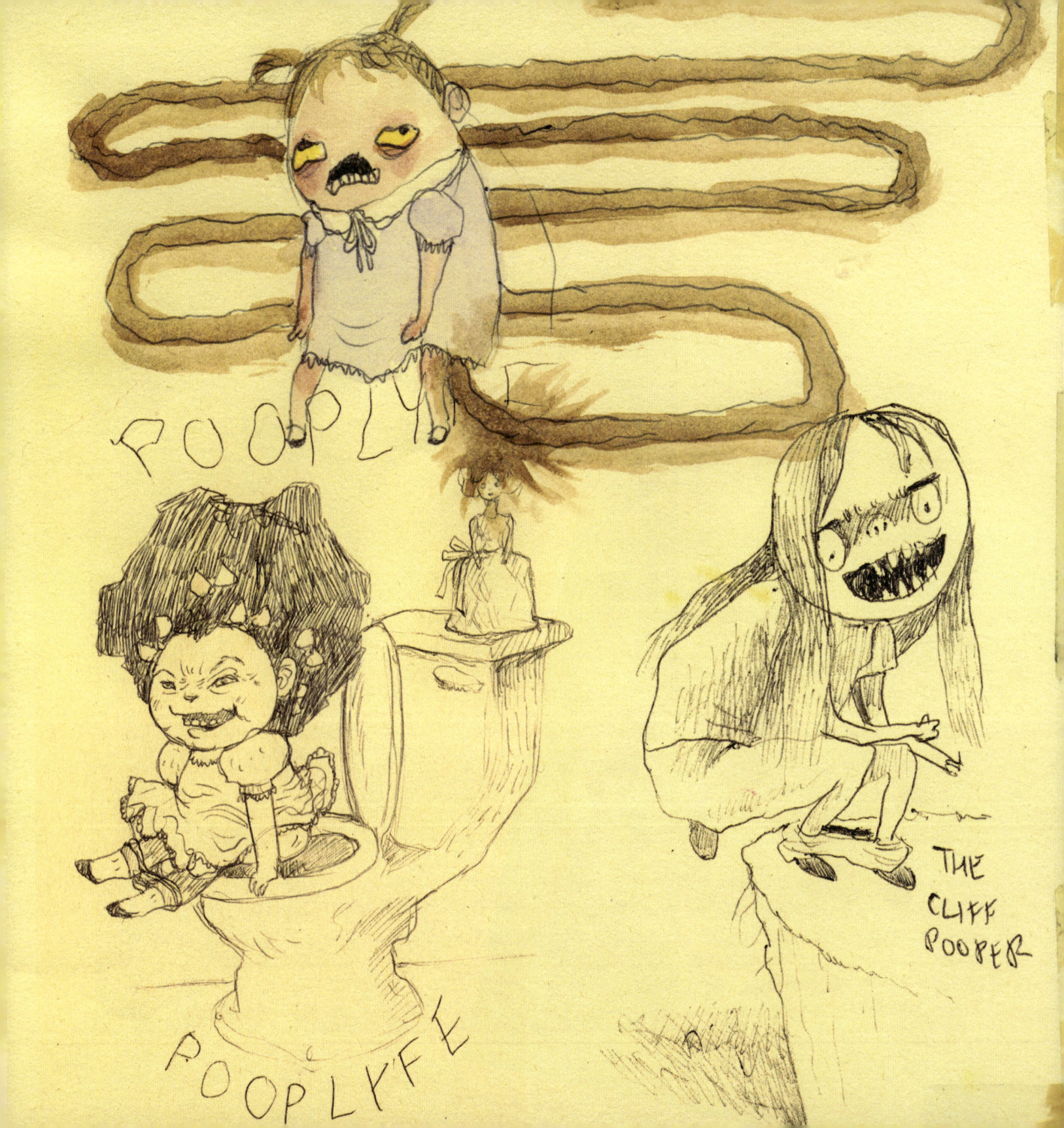

POOPLYFE

POOPLYFE

THE CLIFF POOPER

I like this one for the shading. I was allowing the colour in. It was a study in shade, and then he happened to look like he was sitting on a big turd.

PART II:
GET INTO MY BRAIN, WE'RE GOING TO HELL!

WERE you gonna EAT THAT?

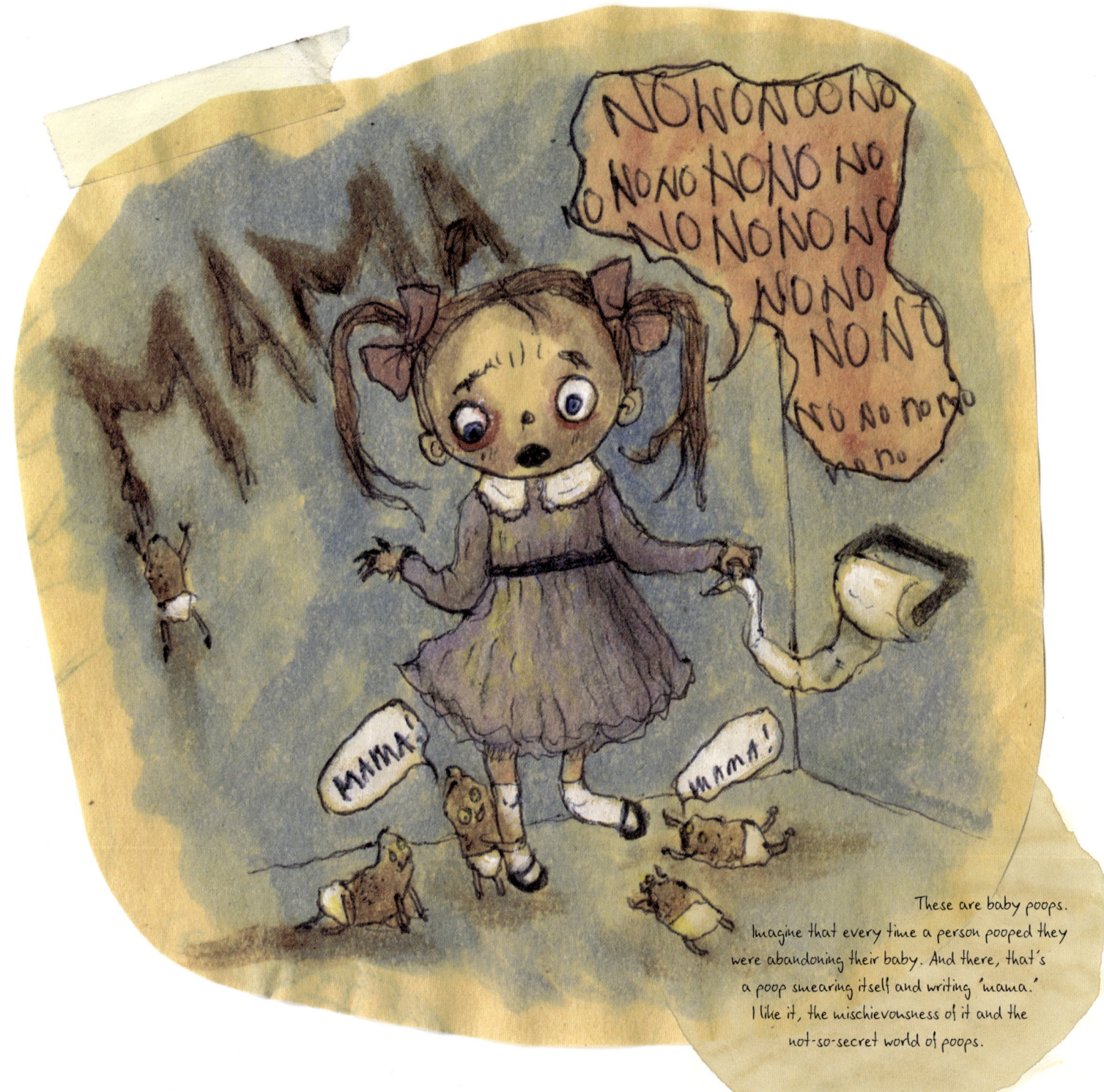

These are baby poops.
Imagine that every time a person pooped they
were abandoning their baby. And there, that's
a poop smearing itself and writing "mama."
I like it, the mischievousness of it and the
not-so-secret world of poops.

I saw some drawings with hair creatures, and I thought they were very interesting, and I'm really into hair (as is obvious by now), and then I thought, "Hey, what if the ass was on the top?" That was my inspiration. If someone tells me that a piece like this is too vulgar, that's basically saying I can't do what I do, which is a challenge, which means I'll do it. And I'll do it over and over again. My response is always, "Okay. Here comes more!" This art is about having nothing sacred. I don't care about propriety. I can make a poop cute; I can pull it off, don't worry about it.

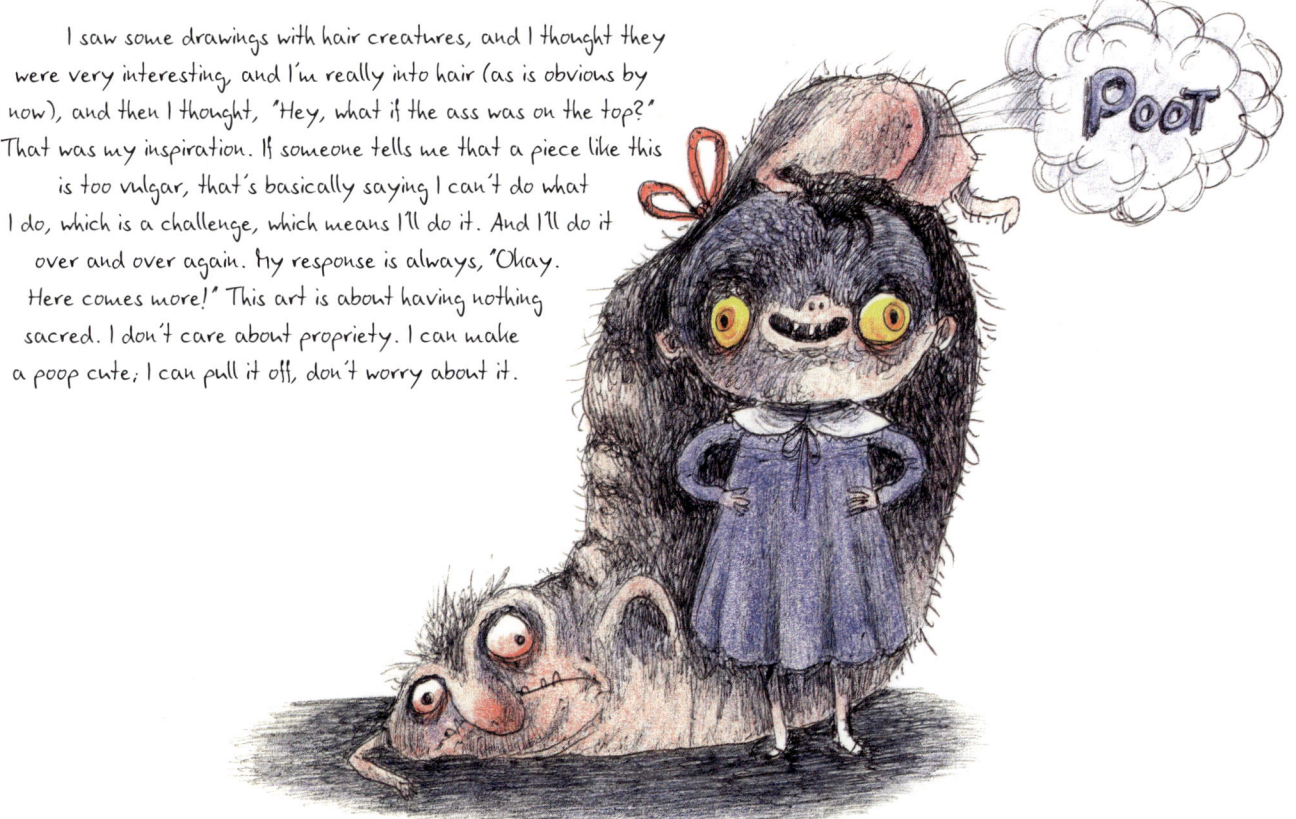

POOP! I DRAW POOP BECAUSE IT'S FUNNY! I DRAW IT because I'm not supposed to. I've never seen "real" artists draw this much poop. But I'm selfish. I don't like rules. So I draw Poop Girl and poop people because I make myself laugh and that's what it's all about. I throw expectation and propriety in the face of anyone who shies away from poop because we have to face it: everyone poops!

I'm especially attached to the little poop people who have this whole weird mythos about them that exists in my head and comes to life in my art. The little poops gather around when someone is sad, and they cheer that person up because they are silly or strange or charming. It's absurd and laughable. Mischief is at the root of why I love drawing poop and vaginas and all the period blood, these personal, secret, "sacred" things. My partner says I'm only happy when I'm causing mischief, and he's totally right. I love to stir up shit (pun intended!). I send Poop Girl out to everyone. Adding little poops or pushing the moment to such an extreme that it would cheer me up is a way to cope with the most miserable moments in life.

I always draw on the envelopes or wrapping for the art I send out. I've had messages from people who couldn't open their envelopes because they'd destroy the envelope art. People are like (read this in a squeaky obnoxious voice, sorry fans), "Oh no, I ripped the envelope to get my order—I had to open the envelope to get the art inside, but your drawing was there." And my response, inside my own mind anyways, is always,

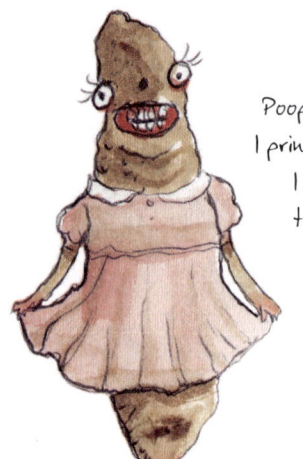

Poop Girl! She's adorable. I love her. She's got a pretty dress.
I printed her out and sent her off with my packages for a long time.
I made a little ornament for people. My thought process was, 'Here's a little poop too, you should probably hang it up. Don't worry about it. We all poop.' I think this one succeeds in making poop cute. To further desecrate everything sacred about shitting, I drew this one on the front page of my favourite serious poetry book. Why? Because it was funny. Poop Girl is art just as much as the poetry, but which one is really better?

express yourself ♥

I keep telling my son that I'm from the sewer. He's too smart, he doesn't buy it. I sing songs about how I'm from the sewer and how that makes him a sewer child. I find so much joy in that and in his reactions. I like to add some absurdity to my son's life, he's so straight-edge. I mean, he's funny, and he's into horror, but I think we, my partner and I, we bullshit so much in the house to lighten him up, to let him know that human beings are weird and gross and that's okay. He has to be the parent a lot, which is fun, it's reverse parenting. I also enjoy that this girl's dress is all covered in sewer water and shit. Charming.

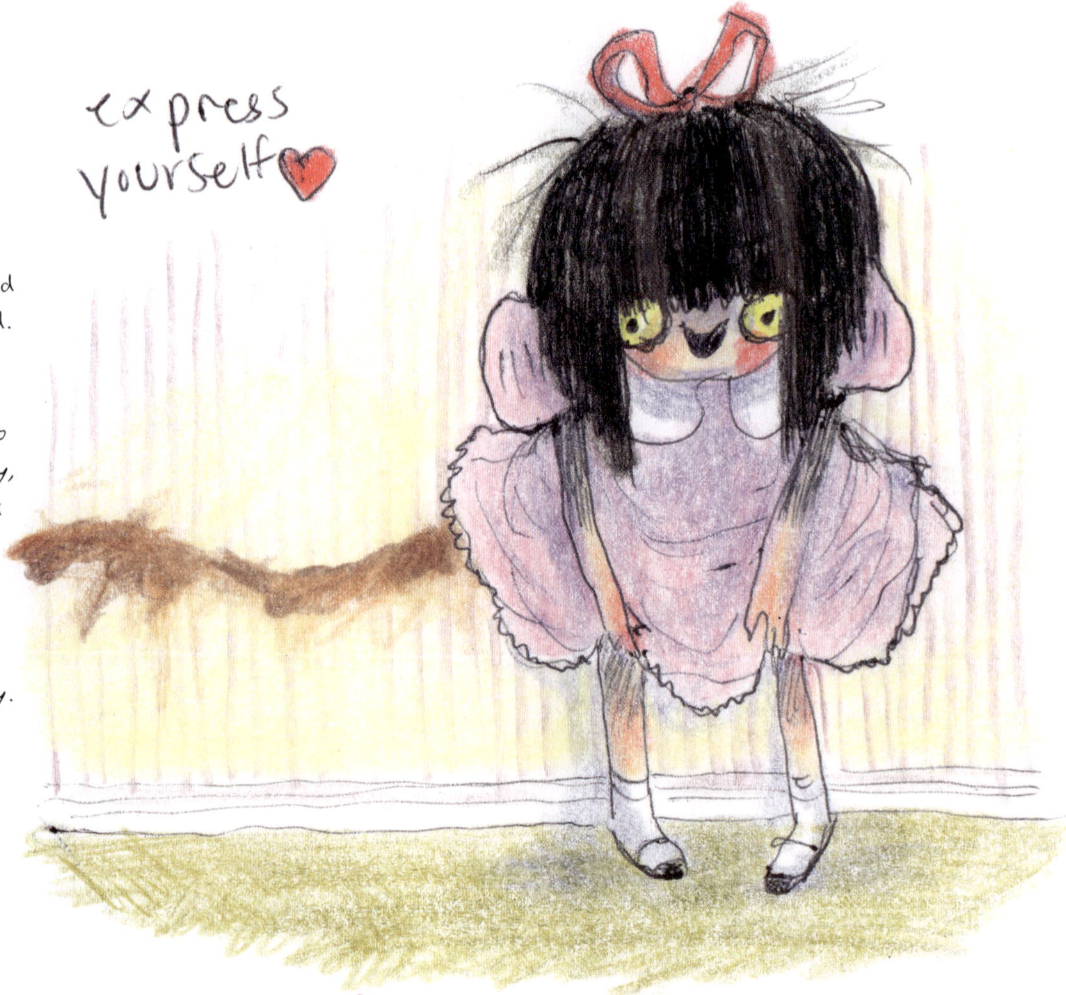

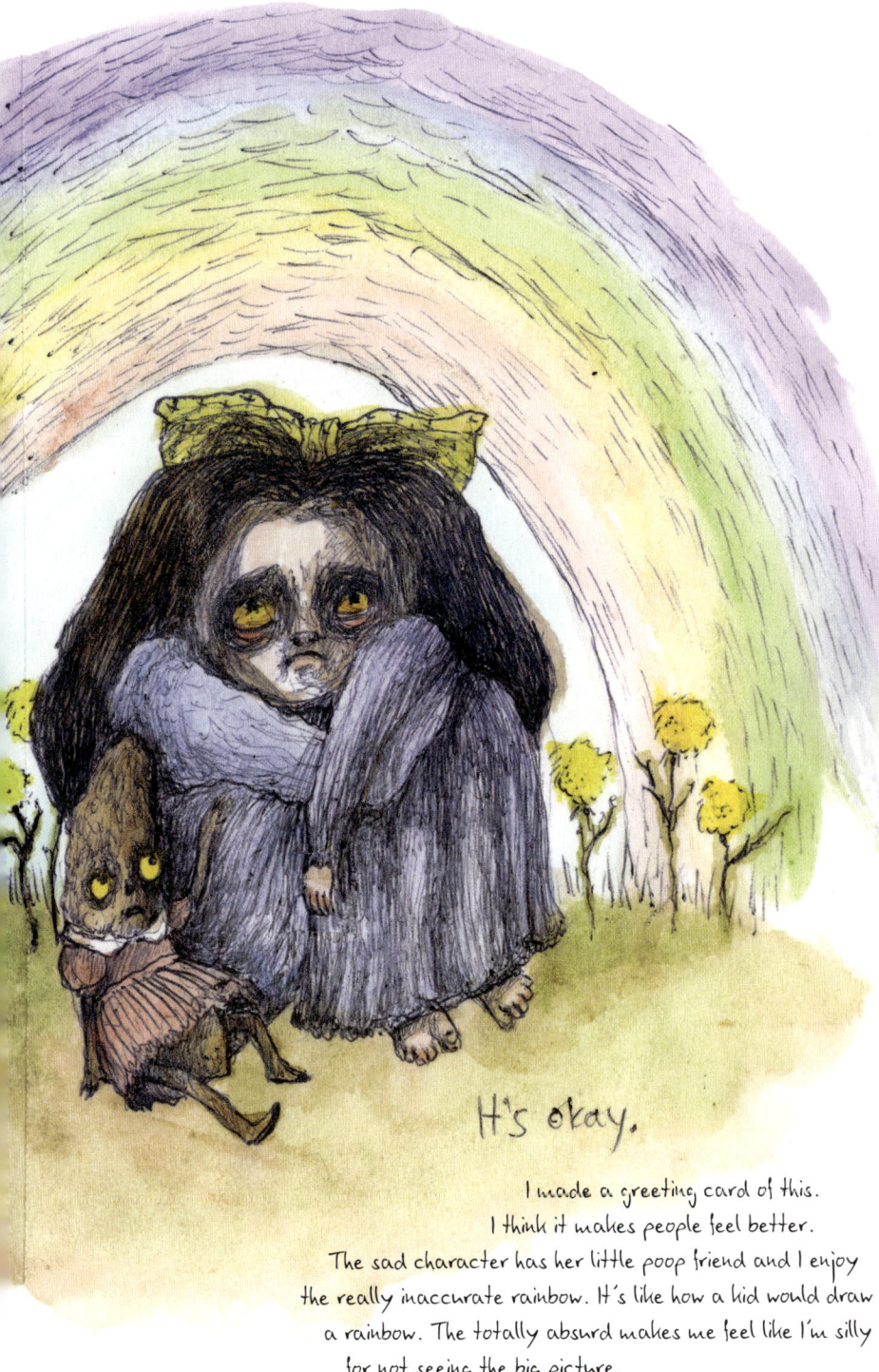

H's okay.

I made a greeting card of this.
I think it makes people feel better.
The sad character has her little poop friend and I enjoy
the really inaccurate rainbow. It's like how a kid would draw
a rainbow. The totally absurd makes me feel like I'm silly
for not seeing the big picture.

"Good. Art is temporary, everything is fleeting. Good." I love the idea that people don't know what to do when they receive their package and realize that to get to the original piece they have to rip through more original art! It's mean, but it's funny, I have this horrible glee at the thought. I get the same feeling when I send poops out into the world too; it's a horrible, mischievous glee.

I'm inspired by real life to draw poop because, let's face it, we all poop and it's always awkward and hilarious. So I was pooping in an Old Navy recently and the fire alarm went off and, naturally, I thought, "Fuck. Fuck this. I'm not going. I'm just going to stay here and shit on the toilet and burn." I kept picturing store employees searching the bathrooms and finding me, or firemen finding my pooping corpse. When I was finished (and, yes, I washed my hands) and left the bathroom, I found that no one had left. No one had left the store. I thought to myself, "Jeez, good decision-making, people. Never leave a burning building." They were all bargain hunting and ignoring the alarm meant to save their lives. I should have known better, it was morning, I'd just dropped my son off, and I'd had my first coffee. I didn't make it home on time to shit because I decided to browse cardigans.

I drew this the same week as the sad girl under
the childish rainbow. They sort of go
together. Her hair is a big frizzy fro,
untamable. Here too is a reference to
the *Smurfs* and *Care Bears* where
these little child-friendly creatures
can make everything better
with a healing stare, like
all eighties children's
cartoons that
I used to like.

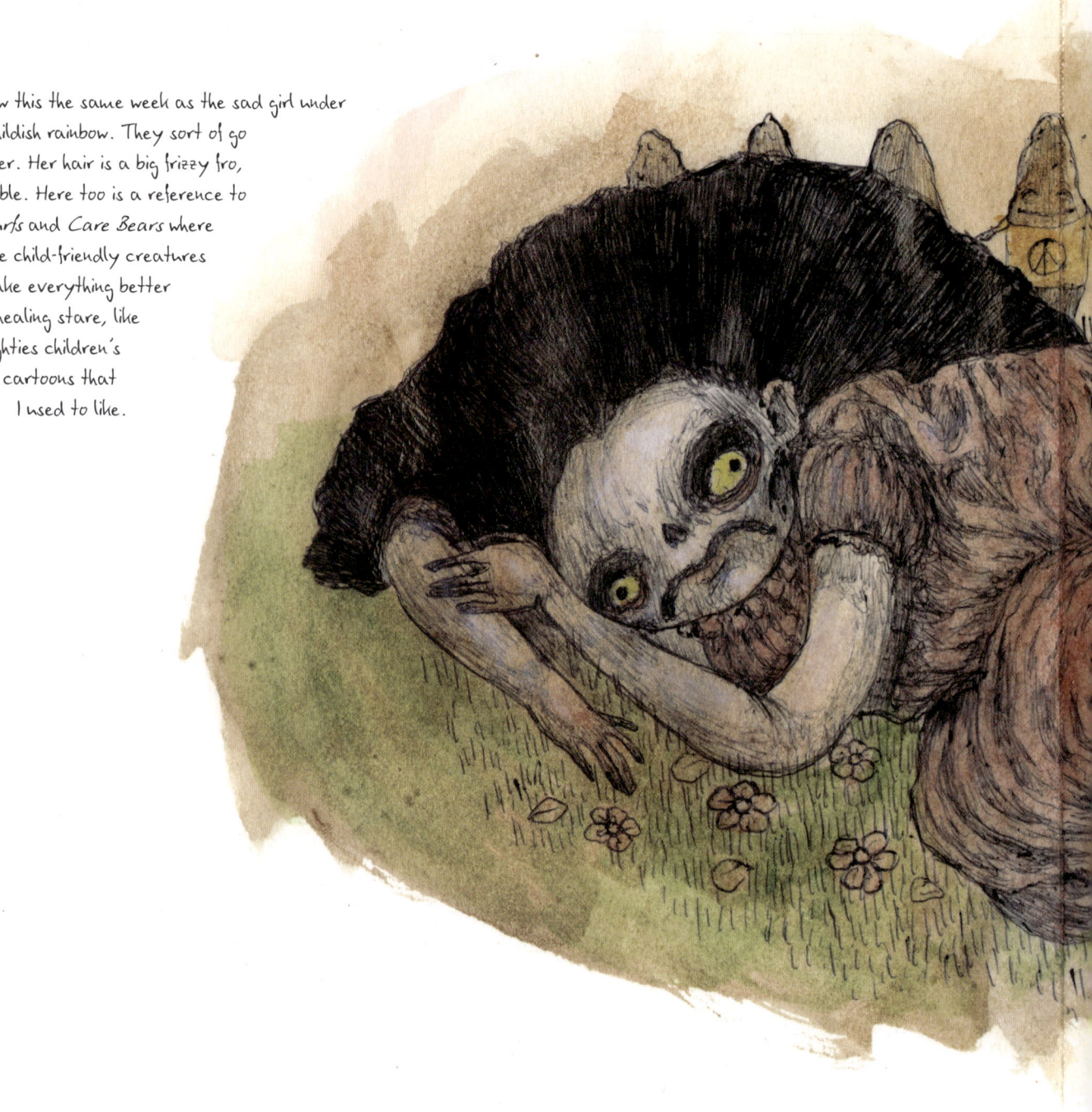

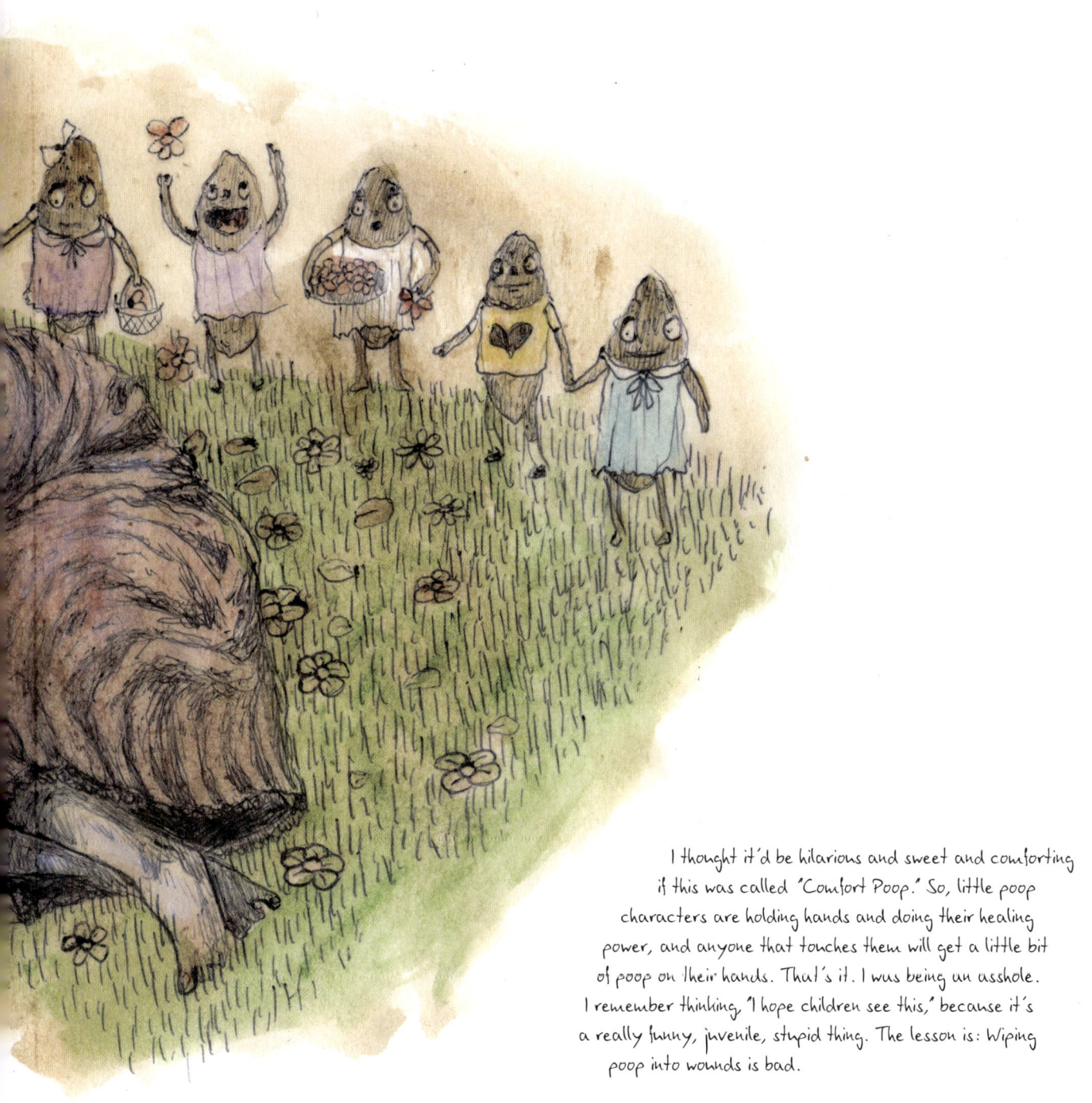

I thought it'd be hilarious and sweet and comforting
if this was called 'Comfort Poop.' So, little poop
characters are holding hands and doing their healing
power, and anyone that touches them will get a little bit
of poop on their hands. That's it. I was being an asshole.
I remember thinking, 'I hope children see this,' because it's
a really funny, juvenile, stupid thing. The lesson is: Wiping
poop into wounds is bad.

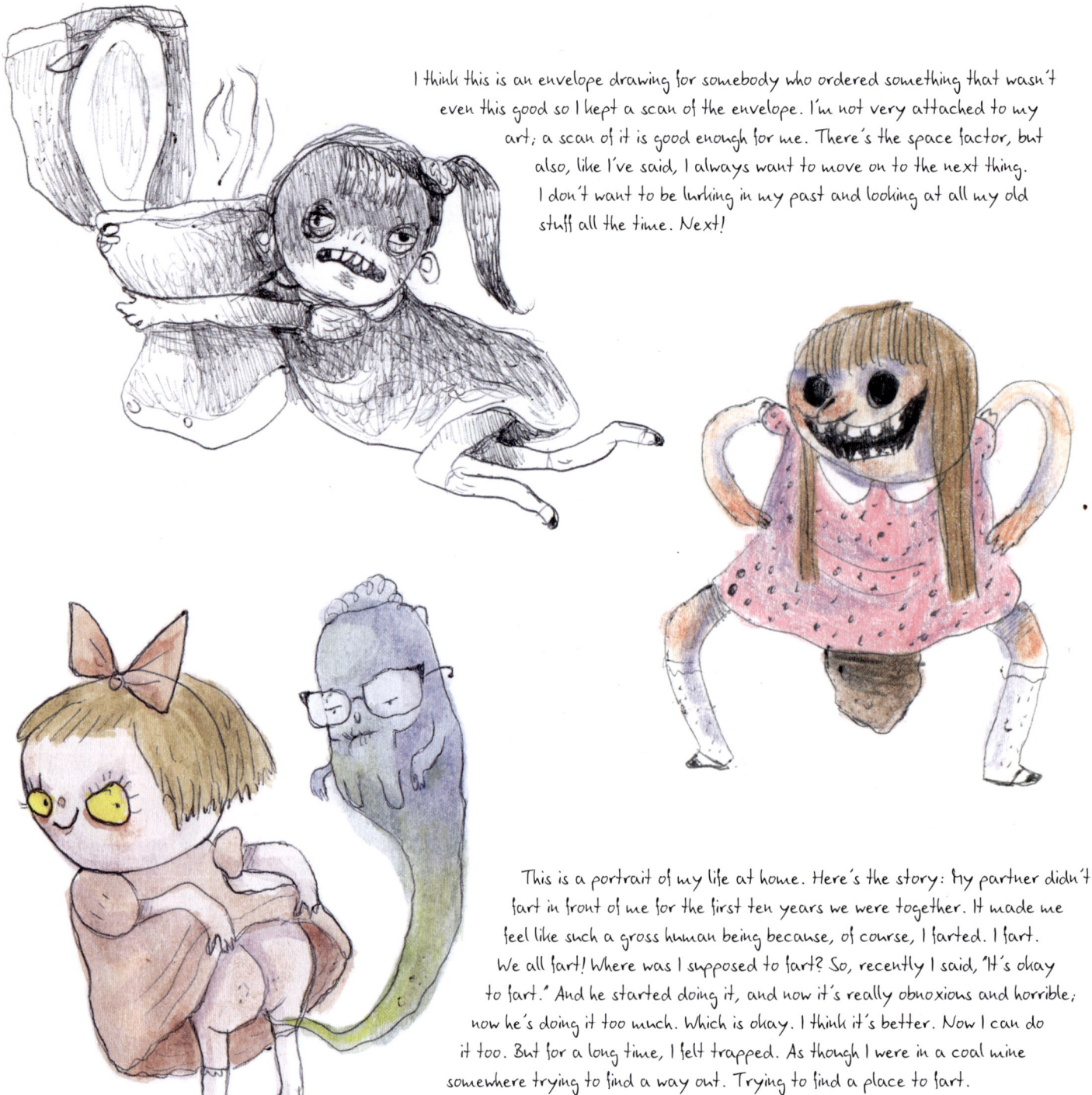

I think this is an envelope drawing for somebody who ordered something that wasn't even this good so I kept a scan of the envelope. I'm not very attached to my art; a scan of it is good enough for me. There's the space factor, but also, like I've said, I always want to move on to the next thing. I don't want to be lurking in my past and looking at all my old stuff all the time. Next!

This is a portrait of my life at home. Here's the story: My partner didn't fart in front of me for the first ten years we were together. It made me feel like such a gross human being because, of course, I farted. I fart. We all fart! Where was I supposed to fart? So, recently I said, "It's okay to fart." And he started doing it, and now it's really obnoxious and horrible; now he's doing it too much. Which is okay. I think it's better. Now I can do it too. But for a long time, I felt trapped. As though I were in a coal mine somewhere trying to find a way out. Trying to find a place to fart.

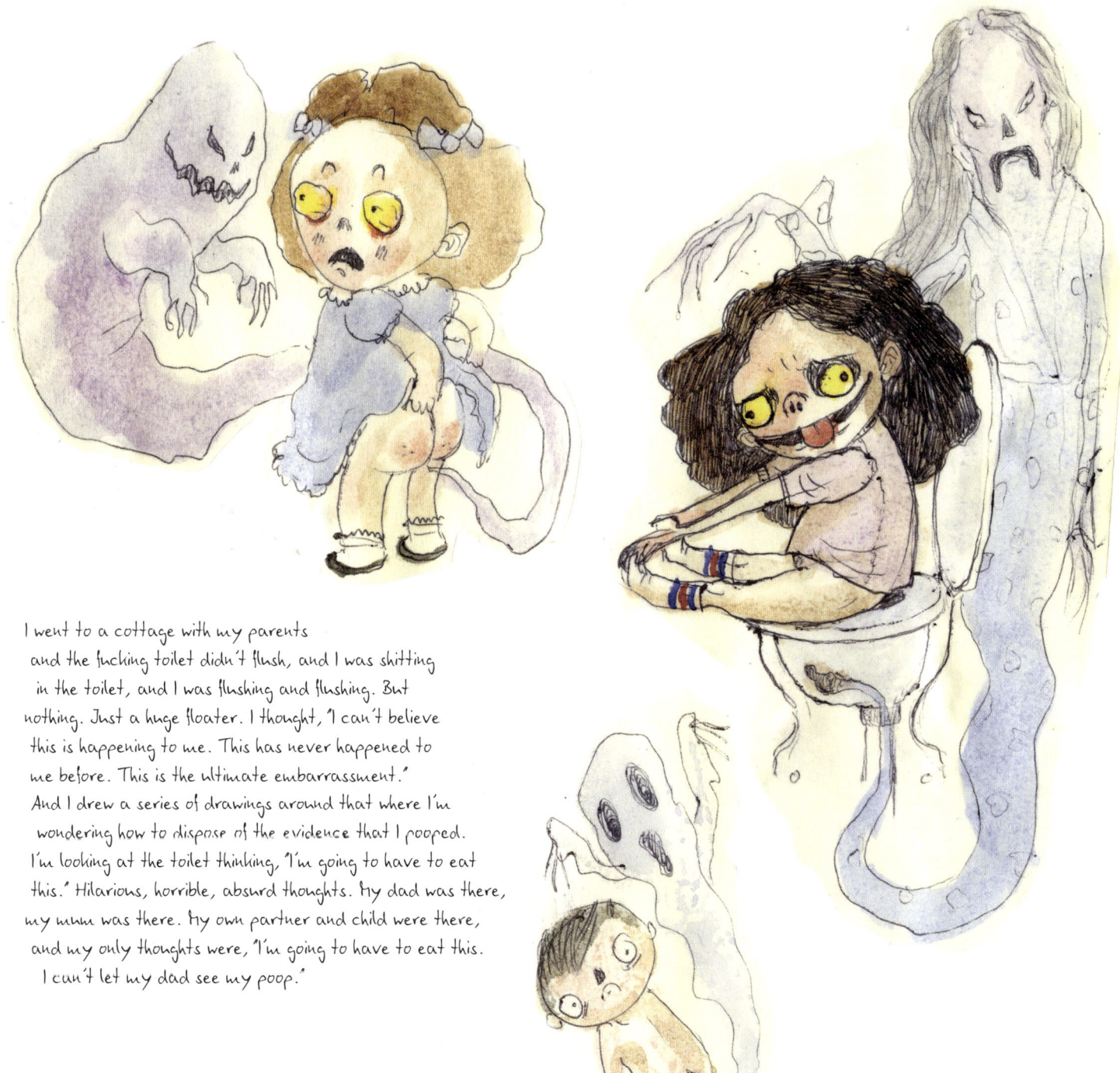

I went to a cottage with my parents
and the fucking toilet didn't flush, and I was shitting
in the toilet, and I was flushing and flushing. But
nothing. Just a huge floater. I thought, 'I can't believe
this is happening to me. This has never happened to
me before. This is the ultimate embarrassment.'
And I drew a series of drawings around that where I'm
wondering how to dispose of the evidence that I pooped.
I'm looking at the toilet thinking, 'I'm going to have to eat
this.' Hilarious, horrible, absurd thoughts. My dad was there,
my mum was there. My own partner and child were there,
and my only thoughts were, 'I'm going to have to eat this.
    I can't let my dad see my poop.'

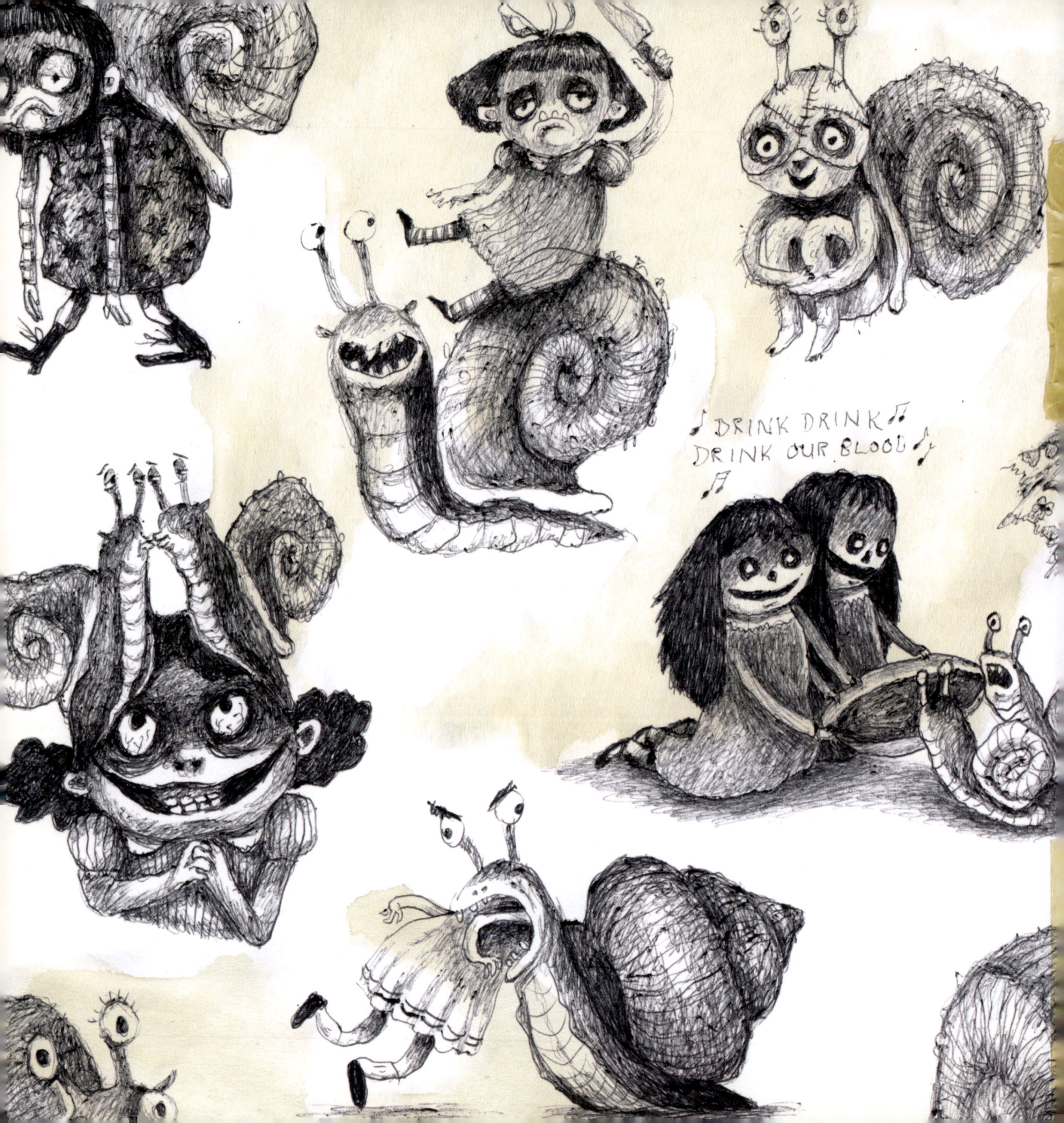

♪ DRINK DRINK ♫
DRINK OUR BLOOD ♪

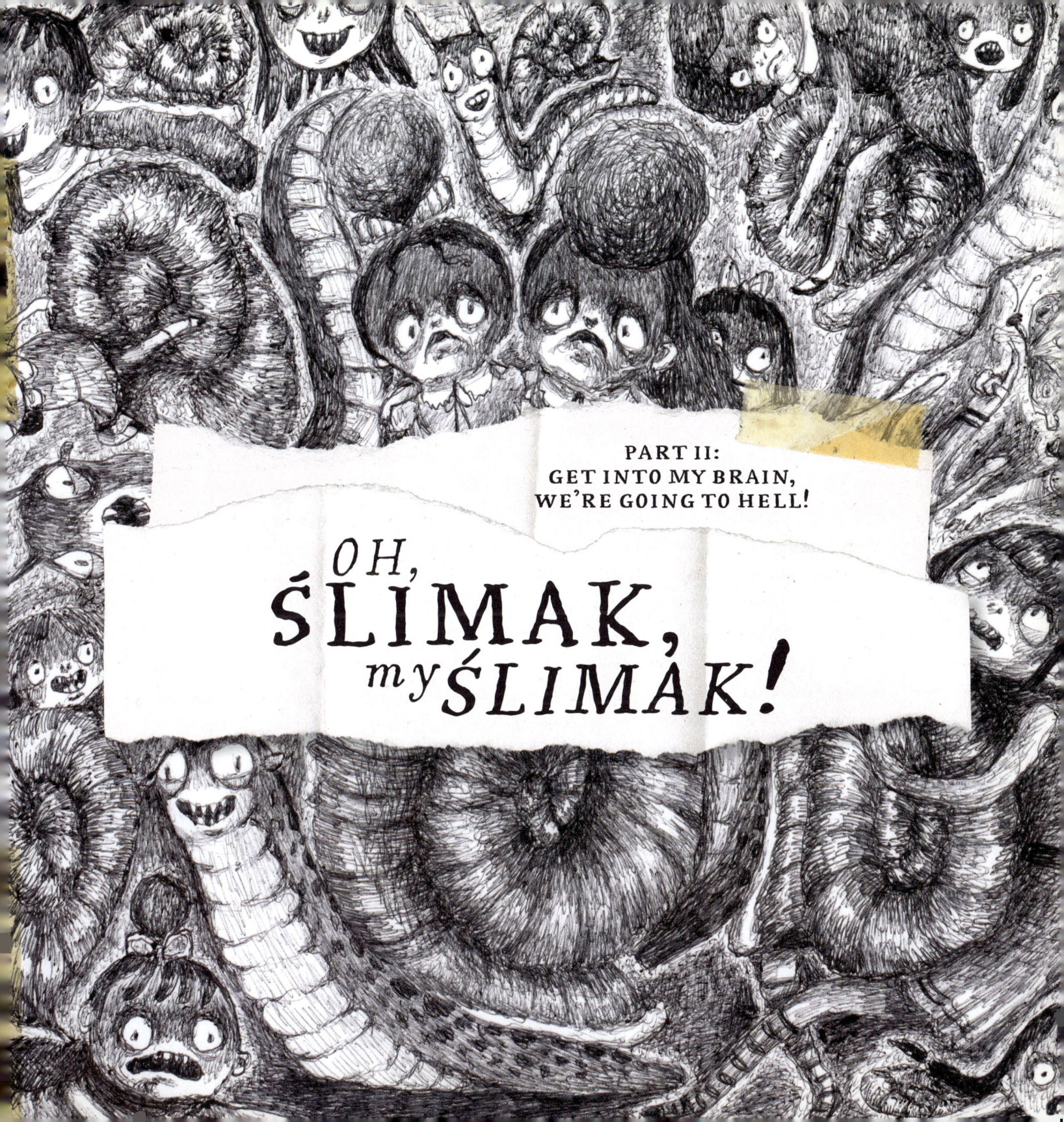

PART II:
GET INTO MY BRAIN,
WE'RE GOING TO HELL!

OH, ŚLIMAK, myŚLIMAK!

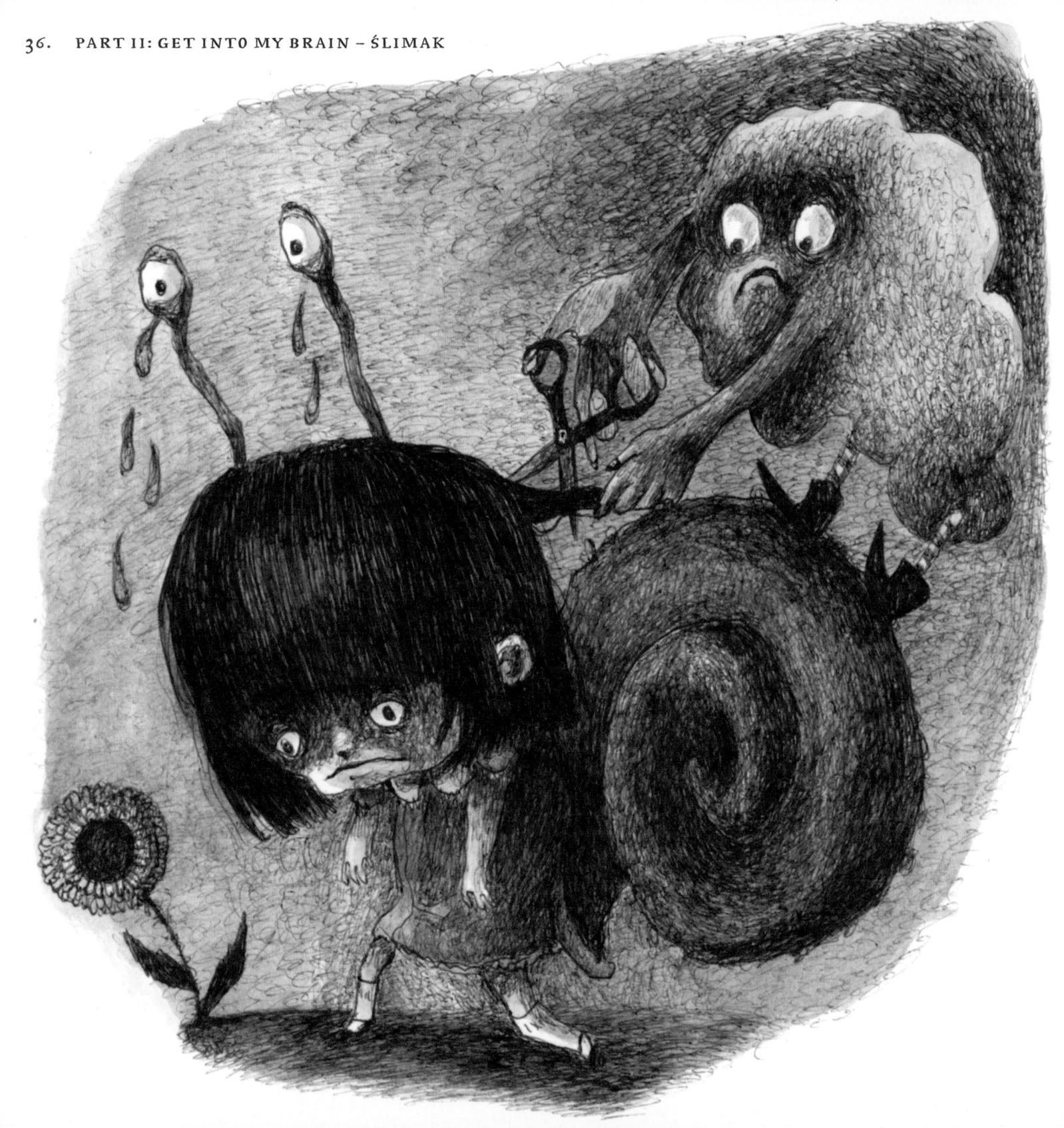

I LOVE SNAILS. THERE ARE CERTAIN ANIMALS THAT ARE amazing to draw because they can be really exagg- erated and easily transformed, for me that's snails and wolves. I think a lot of artists find snails interesting. A lot of the Eastern European cartoons that I watched as a kid had snail and mushroom characters in them. They were very environmental, looking back on it. There were a lot of little characters in the forest and everything was sort of strange, even a little bit gross, but always visually pleasing. Beautiful-gross is kind of my theme. Snails end up in scenes frequently as a sort of "people." They are sympathetic helper-creatures that help others who are sad. They visit little sad girls and help them. Like the little poop people, and later the forest sprites, I have a lot of little characters in my drawings that act like little helpers, little happiness creatures. The snails are a weird, slimier version of fairies, I guess. I love watching nature shows to learn about how nature protects itself and expresses itself. Nature is so interesting, natural camouflage is fascinating, the way that animal bodies work can be so wacky. So, after I'd already started sketching and drawing and was moving into more absurd, weird, dramatic, unrestrained stuff, that's when snails appeared.

There was also a little book series that I read to my son when he was young and learning how to read. It was Mercer Mayer's *Little Critter* stories. The boy-critter is a little brat with a little sister and I felt like the stories were always about how unfair life was. Especially as a kid. I took care of my sister a lot and maybe I can relate to the boy-critter and the unfairness of sharing everything with another selfish child. There's an element in the books that I know I've held onto, and that's the little helpers. Small critters that appear in the images and seem to be on the boy-critter's side but don't say anything. Usually it's a spider, but there are frogs, dragonflies, grasshoppers. I use them too. The helper-creatures are small, maybe half-a-foot tall, they come in groups, and they are natural and neutral.

These are my snail people. They have a creepy stare. The stalks on these ones have decoy eyes, which I thought was cool. This is a cute, weird poem from my childhood that really informs my own sense of Polish identity,
   I remember my dad reciting it:

Ślimak, ślimak, pokaż rogi,
Dam ci sera na pierogi,
Jak nie sera, to kapusty,
Od kapusty będziesz tłusty.

Snail, Snail, show your horns,
I'll give you cheese for pierogi,
If not cheese, then cabbage,
From cabbage you'll be fat.

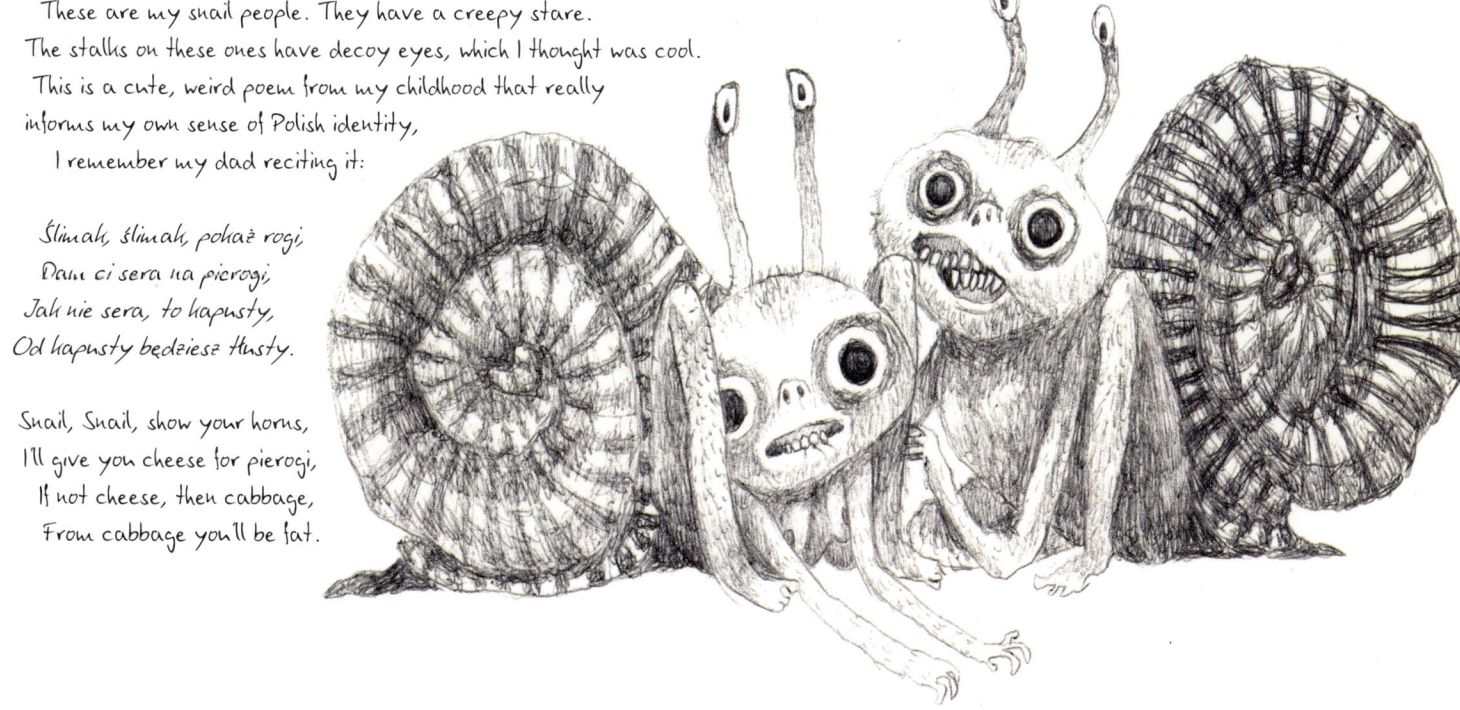

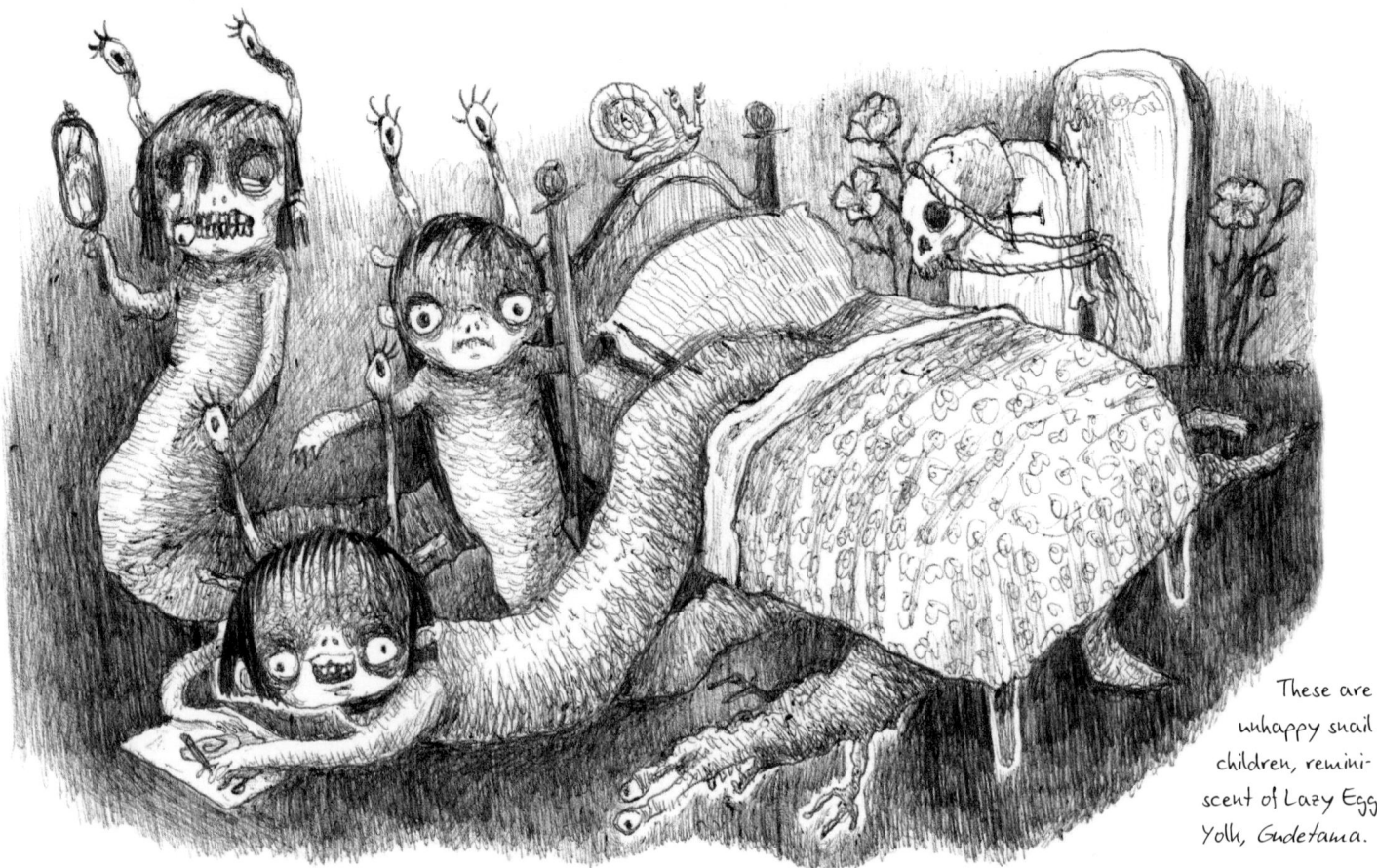

These are unhappy snail children, reminiscent of Lazy Egg Yolk, Gudetama.

I'm obsessed with Hideshi Hino, a Japanese artist. Hino and Edward Gorey have been my two inspirations since I was a kid. Hino is a manga artist for kids, but he draws horrific things. I think it may have been more acceptable twenty years ago when he was popular. He's got these amazing, amazing characters that have stayed with me and still inspire me. One is a slug girl. She deals with bullying or helping the down-and-out kid. Together the snail girl and whoever she's helped usually get their revenge or they die in a tree stump and then turn into butterflies. It's strange and beautiful, and I love it.

There's this concept of the *Gudetama* or "Lazy Egg Yolk" in Japanese culture. It is such a cathartic thing for a society to relate to! Seeing a character that is free to be apathetic or to curse and be rude is so freeing. I love watching that little thing. We have adult cartoon comedies here in North America, like *The Simpsons* or *Sponge Bob*, but I don't think we have a "Hey, it's okay, I feel like I want to kill myself" girl. That's what I'm trying to make, a fun little cathartic character.

I was three when I left Poland, but it's such a big part of me. It's weirdly a big part of me. We would go for forest walks as a kid in Poland and I always saw snails and little frogs, and berries. In Poland they're not called strawberries, they're a forest fruit called *poziomka*. A wild forest strawberry. It's more of a scent memory that takes me right back to Poland, to my childhood. I used to hate my Polish-ness. My parents would keep that alive in the home. We'd only speak Polish, and they talked about *poziomka* or the church or the river we lived close to, and my grandparents would come visit. After we moved to Canada we went back to Poland twice, and I hated it both times. I mean, I loved actual physical locations, but I didn't like all the people assuming I loved them or knew them because we were family. And I always had to kiss everyone. They were very touchy. It was awful. Eventually, I accepted my Polishness, but when I was going to school I would make an effort not to hang out with anybody Polish because I was sick of it. I couldn't express these complicated ideas or feelings. I was quiet. I needed to draw it. I needed a little snail friend.

Normally, I hate when I'm naked, and I hate when I'm flashing too much skin. But at the end of the night, I'm usually tired and feeling silly, and I certainly don't want to do anything responsible. I have been known to lift up my dress and stomp over to the bathroom saying, "I'm going to fucking brush my teeth now!" or "I'm gonna brush my toof!" (emphasis on 'toof') I think that's what happened right here. Irresponsible flashing and toof brushing.

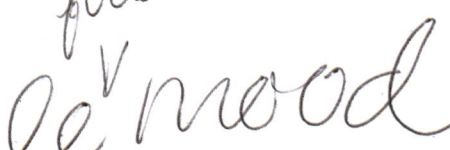

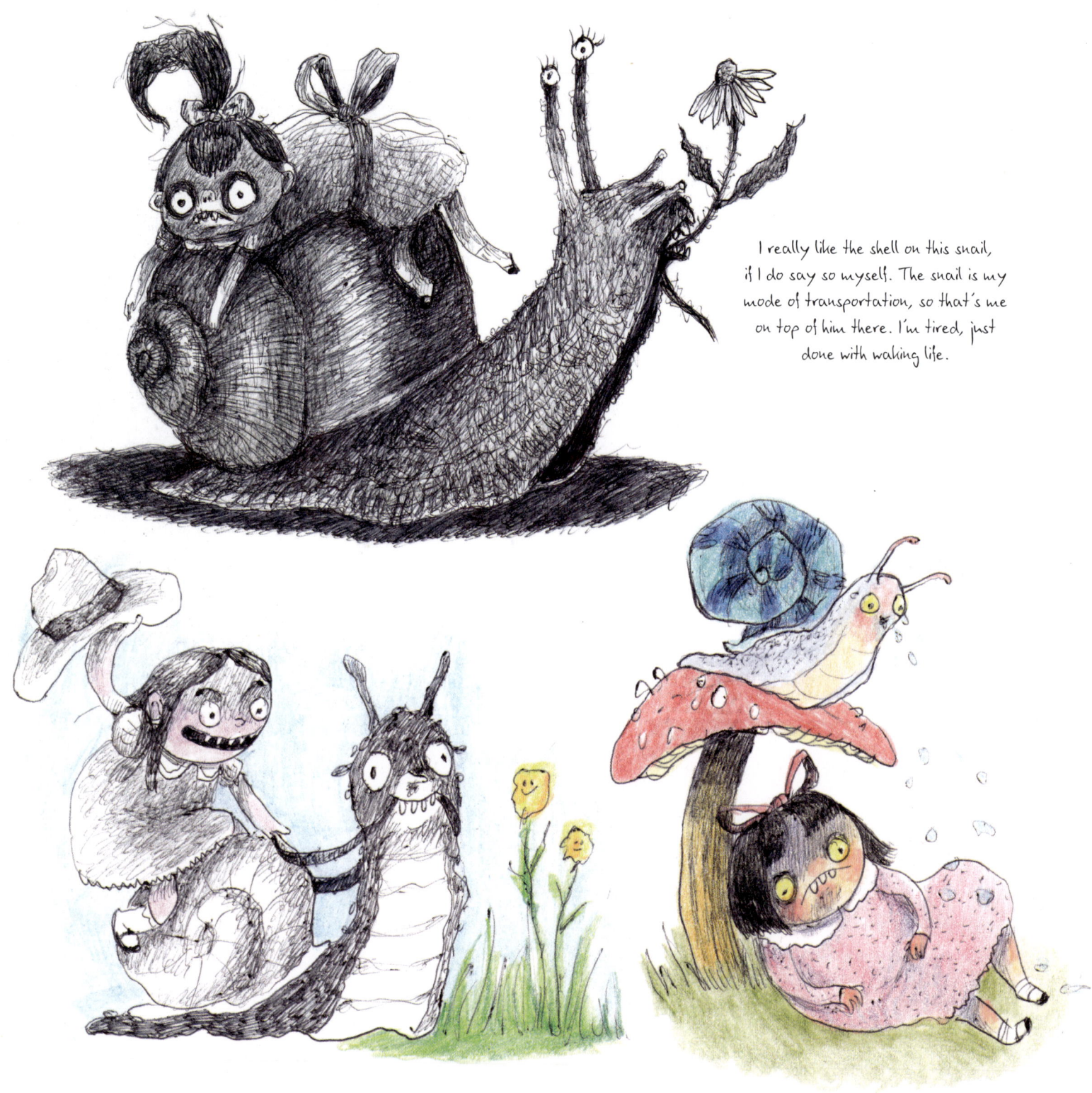

I really like the shell on this snail,
if I do say so myself. The snail is my
mode of transportation, so that's me
on top of him there. I'm tired, just
done with waking life.

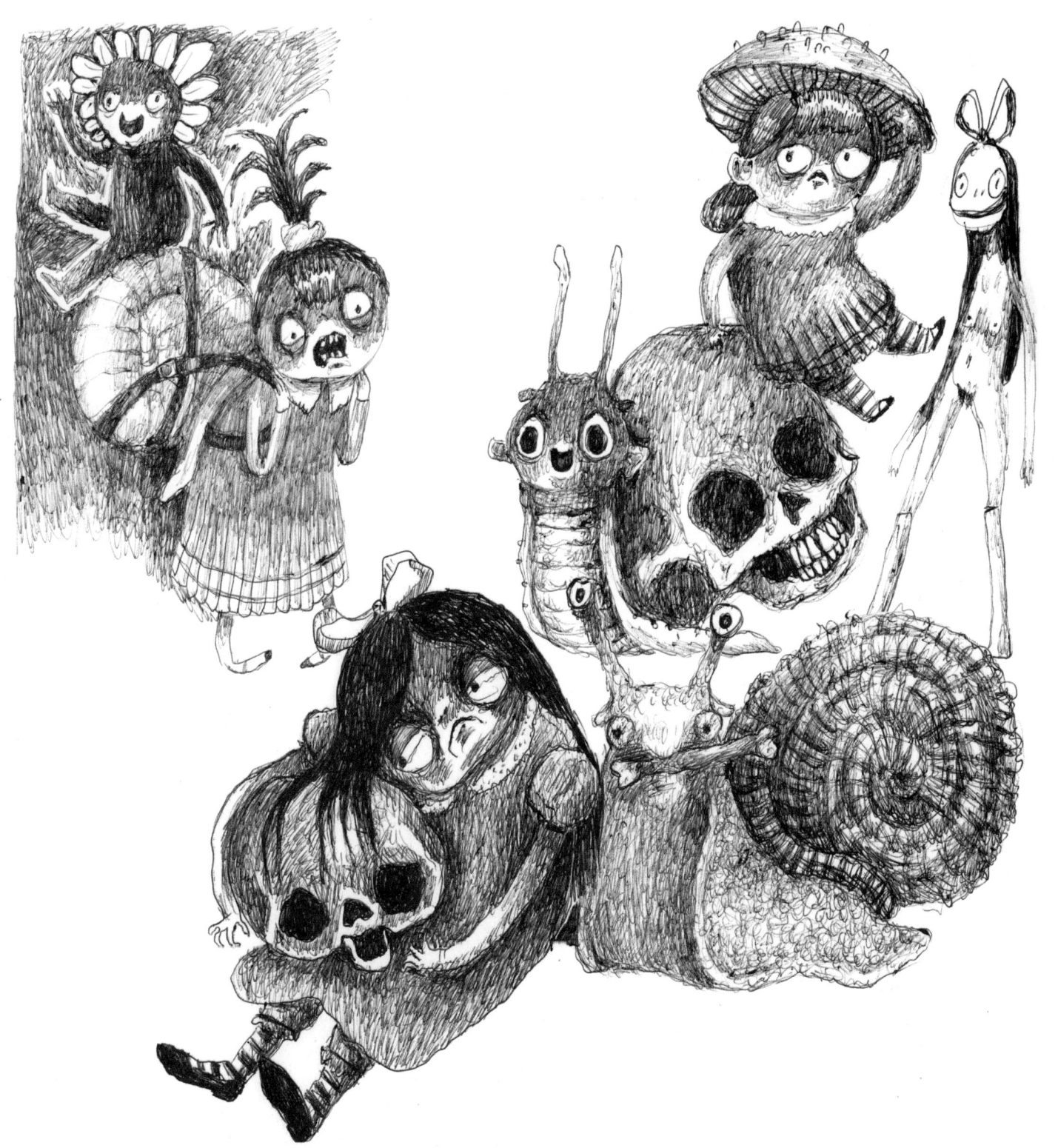

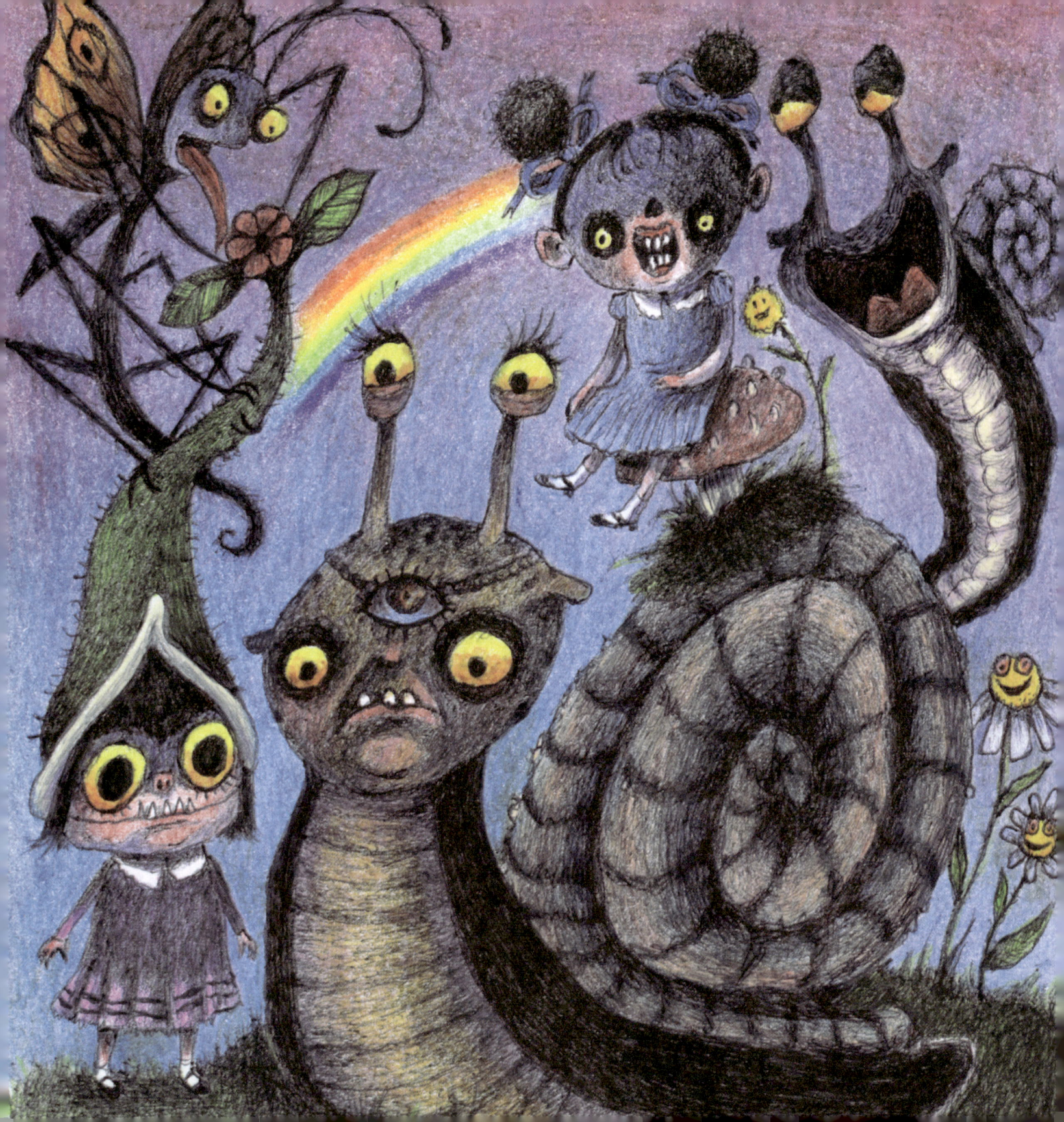

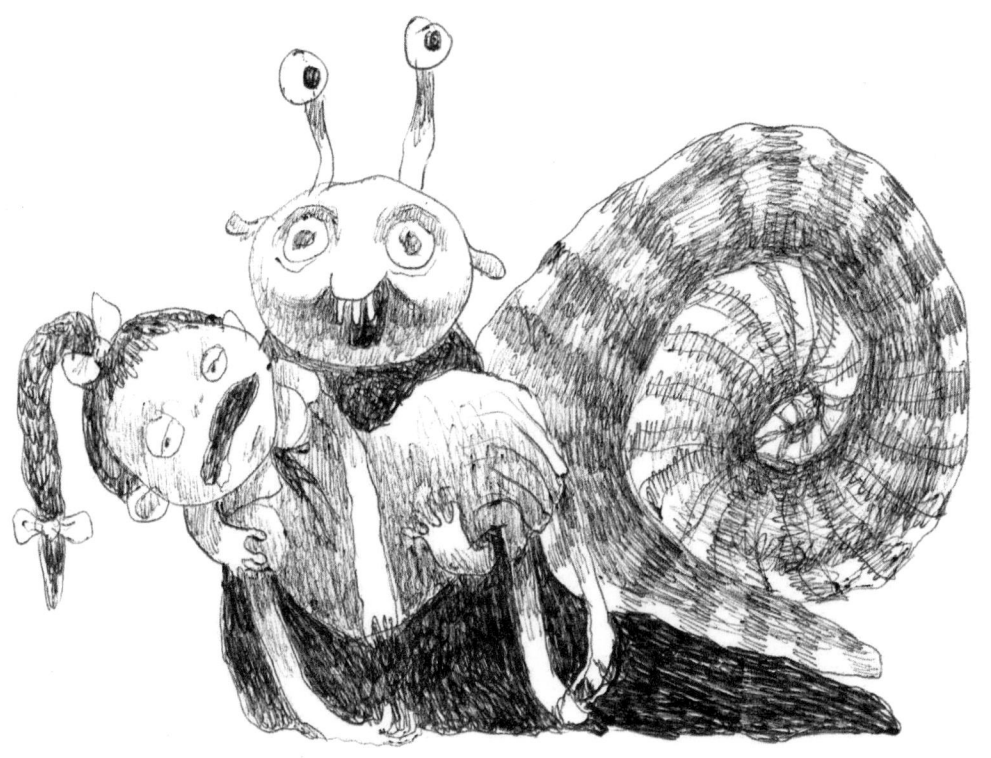

This is a snail friend helping me out. I create all these little creatures and images, and it helps me cope when I'm tired, or when I want to give up. But I swear, I'm happy most of the time. I'm fine.

This one's on a grave, probably mother or sister of the little character there. Somebody she loves. And helper snail friend is there, and he says, "Don't cry, I love you." He'll make her feel better and tell her that she'll feel like shit for years and she won't get over it, but she will learn how to deal with it. I like this because I think we don't accept that part of life. We need more shows and art and books that deal with death in a responsible way. They did that on *Sesame Street*, though, when that shop owner, Mr. Hooper, died. They all addressed it, Big Bird, Elmo, Snuffleupagus They all talked about it and it was really healthy and beautiful.

don't cry I love you

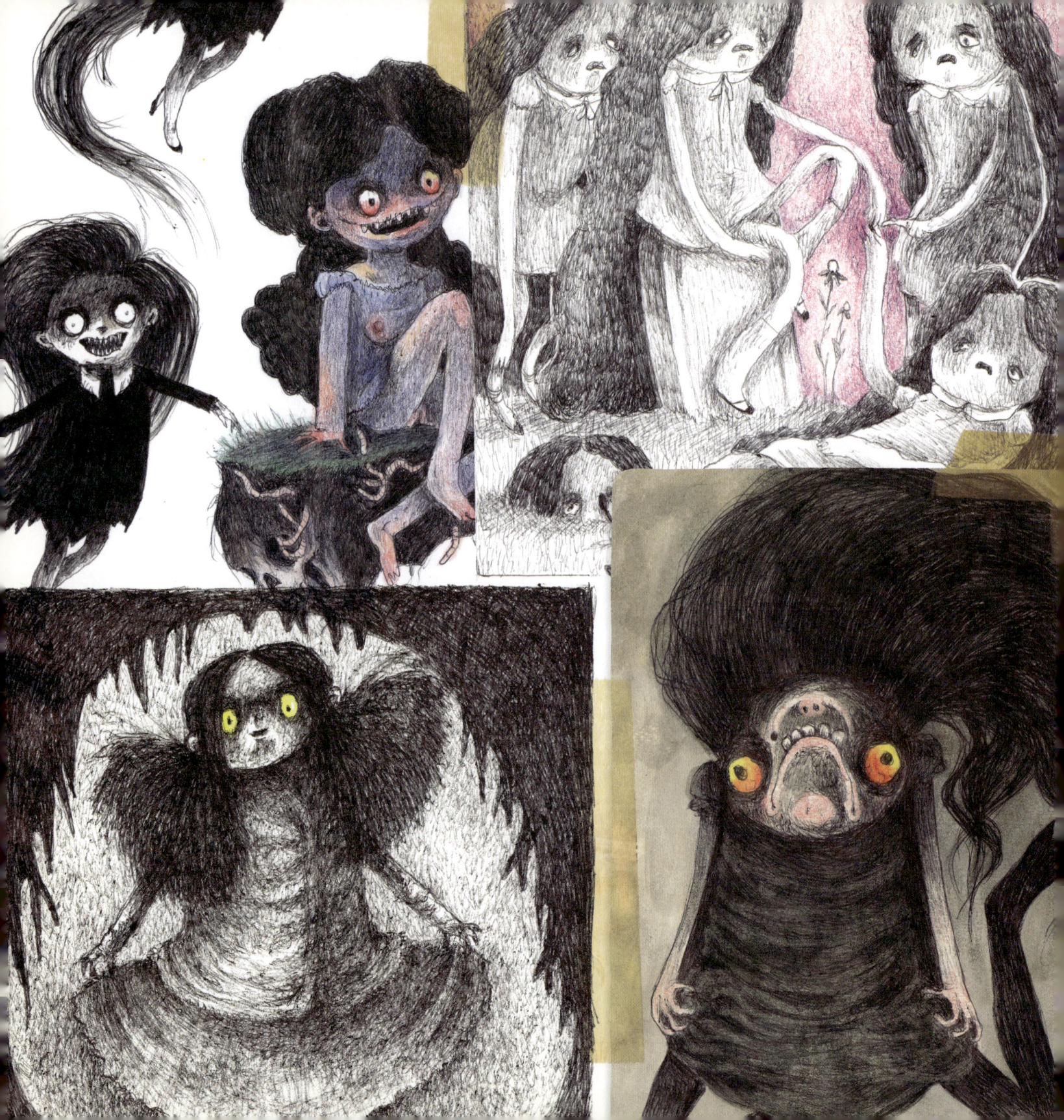

PART II:
GET INTO MY BRAIN, WE'RE GOING TO HELL!

HAIR CURTAINS/
NATURE'S BOOB
SHADES

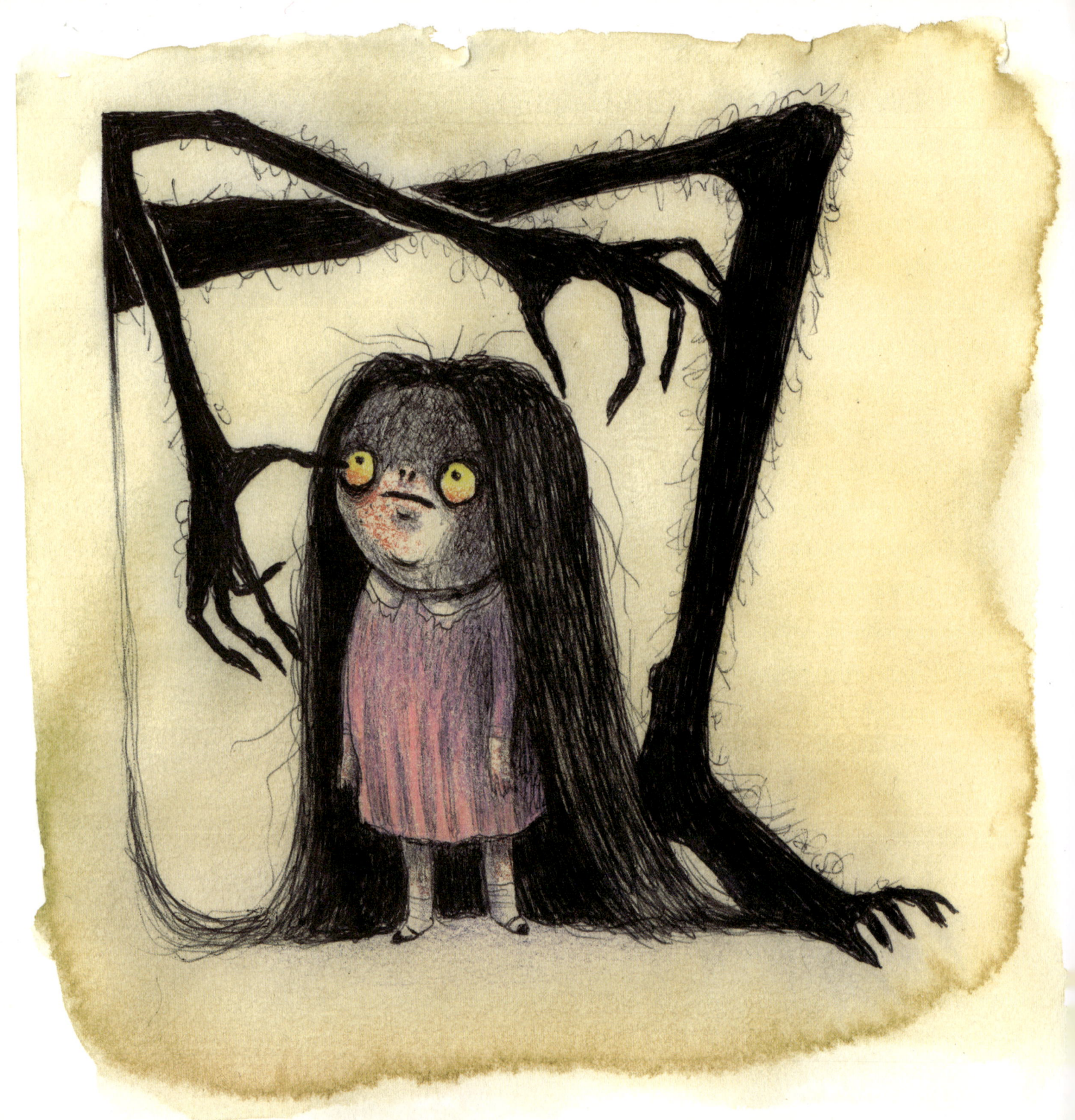

ILOVE HAIR: BIG HAIR; LITTLE GIRLS WITH BIG-BIG PUFFS of hair; and crazy hair; and frizzy hair; and hair all the way down to the floor, in long hair curtains; and combined hair between groups of people; and nets or blankets of hair. It's about being feral. It's about rebellion against the norm of "civilized" and about being unkempt and wild. I love it. Like with my garbage children, who are wild and savage, figures with wild hair are very attractive to me. In horror movies the woman always has long, unkempt, undomesticated hair to show she's unhinged or crazy or open to the supernatural. Wild hair is such a great design element that can be shaped and used to communicate so many things. Hair could come alive, like in *Mama*. A lot of these images are me learning and practicing how to work with my pen. With hair, it's all about the pressure on the pen.

As a child, I had wild and frizzy hair. Very frizzy. I don't think my mom knew how to control it because she had smooth hair. There was a neighbourhood boy I had a crush on that would tease me and tell me my hair was messy and gross. That harsh judgement has stuck with me—hair has power, it is character defining. I grew my own hair out as a rebellion against the world. I refuse to have cropped and tamed "mom hair." I want to be wild! I want to be a heroine in a horror film, free to be unkempt. I brush it every three days, I braid it when it's wet. There are a lot of braids in my work,

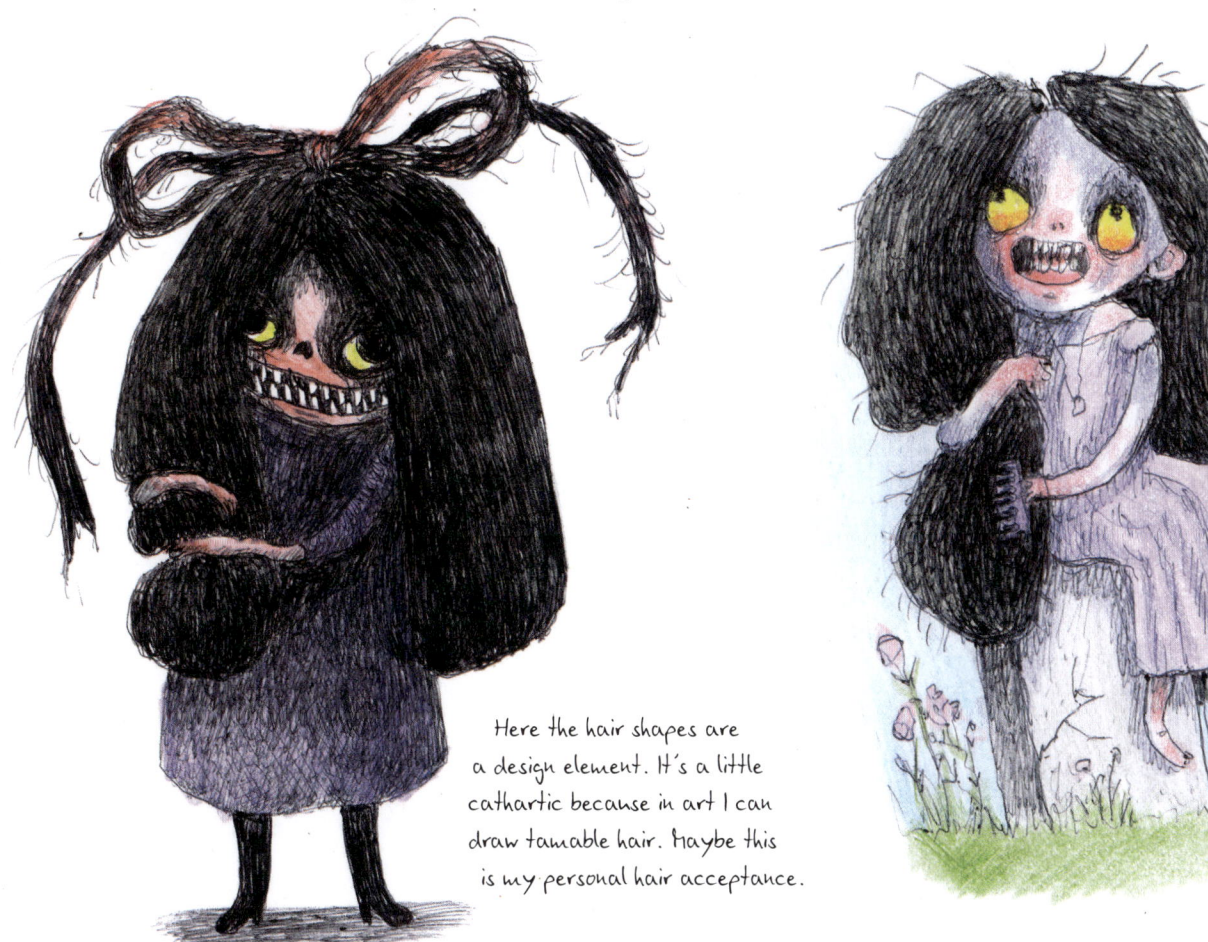

Here the hair shapes are a design element. It's a little cathartic because in art I can draw tamable hair. Maybe this is my personal hair acceptance.

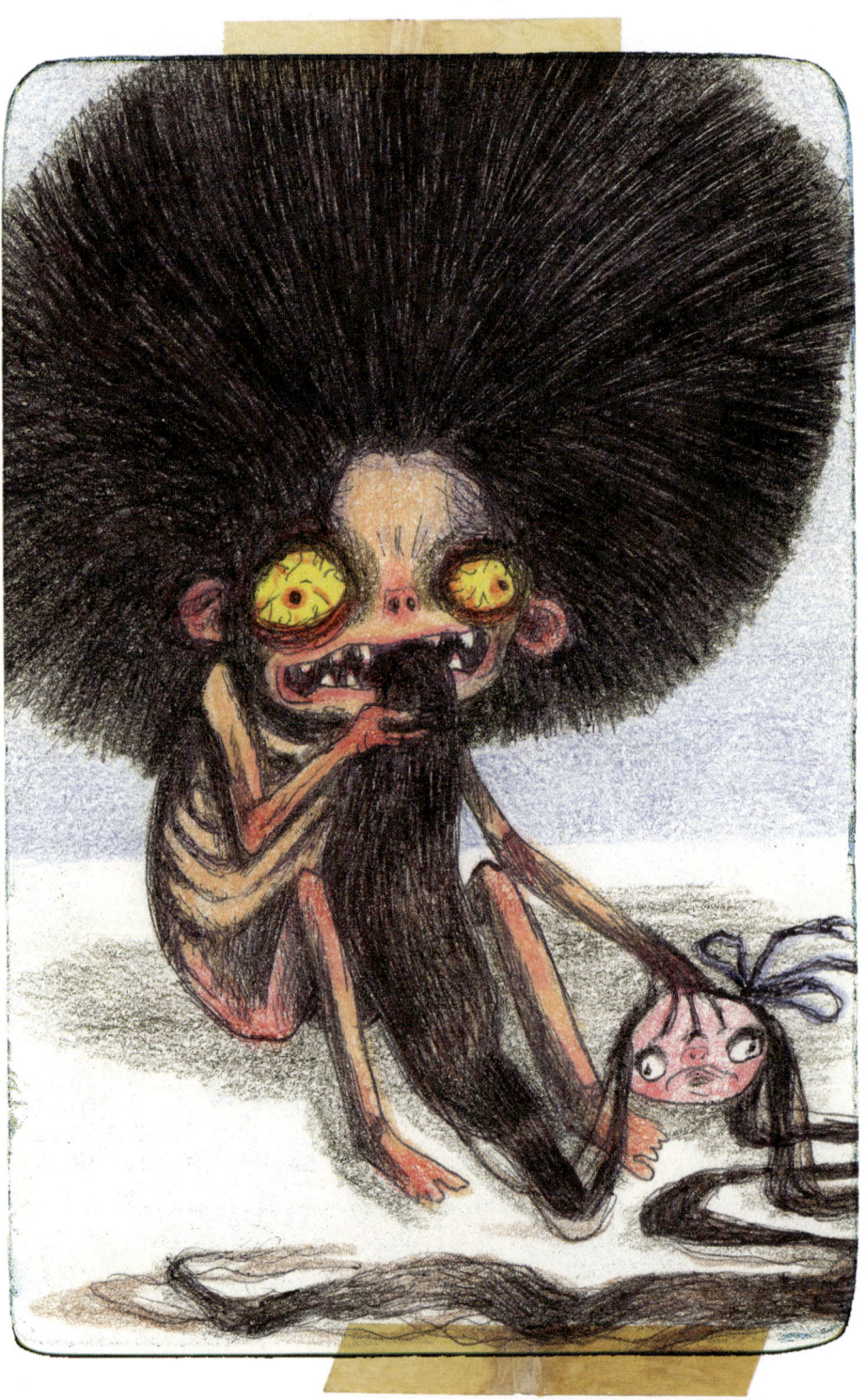

I like the look of it. My grandma always used to put me in pigtails. Two pigtails, really high on my head and in braids. I draw it a lot. It's a great way to deal with kid's hair. My dad, everytime I wear braids, two braids, says, "Oh, it's part of your tradition." So, it's in my blood, but in a comical way. My Polish roots are not as annoying as they used to be. I just work with what I've got.

When I was little, my grandmother came to live with us in Canada for a couple of months, to help take care of me. So, to make grandma's life easier, and I guess a lot of older people do this too, she had her hair cut. Cut all the way short, permed, and dyed red. I'm not sure if those last were really helpful. But I know I hated it. She'd had long, thick, grey hair that when it was down it was just awesome. Such a traditional Polish look, and I was attached to that. I clung, I guess I still cling to, what was familiar and traditional. I think Polish stuff helped me develop a lot of my visual language. That was the last visit from my grandma. I didn't see her again after that. I really missed her and her stories about the Devil and about ghosts and all things horror (but in her mind she was probably just telling me the truth or urban legends), but I also really missed that hair.

I remember my mother's scream when my grandmother died. We got a phone call and she just screamed, not a horror movie scream, but a scream of true, guttural pain. It was the first time I'd heard that; it was a turning point in my life, a moment that's always with me. At that moment, I knew the suffering and the darkness in the world. I eventually found out that my grandmother had hung herself. It shows up in my pieces. It must be linked, my grandmother, and hair, and death by hanging. I don't like to think about it, but I can see that I am right there in my art. I'm allowing myself to be freer and more absurd, and that has also led me to darker places, and some of them are shown with hair.

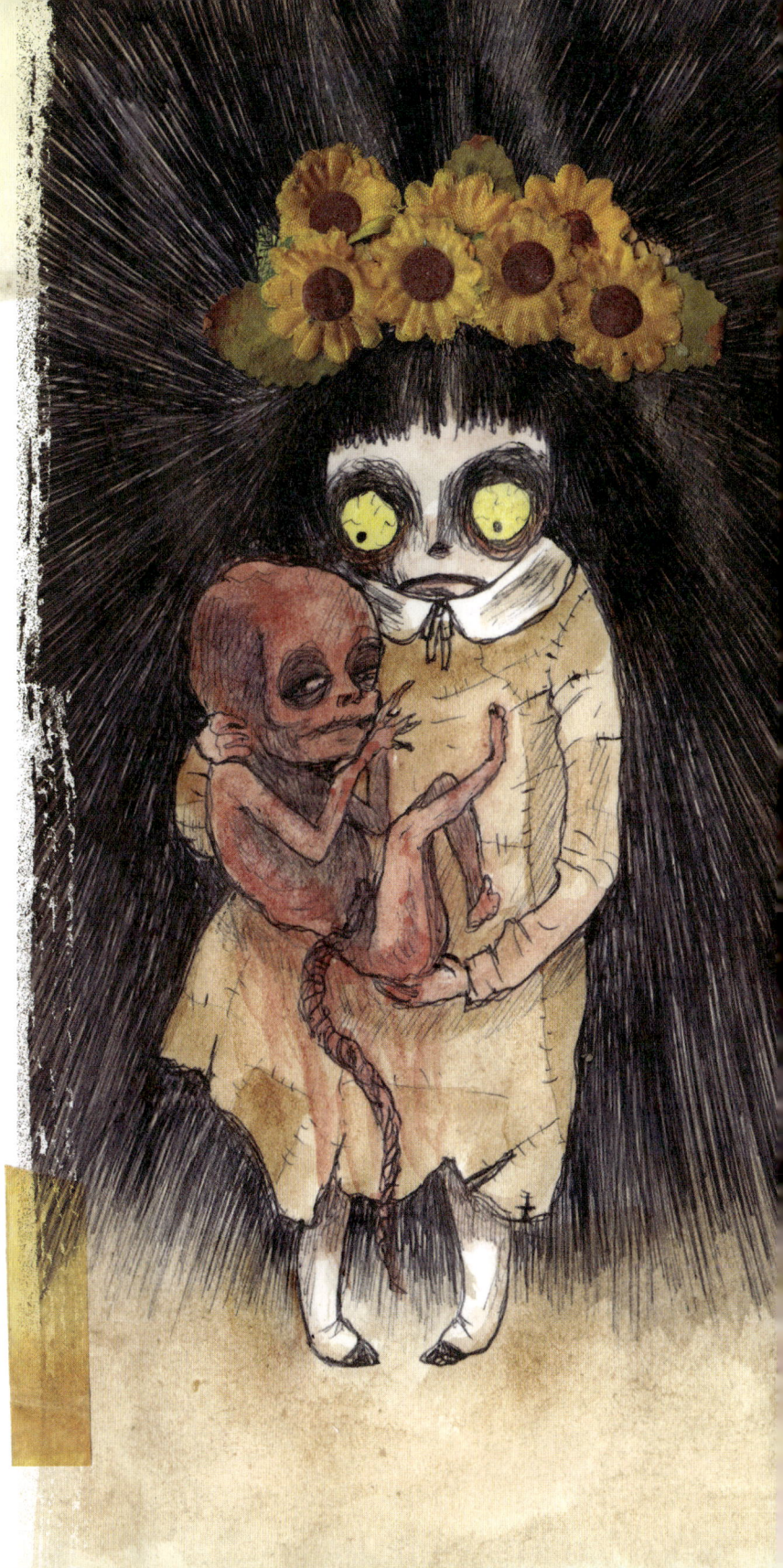

I used little fake flowers in this picture. I was still experimenting with drawing on less-than-precious things, i.e. garbage. To get 'arty' this is mixed media and I was just being very open to any and all techniques when 'finding myself' as I was drawing more and more. My favourite movies and books have always been a great source of inspiration whether I was aware at the time or would realize after the fact. The fetus in this picture definitely looks more wise and mature than it's mother or caretaker, still a girl. The idea of the all-knowing, almost-sacred baby definitely comes from all those religious pictures of all-knowing baby Jesus. Also Alia Atriedes, character from the *Dune* series, the abomination born (or 'preborn') with all the wisdom of her elders that came before her.

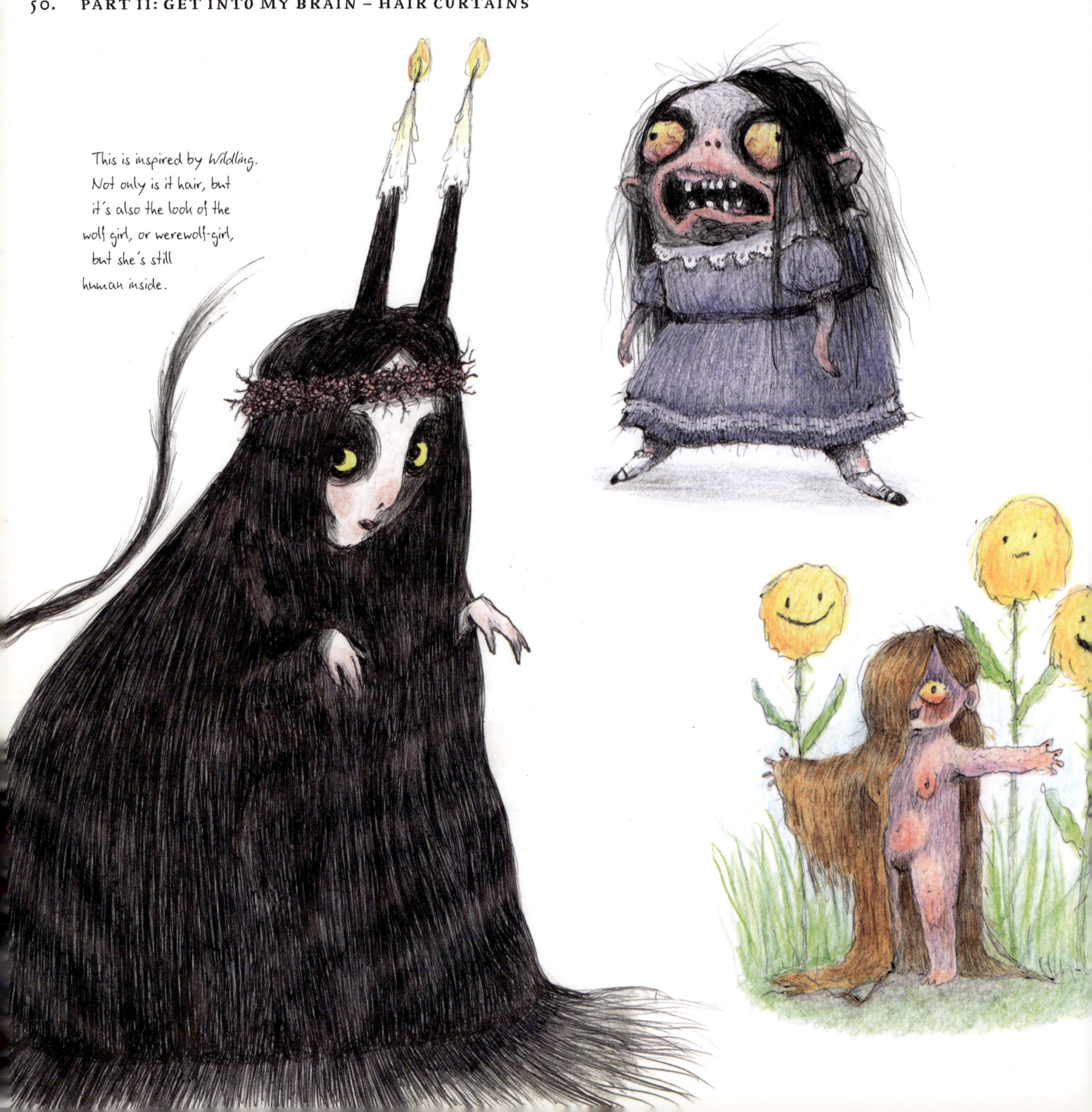

This is inspired by *Wildling*. Not only is it hair, but it's also the look of the wolf girl, or werewolf-girl, but she's still human inside.

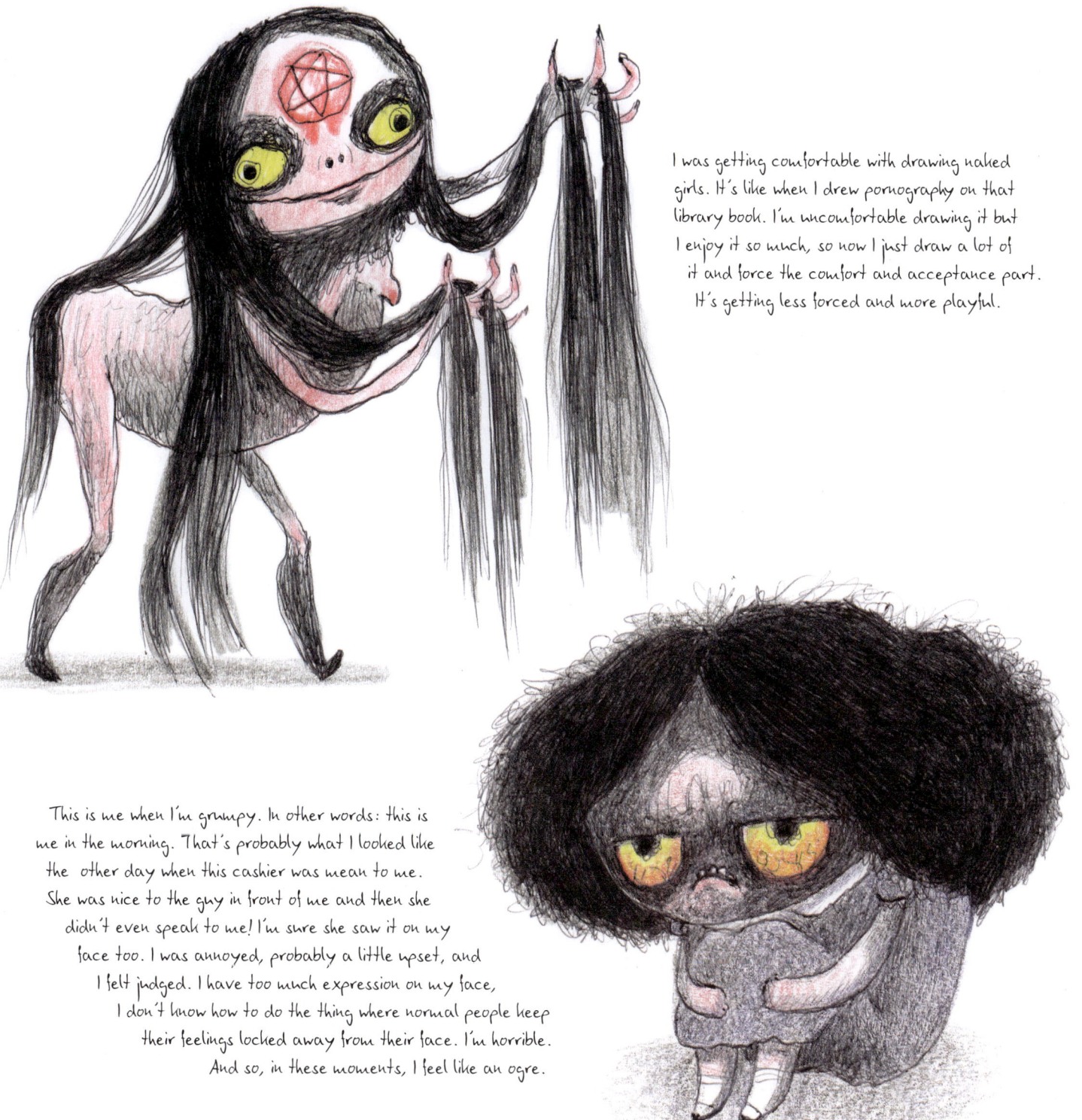

I was getting comfortable with drawing naked girls. It's like when I drew pornography on that library book. I'm uncomfortable drawing it but I enjoy it so much, so now I just draw a lot of it and force the comfort and acceptance part. It's getting less forced and more playful.

This is me when I'm grumpy. In other words: this is me in the morning. That's probably what I looked like the other day when this cashier was mean to me. She was nice to the guy in front of me and then she didn't even speak to me! I'm sure she saw it on my face too. I was annoyed, probably a little upset, and I felt judged. I have too much expression on my face, I don't know how to do the thing where normal people keep their feelings locked away from their face. I'm horrible. And so, in these moments, I feel like an ogre.

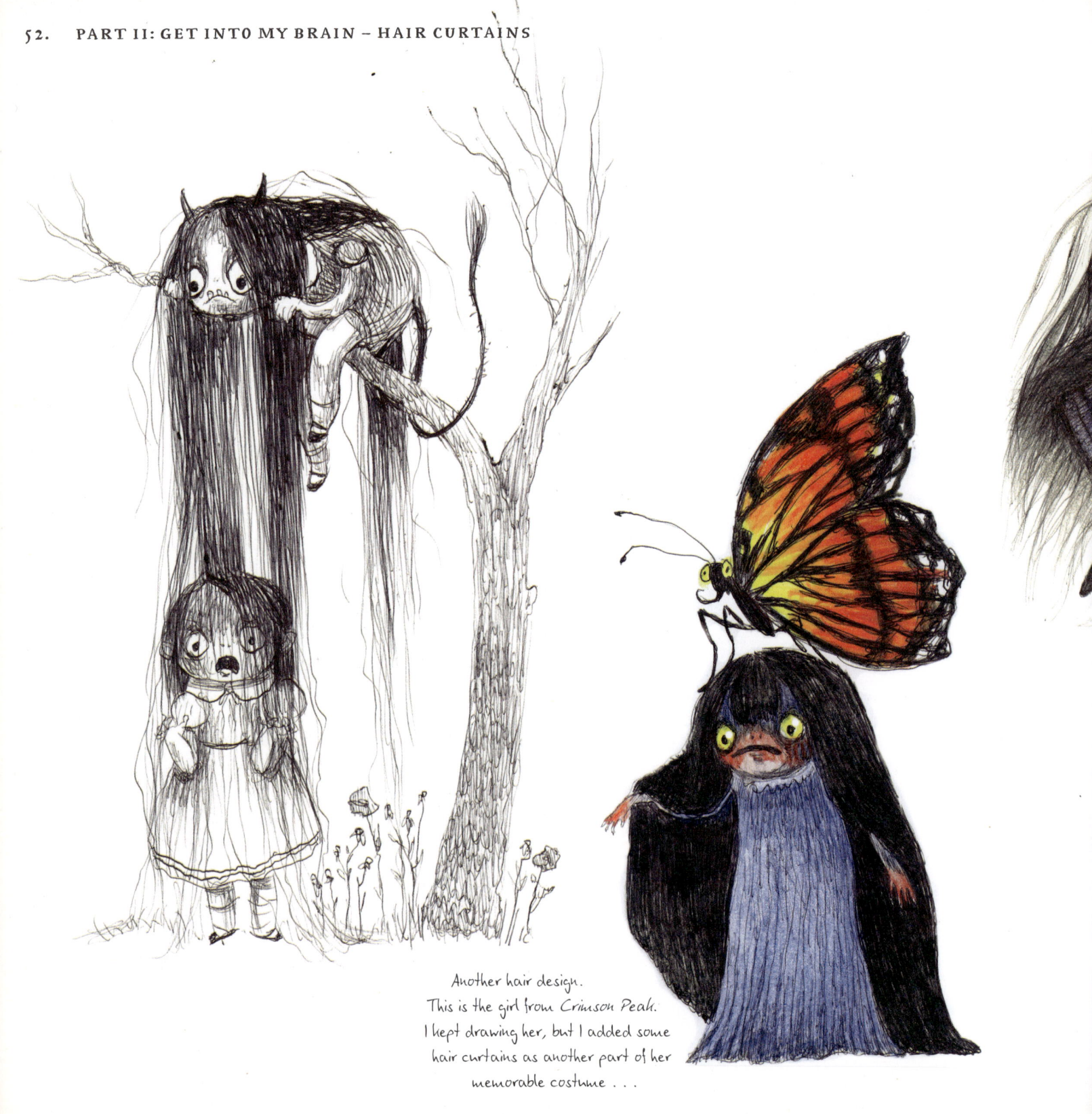

Another hair design.
This is the girl from *Crimson Peak*.
I kept drawing her, but I added some
hair curtains as another part of her
memorable costume . . .

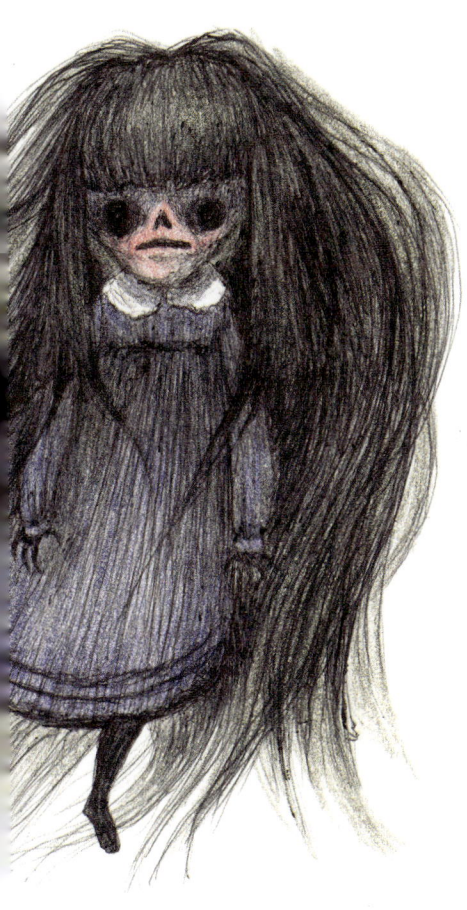

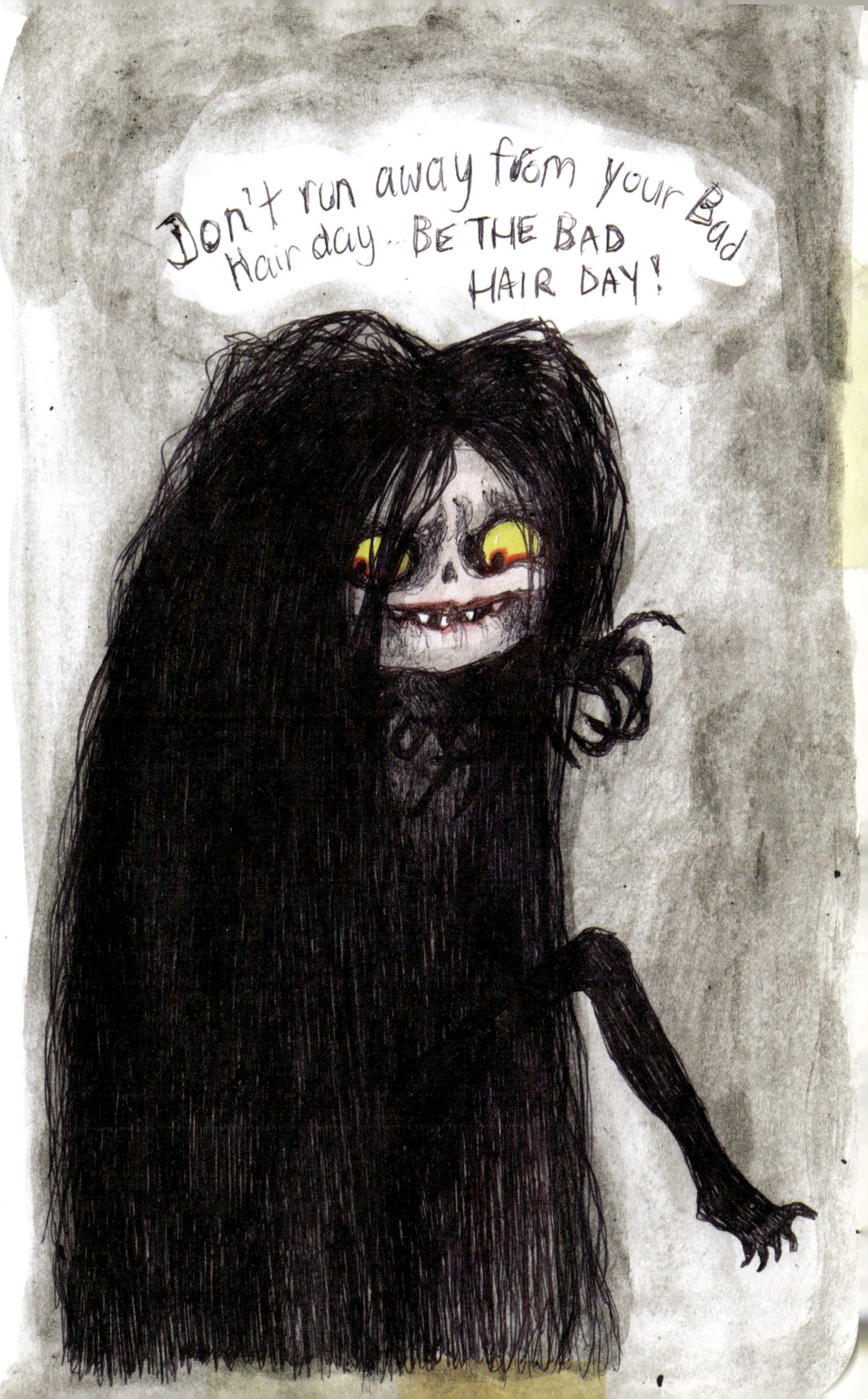

"Don't run away from your bad hair day, be the bad hair day!" Probably a lot of things could be solved with a shower in my life, and maybe yours too? This one was about accepting my hair looked terrible that day and I didn't feel great, but I was too lazy to do anything about it. I think this resonates with a lot of people. It's about self acceptance . . . and showering. Tapping into my inner Gudetama here.

Naked ladies adorned in nothing but their beautiful, unwashed, stringy hair and winning smiles! I think drawing collages was a great way for me to draw without having to stress out about what scene or idea I was drawing. It could be anything. Just pure, joyful drawing with no other purpose than practice.

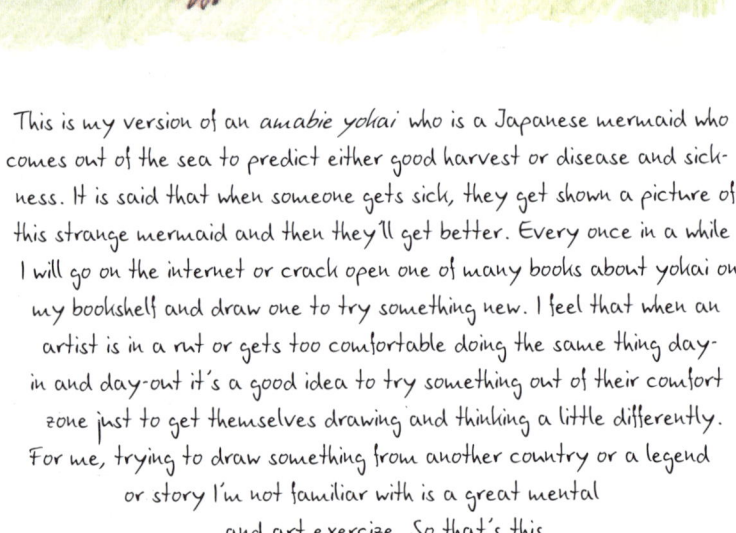

This is my version of an *amabie yokai* who is a Japanese mermaid who comes out of the sea to predict either good harvest or disease and sickness. It is said that when someone gets sick, they get shown a picture of this strange mermaid and then they'll get better. Every once in a while I will go on the internet or crack open one of many books about yokai on my bookshelf and draw one to try something new. I feel that when an artist is in a rut or gets too comfortable doing the same thing day-in and day-out it's a good idea to try something out of their comfort zone just to get themselves drawing and thinking a little differently. For me, trying to draw something from another country or a legend or story I'm not familiar with is a great mental and art exercize. So that's this.

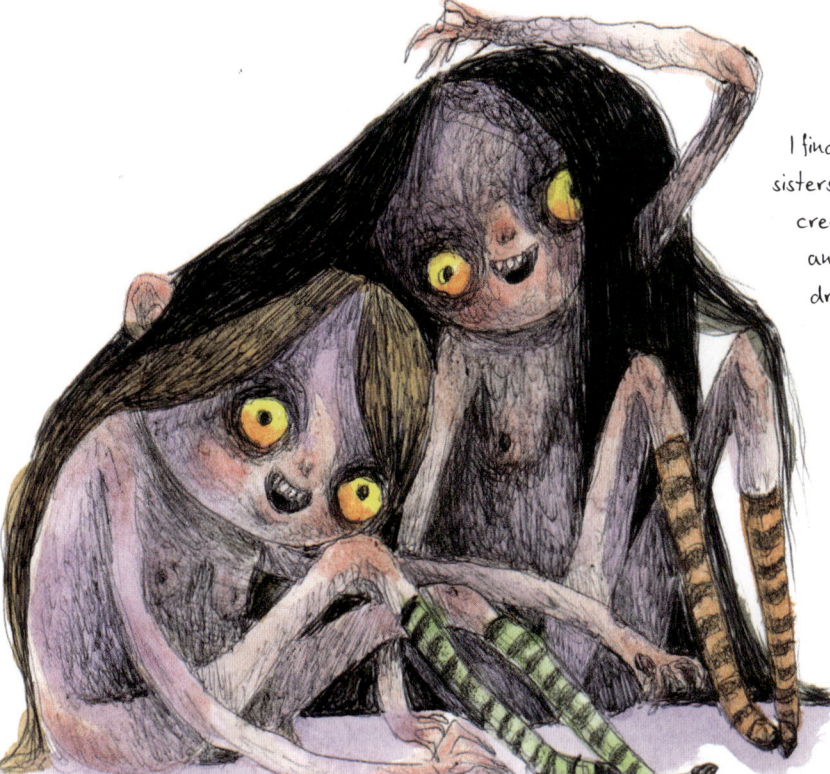

I find families fascinating, and within that, sisters can be so intense and interesting and creepy. They are often a horror element in story and film. This particular picture is affectionate, draping and protecting a sister with hair. When I look at this, I also think that the hair curtain here could be hiding or covering the fact that I'm frigid toward my own sister and mum.

My sister and my mum make fun of me all the time for being unaffectionate. My sister is this beast that cuddles things, and it's a lot of hugs, and that's weird to me. I don't cuddle with anyone but my son and my partner. I don't even want to hold hands or link arms, I'm always like: "This is horrible. Please let go."

Little demented sisters with the draping hair and creepy snuggling.

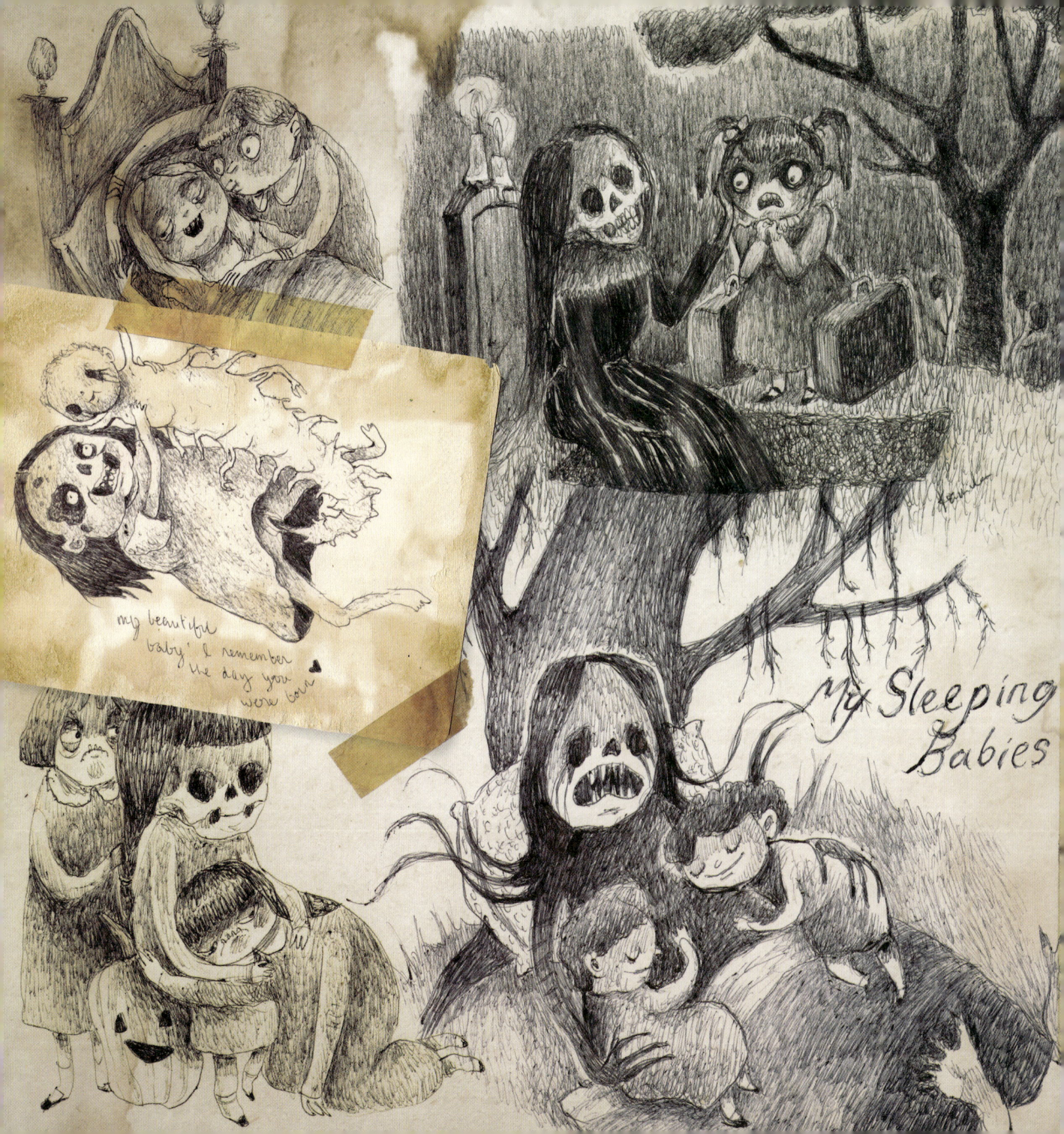

My beautiful baby! I remember the day you were born

My Sleeping Babies

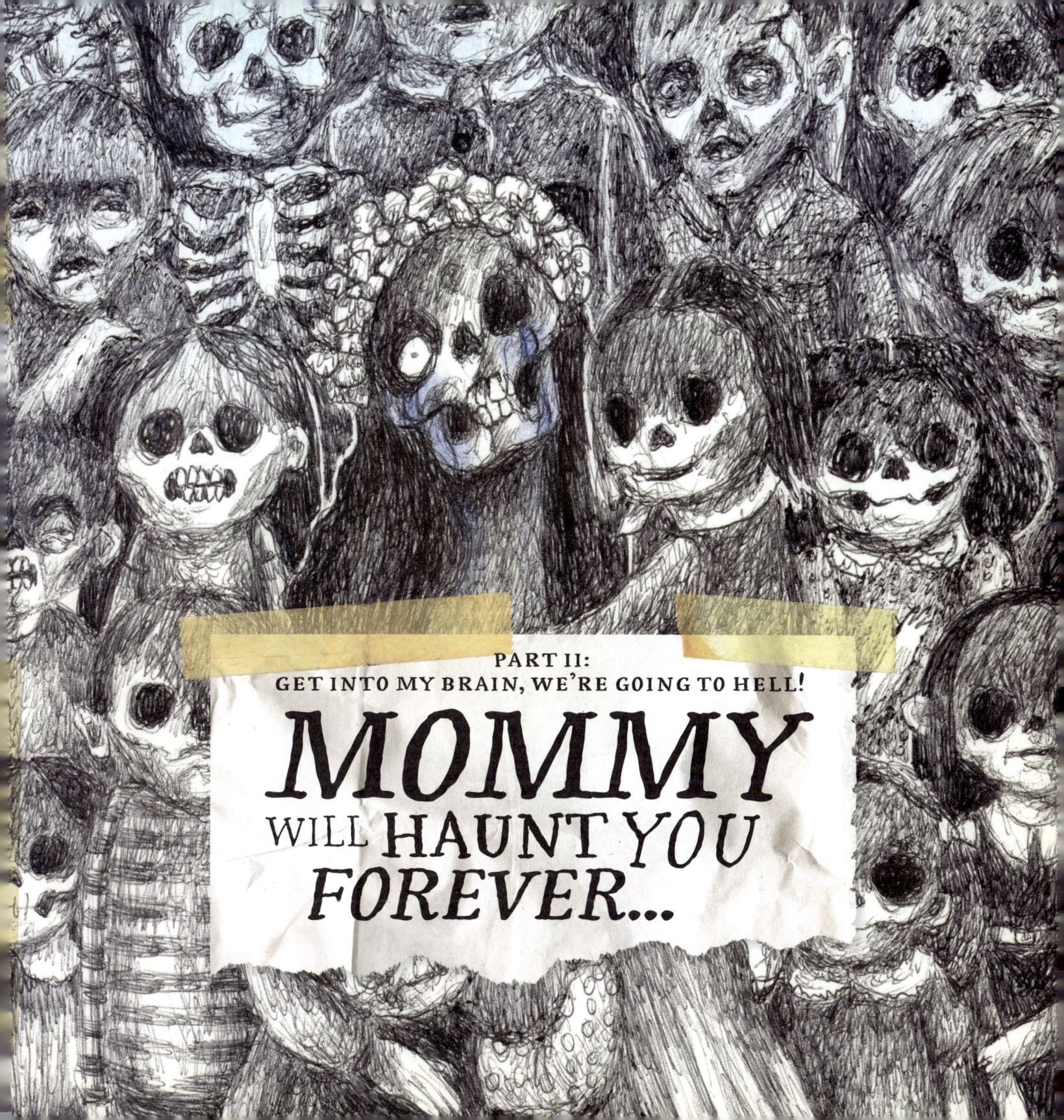

PART II:
GET INTO MY BRAIN, WE'RE GOING TO HELL!

MOMMY
WILL HAUNT YOU
FOREVER...

Mama's Goodnight Song

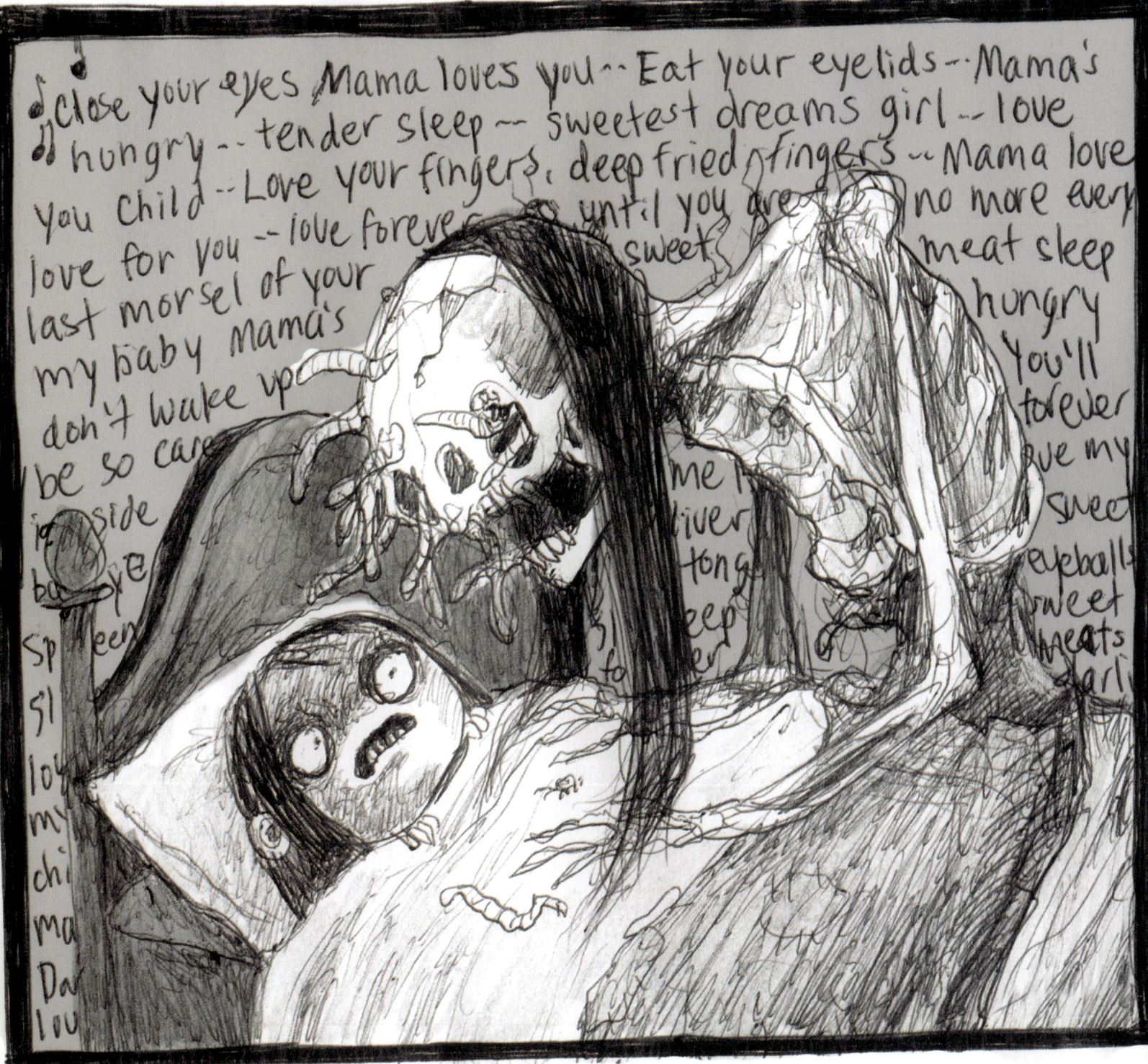

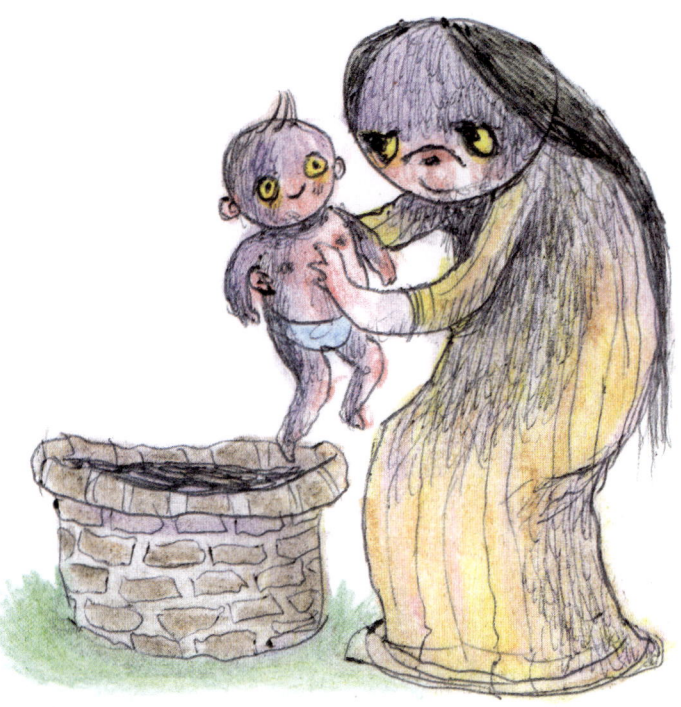

BABIES ARE ONE OF MY WEAKNESSES. I LOVE THEM. I love drawing them, I especially love drawing horrendous babies being loved by their mothers. Happy little babies being eaten or cooked up in soup. The only time I draw normal babies is when a witch is eating a cute, normal baby, and then they're smiling anyway so it doesn't feel like they're actually getting cannibalized. It's like in cartoons, when an anvil falls on a character's head they are usually still smiling as their teeth fall out and they crash into the ground leaving a physical outline all while delivering a closing line like, "Bye." It's cartoon logic. The witch is doing her job, the babies are delicious. It's all a fantasy or horror story. Maternal love is so strong. I think that if my son turned out to be a murderer, I would still love him, I'd help him hide the bodies. If my child turned into a zombie, I would sacrifice myself, or I'd murder so that he could eat. Of course I would. These questions are incredibly simple in my mind.

The first time I felt like I had a real conversation with my mum was when she was in the hospital. Usually, somebody else was around, but we found ourselves alone once and we didn't know what to talk about. Then I broached the subject of how weird I am, and she just laughed. She agreed that if we were still living in Poland I'd be dragged out in front of the church and burned at the stake. We talked about how good it was that we left. Even though she had to sacrifice a lot, and even though it affected me because it was a very chaotic time in my young life, in Poland, I probably wouldn't have been able to really be my true self. Here, I can be myself (even if everyone I know isn't quite dead yet!). The conversation was so funny and true, it's stuck with me. I think there are echoes of that moment in the sentiment of these images.

Horror is wonderful when it's layered with a mother's love. There's an emotional depth that is palpable and relatable to nearly everyone except, maybe, psychopaths. It has the potential to be the most touching and horrifying because it's so real. A good horror story can have an almost magical way of capturing all the elements of motherhood. It can be made so clear how a person could slip into a state of being where they treat everyone in a horrible way. Unfairness can account for most of the real horror in the world. The world is so unfair.

I think I almost exclusively draw children because it lessens how horrific my art can be. Another aspect, I think, is that it's just a basic truth that kids are simultaneously violent and innocent. I find that violent-innocence fascinating. I love to play with that as a characteristic. I think it's relatable because it's nostalgia for childhood. Kids don't know the real world yet. They don't know that nothing fictional could ever equal the fucked-up shit that goes on in the real world. They think

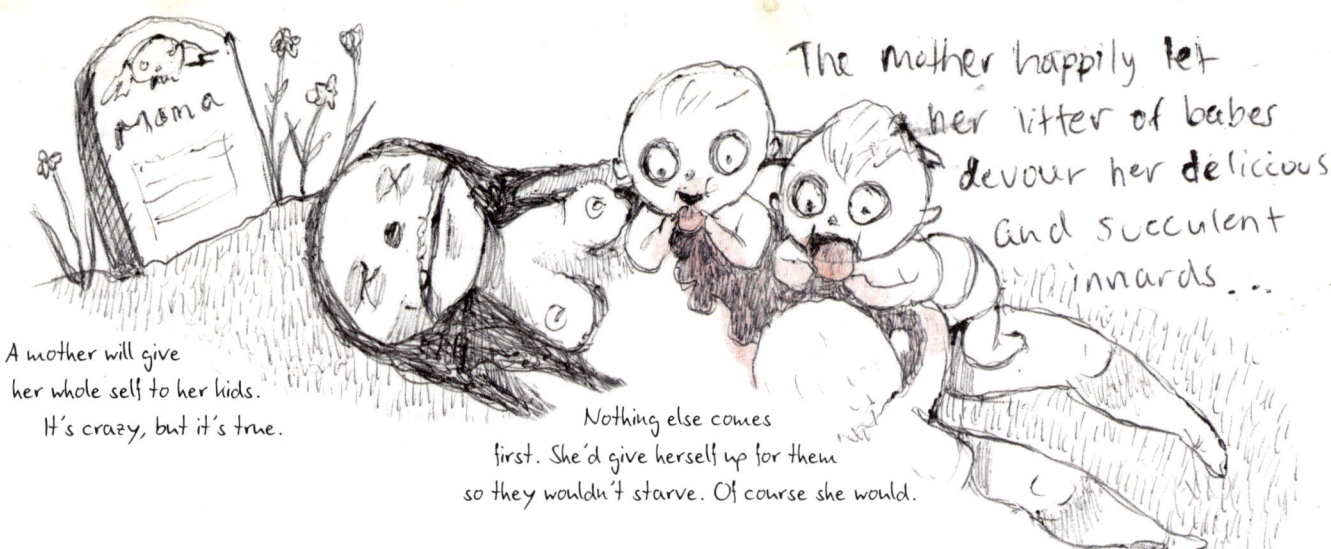

The mother happily let her litter of babes devour her delicious and succulent innards...

A mother will give her whole self to her kids. It's crazy, but it's true.

Nothing else comes first. She'd give herself up for them so they wouldn't starve. Of course she would.

everything is funny. It stops me from making something too serious. If adults were the characters in my images, then it would be way too heavy, too loaded with history and issues and baggage. When children are doing evil or sadistic things, it feels story-like. That's the way my mind gets around it. When I draw serious things, or when I draw somebody actually getting murdered or something, it's dark and gory and there's no joy. I always want joy in my drawings. Children do that.

I think that my parents were, are, too serious, which is why I ended up being so not serious. My son is basically my dad now, serious, stubborn, and charming. I can't convince him that there's anything hiding under the bed or creeping outside the window, he's way too hard to scare. But he can scare me so easily it's laughable. Seriousness skipped a generation. People always say, "time flies" or "children grow up too fast." It's annoying, but it's true, and I'm feeling it. So, it's my practice to slow things down a little and capture memories. A lot of these images are my favourite memories of myself and my son, or my favourite tropes of motherhood, and there's a lot of horror influence here too. Motherhood

in horror films, as I've said, is fascinating because it's truly horrifying to me.

In here too there's a lot of daily angst. I try to stay in the moment, but it's hard not to relive horrible moments from the day, the week, the month, the year, my life. For instance, "Remember that one time at the grocery store, you were at the self-checkout, and you had to run and get something. When you got back, you'd thought someone else had taken your lane, and you went up to him and said, 'These are my groceries!' And then you realized your stuff was one lane over." Ugh. I think about this episode every day still. I felt as though my head should have sunk into my neck. So embarrassing and horrible. I can't let it go. Then my son will say or do something so innocent, but so wise. I went shopping with him and he saw me get really frustrated with the crowds and the aisles and the noise and the lights, and when we got back in the car I said, "I'm really sorry. I can't. I don't like crowds." And he said, "That's okay, Mummy, it happens." It was then and there that I decided I needed to try meditation. I need to get to his level of calm. Who is this kid?

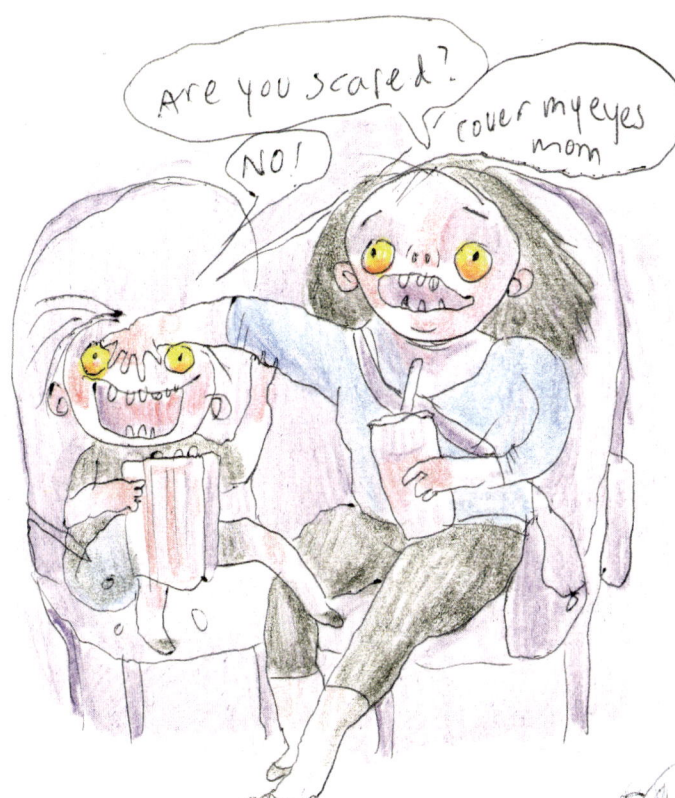

I take my son to the movies all the time to see whatever he wants to see, and it's usually horror. Not psychological horror or anything, but standard horror like *The Nun*, one of his favourites still. Anyway, when we're at the theatres and I think a scary thing is about to happen I'll ask if he's scared and he'll almost always say, 'No!' but still drag my hand over to his forehead so he can peek through but still be touching me.

This is mom-butt. Let me explain: when a mom bends over to talk to their child, squats down to be at their eye level, bends to pick something up, leans over to close the car door, or whatever mom motion that moms do, mom-butt appears. Before momhood, a woman would rarely enter these unflattering positions. Often they are uncomfortable and show way too much skin (unless wearing "mom clothes"). So, there's this postcard that I bought that reminded me of the shape of mom-butt. It gives me a warm fuzzy feeling; this is my version of that.

This is a memory I have of the first time my son said he was "just thinking." He was lying on the floor day-dreaming. But the awesome thing was, he knew it! It was the first time he acknowledged that he was doing something cerebral and I imagined him in his own mind floating around in this liquid and being happy and comfortable.

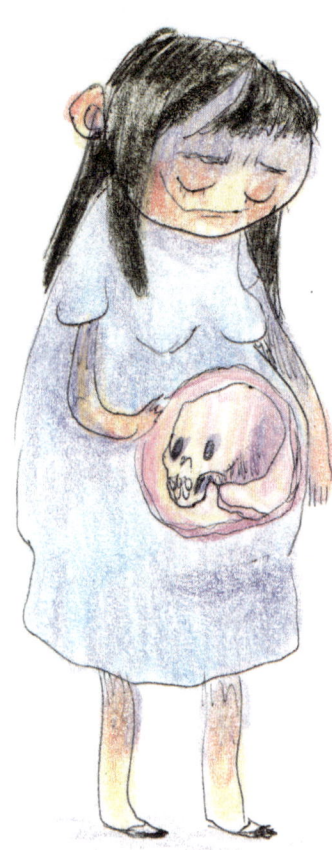

This one was an expression of some
dark anxiety when I was pregnant
with my son, self-explanatory.

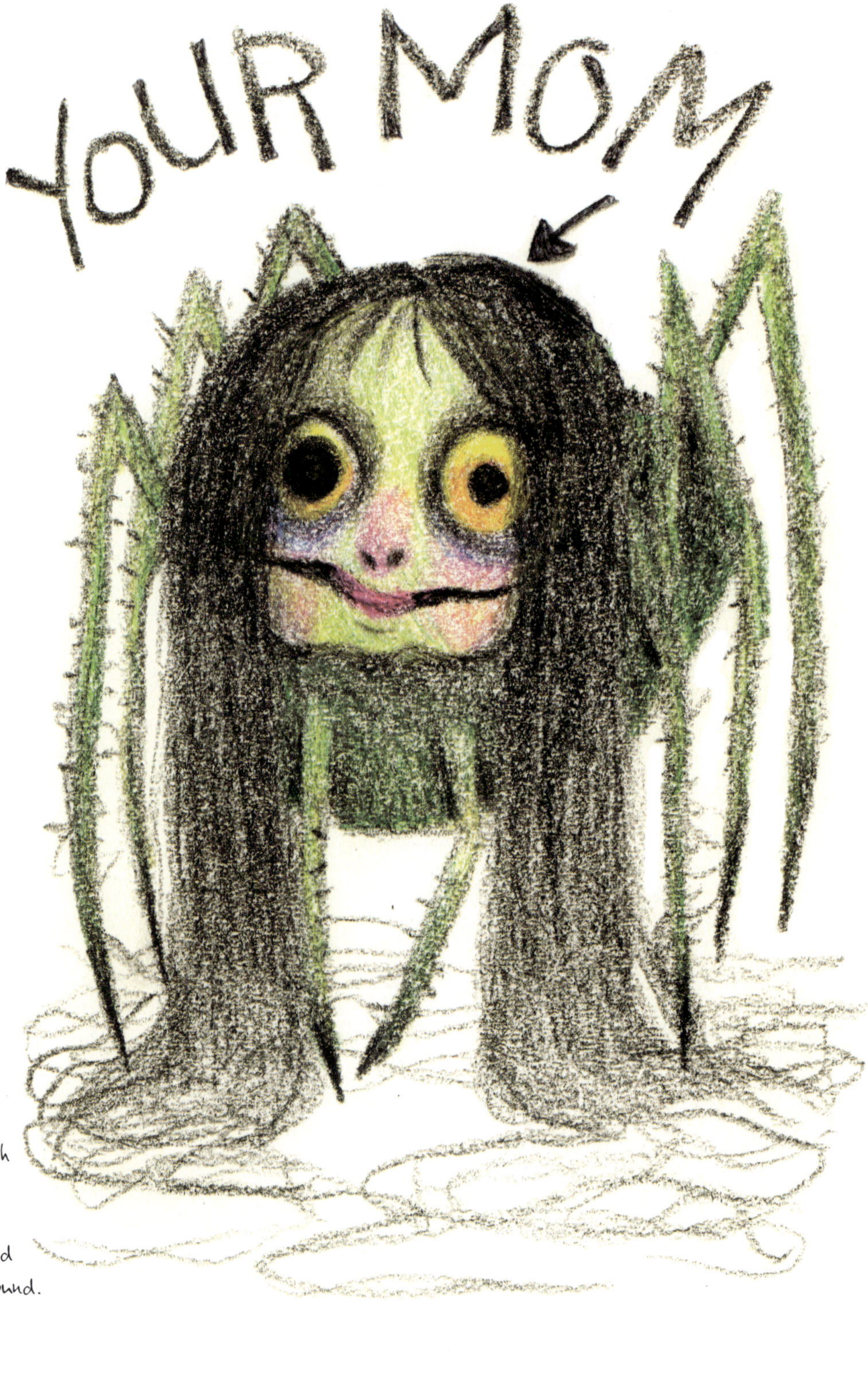

YOUR MOM

I'm a big fan of "your momma" jokes and so
is my son, and sometimes we exchange them
until he realizes I'm actually his momma,
so he'll say something serious and sweet like,
"Your momma is so beautiful and nice." He's such
a sweet boy. Anyway, this is supposed to be
a joke. If I'm not feeling creative, I'll stick
"your momma" onto tombstones or carved
into a tree somewhere in the background.

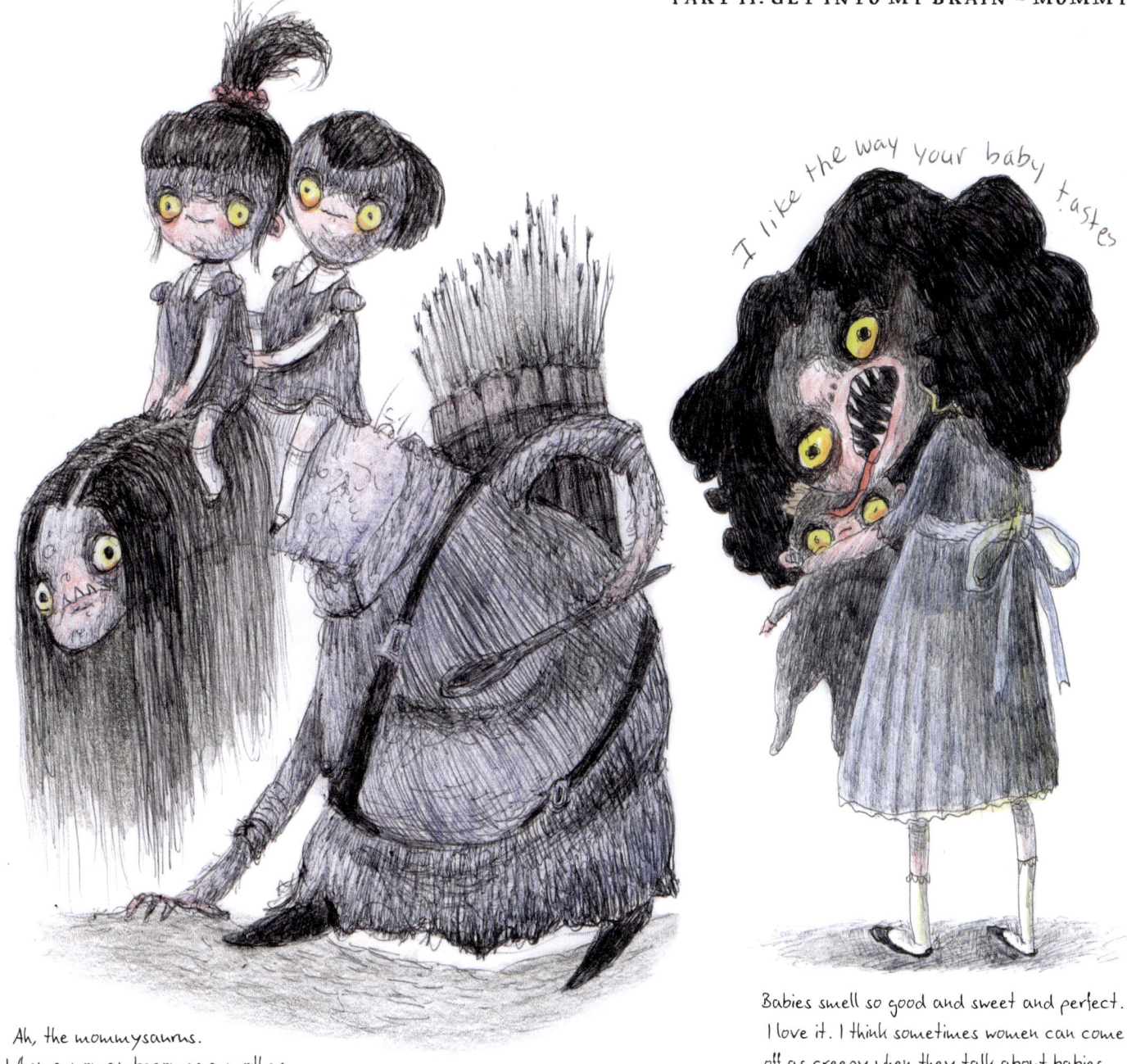

I like the way your baby tastes

Ah, the mommysaurus.
When a woman becomes a mother,
they stop being an entity of their own and are simply this lumbering thing
that protects and cares for the children. She's having a bout of mommy-
brain here because she's packed her enormous quiver of arrows (why are
quivers of arrows always empty-looking in movies and on T.V.?)
but forgotten her bow. She does have a wooden spoon though . . .

Babies smell so good and sweet and perfect.
I love it. I think sometimes women can come
off as creepy when they talk about babies,
how they'd eat them up or want to bite them
and squish them, but it's a natural impulse to
be overly close and protective.

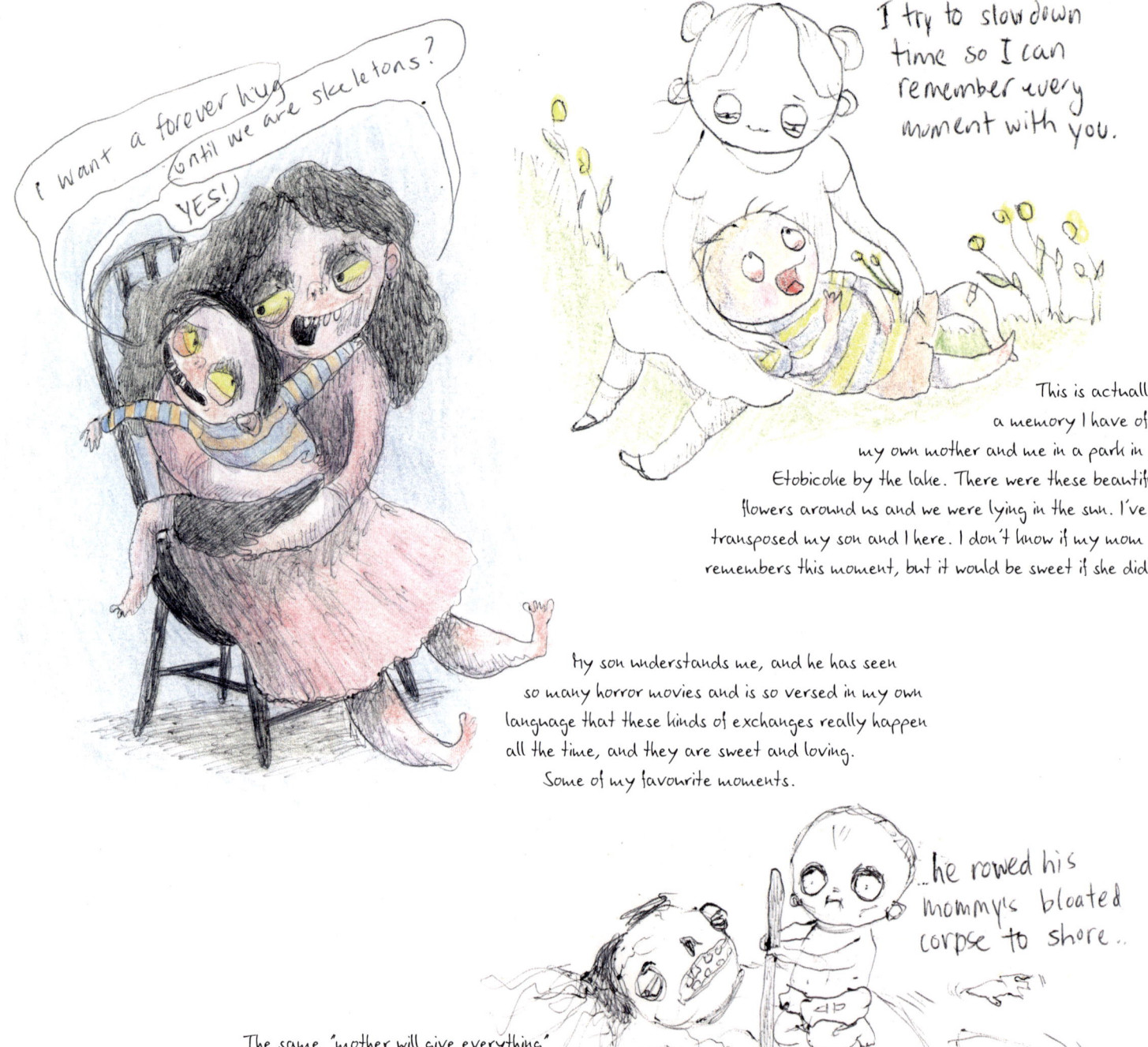

I want a forever hug until we are skeletons?

YES!

I try to slow down time so I can remember every moment with you.

This is actually a memory I have of my own mother and me in a park in Etobicoke by the lake. There were these beautiful flowers around us and we were lying in the sun. I've transposed my son and I here. I don't know if my mom remembers this moment, but it would be sweet if she did.

My son understands me, and he has seen so many horror movies and is so versed in my own language that these kinds of exchanges really happen all the time, and they are sweet and loving. Some of my favourite moments.

...he rowed his mommy's bloated corpse to shore..

The same "mother will give everything" sentiment here. Even to her last, she gives everything, her life and physical form, so that her child can survive.

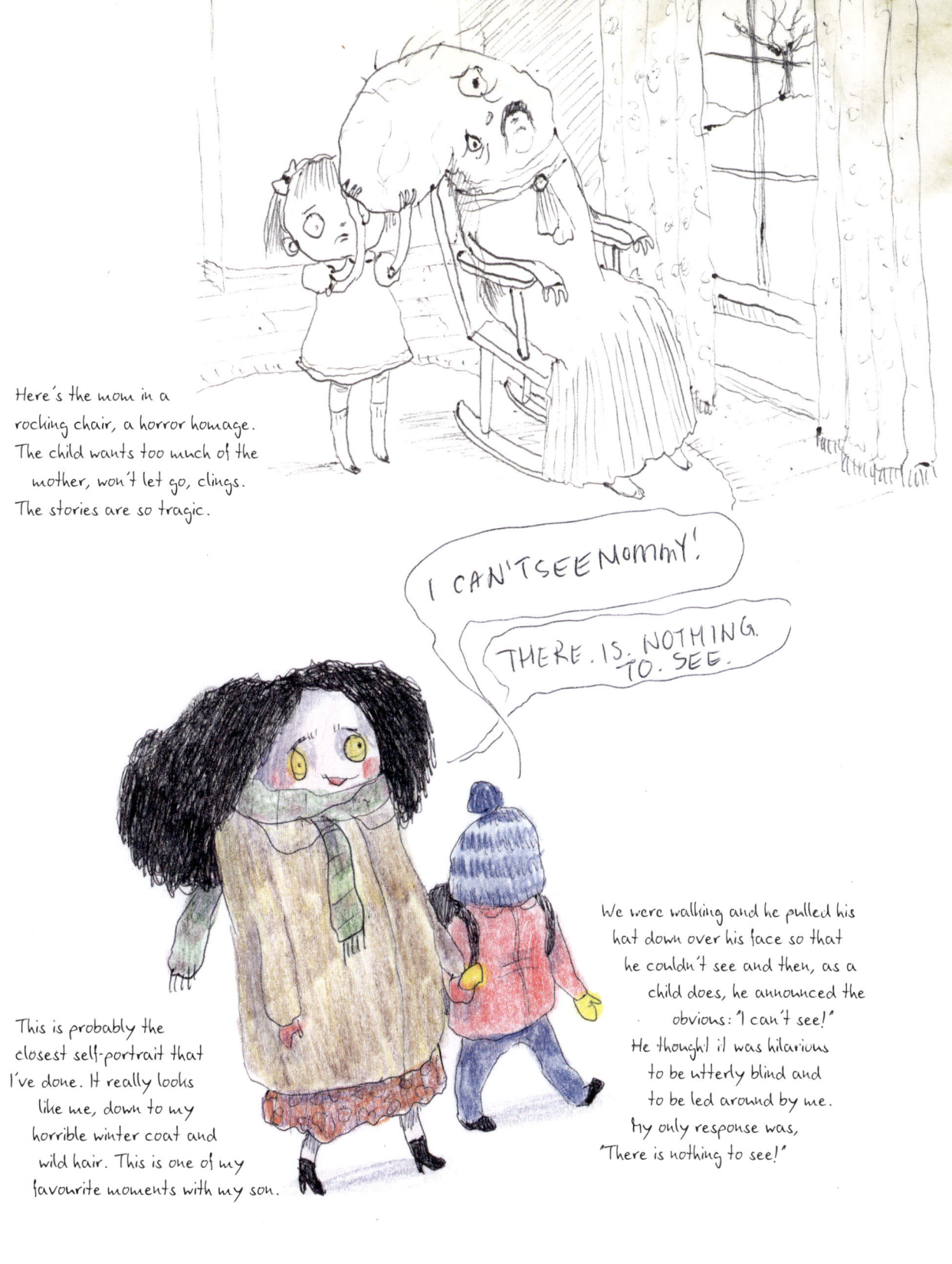

Here's the mom in a rocking chair, a horror homage. The child wants too much of the mother, won't let go, clings. The stories are so tragic.

I CAN'T SEE MOMMY!

THERE. IS. NOTHING. TO. SEE.

This is probably the closest self-portrait that I've done. It really looks like me, down to my horrible winter coat and wild hair. This is one of my favourite moments with my son.

We were walking and he pulled his hat down over his face so that he couldn't see and then, as a child does, he announced the obvious: "I can't see!" He thought it was hilarious to be utterly blind and to be led around by me. My only response was, "There is nothing to see!"

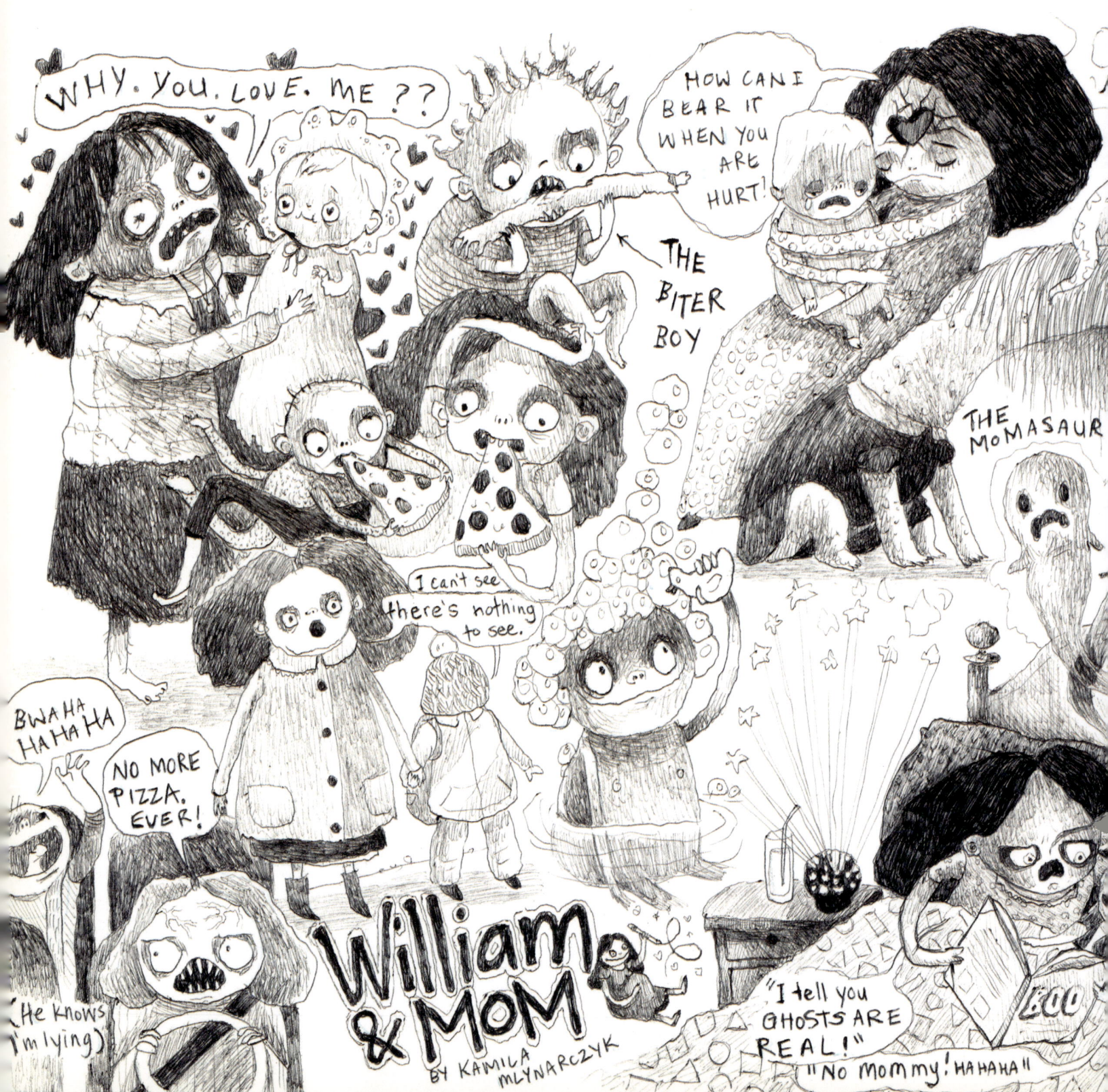

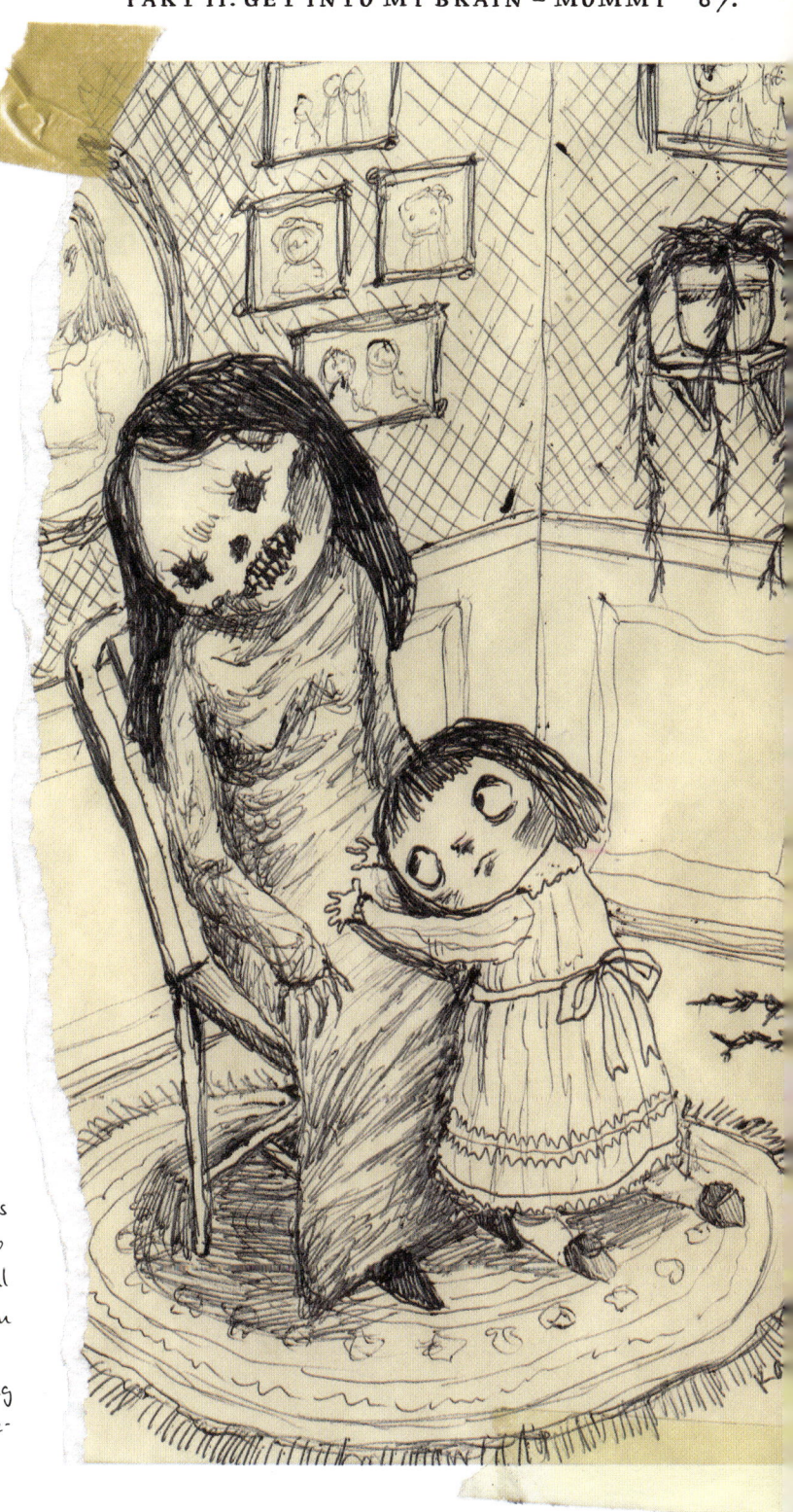

This is a collection of some of my favourite moments with my son. There's me just holding him, selfishly holding him. A mom doesn't ever really want to let go of her baby after carrying it for so long inside of herself. Here's my son as a biter. I think all children go through a biting phase. Here's that scene again where my son pulled his hat down and there was "nothing to see." It's my scrapbook, a styled, cheaper, faster version.

This is an early one, an homage to horror and how often there is an unhealthy attachment to a mother figure, and how often the mother was actually dead all along. I'm also playing with clichés here, the special chair in the corner of the nursery room in an old house with wallpaper. I have an image where the chair is a rocking chair with a blanket. It's such a give-away when watching horror films.

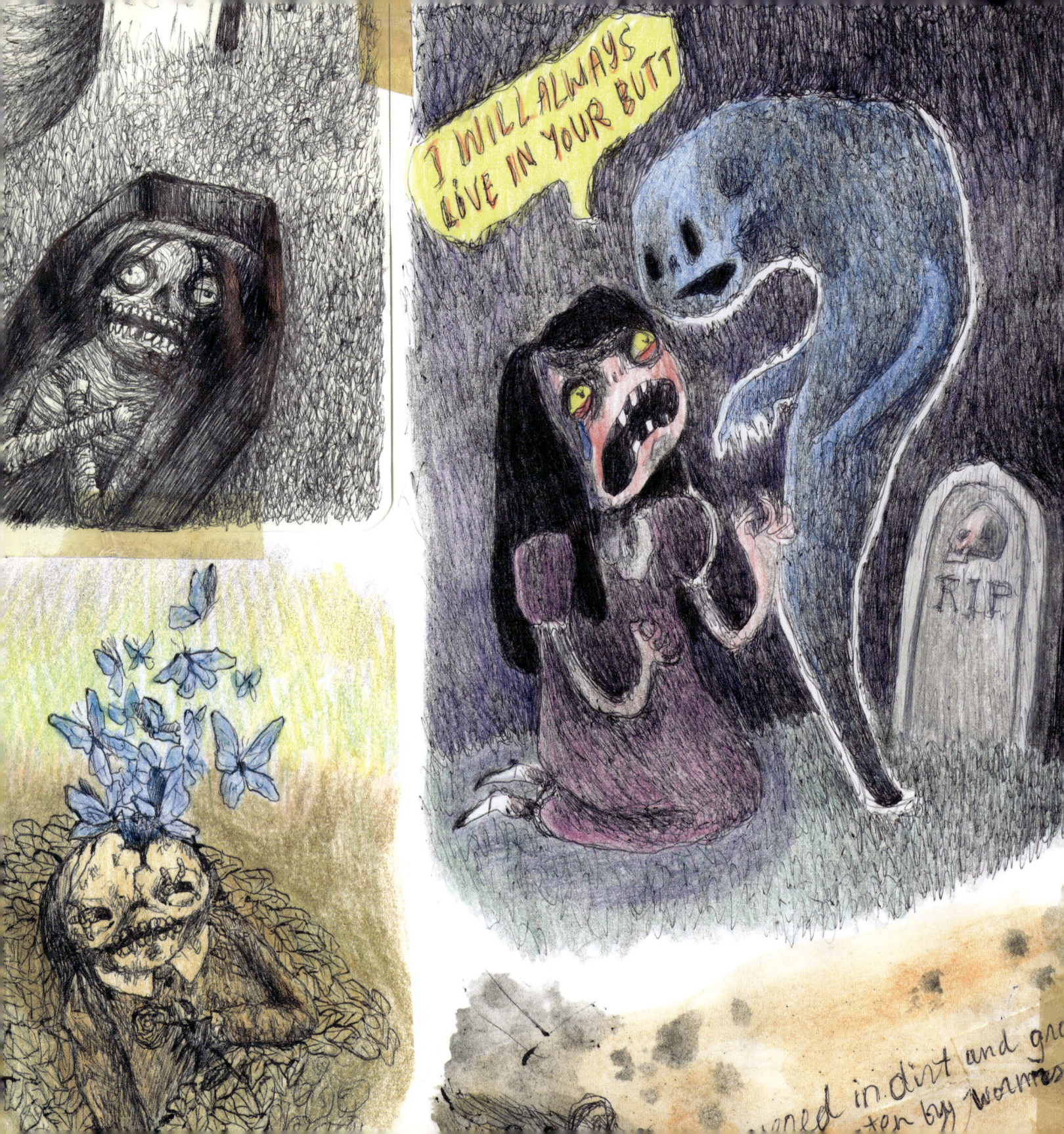

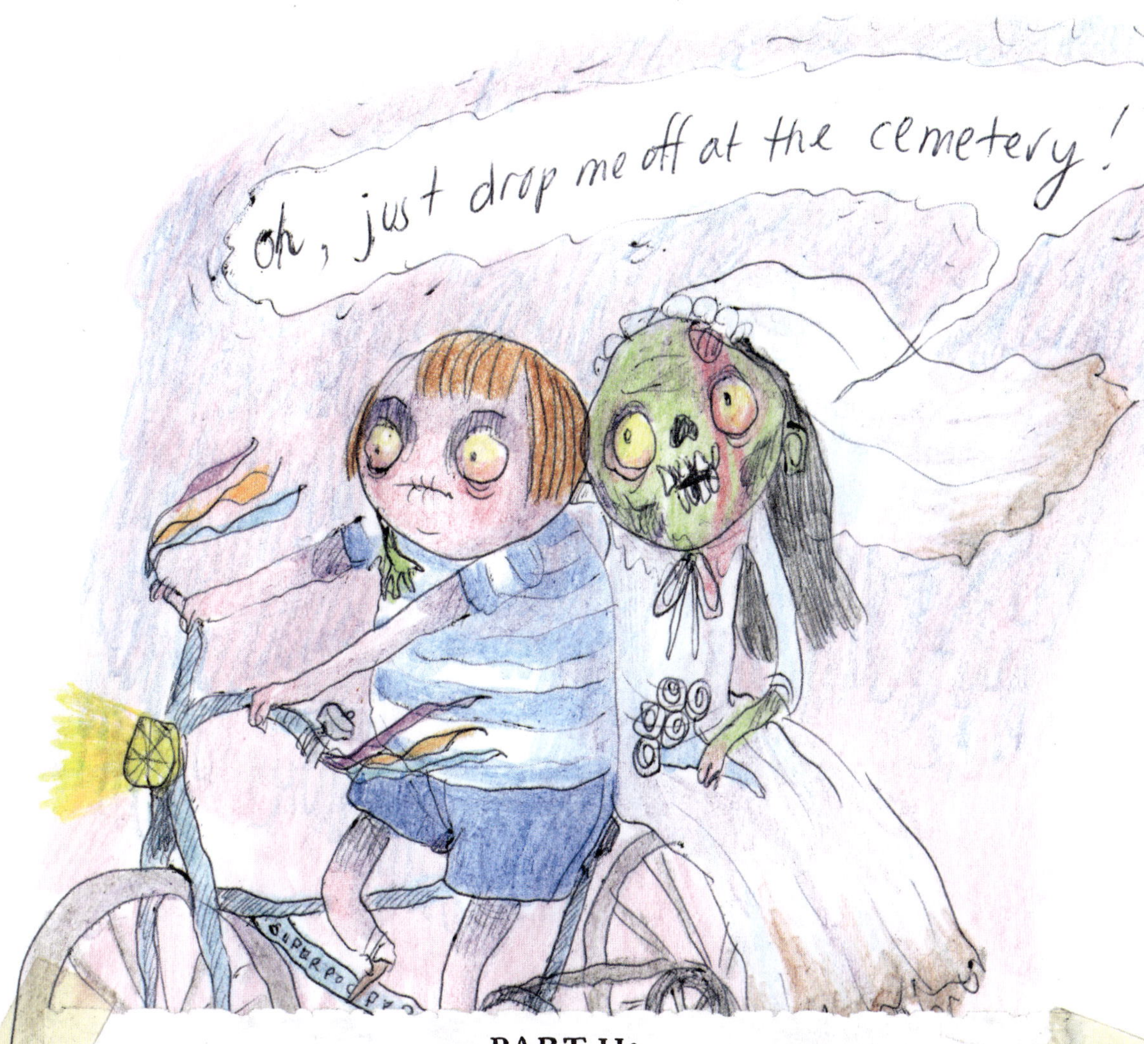

PART II:
GET INTO MY BRAIN, WE'RE GOING TO HELL!

DON'T give RIDES to
BLOODY BRIDES,
SAD GHOSTS

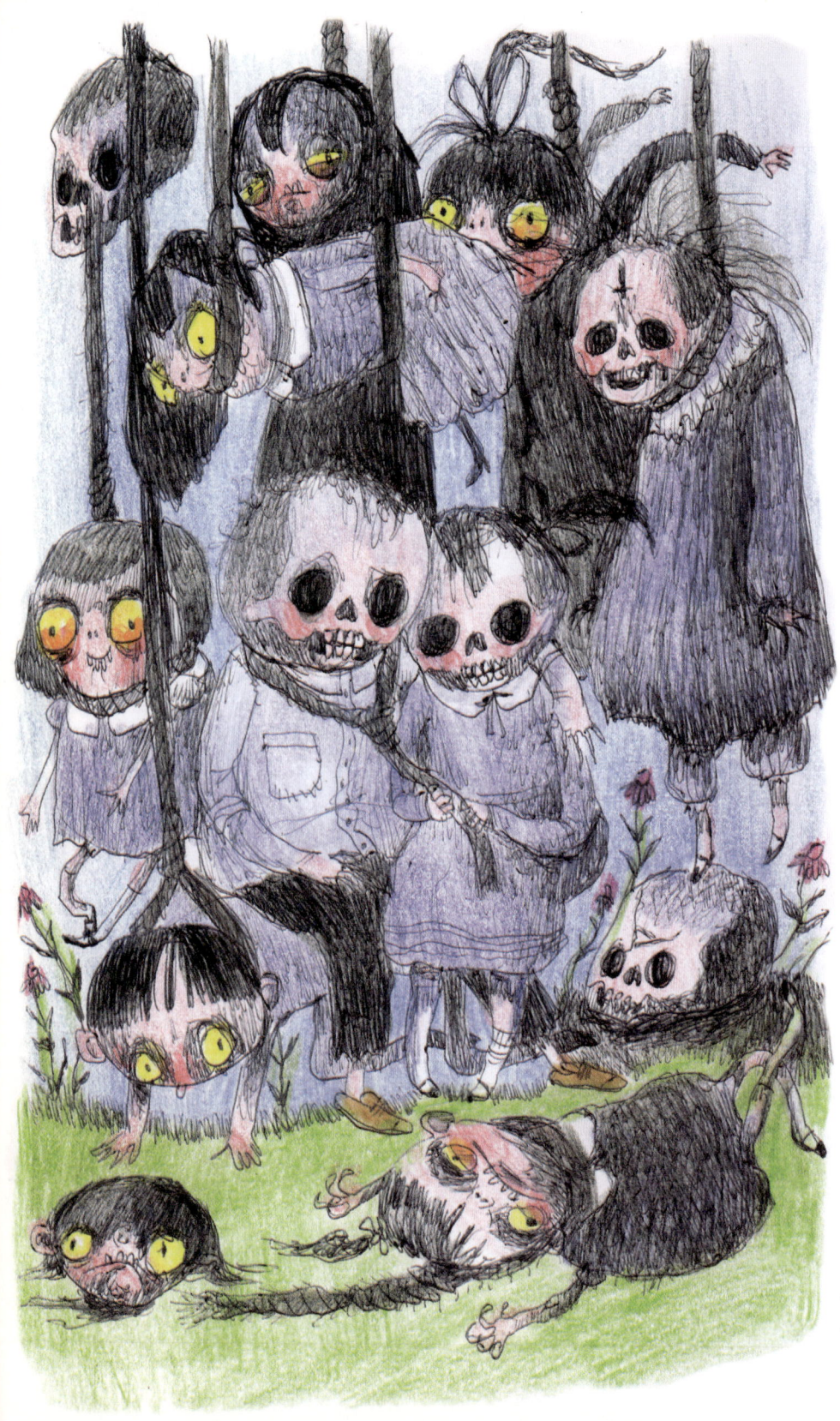

WHEN I WAS LITTLE, I USED to have this thing where I would pretend everyone I knew was dying or dead. Like, if my parents came home late, I would have been convinced they'd been murdered and wound myself up into a tragic and fantastic little story. I think I read too many young adult novels; they always seem to start with a tragedy. I'd imagine living in another country, having an adventure, finding love and so on and so forth. But it was always tinged with a heavy sense of worry and fright. The sentimental ghosts are not random ghosts, they're ghosts I know or that are known to the characters in the drawings. They're memories. And memories are sentimental, made lovely by our minds. These are the missing ghosts, mothers or sisters or someone who is no longer there but should be. They are the romantic and terrifying idea of being haunted. Hauntings can happen in many different ways, and

Kids hanging out. Literally. But they're all together, so it's not so bad. I'm playing with the black eyes thing here too. Some of the kids have black eyes that can see forever. These are true eyes, they aren't the eyes of someone who is always smiling and fake; these have real sight and insight.

it never really has to do with the paranormal. It has to do with emotions and desires. "A ghost is a wish," is such a great line from *The Haunting of Hill House*.[1] Having a dead relative come back is a dream come true, but it's never what anyone expects. From Waterhouse to Gorey to Hideshi Hino, I have been shown that it's okay to draw morbid things and keep morbid things. My sentimental ghosts are my morbid things.

I have a really hard time with my conscience, or maybe it's my inner voice which is just mean and awful. I've tried mindfulness and self-help, all that "love yourself" crap. What works for me is drawing it out. That's my meditation. I can be kind to myself by drawing something real but externalizing it and making it charming. My sentimental ghosts are helper-creatures. It's nice to be haunted; it's romantic, it's never lonely. I don't feel guilty about being kind to myself, because it's just a picture. I think this could be where my twisted sense of the romantic and tragic comes together.

My Polish childhood is, as is probably obvious by now, a great source of inspiration for me. The church that I went to all the time in Poland, for instance, is something that crops up a lot with these sentimental ghost drawings. The church is a very good representation of my childhood in Poland. I went to church a lot. And when I went back to visit, I was made to go to that church every night. Poland is very Catholic. It's full of God and Satan and angels, and holy ghosts, proverbs, superstitions. It's full of churches. I know it means a lot to my parents too, but they identify with that Church in particular. So do I, I guess, but not in the religious way. In a sentimental, nostalgic way. My parents have a chandelier that looks exactly like the chandelier from the church. I see it every week. My past, my memories, are always haunting me, and it's always in such a sentimental light. Even if I'm being trite or ironic, there is sweetness there.

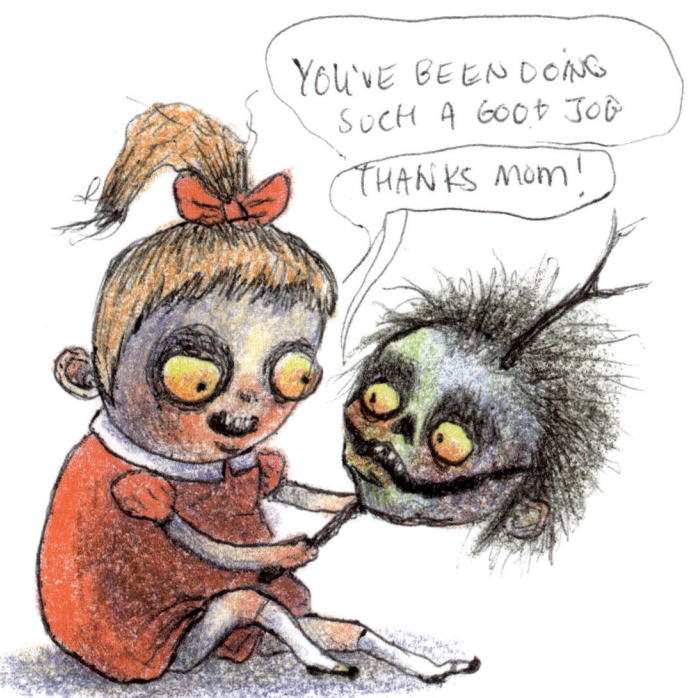

This is a fan favourite of mine. I did it for Mother's Day. It's that 'missing mother that's always so proud and says it at just the right moment' cliché, but the sentimental ghost version. A lot of people messaged me about this to say how much it cheered them up on Mother's Day because their mom was dead.
Now, I'm opening a whole market for dead Mother's Day cards.
Why not?

One of my earliest childhood memories is of my grandpa cutting a field with his scythe. I remember watching him sharpen it too. My grandpa always used to have a scythe; I think that could be why I'm attracted to edged weapons. To knives and the slashing motion. I feel like I grew up in medieval times, and in the eighties in Poland, it was really like that: no phones, T.V., everyone was poor. My grandpa passed away after I moved to Canada and before I visited Poland again, so I have a hard time remembering him. I remember he liked fishing, and he liked to call me *Marchewka* or "carrot," because I had jaundice when I was a baby. My mum was really sick

1   *Haunting of Hill House*, season 1, episode 1, "Steven Sees a Ghost," dir. by Mike Flanagan, aired October 18, 2018, on Netflix. https://www.netflix.com/watch/80189222.

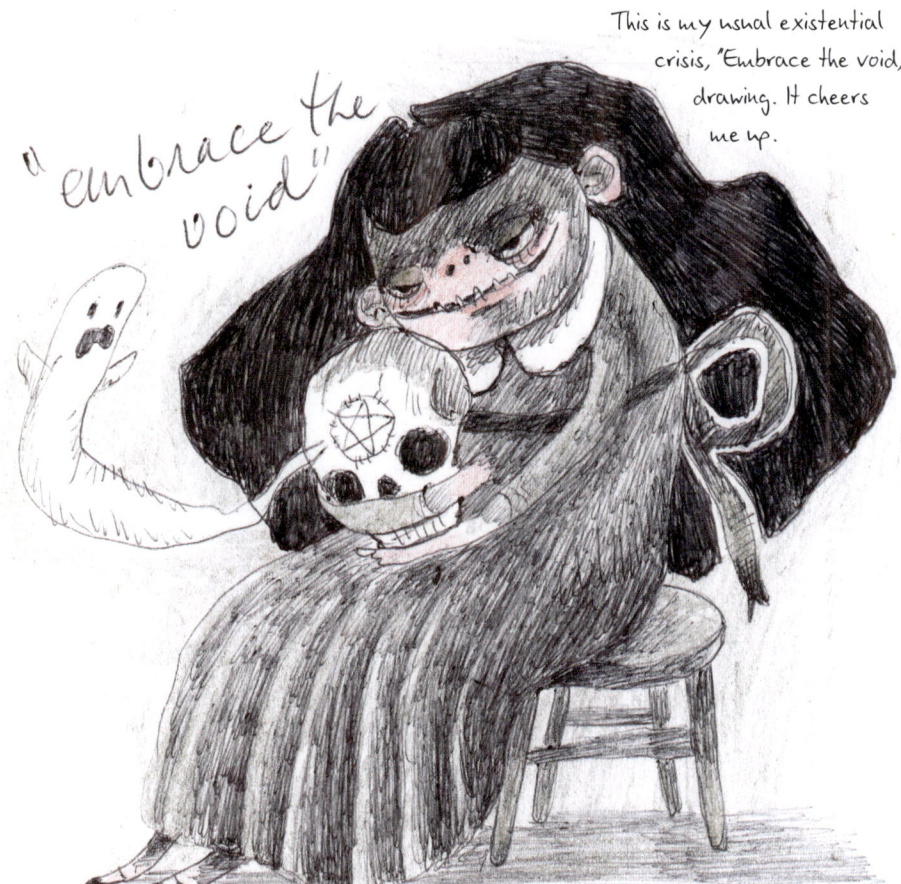

"embrace the void"

This is my usual existential crisis, "Embrace the void," drawing. It cheers me up.

This one is reminiscent of an Art Doll that I did that had a Glasgow Smile, which is when a person's face is cut from the corners of their mouth to their ears with a knife. Like the Joker from *The Dark Knight*.

in the hospital when she was pregnant with me and she went into premature labour at five or six months. They had to keep her on bed rest after that, and my dad would always ride his bike to the hospital, which was two towns over, and he would bring my mum fresh carrot juice. Carrot-apple juice. My grandpa would say something like, "You have this colour from the carrot juice!"

People ask me sometimes, "Have you ever seen a ghost?" I say, "No." But after my grandma died, and after my uncle died, I started seeing them. I see people that look like them everywhere. After my uncle died, I saw him in crowds in Toronto. I saw my grandma, too. I know, in my rational mind that it wasn't the ghost of my grandma, I just had a dirty rear-view mirror. A very specific smudge, so that when I looked at it at night, it looked like the outline of my grandma's old, long, grey hairstyle, sitting behind me in the car. It was comforting in a weird way to have her there. I mean, I've always loved ghost stories. I've always collected them. I'd scare neighbour kids and people would ask that I not come over anymore. I don't actually believe my grandma was in the backseat, but I believe it's a nice thought. It's sort of sweet that she'd be there watching over me, so I put it in my art.

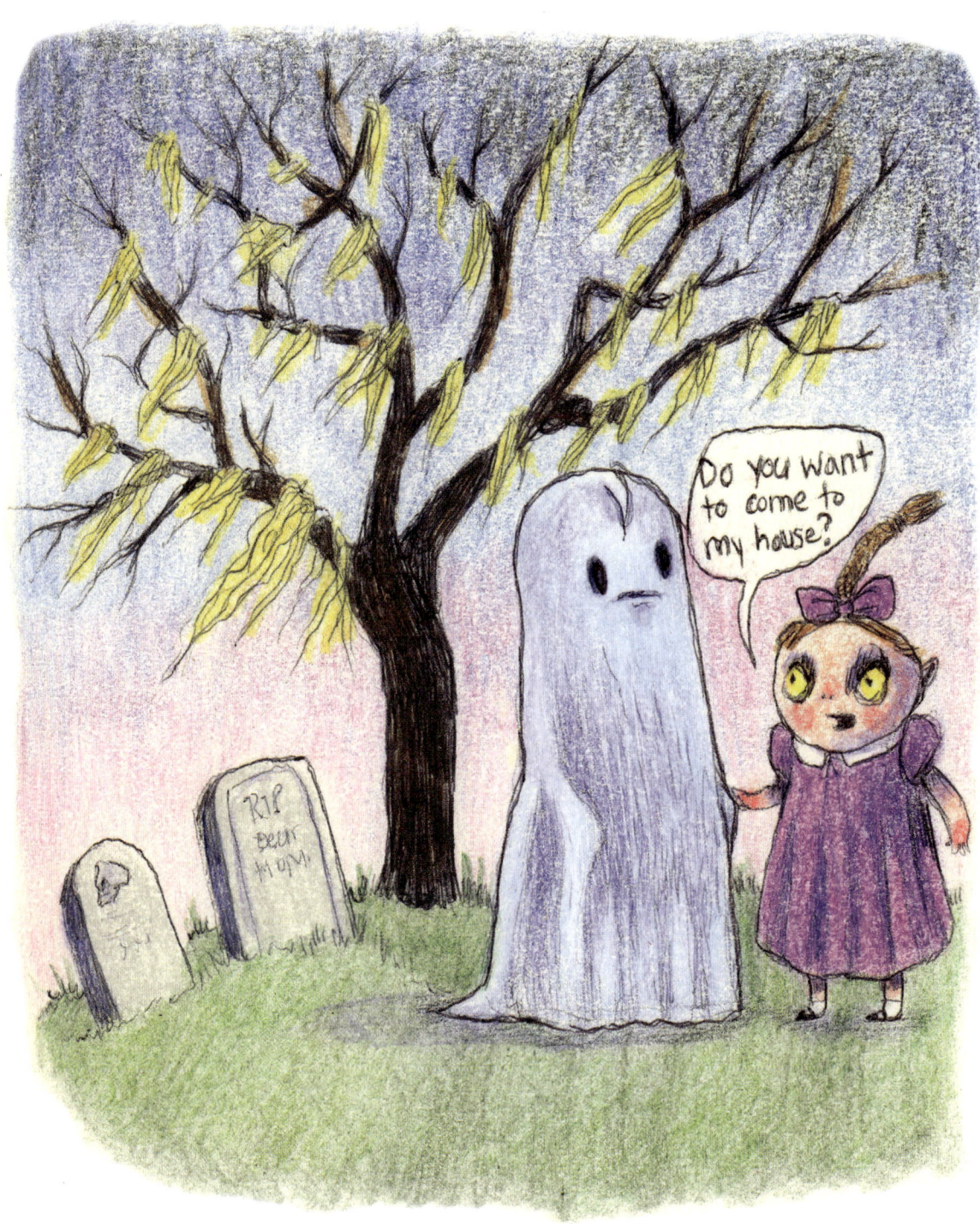

My grandma would say, "Don't pick a flower from somebody's grave, or a ghost will follow you home." In this version she wants the ghost to come over to her house anyway, so she picked the flower.

I've always been a really big fan of death in the water, or the idea of the 'River of Death.' Like 'The Lady of Shallot' or Ophelia from *Hamlet*. Even *Lord of the Rings* has that scene with all the death-people sweeping over the river. Bodies are dumped into rivers, a river is crossed to get to the underworld.

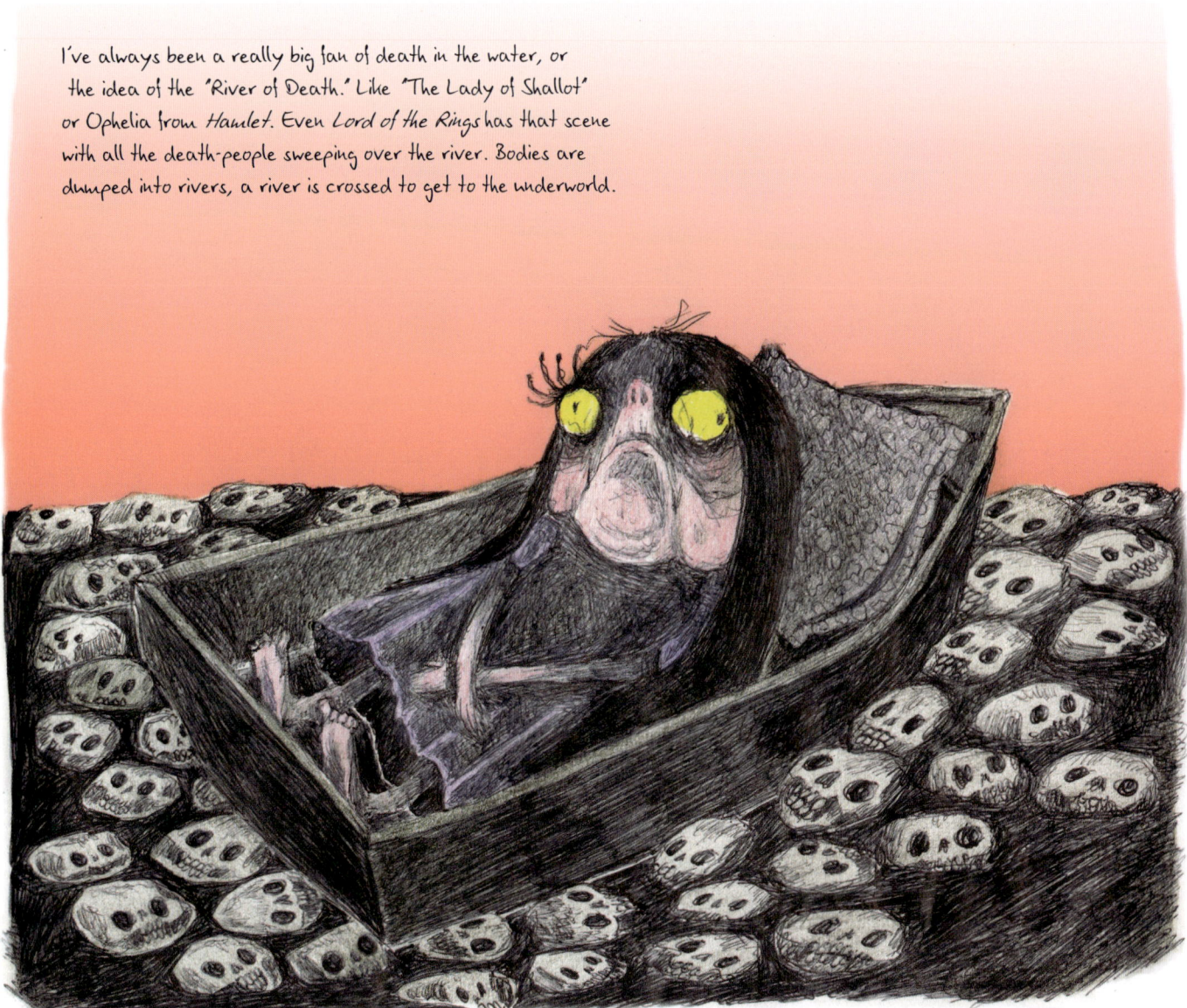

Water is part of death, and death near or in water is romantic and fascinating. Water was a big part of my grandfather and his mythos in my life, too. He'd say, "There's a river next to our village, and there's a forest." My grandfather fished in that river. My grandfather watched someone drown in that river. There's this one spot where people drown, and I'm sure it has something to do with water currents. In Polish, it's called a *topielec*, which means drowned water spirit. It's a spot that is known as a place where people drown, like they are pulled down by the spirit to drown too. Apparently, my grandpa almost got sucked into it. He said he was in a daze and didn't realize he was swimming toward it, but he snapped out of it in time and came back.

It's a really cool and cryptic story from Poland that always stuck with me.

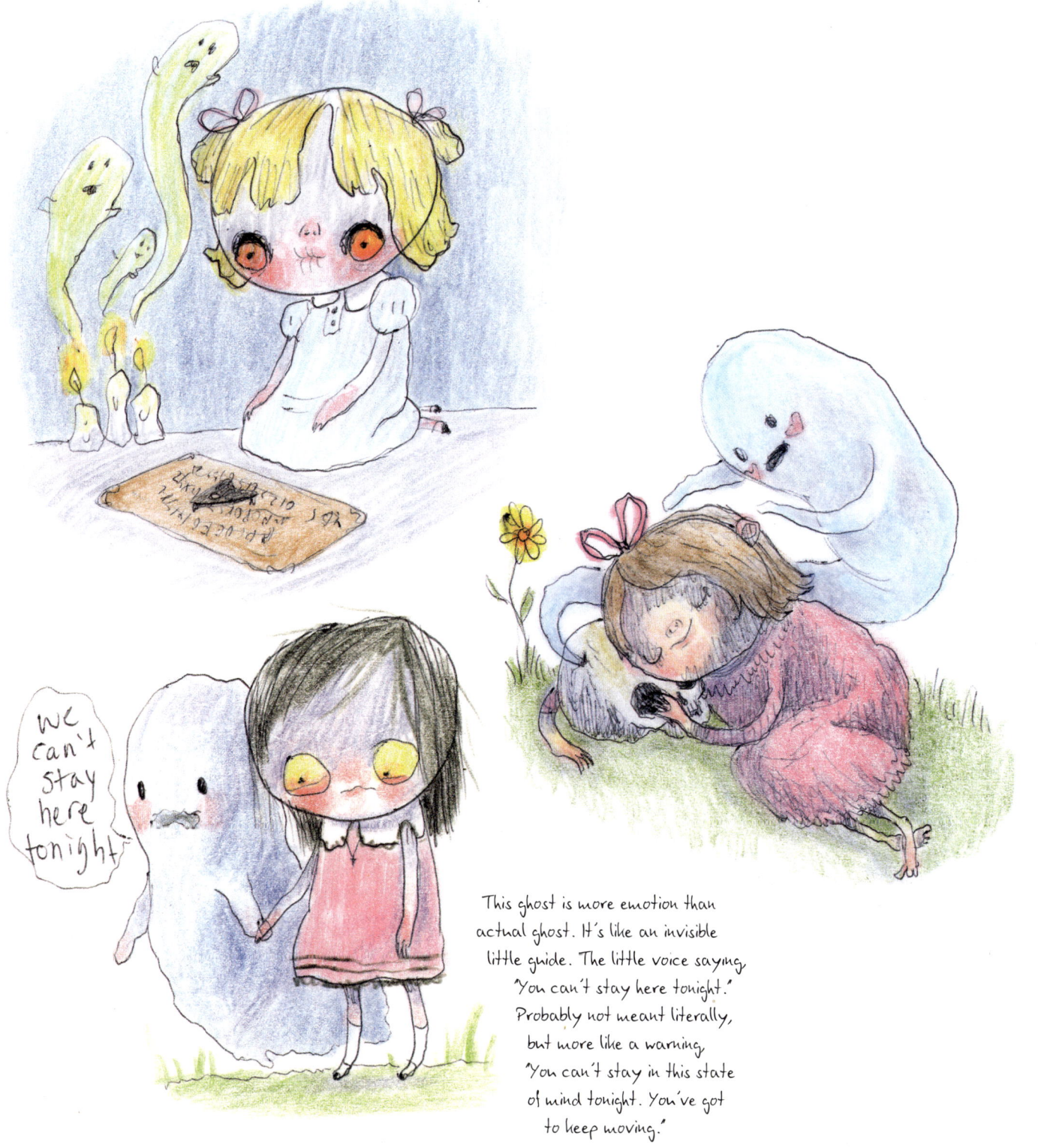

we can't stay here tonight

This ghost is more emotion than actual ghost. It's like an invisible little guide. The little voice saying, "You can't stay here tonight." Probably not meant literally, but more like a warning "You can't stay in this state of mind tonight. You've got to keep moving."

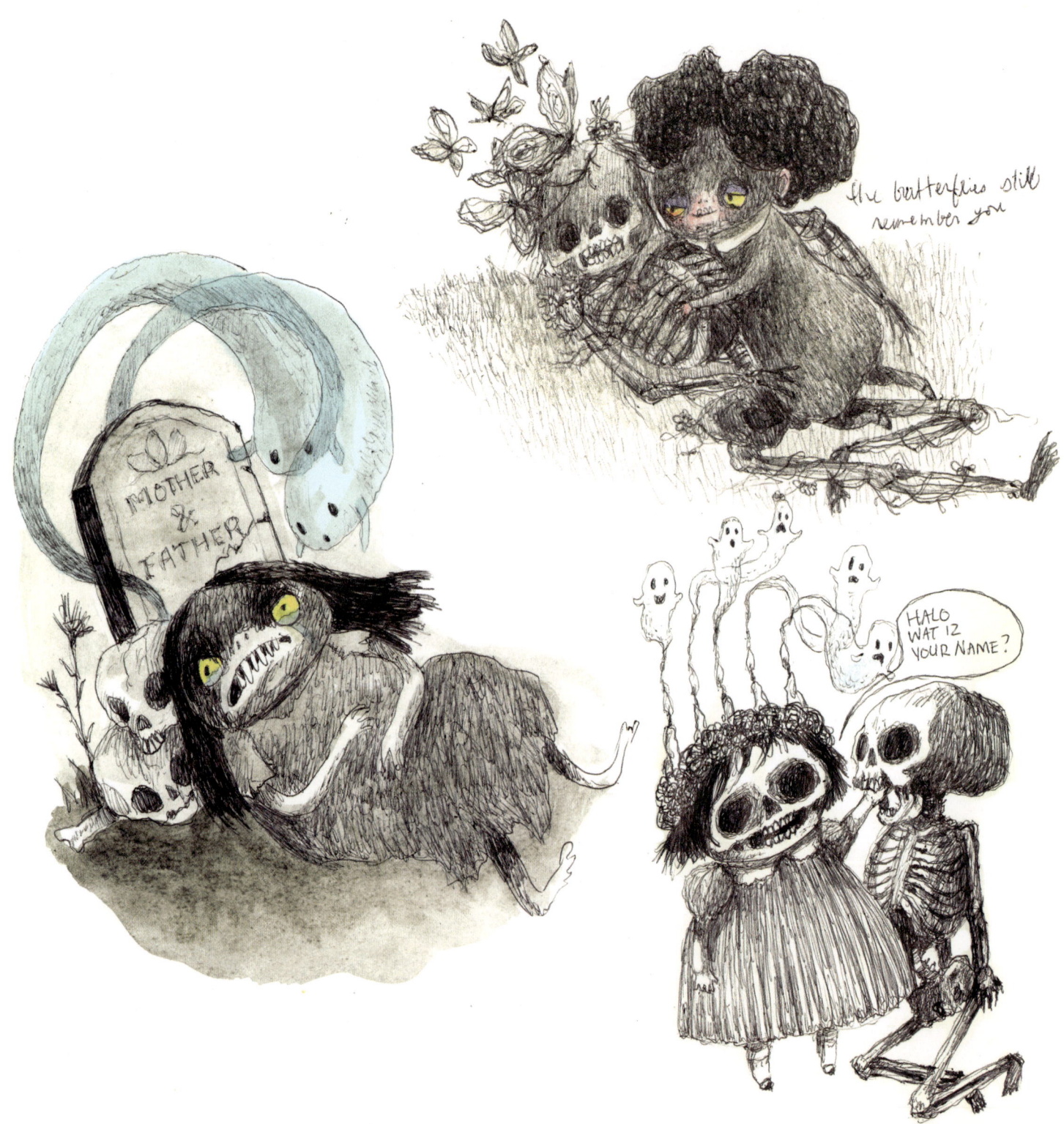

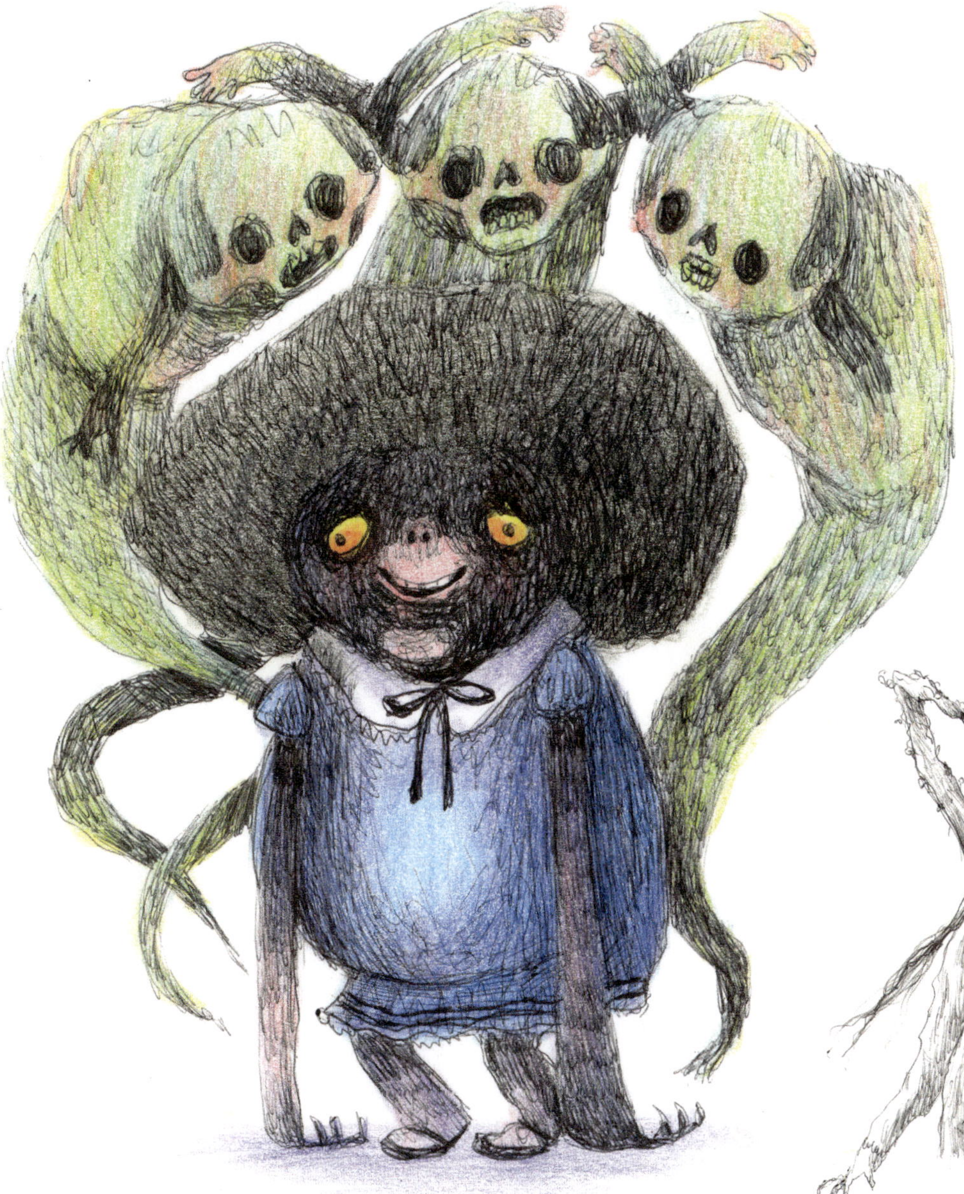

Some of the ghosts I draw are actually doppelgangers, dead versions of myself. It follows a line of thought I've had for ages, this idea that when I'm dead, maybe I could visit my past self and change things.

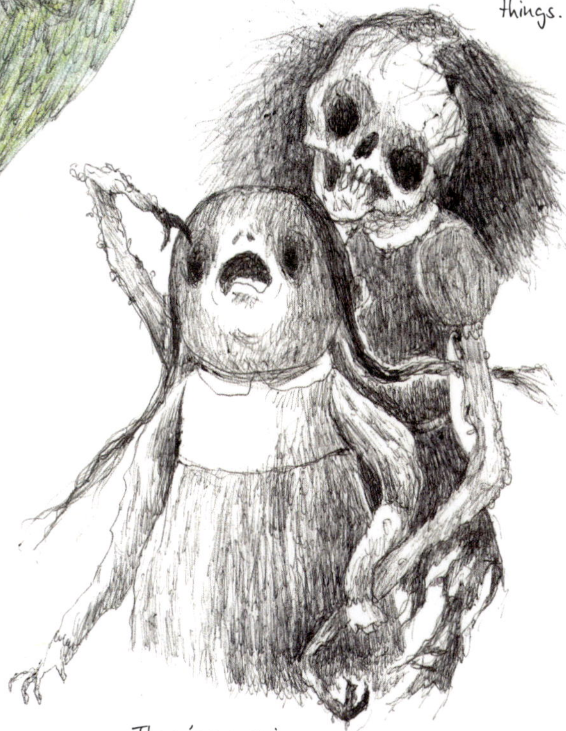

There's a movie from the '90s called *Doppelganger*, and the first thing a person has to do is kill their doppelganger. But over the years I've become less fearful of mirrors and the idea of doppelgangers. I'm okay with facing myself now. Sometimes it's scary, but sometimes it's sweet and wistful—I love this drawing.

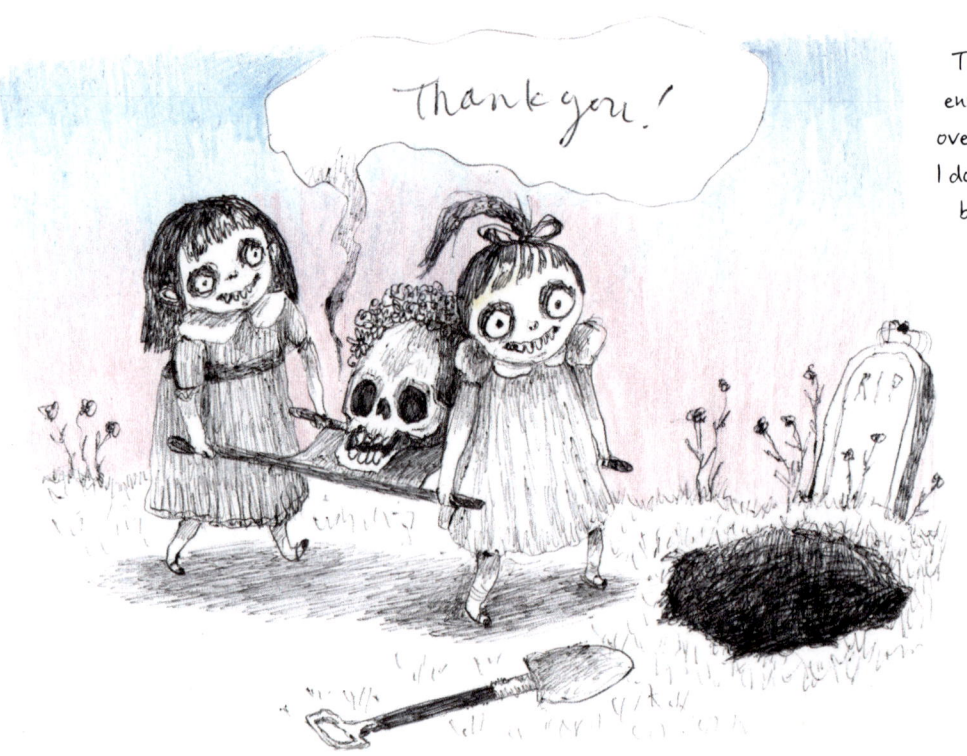

Thank you!

This is part of a thank you envelope. A really elaborate, overdone thank you envelope. I don't know why I did that, but I enjoy this one.

Ultimately just waiting to die.

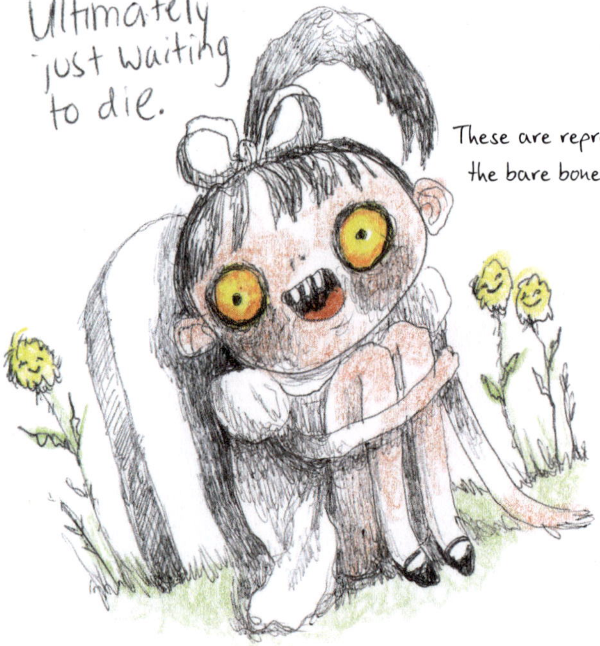

These are representing the bare bones of life.

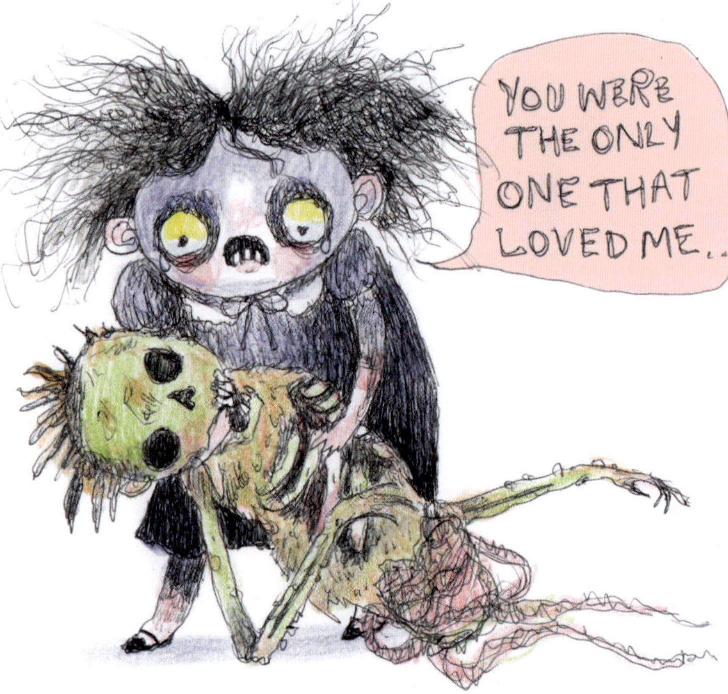

YOU WERE THE ONLY ONE THAT LOVED ME...

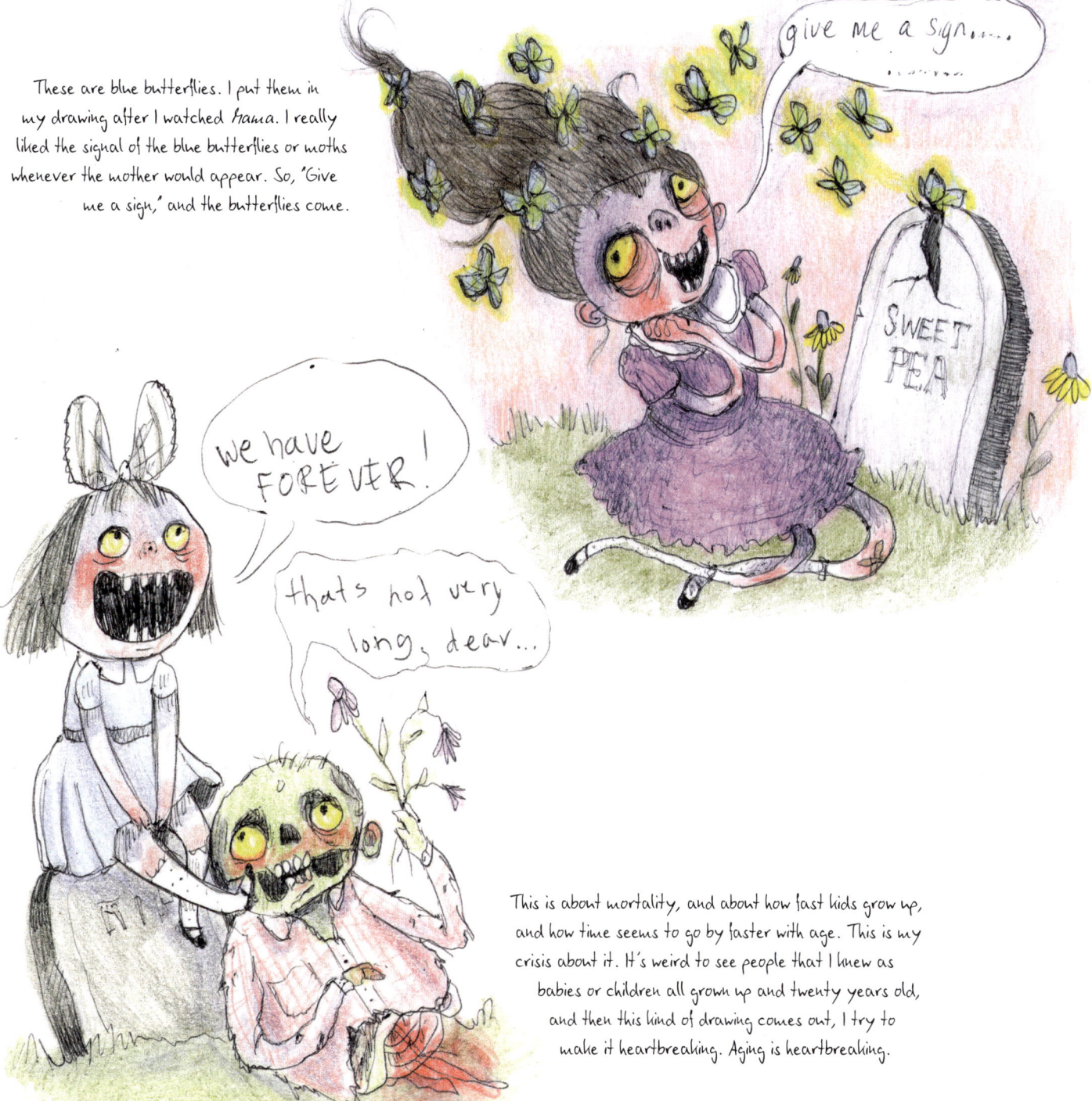

These are blue butterflies. I put them in my drawing after I watched *mama*. I really liked the signal of the blue butterflies or moths whenever the mother would appear. So, "Give me a sign," and the butterflies come.

give me a sign.....

SWEET PEA

we have FOREVER!

that's not very long, dear...

This is about mortality, and about how fast kids grow up, and how time seems to go by faster with age. This is my crisis about it. It's weird to see people that I knew as babies or children all grown up and twenty years old, and then this kind of drawing comes out, I try to make it heartbreaking. Aging is heartbreaking.

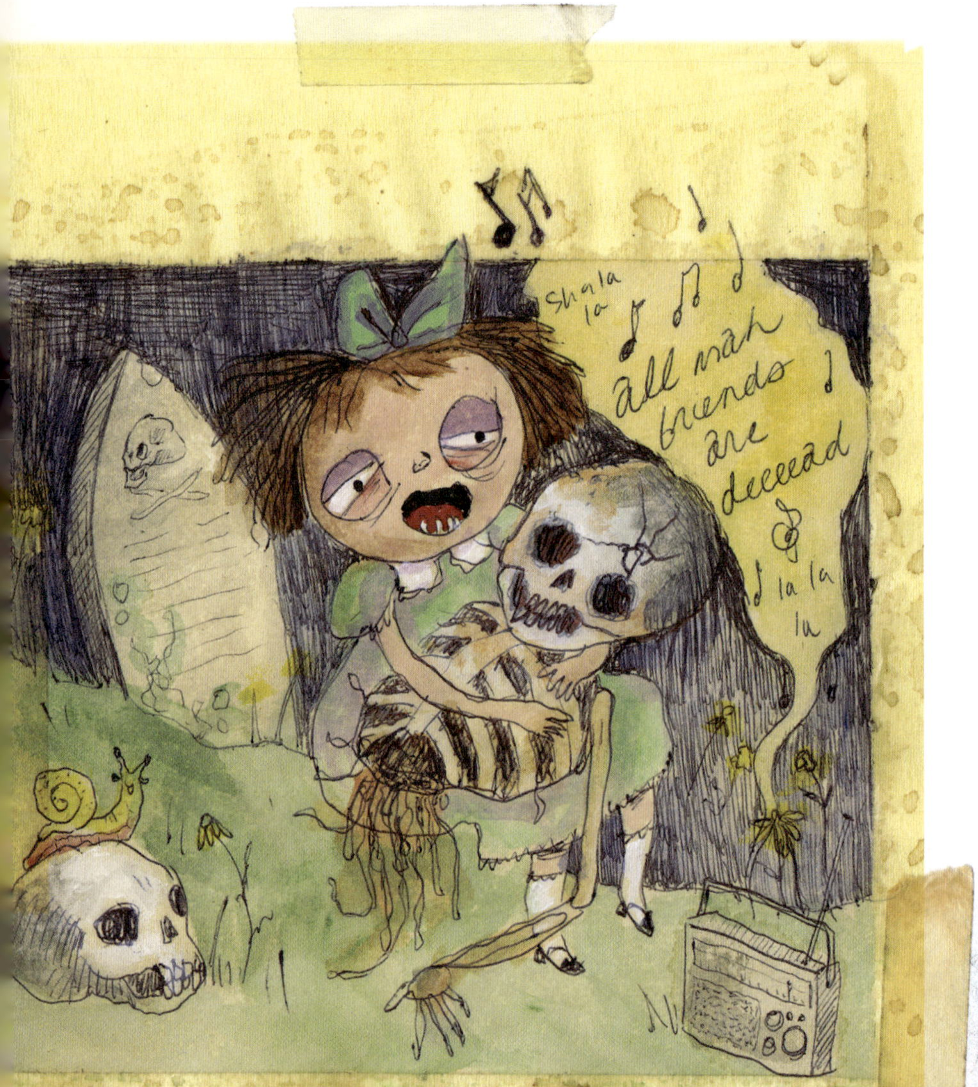

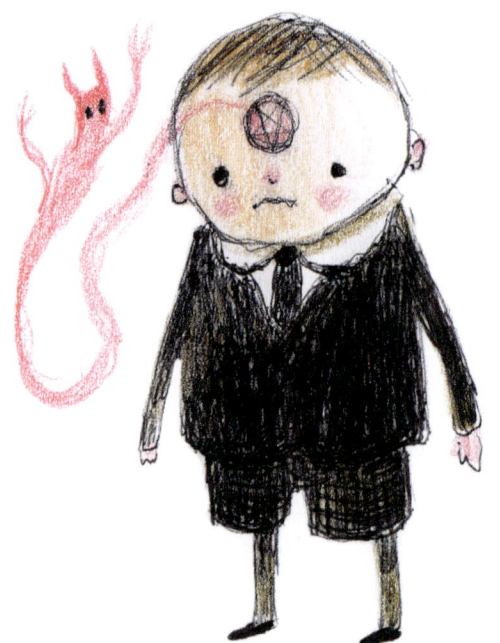

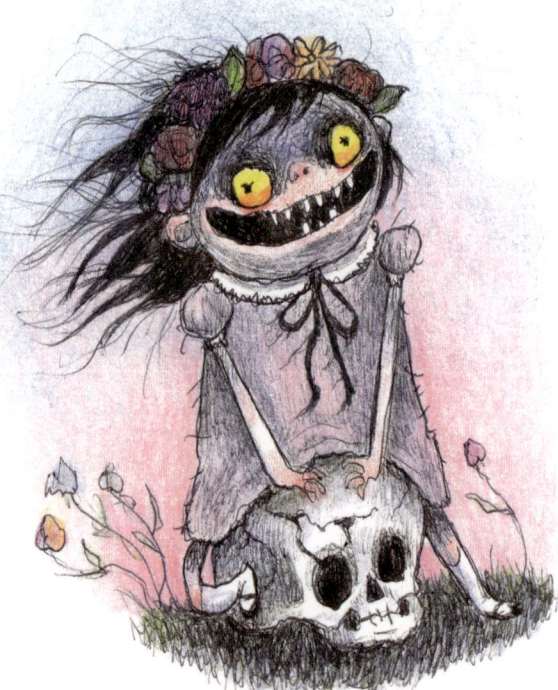

This is angst about lost friendships. I lost touch with so many people and never reconnected. Everyone has, I think. Anyways, I think it's funny to keep drawing and noting that all my friends are dead. I think it's a popular trope, and it's also something universal,

we all have friends that we have lost so entirely that they could be dead. We all also probably have friends we wish were dead.

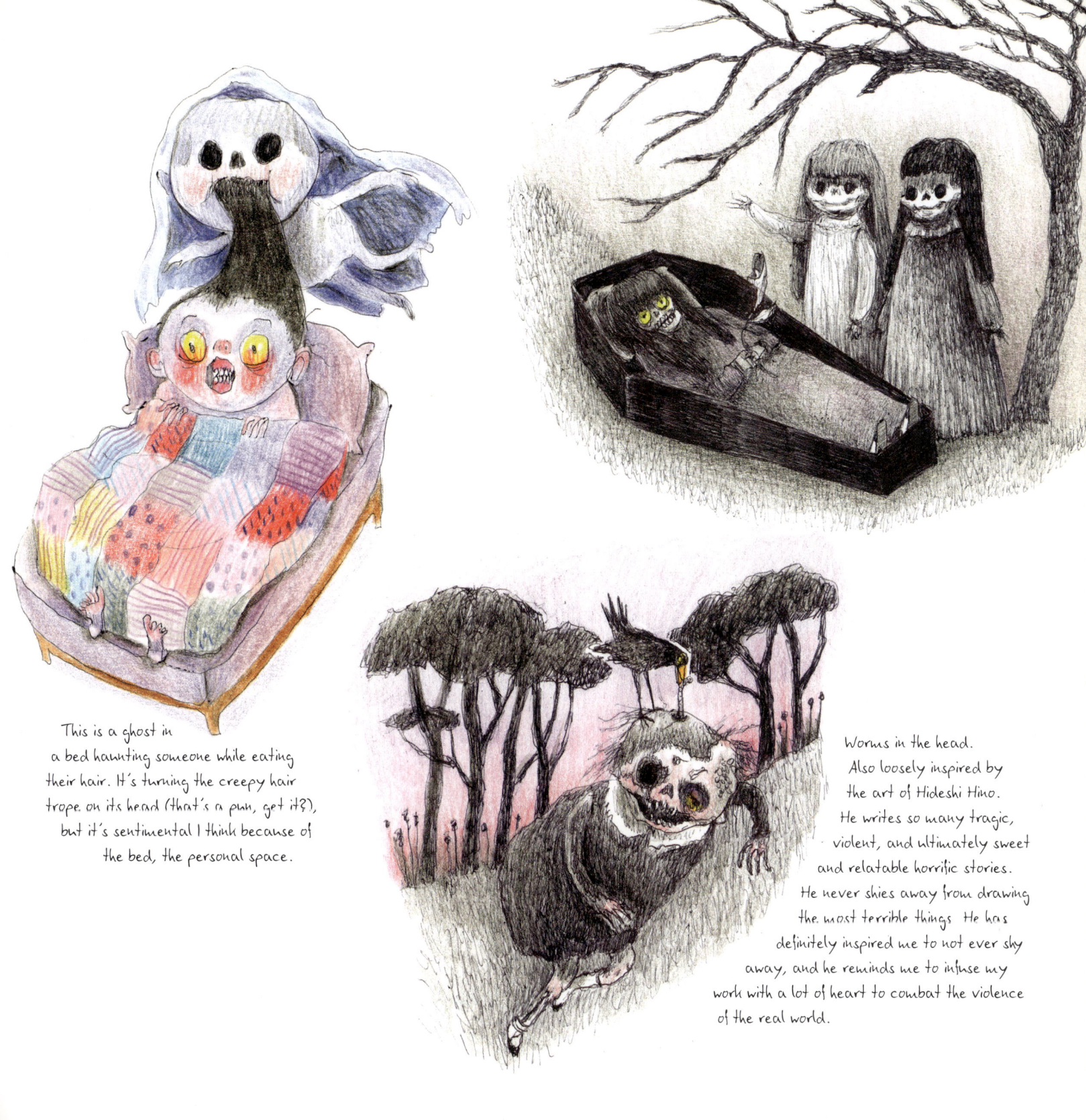

This is a ghost in
a bed haunting someone while eating
their hair. It's turning the creepy hair
trope on its head (that's a pun, get it?),
but it's sentimental I think because of
the bed, the personal space.

Worms in the head.
Also loosely inspired by
the art of Hideshi Hino.
He writes so many tragic,
violent, and ultimately sweet
and relatable horrific stories.
He never shies away from drawing
the most terrible things He has
definitely inspired me to not ever shy
away, and he reminds me to infuse my
work with a lot of heart to combat the violence
of the real world.

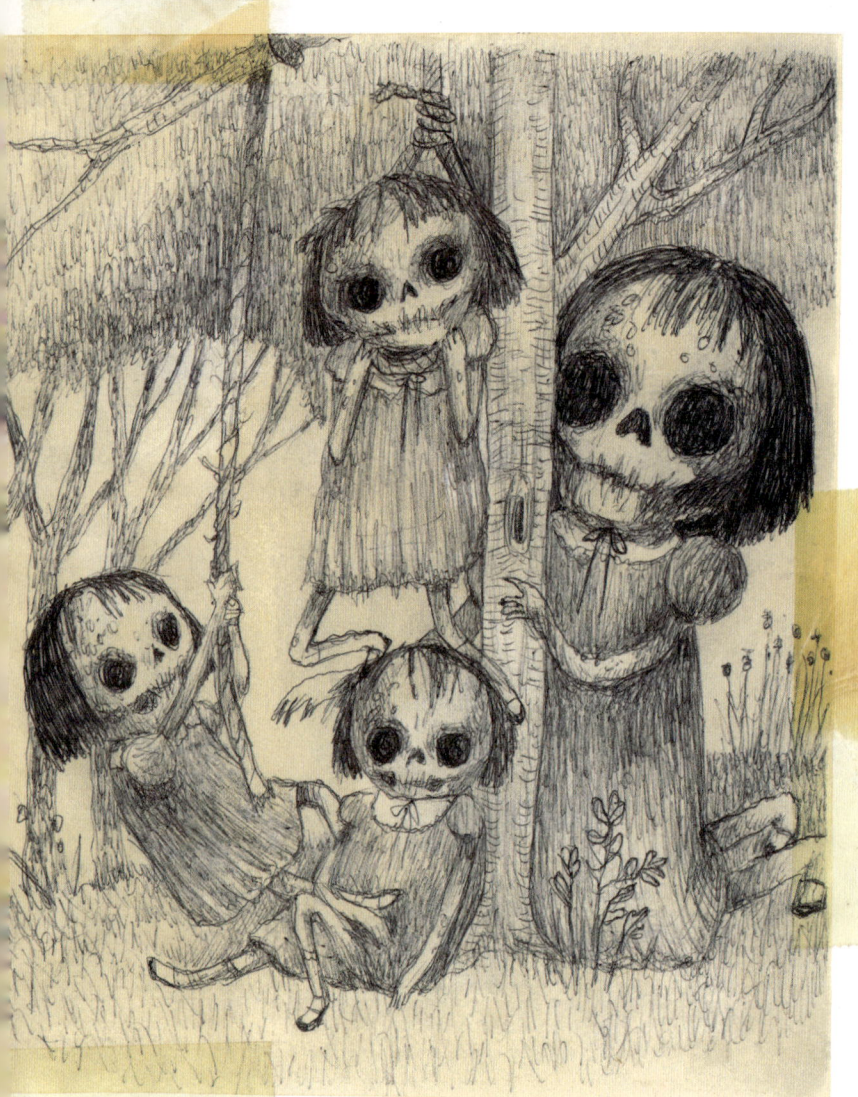

DAD SAID MOM LEFT BUT I FOUND HER UNDER THE PORCH♪

This is actually referencing a Louis C.K. joke. He was talking about God and the Father, but where is the mother? And he said something along the lines of, "Where did mother go? Did God kill her? What, God, what did you do to our mother?" And I think he implied murder for sure and mentioned under the porch. Murdered mother under the porch. She's still there. Always there.

My affinity for hanging strikes again. These are a bunch of dead girls in the forest. This was the way dead children play in the forest, or a way to stay occupied after death: hanging games. Hanging out.

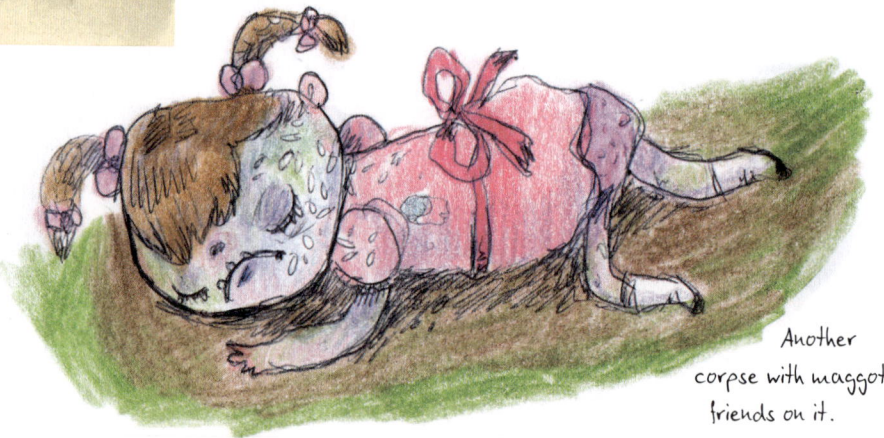

Another corpse with maggot friends on it.

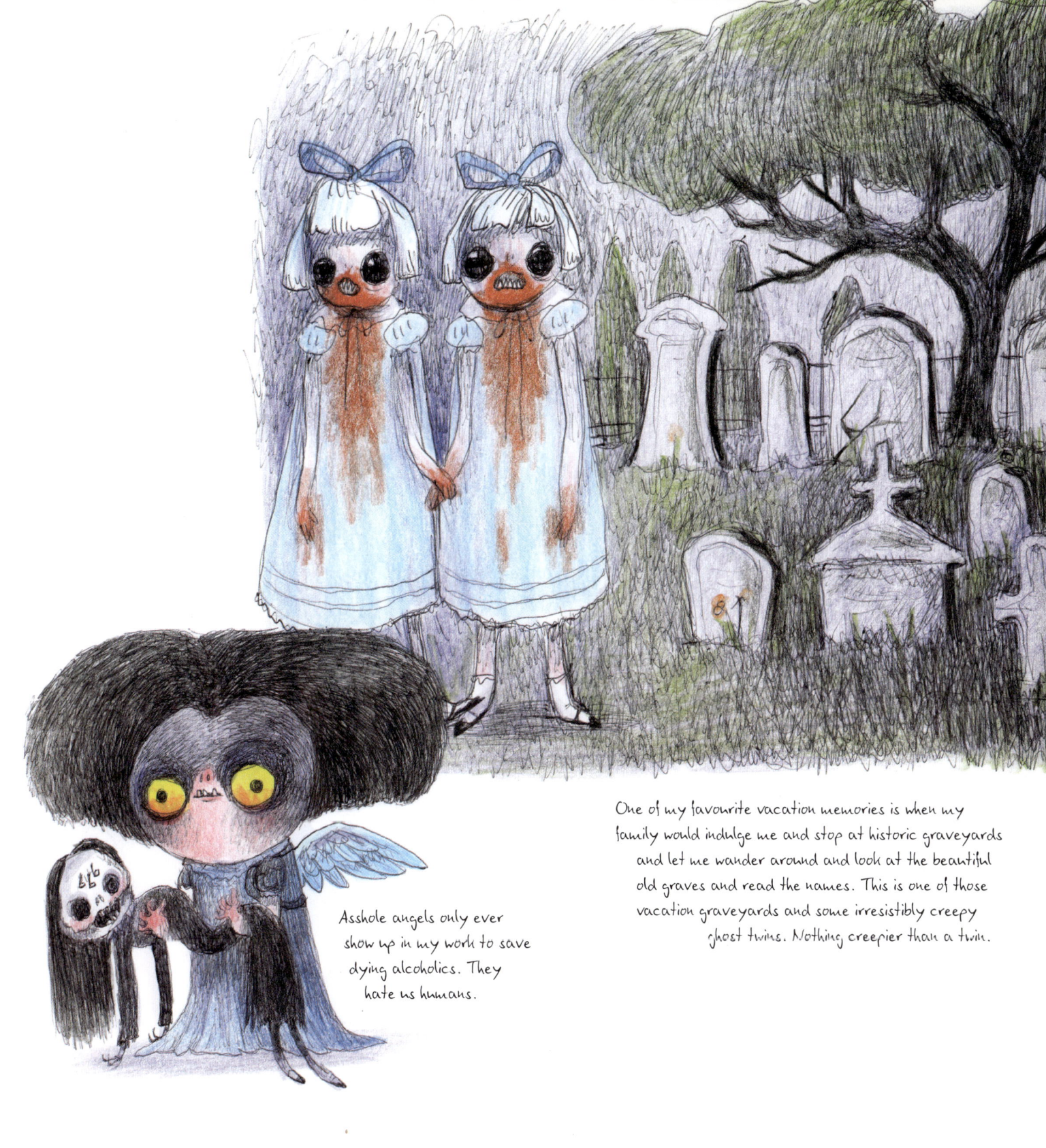

Asshole angels only ever show up in my work to save dying alcoholics. They hate us humans.

One of my favourite vacation memories is when my family would indulge me and stop at historic graveyards and let me wander around and look at the beautiful old graves and read the names. This is one of those vacation graveyards and some irresistibly creepy ghost twins. Nothing creepier than a twin.

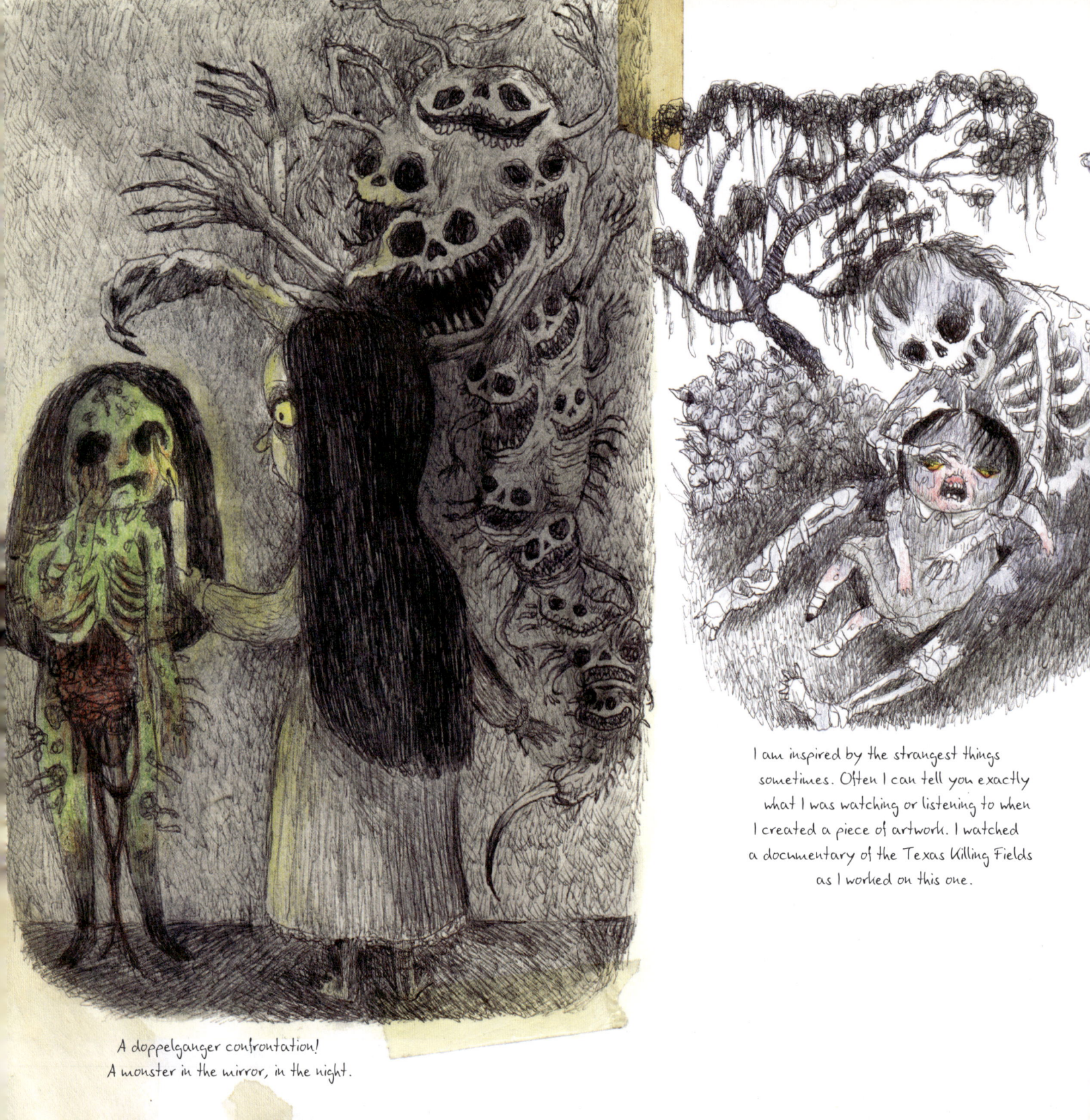

I am inspired by the strangest things sometimes. Often I can tell you exactly what I was watching or listening to when I created a piece of artwork. I watched a documentary of the Texas Killing Fields as I worked on this one.

A doppelganger confrontation!
A monster in the mirror, in the night.

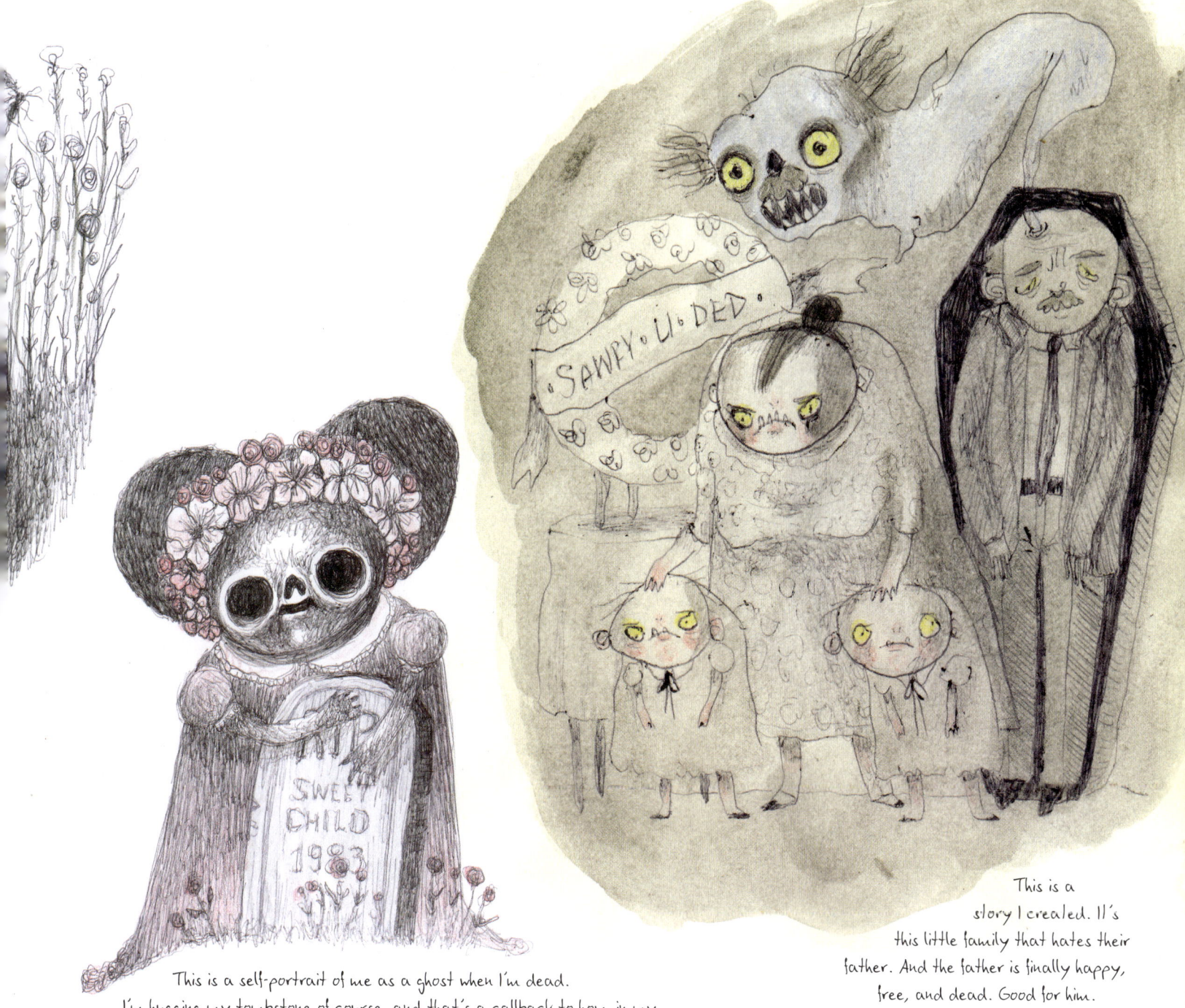

This is a self-portrait of me as a ghost when I'm dead.
I'm hugging my tombstone of course, and that's a callback to how, in my
family anyway, we always had to visit graves of dead family members and
take a picture. See my artist photo at the back of the book, it's a true story.
Maybe I was supposed to hug their tombstone or something.

This is a
story I created. It's
this little family that hates their
father. And the father is finally happy,
free, and dead. Good for him.

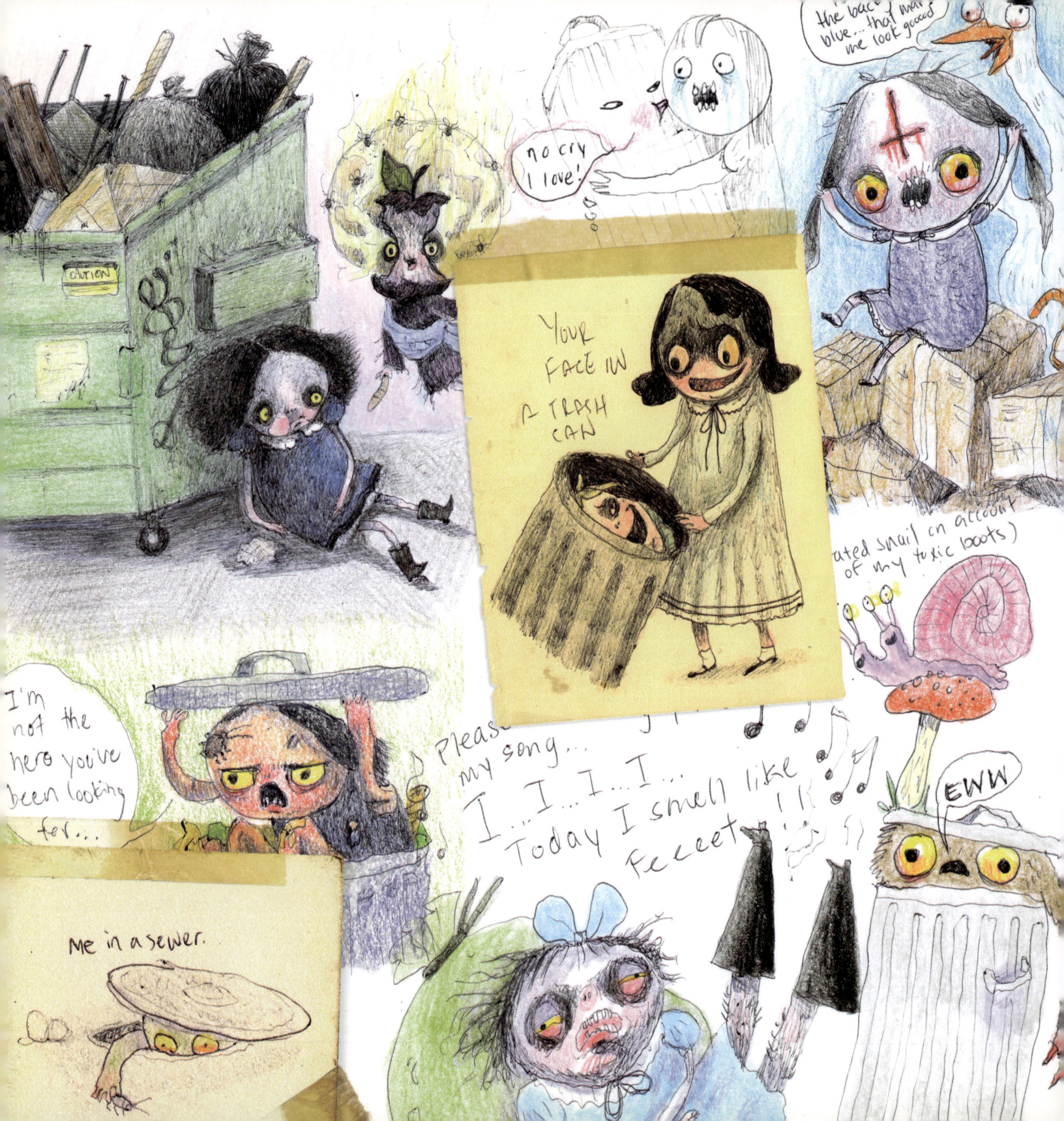

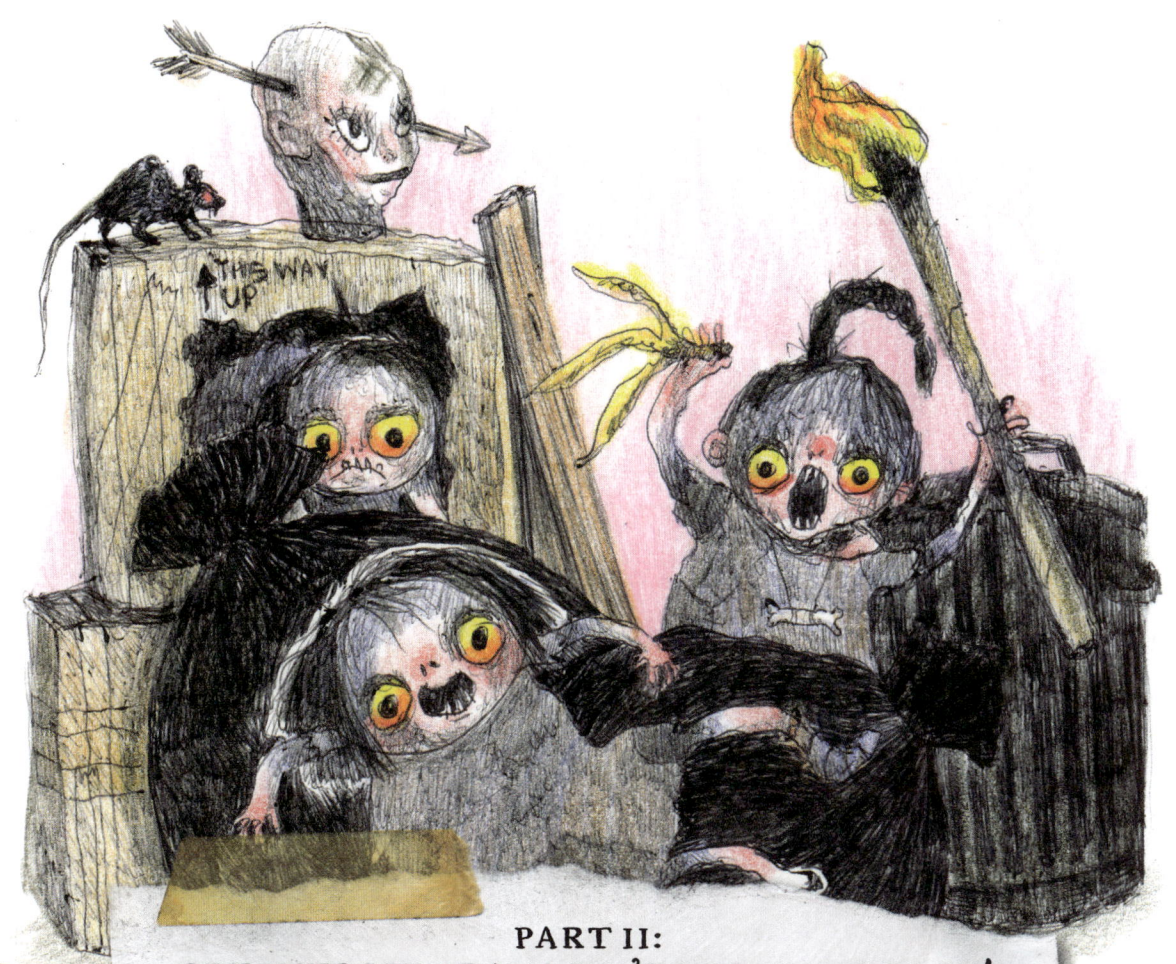

PART II:
GET INTO MY BRAIN, WE'RE GOING TO HELL!

HEY KIDS,
YOU GET AWAY *from that*
DUMPSTER!

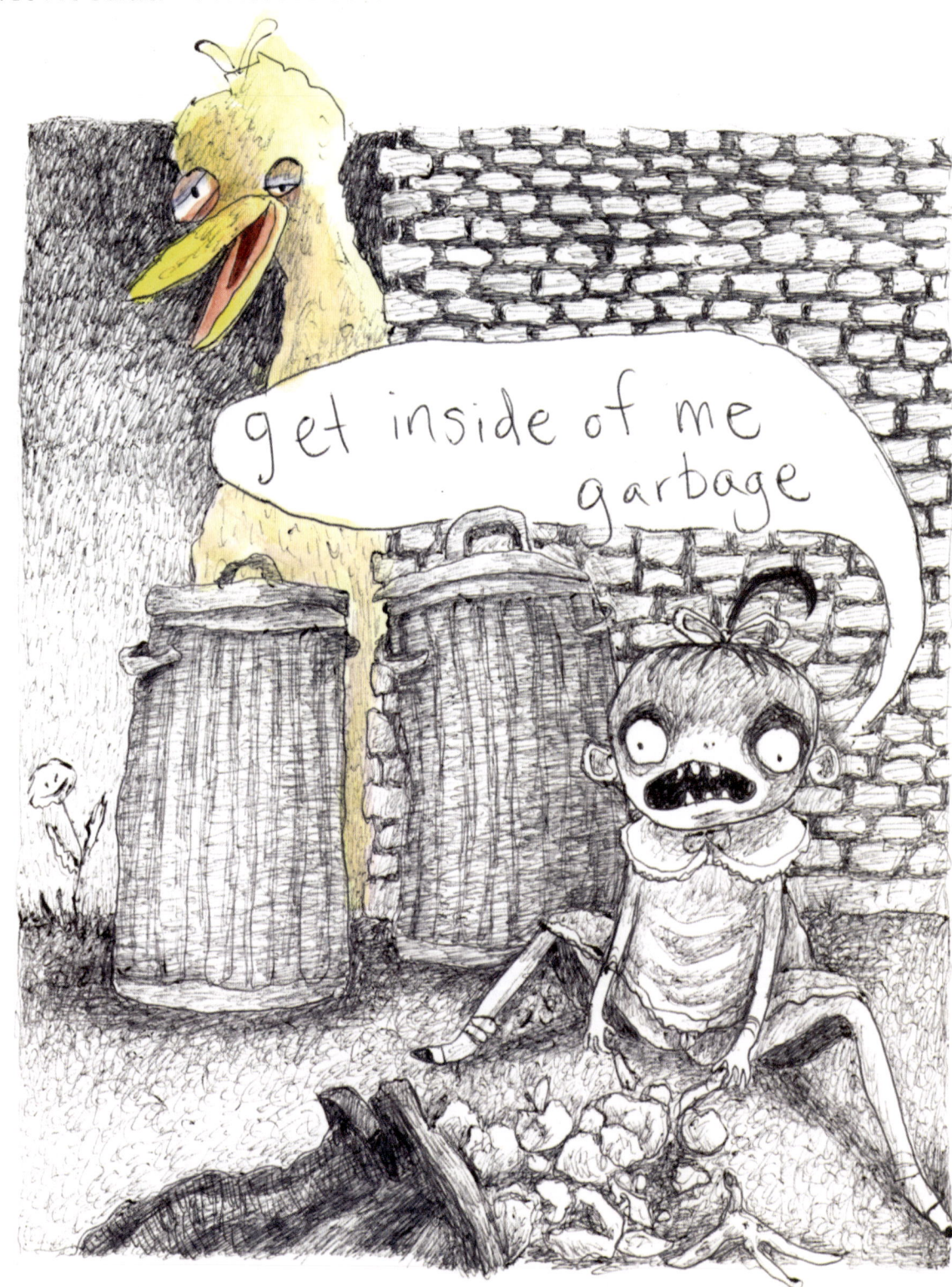

This is garbage world's Big Bird. He's perverted. I've always thought that Big Bird was annoying, so my version is.

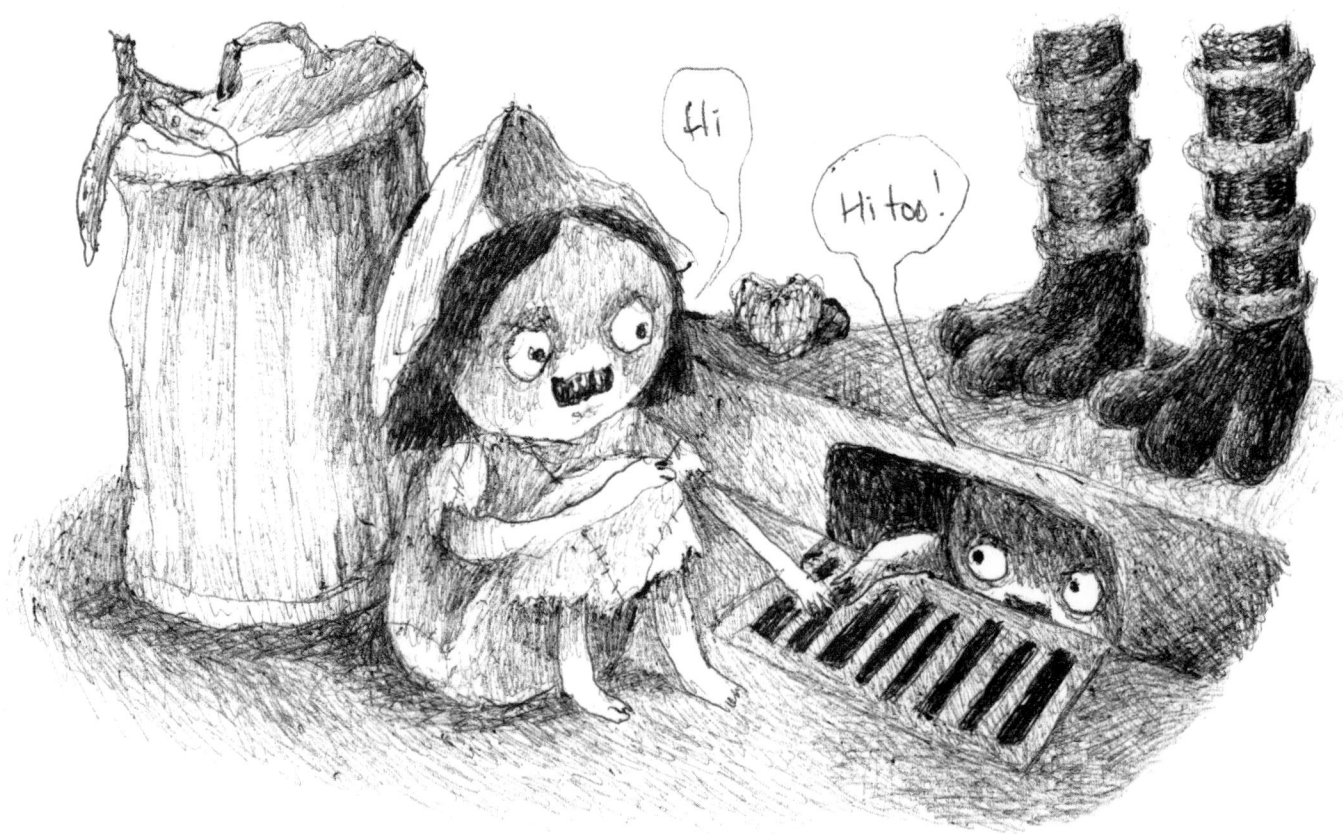

IT COMFORTS ME TO IMAGINE MYSELF DESTITUTE AND under a cardboard box somewhere. It helps put my problems into perspective so that I can realize how silly I'm being. These pieces are mostly self-portraits. I'm making fun of myself, lightening my own mood. It's cathartic, I think, but definitely not serious.

When I was six, I had a nightmare of evil Ronald McDonald trying to push my parents off a bridge. My garbage kids are unfortunate little kids in danger. These images are full of evil eighties cartoon or puppet characters, unfortunate Gorey children, and Hideshi Hino's tragic characters. I found myself combining *Sesame Street* or *Care Bears* or *The Muppets* with this horrible garbage life. It's not meant to reflect reality at all. I actually think I've created my own sort of "garbage universe" where everyone is a

garbage kid. To me, shows from the eighties were always kind of for adults. Sure, children would be entertained but there's a lot of innuendo and adult stuff going on as well. The characters were all sort of neurotic, hiding an aspect of adulthood behind their childlike veneer. Big Bird always seemed on the edge, so sensitive and ready to snap. The *Care Bears* had so much pressure to be good and to heal everything with their stomach tattoos. It was an interesting time in television for children, and it was obviously impactful on me.

My dad, too, gave me permission in the physical world. He would bring me to his construction sites, and I would have to amuse myself, so I'd play in the rubble and the garbage, and I loved it. I find the smell of construction very comforting. I actually find sweetness

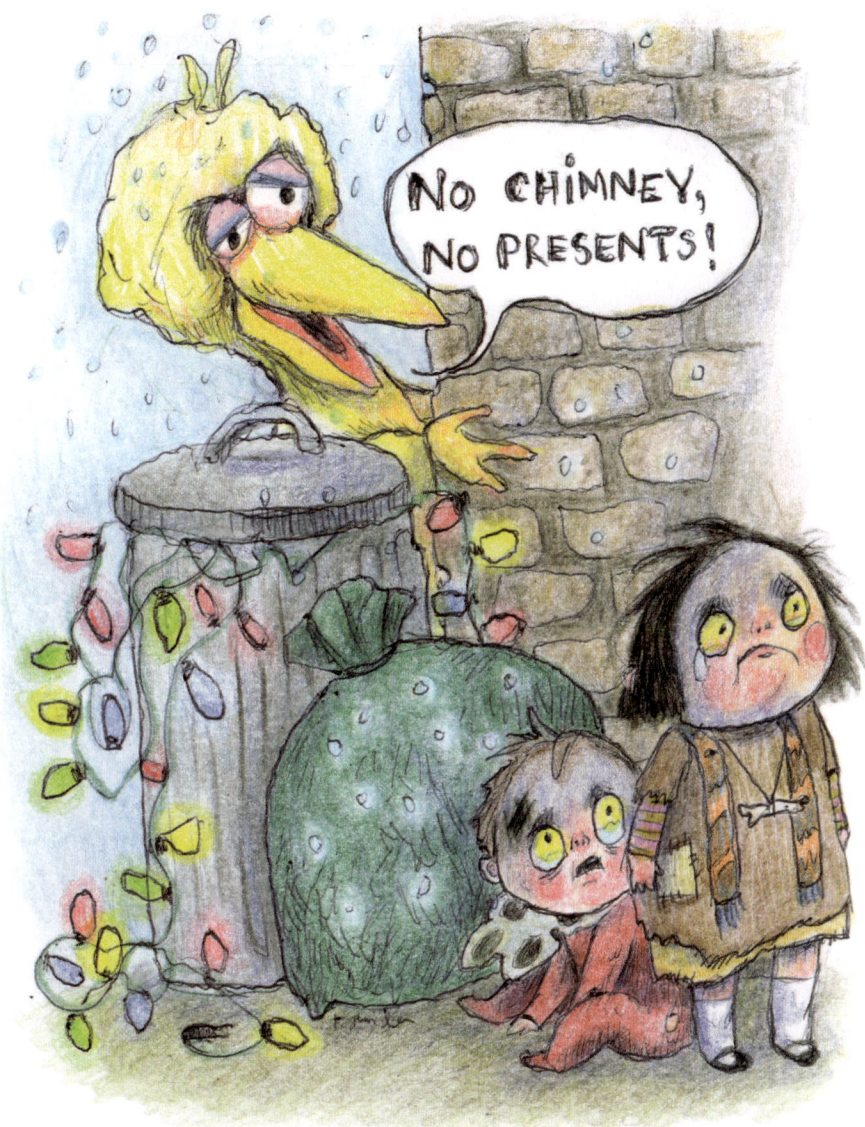

There's a horrible nineties film that greatly influenced me as a child called *Boxing Helena*. It follows this doctor who is obsessed with a woman. She gets in a car accident, and a man takes her into his house and cares for her, amputating her legs. She hates him and he tries to seduce her, and she continues to hate him. She tries to choke him at one point and then he amputates her arms making her into a likeness of the Venus de Milo. It's a surreal modelling of a beautiful woman. He puts her in a box and surrounds her with beautiful flowers. It's grotesquely beautiful. It touched me, that very overt image of the horrible and the beautiful together. She became an object, a horrible, disfigured object that was still lust-worthy but unreachable. I think that's my idea of romance here in my garbage world.

I guess too, I've always been working with garbage, buying shitty pencil crayons, ballpoint pens, drawing on napkins or scrap paper, even garbage. I like it because it relieves the pressure of creating art. Because if it ends up being a garbage drawing, it doesn't matter, right? It's already garbage. If it's good, then it can always be preserved. I think my best drawings were doodles on inconsequential stuff. The nicer the sketch book, the more the pressure and the more I would hesitate to draw or do anything. With garbage, I would dive into it and be free. Maybe that's why people like my garbage kids—they are free, even freer than regular kids. They can just live in their garbage utopia forever without rules.

and beauty in piles of garbage and dumpsters. I take pictures and share them. A lot of garbage chairs in particular, where they are stacked or piled or littered around suggestively, and my mind creates a narrative where they are in love, huddled, or stacked together in the garbage waiting for their doom. There's this image stuck in my head of a grocery cart on its side, lying in a stream, littered with garbage. It was real, in a stream that I walk past. It's just such a melancholy image. I'm trying to find something sweet in something rotten.

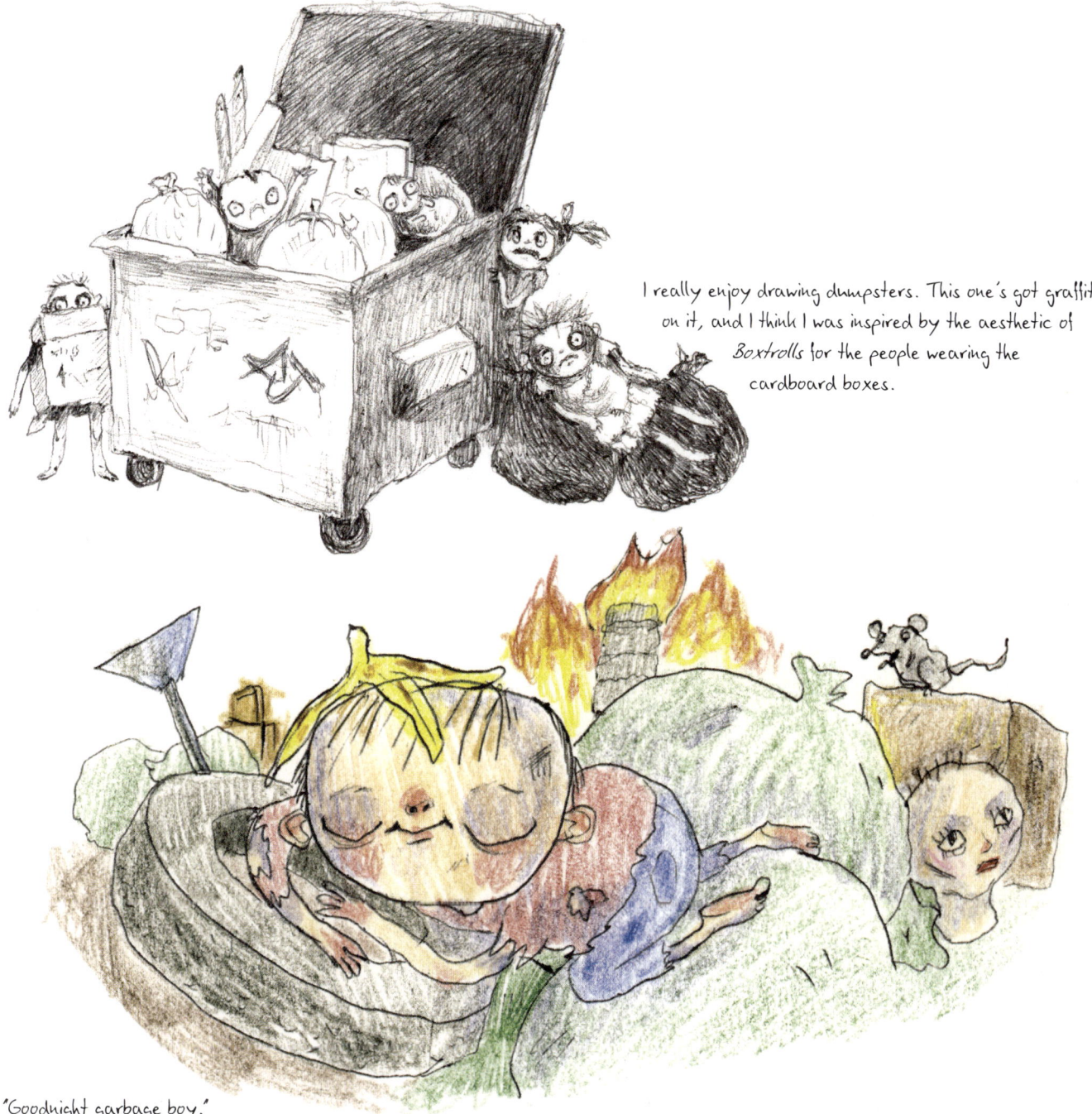

I really enjoy drawing dumpsters. This one's got graffiti on it, and I think I was inspired by the aesthetic of *Boxtrolls* for the people wearing the cardboard boxes.

"Goodnight garbage boy."
I was thinking about that children's book *Goodnight Moon* except with garbage boy. There's a burning garbage fire behind him, and rats, and this lamp. I keep drawing this lamp, because it's the lamp we had in our apartment from when I was a kid; it's the eighties black lamp. Everyone had it in their apartment. I got online comments that people recognized the lamp!

There's a lot of "beautiful" art, almost every-where, and a lot of the same kind of "beautiful," and so when people online see something horrible or something expressing raw emotion in a grotesque way, I think they feel drawn to it and they some-times respond to it. It makes them feel better, it makes me feel better. A lot of people have said that they would join me in living in a garbage can. I think I'll eventually have a little garbage utopia, a little garbage island that I can be mayor of. It'll be awesome.

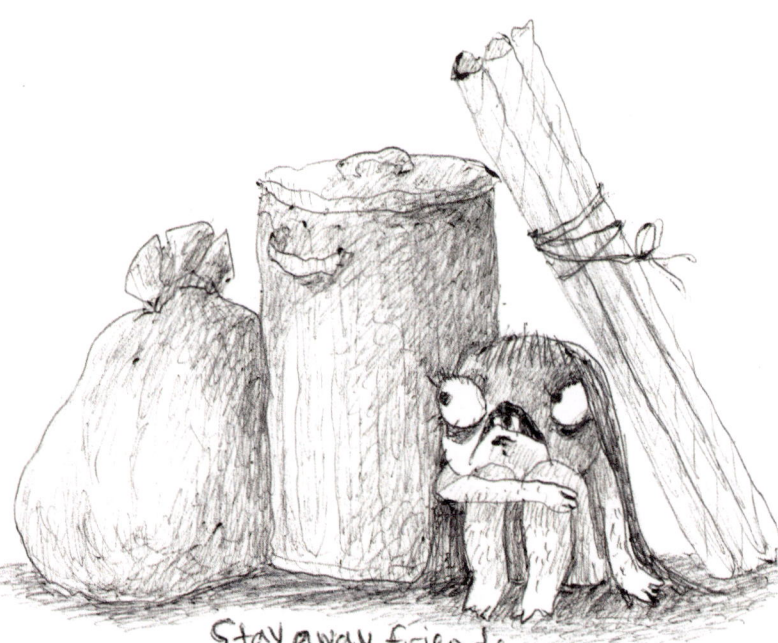

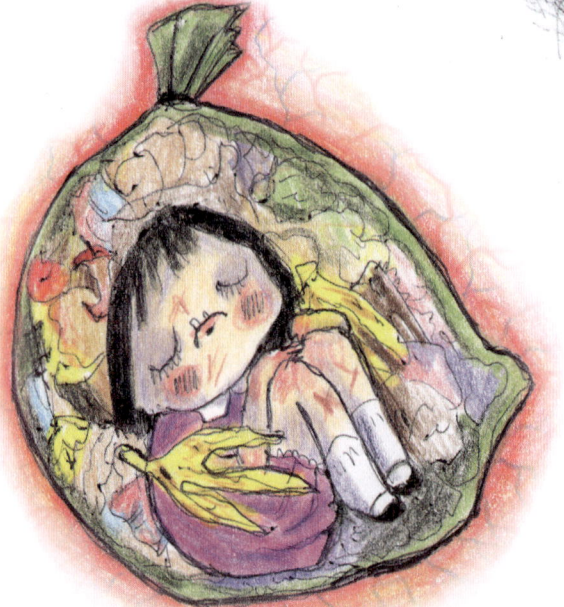

People say this one is disturbing, but that wasn't my intention. It's called, 'In garbage utero.' It's not that the character was born there, just that she's gone back to a safe, contained place. It's a garbage bag in warm uterus-like colours.

Stay away friends.
Safe in my garbage alone.

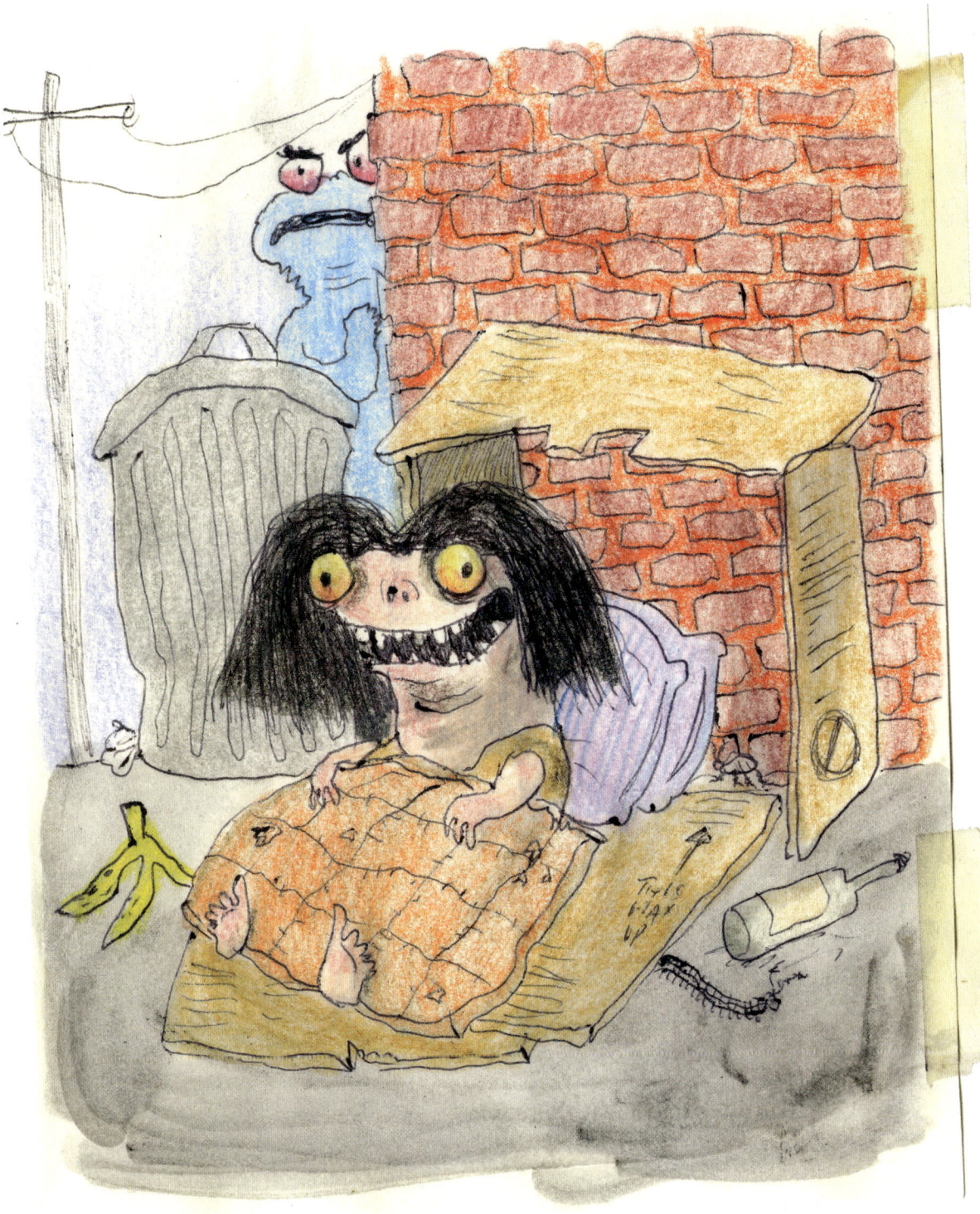

This is one of my favourites. It was drawn very spontaneously. This is a couple of streets away from happy, peaceful *Sesame Street*. It's like bizzaro-*Sesame Street*. The little house that this girl has made for herself looks so cozy; she looks thrilled to be there. She's comfortable. As long as she has her pillows, she'll be fine. But there's alternate, garbage-world Cookie Monster and he's probably going to fuck her up. She's on his turf.

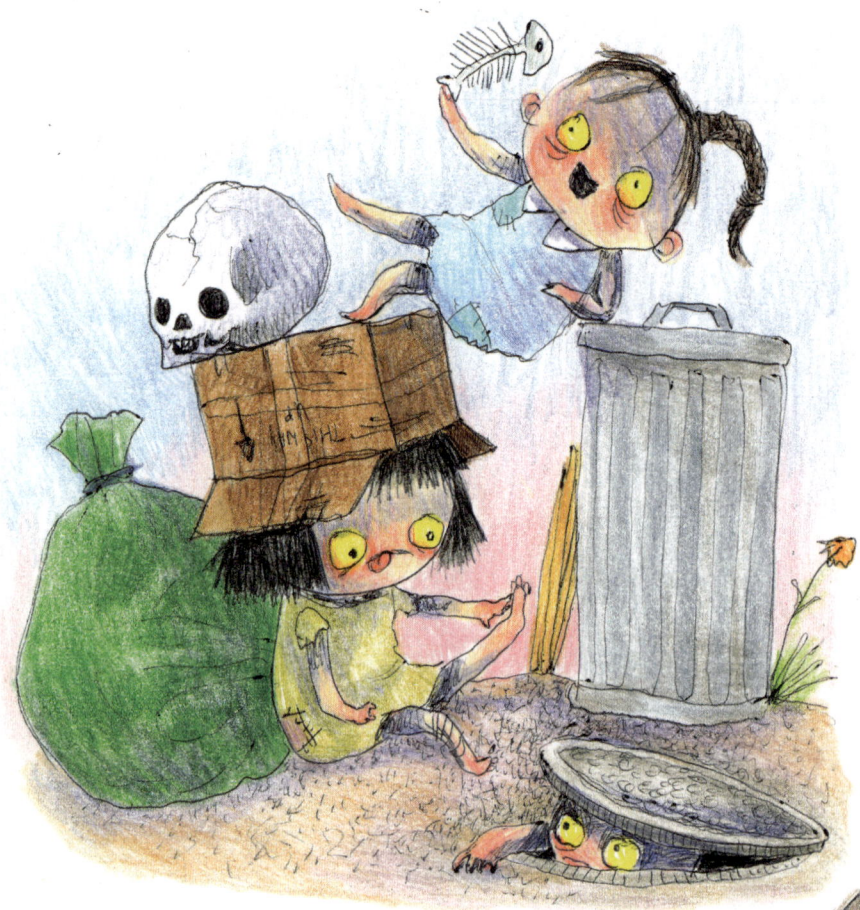

Sewer Boy makes an appearance. I think this is the first time I drew him; I like him. He's one of my recurring characters, he eats bugs and lives in the sewer, and he's the boy, obviously. By my logic, girls are in the garbage dump, and the boys are in the sewer. The skull is probably an old friend, because that's what happens in the dump, the rats clean the meat off the skull, and then the skull becomes a plaything. They have accepted death as totally normal, they are unphased by it, that's just what life in the dump is.

This is Potato Girl, also recurring. She's a miserable little potato. She's me when I feel frumpy and horrible. It relates a little to Japanese Kawaii culture, with *Gudetama*. I think it's wonderful and empowering if overworked people can relate with a caricature that epitomizes the opposite and is sympathetic. They need an outlet! Here in North America, I feel like we're media swamped, we're inundated with sexy advertisements and sex in shows, and things that promote sexual empowerment. So lazy Potato Girl is the exact opposite of sexy, so, like Lazy Egg Yolk, she's empowering.

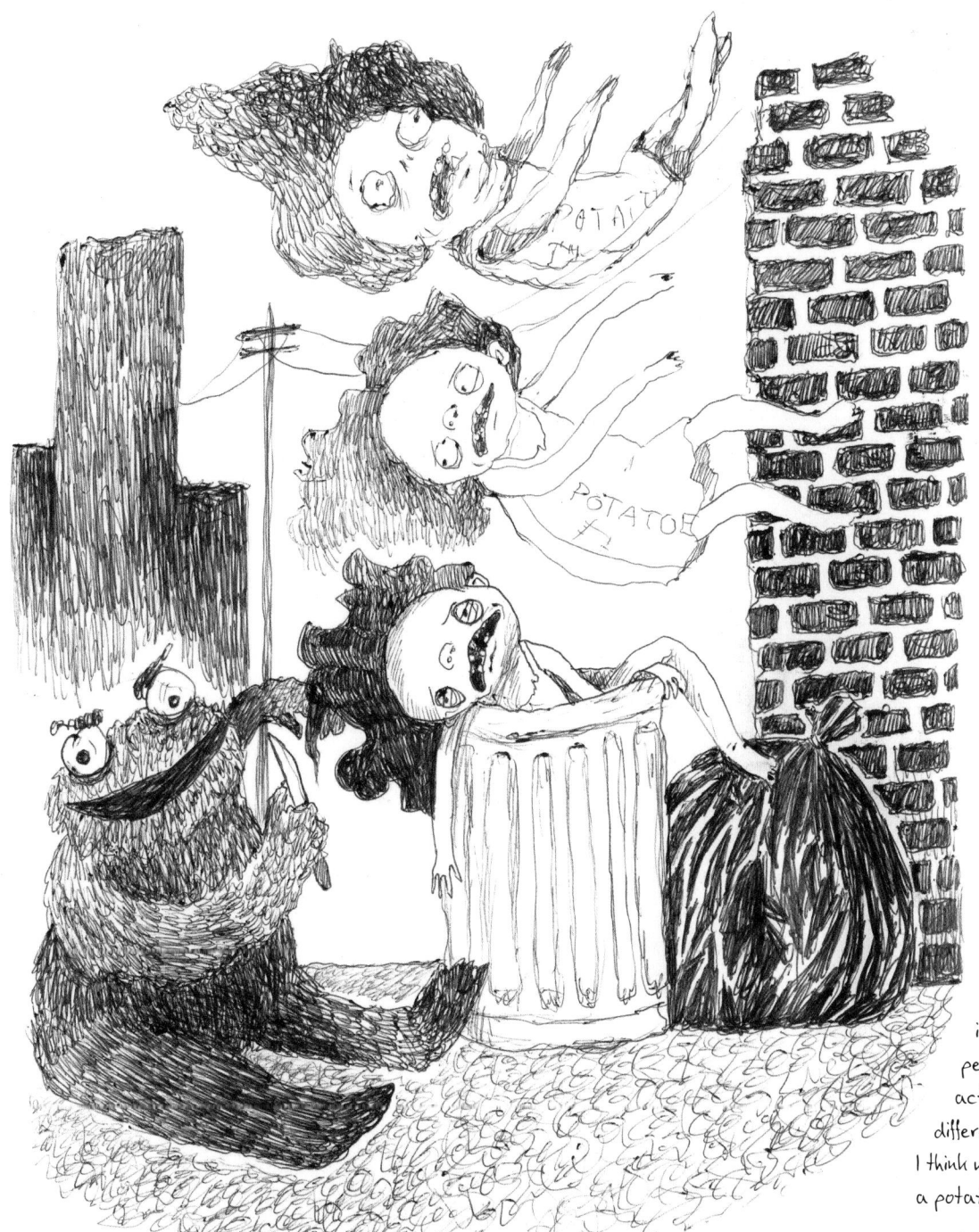

This is before Potato Girl. It's a happy drawing; it's me wearing a potato sack, and this is me slowly losing consciousness and letting go, rising, dying. Garbage world Cookie Monster is there, cutting my hair so he can smell it later, of course. A lot of people thought she was falling, actually, or that it was three different girls descending. I think my final form will be a potato.

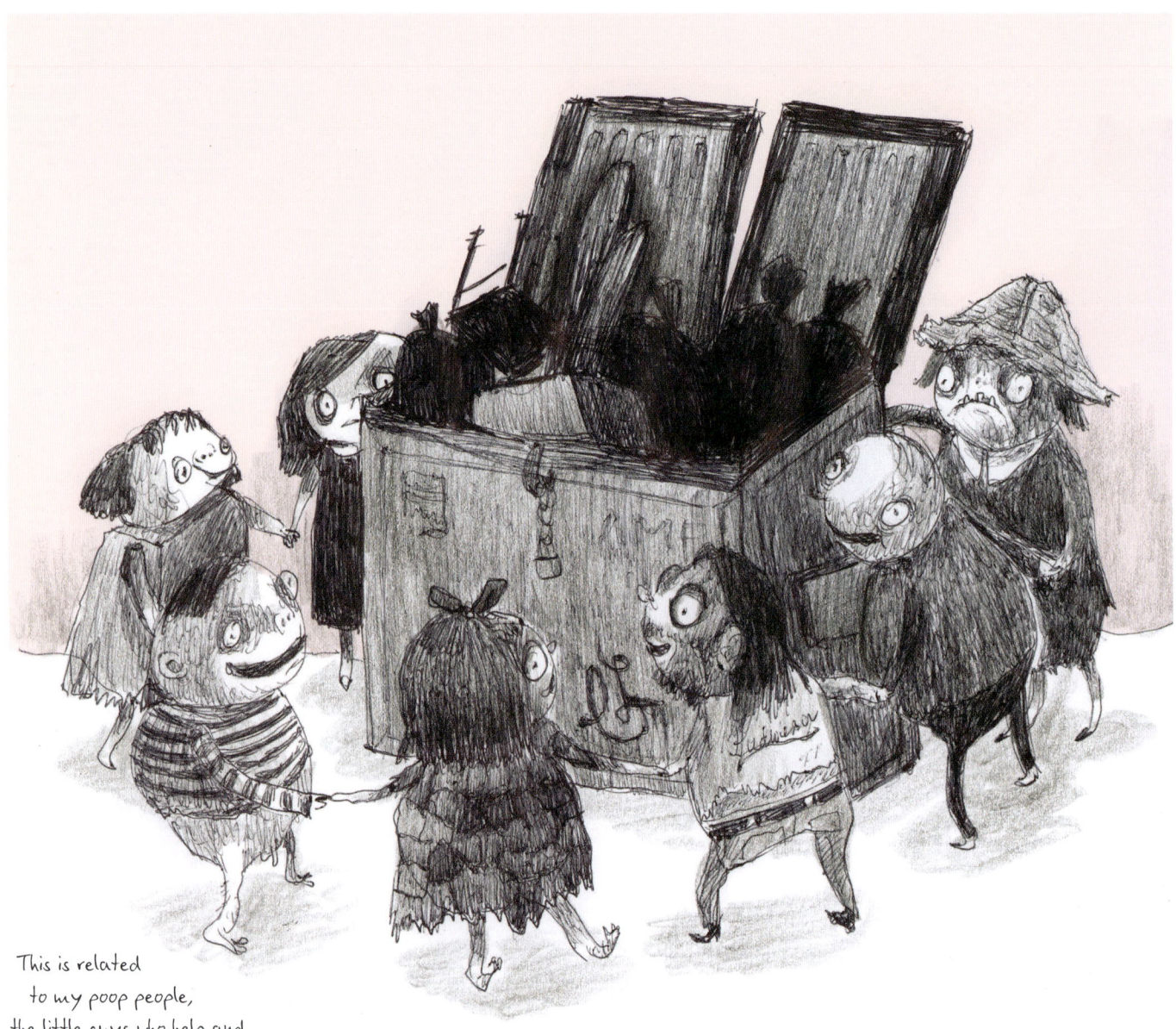

This is related
  to my poop people,
the little guys who help and
  heal, like the *Care Bears* or *Smurfs*. They're trying
  to heal a dumpster, and it's a feel-good garbage cult that's
  really inclusive. By healing the dumpster, they become healed.
In my high school yearbook, I was voted "most likely to start my own
cult" which rankled because I really wanted to be "biggest *X-Files* fan."
  Sometimes I wish I had started my own cult. I mean, there's still time.

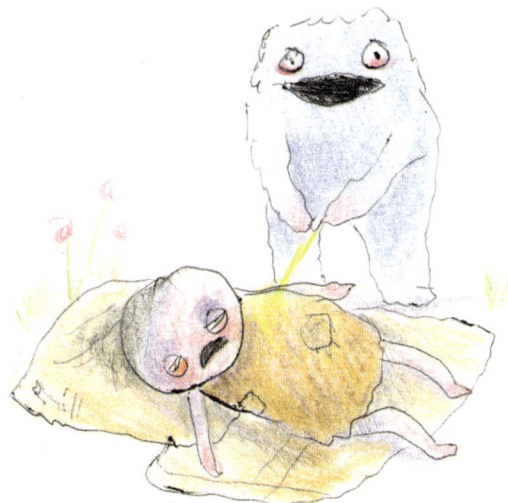

This is of me being
depressed and lethargic and thinking
"I hate everything, I want to lie down and
die." There's a *Sesame Street* sort of
character pissing on me to make the scene
complete. Because I'm a kid and not an
adult here, there is more joy in it, it's not
restrained and menacing.

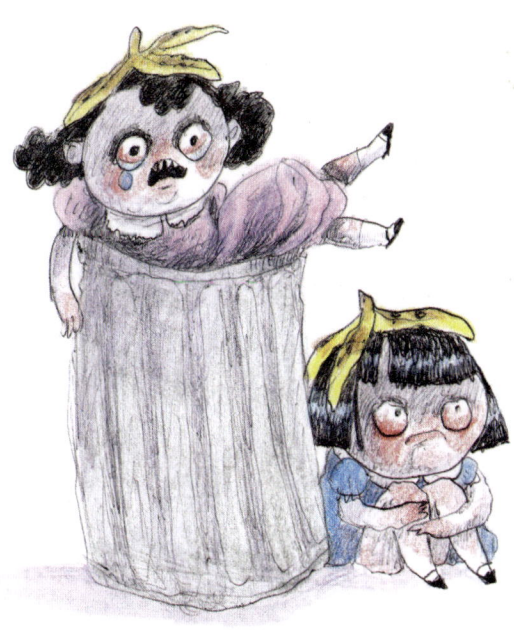

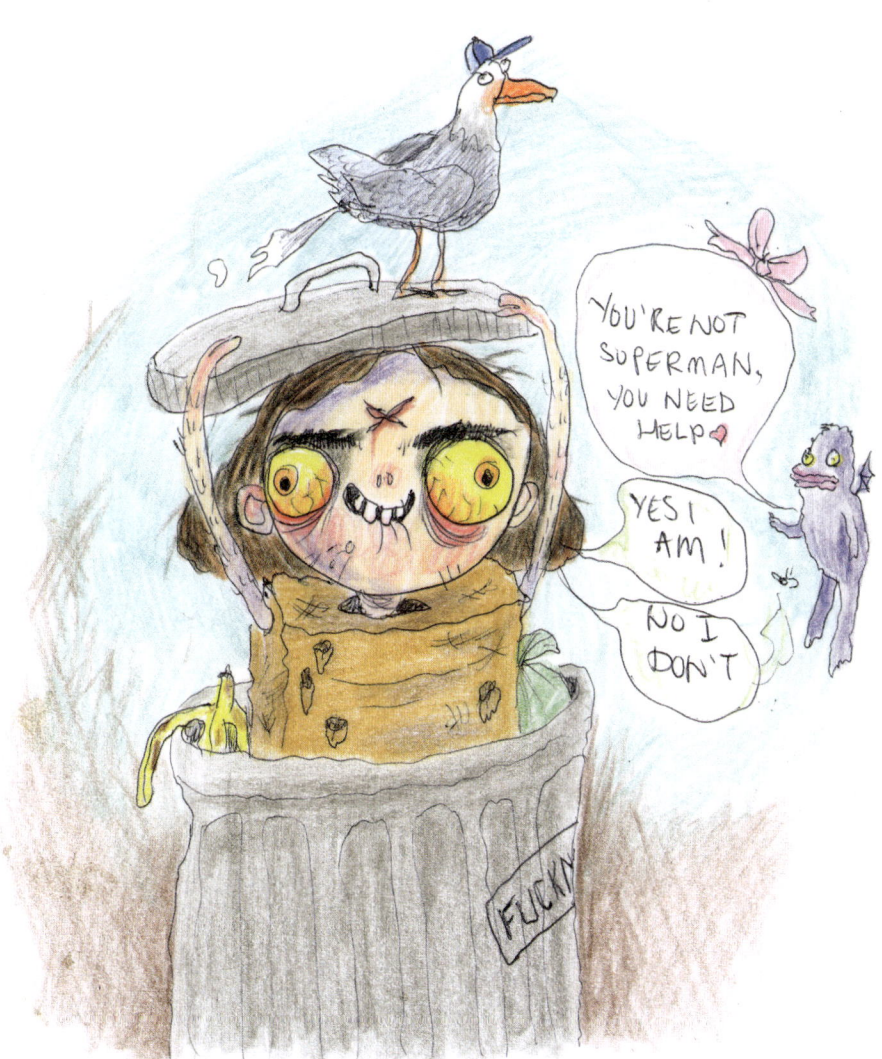

This is me being stubborn and not asking for
help. It's a conversation I had with a friend of mine,
verbatim. It's supposed to be ridiculous. Me in the trash
with a seagull shitting on me all while I decline help.

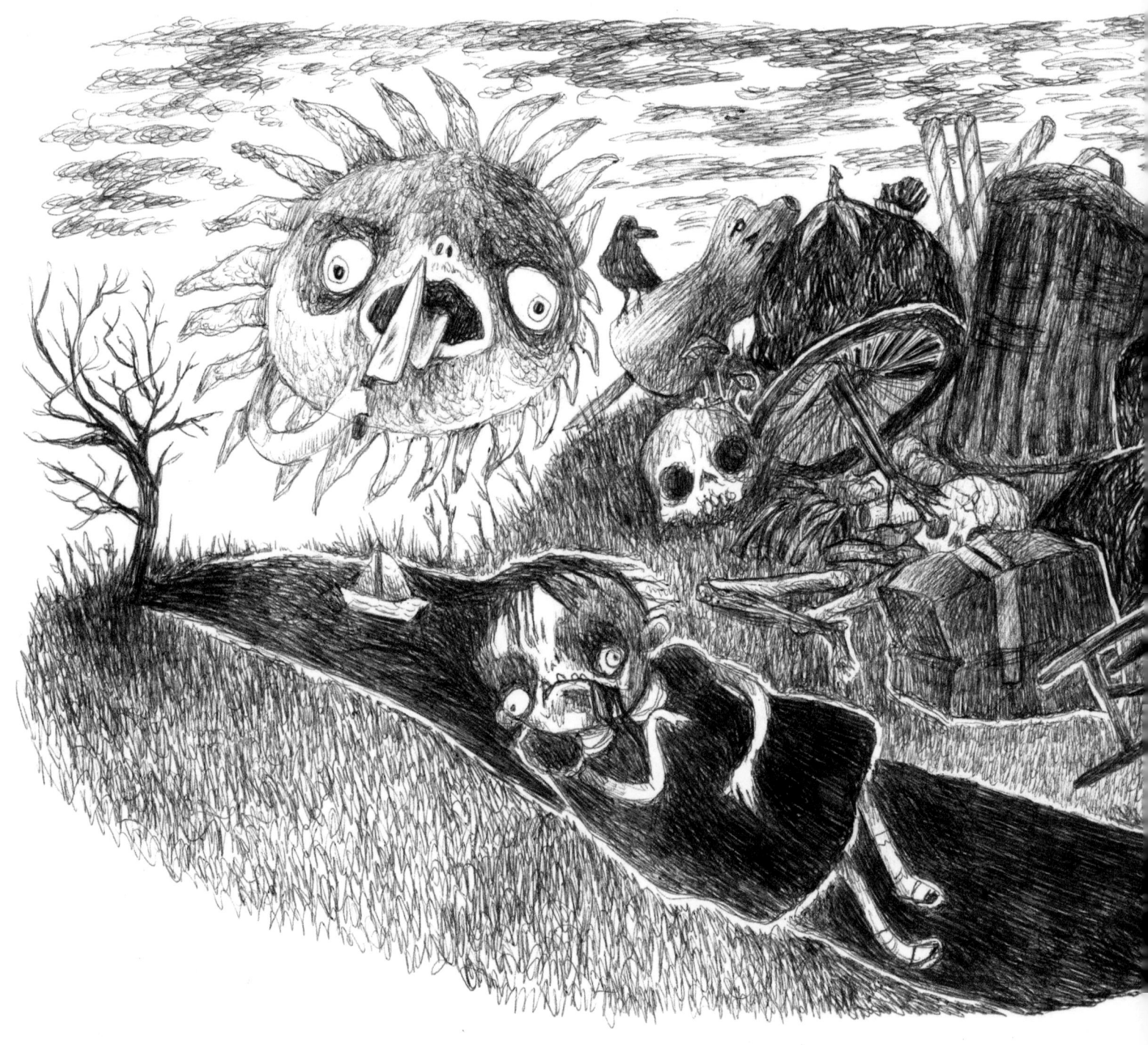

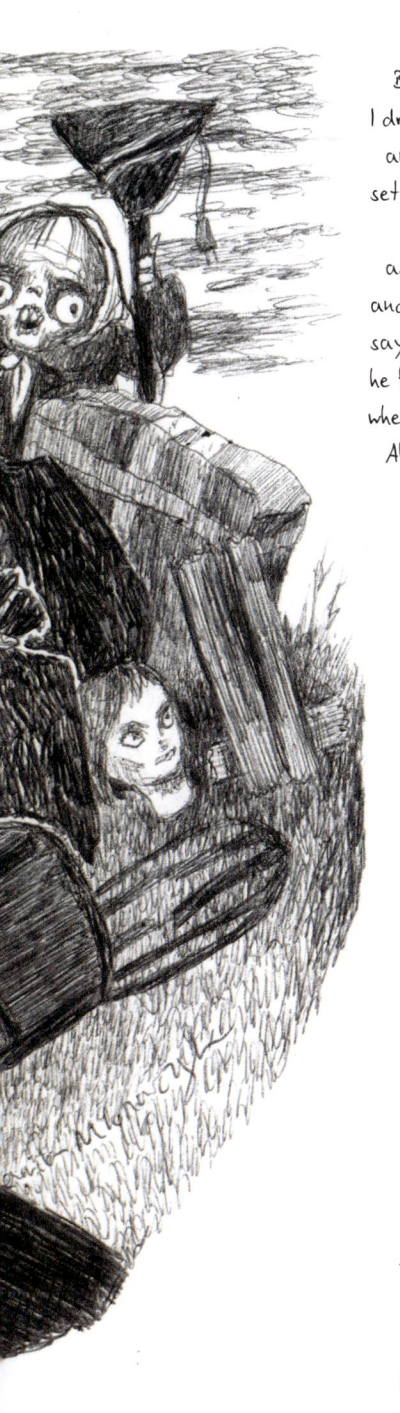

Bastard Sun makes an appearance. He's an asshole and he wants to kill me. See, he's got a knife.
I draw him a lot, even in newer pictures; he's a recurring character. I think I was inspired by *Midsommar*
and also *Teletubbies*. Let me make the connection. With *Midsommar* the whole thing is that it's a horror
set in sunlight, but to me, *Teletubbies* is also a horror set in sunlight. It's the original horror set in sunlight.

Midsommar though is very exciting for me because my childhood, my little village, feels as crazy
as *Midsommar*. Full of weird, stupid rituals and a lot of morbidity, like babcias saying, "Thanks God,"
and, "Thanks God, I'm going to die soon." Old Polish people are incredibly nihilistic and tragic and they
say the most horrible things but they justify it as something normal. Or my dad, again my poor dad,
he fell over in his garden and said, "Oh, just bury me." He's a happy-go-lucky guy and he gets annoyed
when I'm acting tragic and depressed, but he doesn't realize that I picked it up from him.

All this dark stuff, I grew up with it and it was fun, but it was very dark.

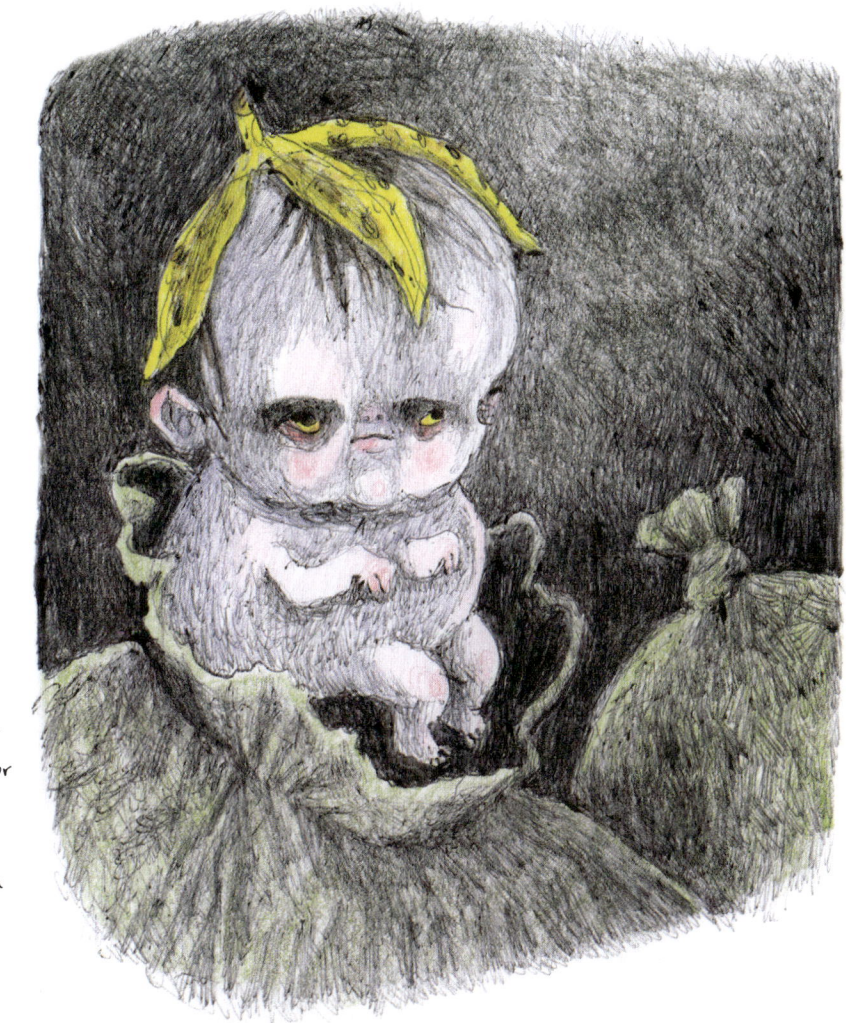

This is the pin that I sent
my son to school with for
days, because he liked
it. The garbage baby.
Very Hino inspired, it's a
lot like *Hell Baby* with his
little banana peel.

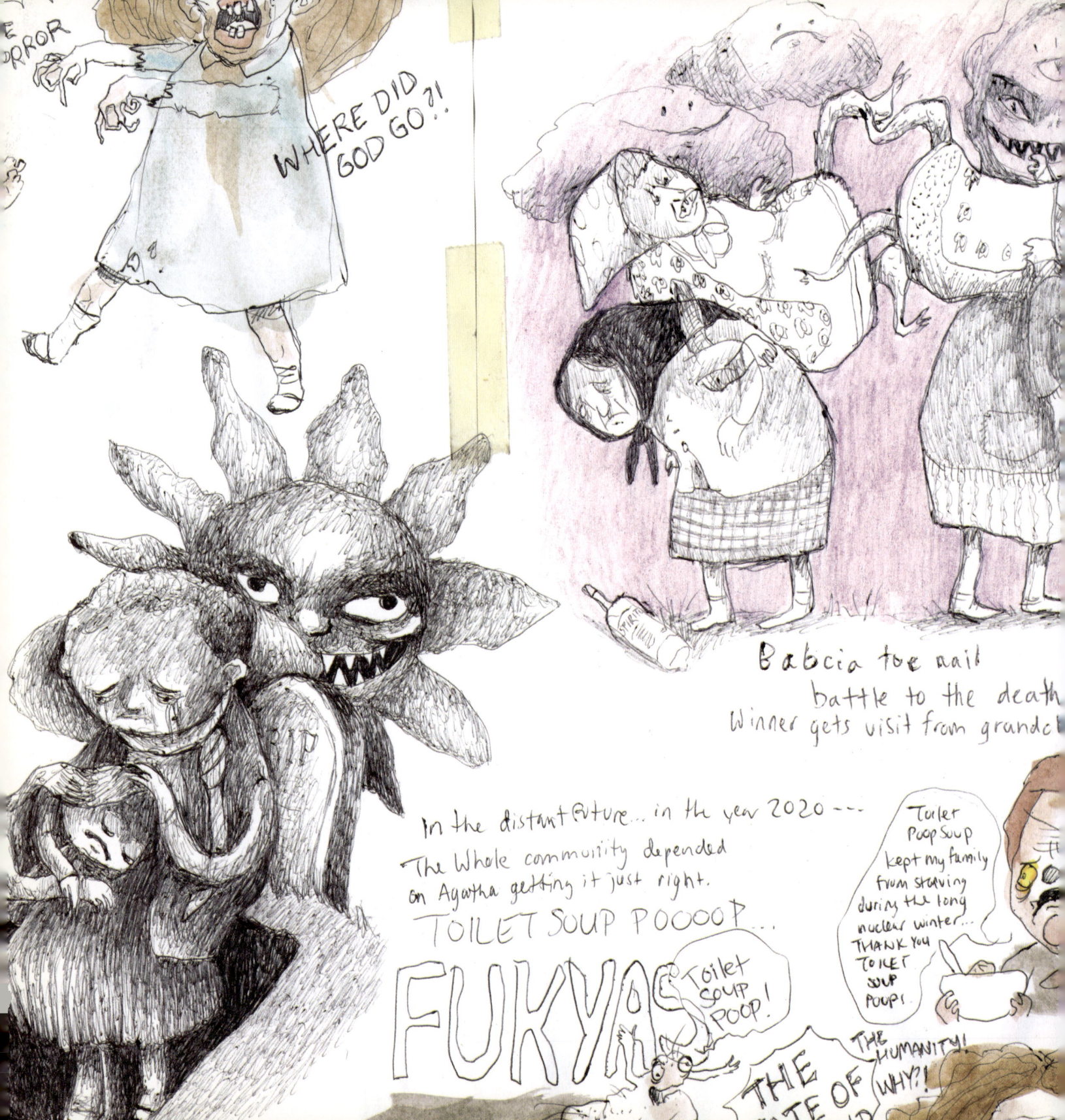

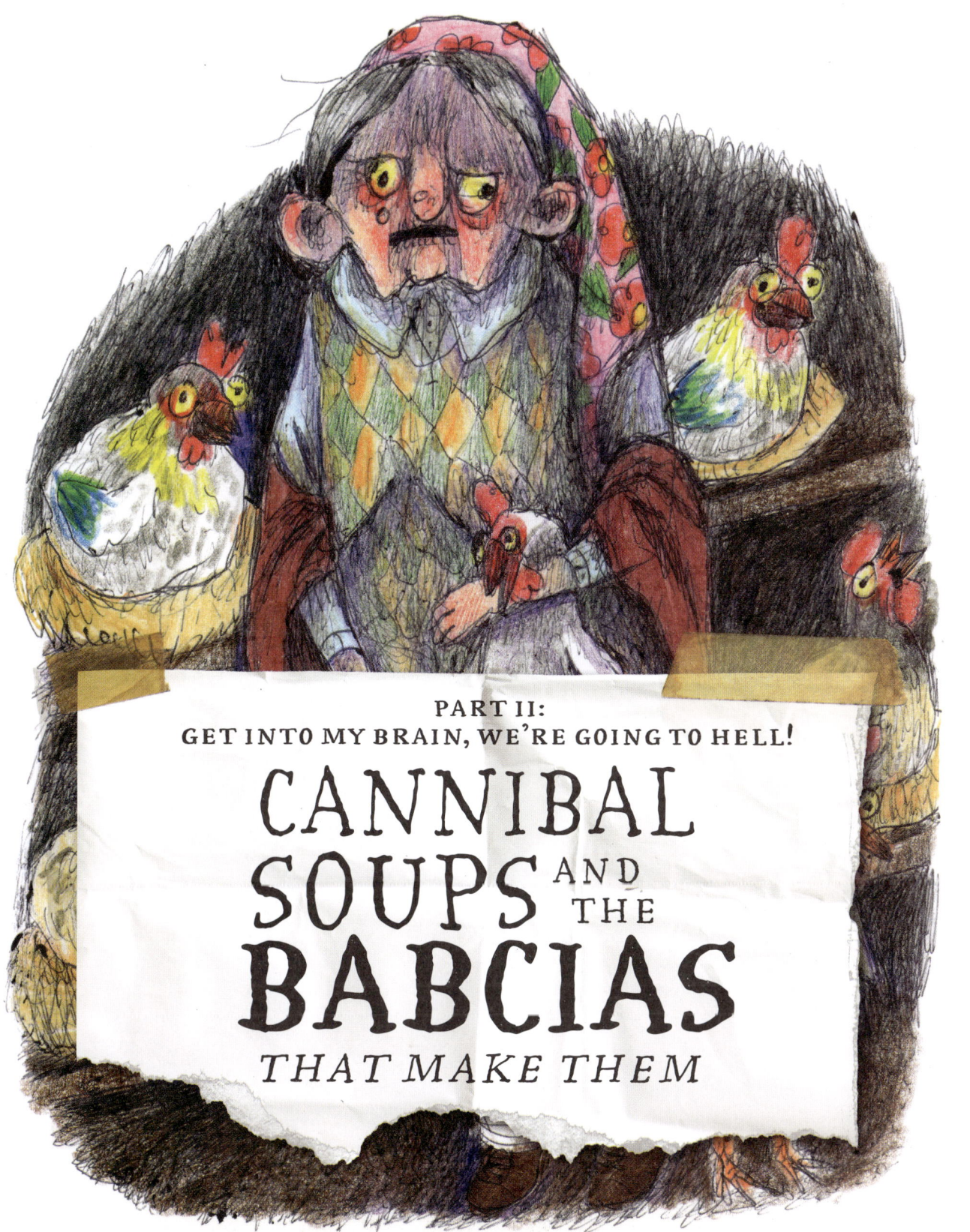

PART II:
GET INTO MY BRAIN, WE'RE GOING TO HELL!

CANNIBAL SOUPS AND THE BABCIAS

THAT MAKE THEM

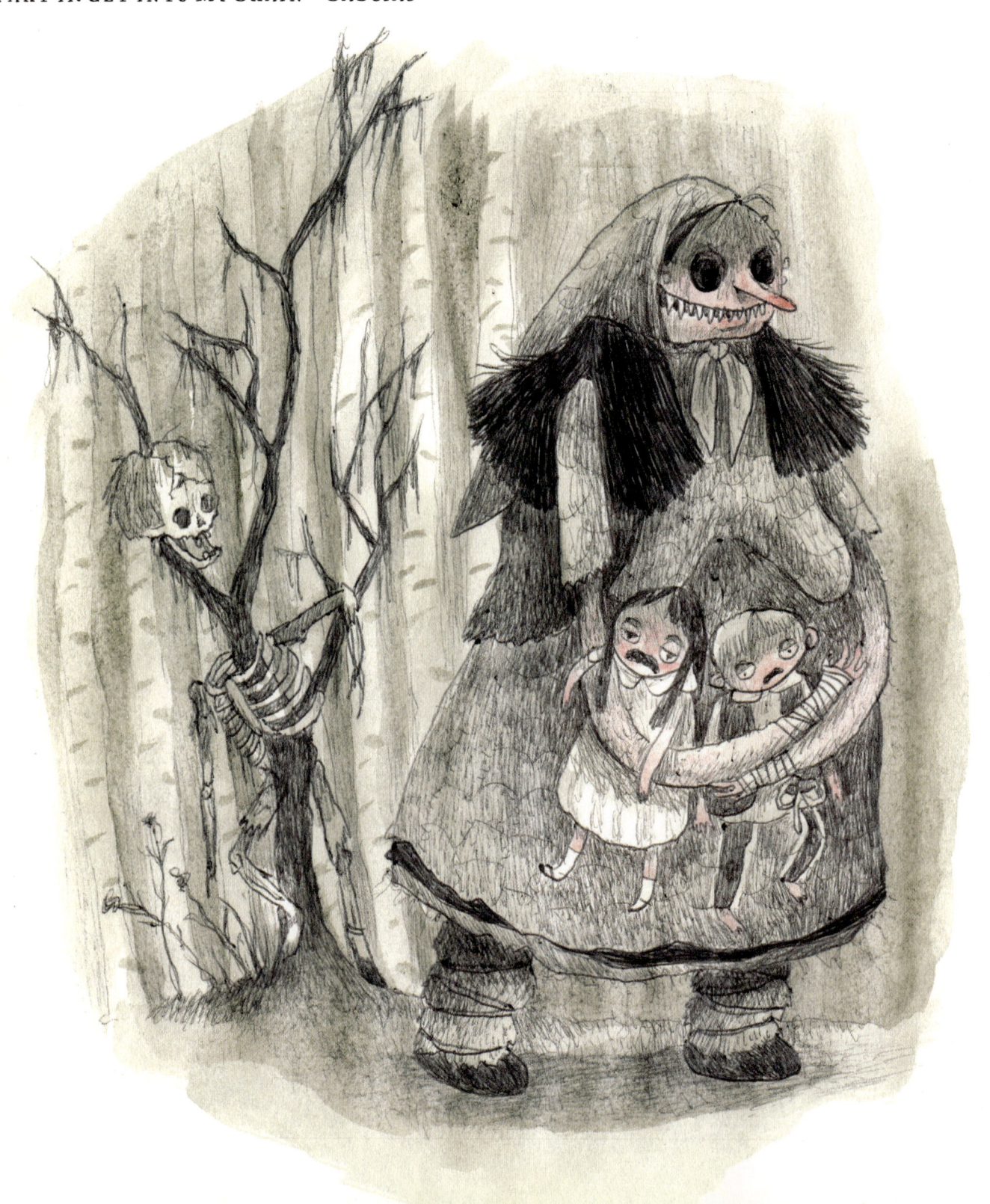

IN MY ART, BABA YAGA CAN BE A SYMPATHETIC CHAR-acter, usually a mix of the "wicked witch" aesthetic and also the traditional Polish babcia. Baba Yaga is a great folkloric character. It's all about cannibalizing babies. She's usually an outcast woman, old, sometimes deformed, almost always "ugly." She lives in a cabin in the woods; sometimes it stands on chicken legs. In some stories she's helpful or maternal, but mostly (and in my art) she's a child-eating monster figure. But a sympathetic one. Who wouldn't sympathize with a lonely, bereft, misunderstood outcast? I have a soft spot for these women. They are "old people" and reflections of my European grandparents. Babcias live to feed and take care of grandchildren; they want to make stuff from scratch and spoil grandchildren rotten. My grandmother always fed me honey on toast, which was horrible for my teeth, but I loved it. Then, at the same time, they're

also manipulative and passive aggressive. They want to save their grandchildren's young souls, and they want their grandchildren to go to church with them, they want more visits, they want *you*. That's where Baba Yaga comes in. I think grandparents can feel all-consuming, but in a sweet way. Grandparents are also generally nihilistic and fatalistic. They're always saying things like, "Oh, I'm going to be dead one day." And then when a young person says the same thing it's weird and morbid. An old lady has permission to say whatever she wants; they have a kind of power.

I told my mum I was going to name a whole chapter after how she forced me to eat soup all the time when I was little. I hated soup. But now I love it. I've embraced soup-making with a passion. I'm a babcia in training. There's actually a picture of me in a cabin angrily sitting

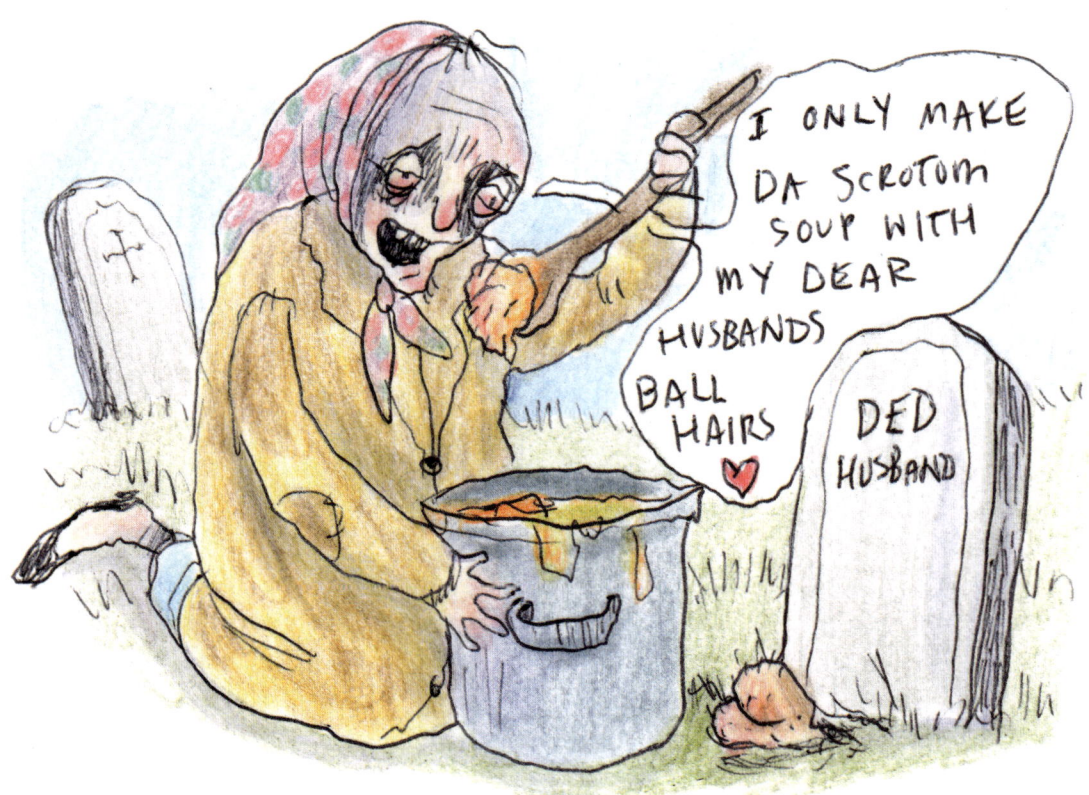

One of my favourite babcias. It seems to me that grandmothers always brag about what ingredients they've used in a soup (or whatever they're especially good at making). This is my internal thoughts on that.

in front of a bowl of soup (see Neil's foreword). I wasn't allowed to leave my seat until I finished it and I wouldn't. My family thought it was so funny that they took a picture of me. And now look at me, I keep drawing soup over and over.

It's my perception that grandmothers are competitive with each other. My grandmothers were. One grandmother wouldn't let me visit the other because she thought I had already had enough time and say things like, "You can't see the other one, you're mine now." So I always had this idea that they were outwardly gentle, but there's an underworld of grandmothers, like a *Fight Club*. In Poland I was told stories about old ladies getting into arguments and how they'd never wear underwear so they'd turn around and flash each other with their butts. So the grandmas would all meet at the Club and flash each other's asses during the fights and scratch each other with their long toenails. Hating each other by night, baking cookies by day.

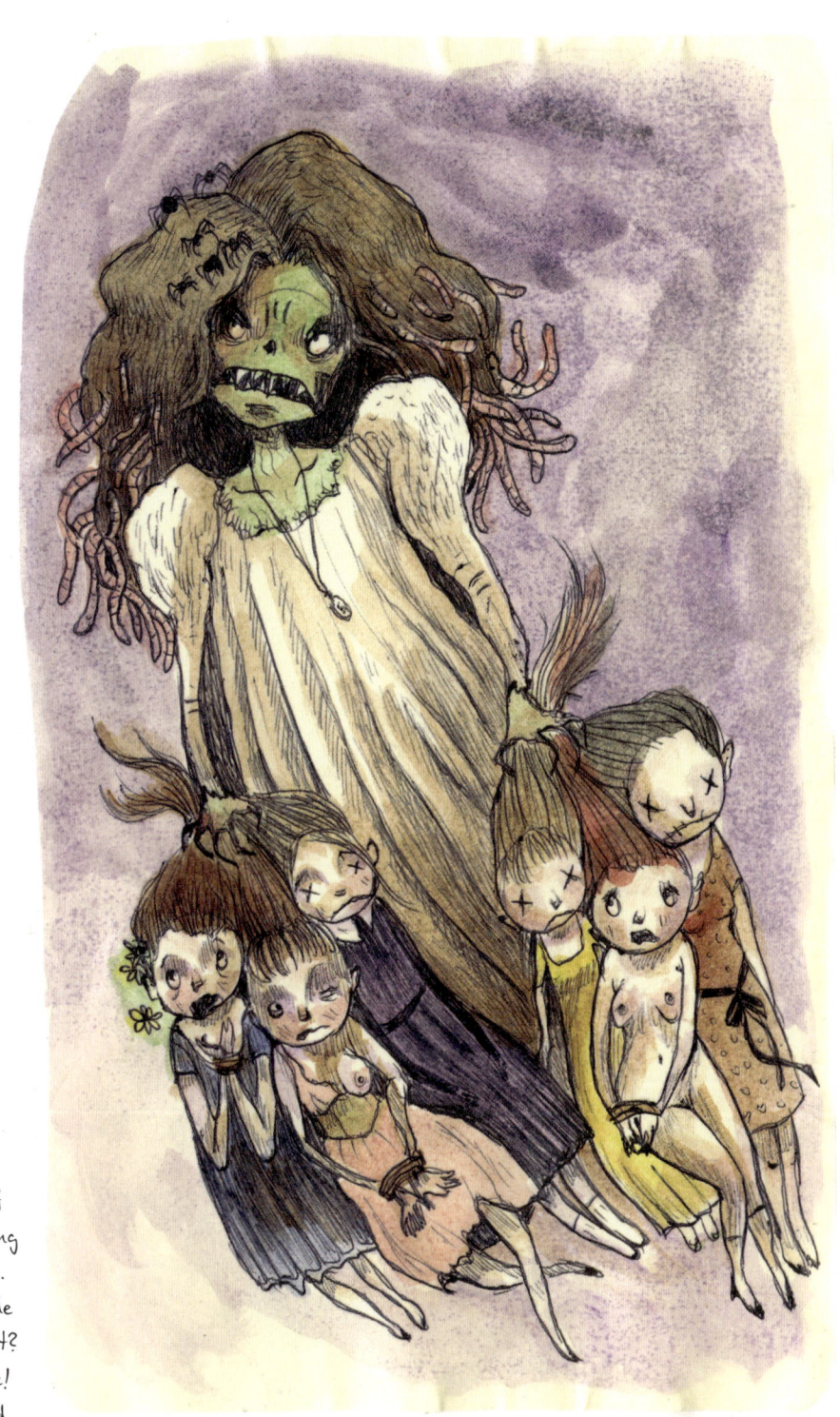

This is me creating my own little Baby Yaga story of a jealous wormy-haired witch flying some pretty young village gals home to her hovel for horrible things . . . breeding program with her hellish imps? Wretched little Cinderellas meant to clean her witch home? Just meat? Who can know these things? Probably all of the above! In my world, Baba Yaga is the main character and everyone else is just meat walkin' around being annoying.

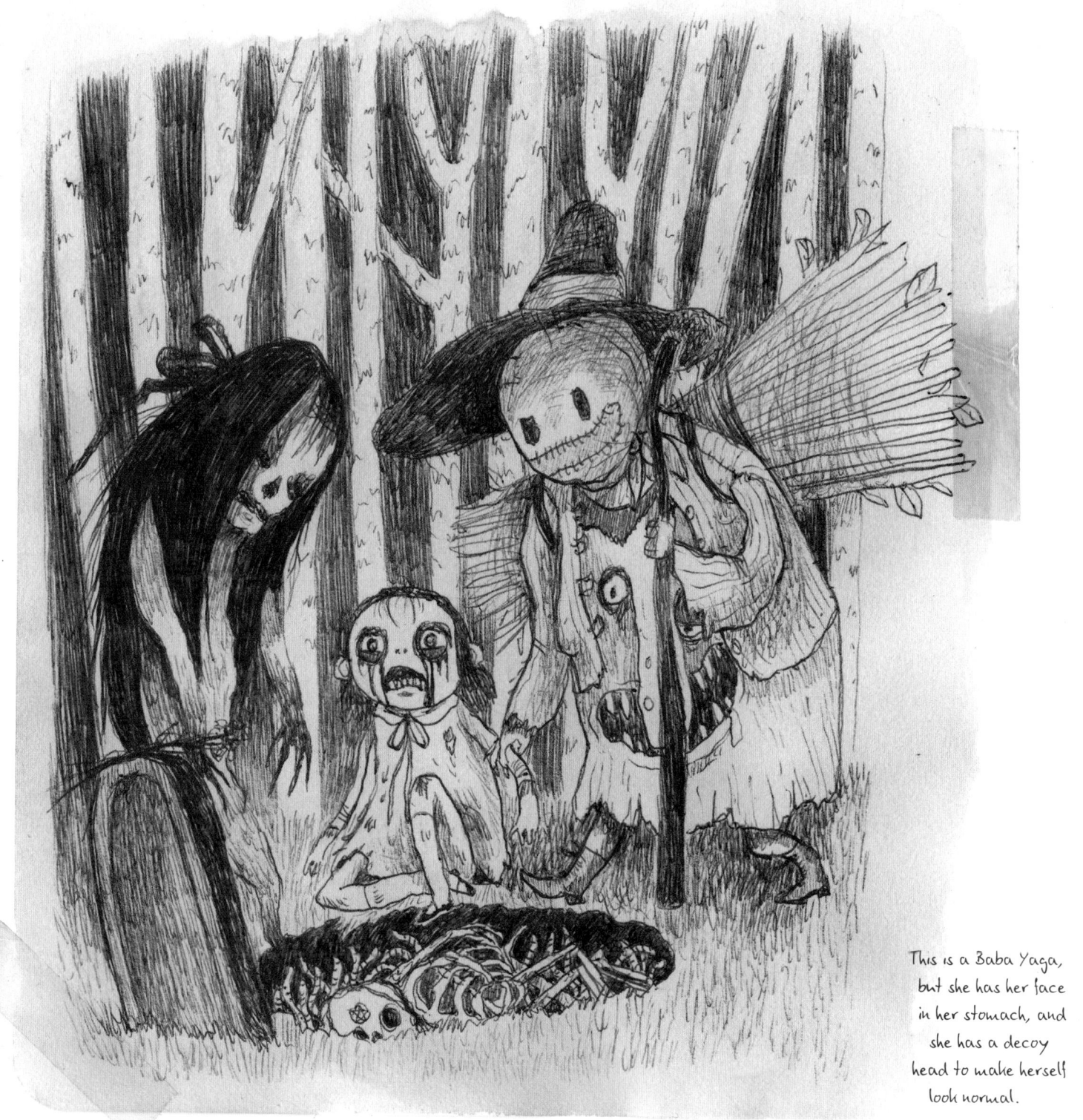

This is a Baba Yaga,
but she has her face
in her stomach, and
she has a decoy
head to make herself
look normal.

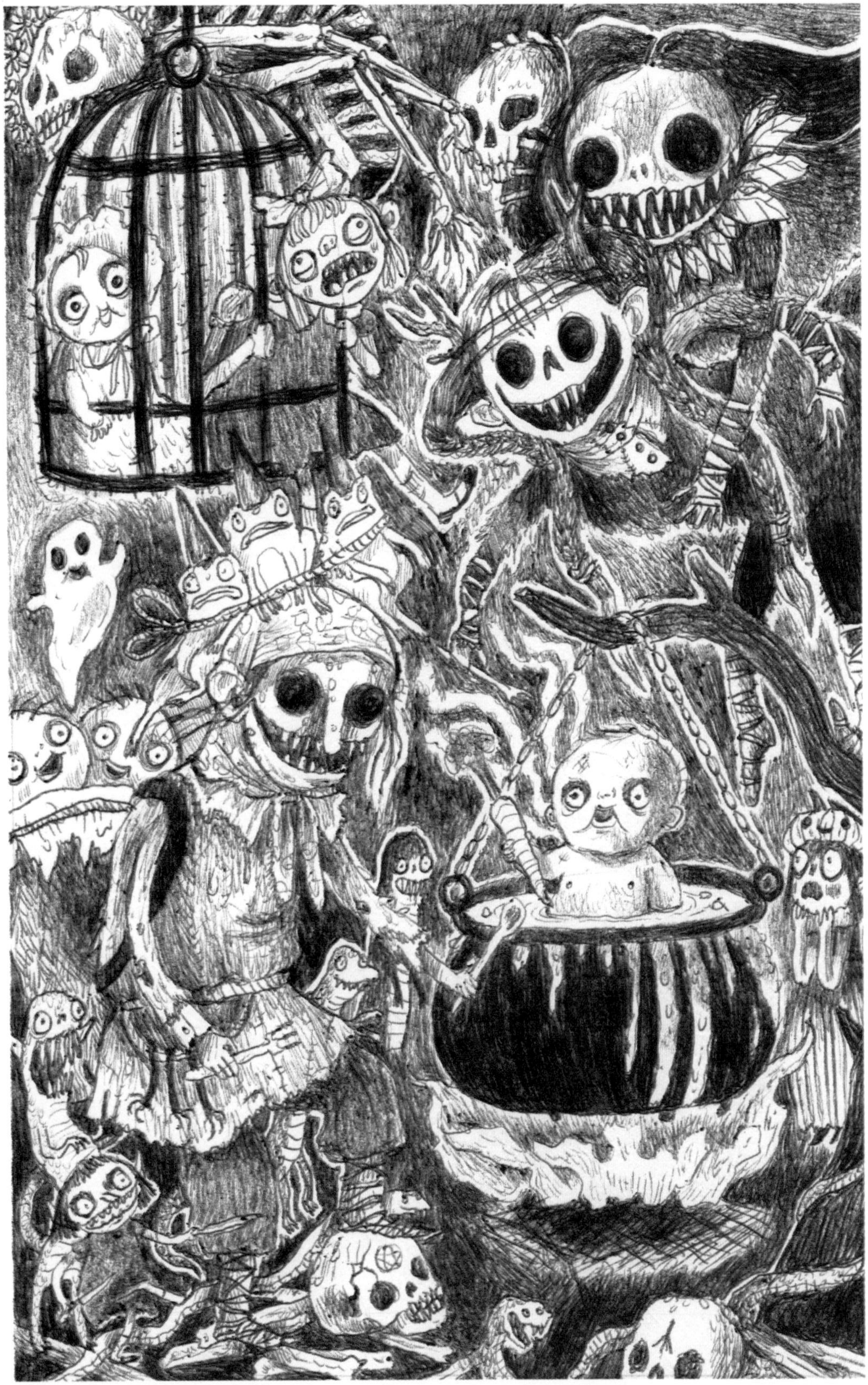

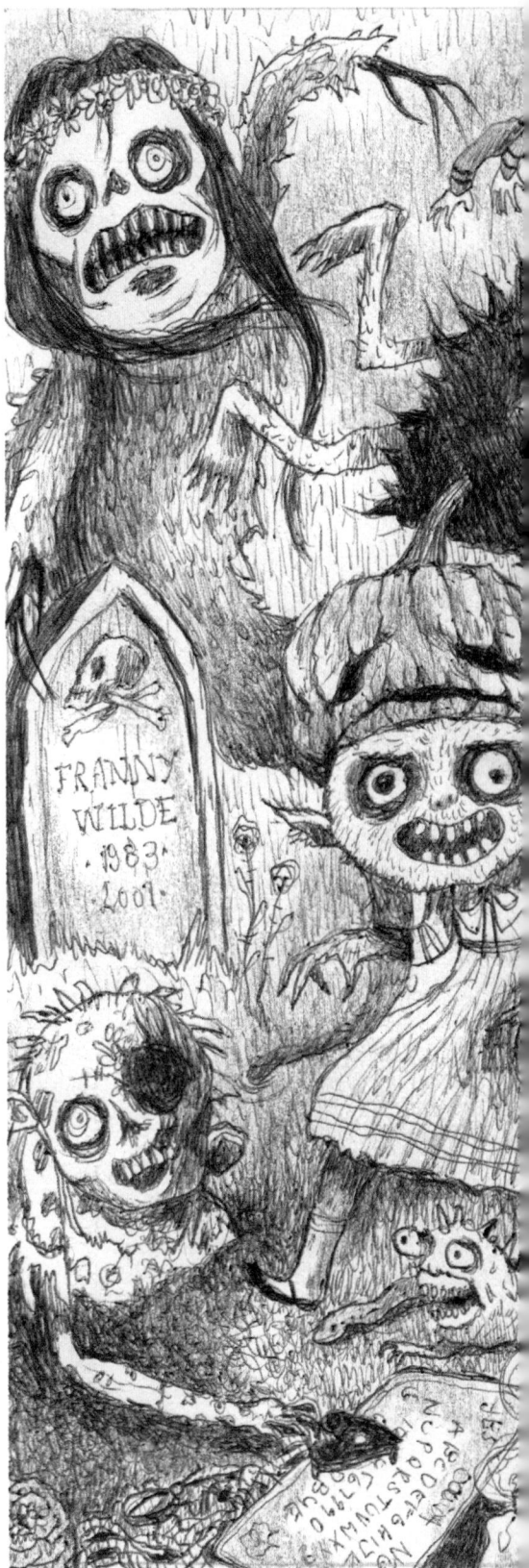

FRANNY
WILDE
·1983·
·2001·

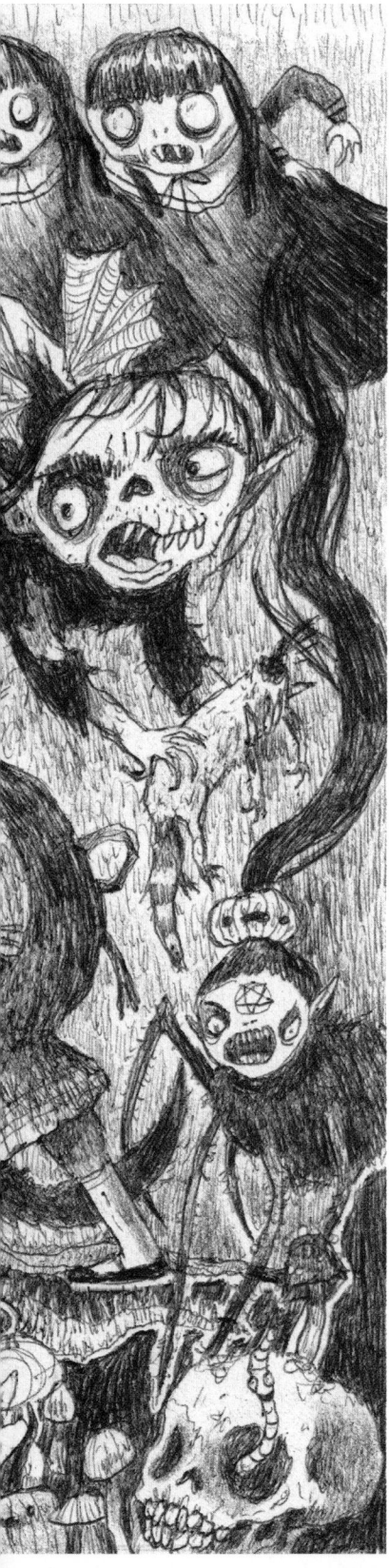

Baby soup. And there's one baby helping,
    see, he's putting a carrot into his own soup
    that he's cooking in. It's a big collage of
    everything, the babcia has more babies,
    the babcias are like, "There are always
    more babies in a basket."

Maybe that's the association with witches, that dual nature, the two-faced-ness of a witch and of a grandmother's outwardly sweet demeanour and their dark, human internal struggles.

There's not a big pantheon of monsters and myth in Poland, so growing up I heard a lot of witch and ghost stories, and a lot about Satan and weird Catholic things. I was drawn to the witches, they resonated with me because I like monsters. I think that's the root of why I do a lot of drawings of witches eating babies. I try not to make it too gruesome, so the babies are usually happy, and the witch is sort of sentimental and grandmotherly. I have a witch aesthetic that I've created: she's in the woods, she's foraging, she usually has a basket where she keeps the babies, and the babies are happy and comfortable in there. The witch has a pact with the Devil, which takes me back to the Edward Gorey story, *The Disrespectful Summons*, which I read in the library when I was too young. It's about a witch who makes a pact with the Devil and even though she followed him, in the end he grabs her by her hair

and takes her down to a fiery hell. I view it as a nice story, a love story. All pacts with the Devil are love stories, there's always something sexy about life pacts. They're like marriages. There's another witch story that I read, it was an Orson Scott Card book, *Enchanted*. The people from the past voyaged to the present, and the witch made extra effort to be mean to anyone that was nice to her. I always thought that was unique and interesting, to have such a spiteful character. It always stuck in my head that her motivation was to make a good person lose their hope and enter into a descent before she (or the Devil) ate or took them.

For me, the striking part is always that the witch, or that Baba Yaga, was cast as an outsider, someone unwelcome. It's the only way the story works. It makes me want to turn the story on its head. To tell horrific stories, but drawn in such a cute way that, even though it's horrifying, it's still adorable. That's why the little babies are smiling as they're going into the witch's mouth. It's meant to be metaphorical. It's meant to be mischievous.

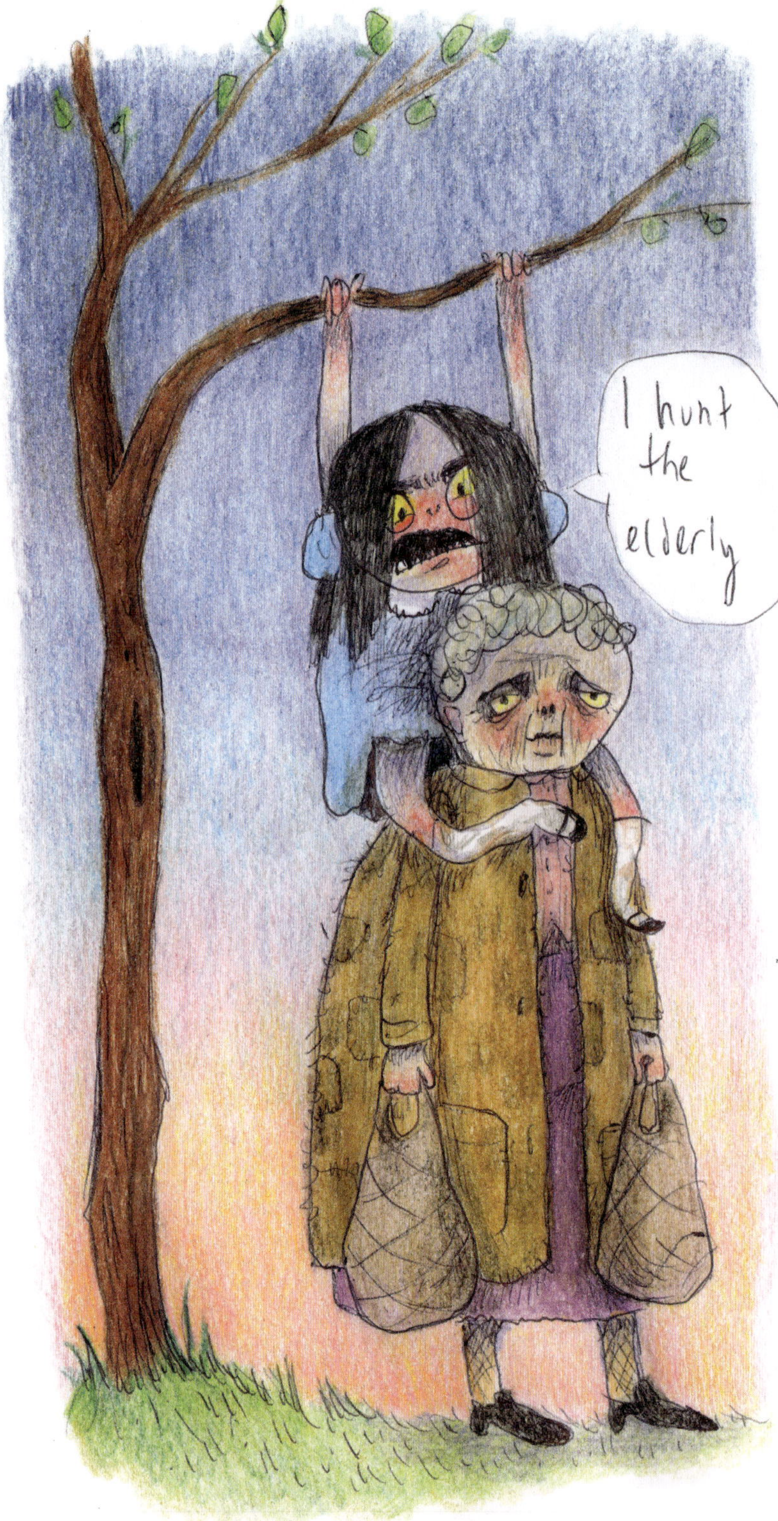

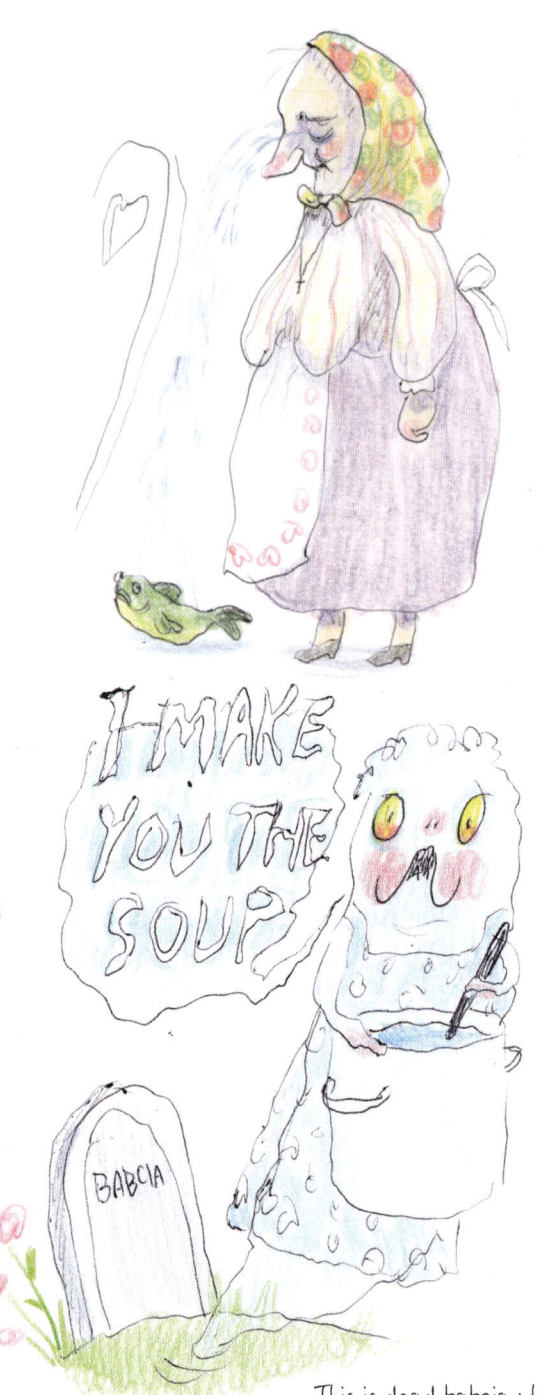

This is dead babcia who's still making soup in the afterlife, only her grandchildren can't eat it because it's in the afterlife. But she doesn't know because she's still stuck in the cycles of the living.

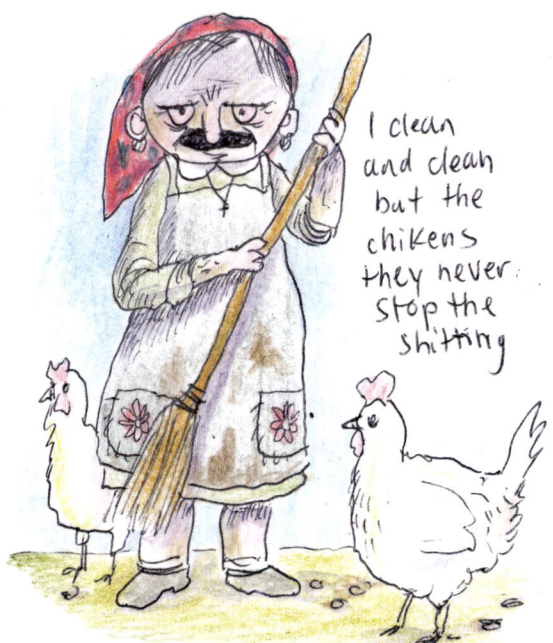

I clean and clean but the chikens they never stop the shitting

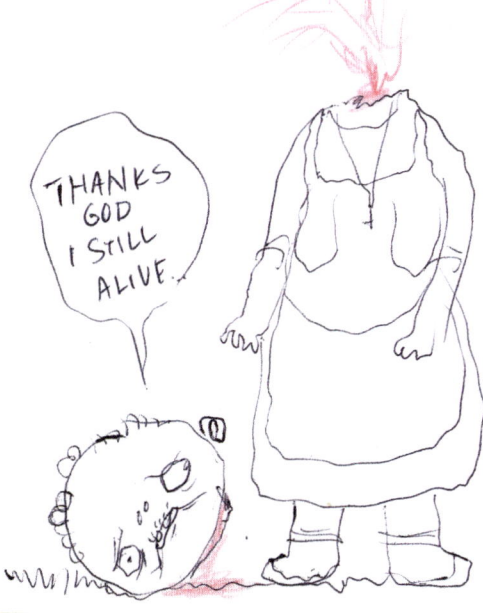

THANKS GOD I STILL ALIVE.

She lost her head and blood is gushing out, but at least, God is keeping her alive.

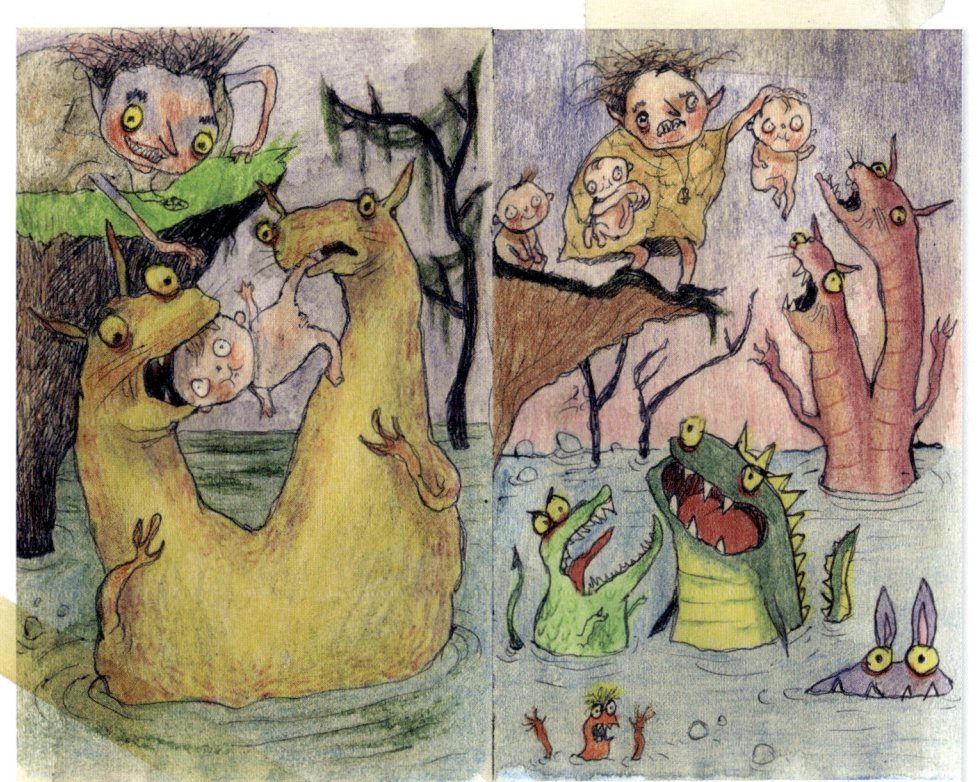

This is a Baba Yaga who is feeding babies to her beloved swamp monster pets. And the babies are happy too, of course, so that now no one has to worry about them. One is literally being torn apart by a two-headed monster, but he's still smiling.

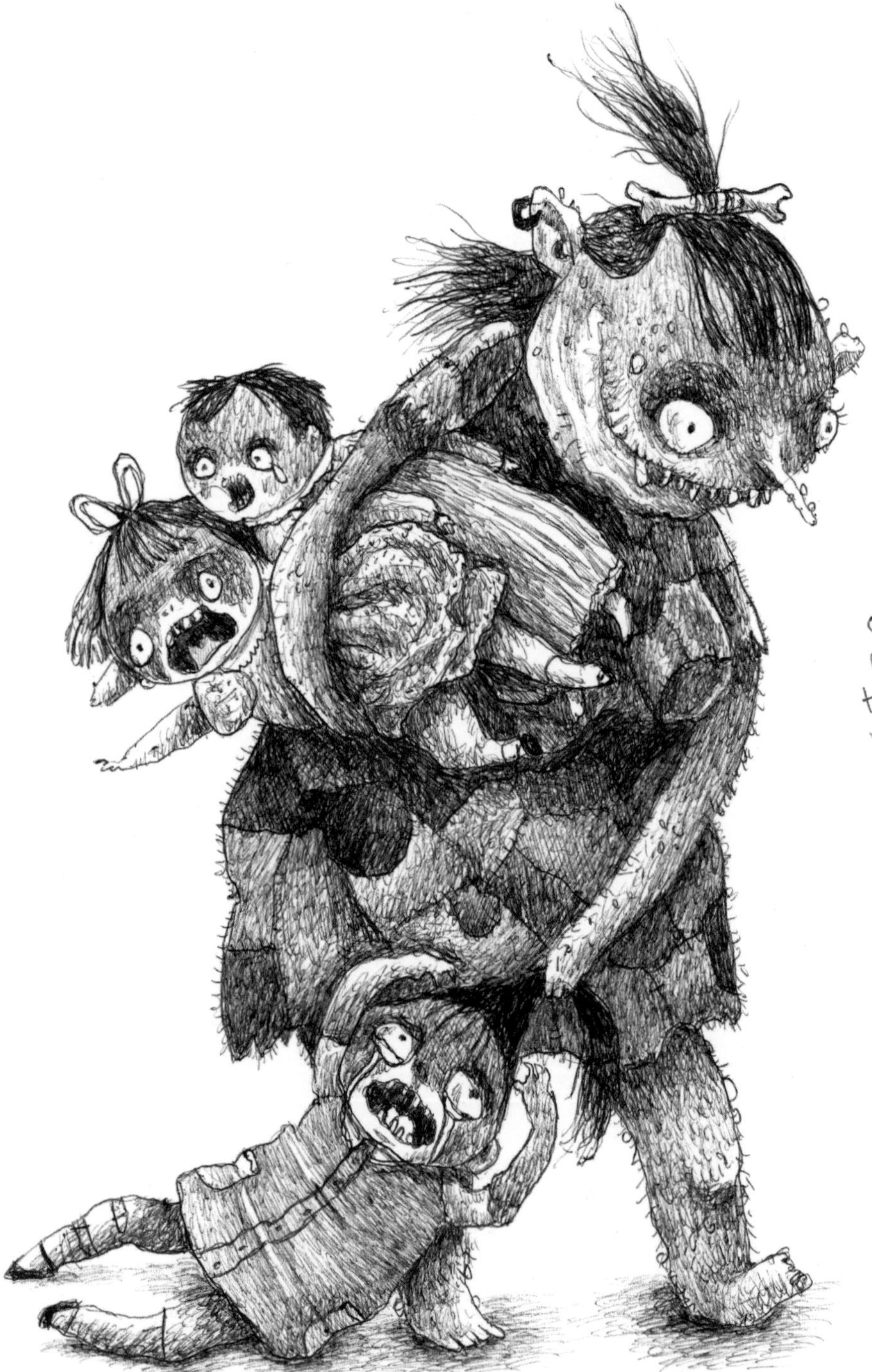

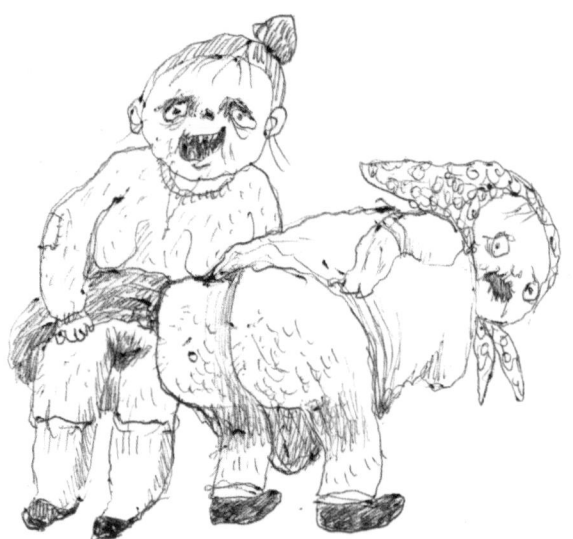

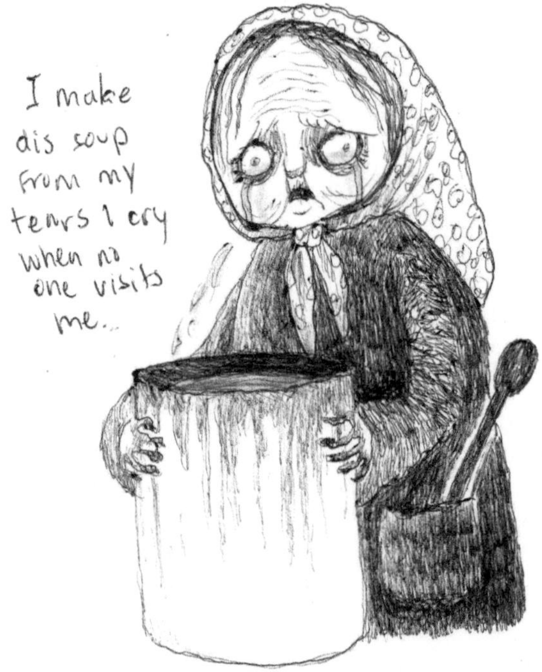

I make dis soup from my tears I cry when no one visits me...

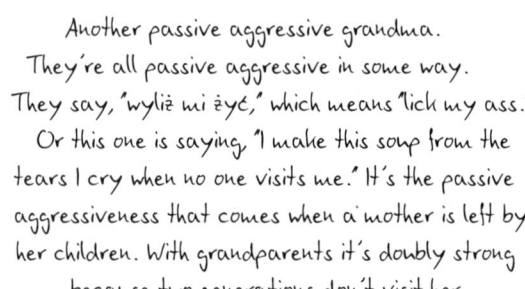

Another passive aggressive grandma.
They're all passive aggressive in some way.
They say, "wyliż mi żyć," which means "lick my ass."
Or this one is saying, "I make this soup from the
tears I cry when no one visits me." It's the passive
aggressiveness that comes when a mother is left by
her children. With grandparents it's doubly strong
because two generations don't visit her.

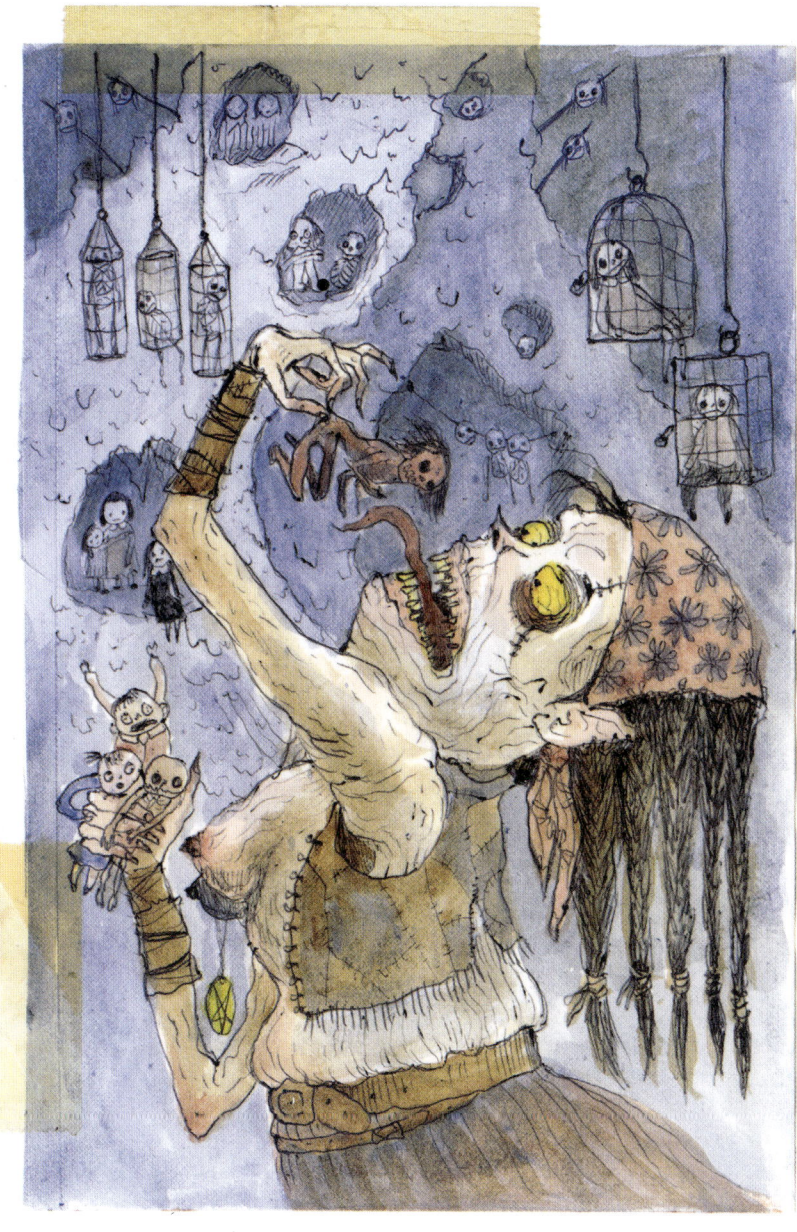

This was inspired by a Spanish movie, called *Witching & Bitching*
which featured a giant witch who ate a little boy, but she was
gelatinous, so he was visible as he was being digested and going through
her. And then she shits him out and he's alive but also possessed by an evil
entity with super evil powers. I loved that. This is fanart for that movie.
They're in a cavern, which is from the film, and they are celebrating
the arrival of this giant witch mother.

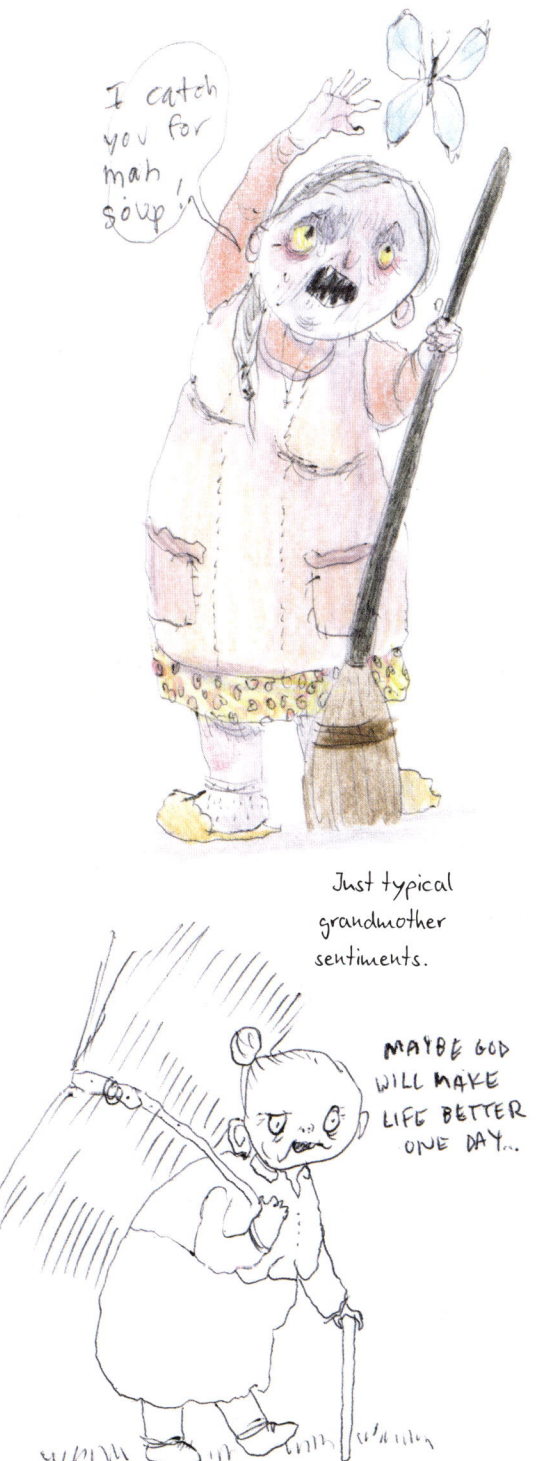

Just typical
grandmother
sentiments.

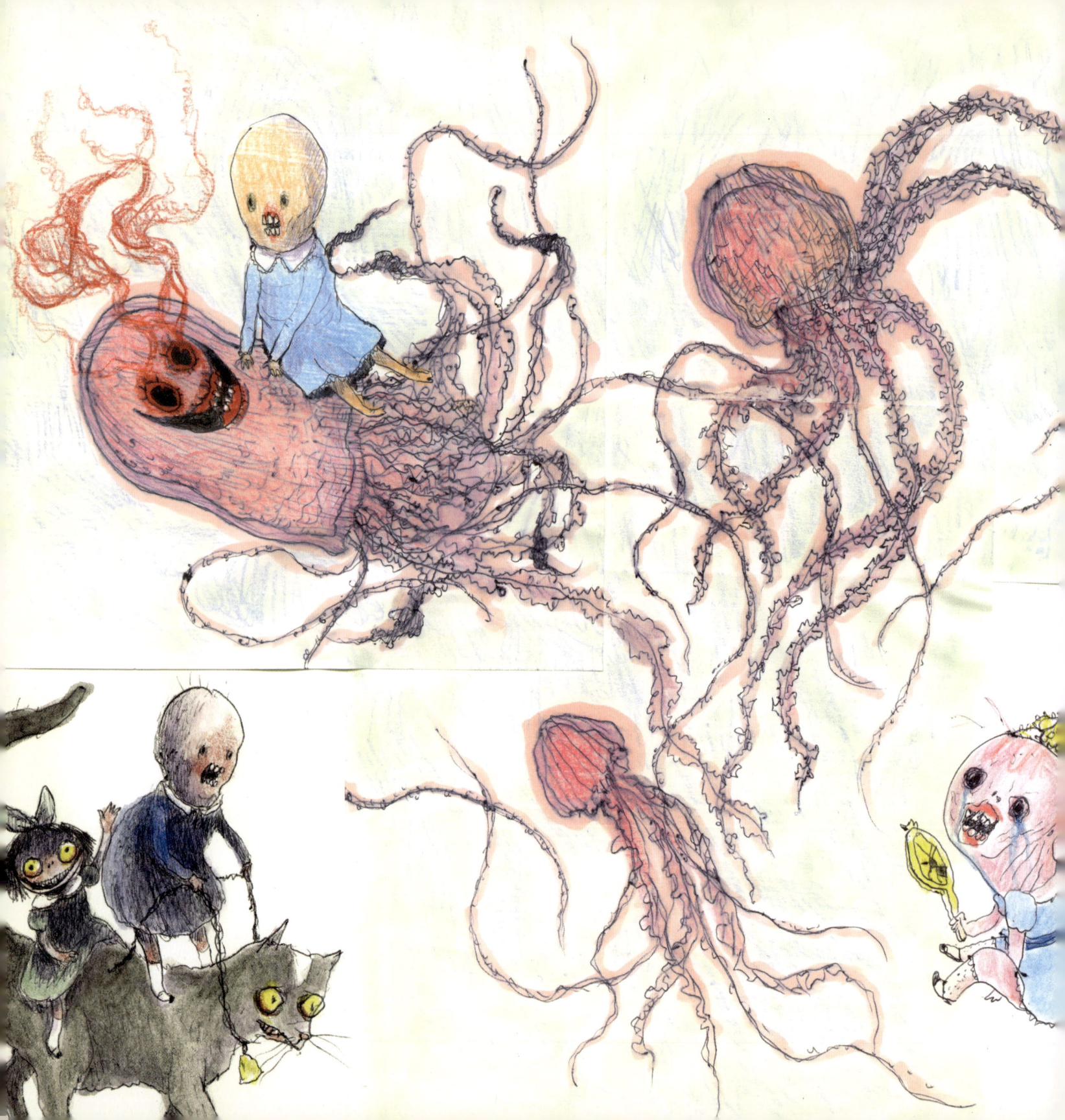

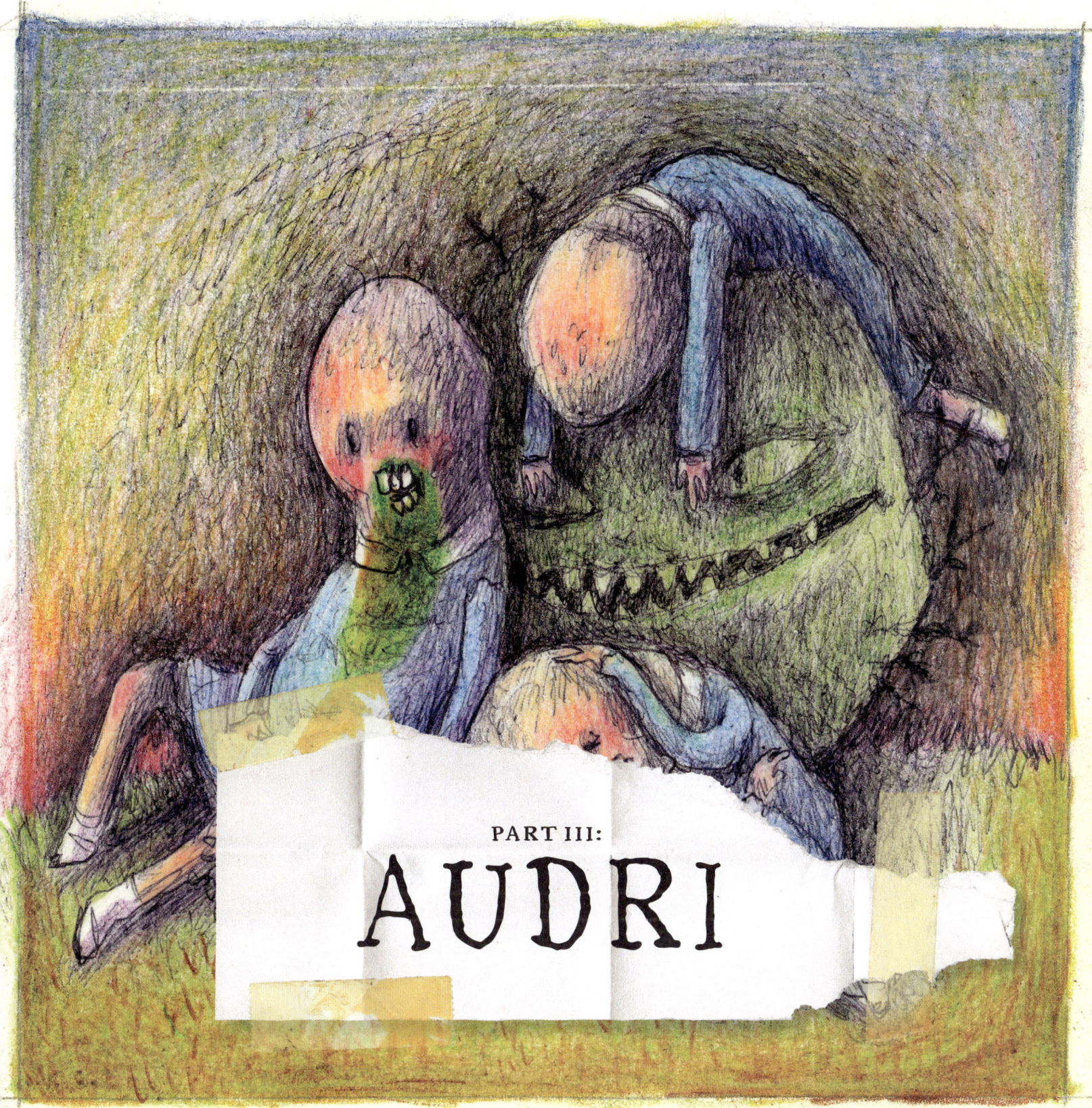

PART III:
AUDRI

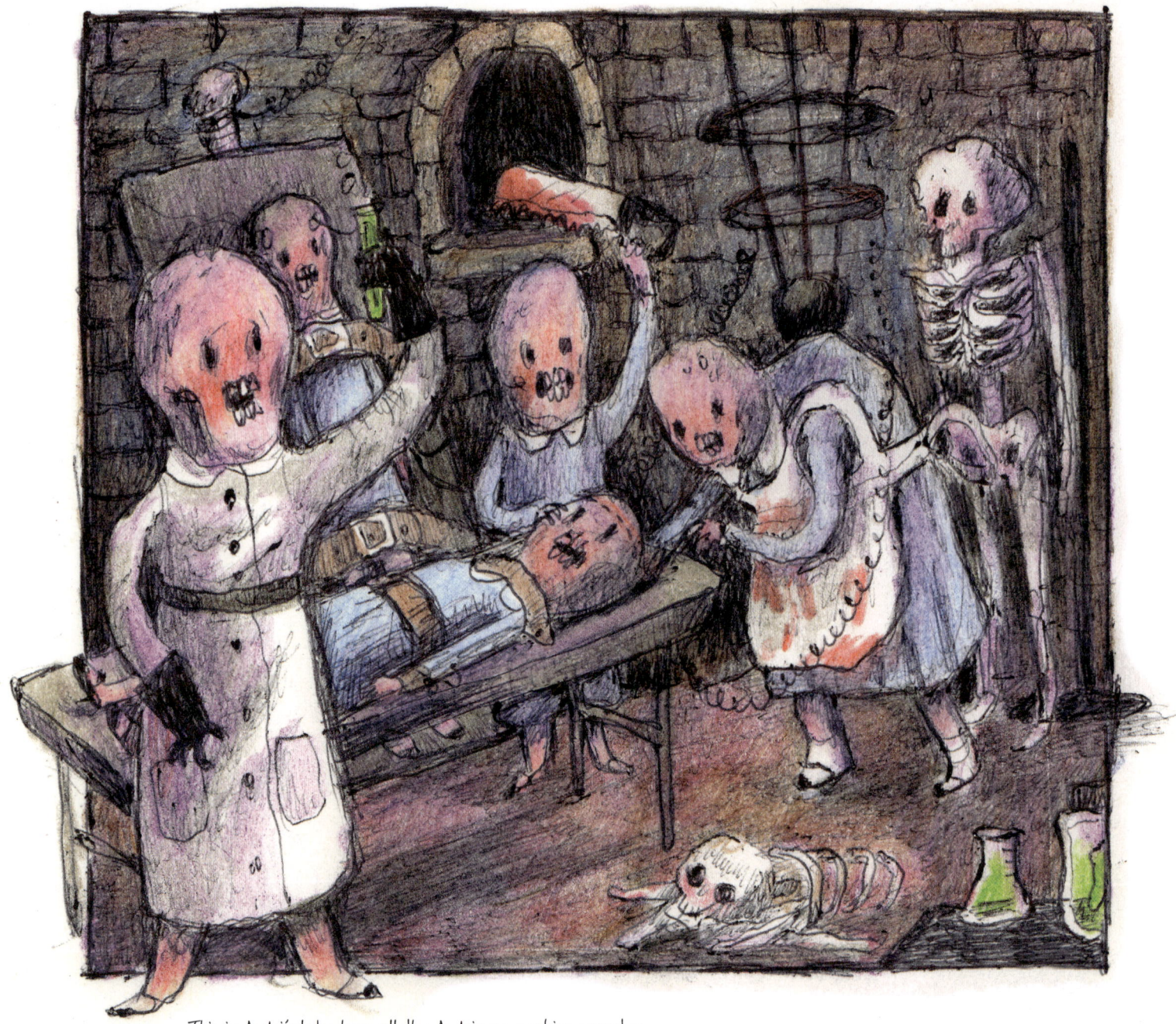

This is Audri's lab where all the Audris are making monster
Audris in these horrible science experiments. Lots of reference
to *Frankenstein*, obviously. This is a completed scene,
the whole story in a snapshot.

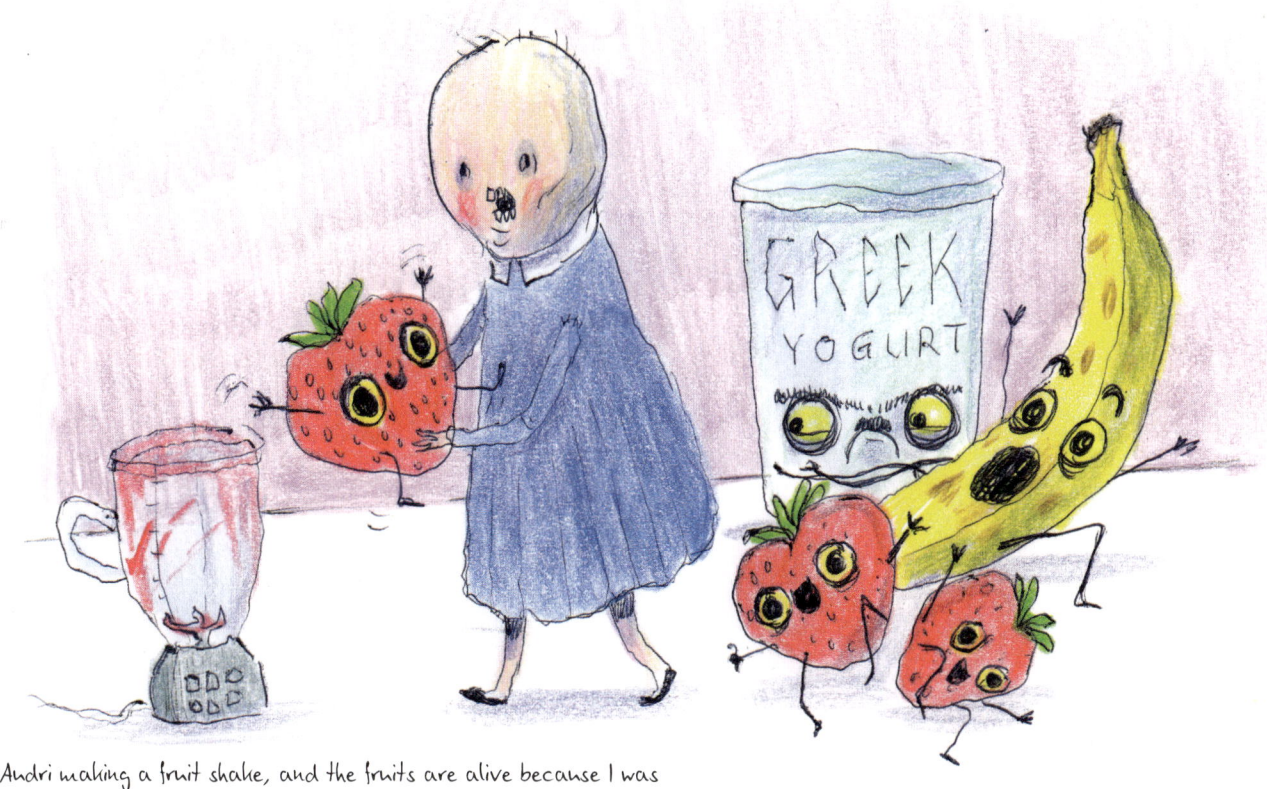

Audri making a fruit shake, and the fruits are alive because I was
making my partner and son eat healthy and I was probably going
overboard on fruit shakes. That's just my life, from real to drawn, the line is blurred.

AUDRI IS THE LITTLE CHILDISH SPIRIT INSIDE EVERY-one. She isn't pretty, she looks like a little burnt girl, which I imagine is how people really feel inside, scared and insecure and ugly. My inner child is definitely a little burnt girl with no hair, or maybe tufts of hair, but no eyes and a potato form. Sometimes Audri is worried about her image so she tries to look pretty. She eats weird things, like, when it rains, she eats all the worms that come up. She's full of mischief and she's curious and plays a lot of pranks or occupies herself by doing strange things, things that only our inner selves or children could think of. She gets to do what none of us can or will. She's sort of a little comic character acting out scenes and delivering cuttingly honest lines.

Audri emerged from several different things. I had been researching World War I images, for reference, and from that I sculpted this burnt boy. Burn Boy ended up being my son's childhood toy. He used to take it to the park. It was so embarrassing. I mean I had made it and it was being flaunted around town, so that was mortifying. Also, it was pretty horrific and gruesome for a child's toy. Burn Boy had one eye, and it was kind of a clouded dead eye while the other was just a burnt hole, and he had all these scars. He had a little striped blue and black shirt and corduroy pants. He was pretty big, half the size of a four-year-old. Then, because it was a homemade sculpture and my son played with it so much the hands and feet fell off of it leaving spikes of wire

Okay. This should perhaps go in "It's a personal problem" but here we go. I have a lot of period troubles. I have low iron because I bleed so much, I have cysts, hormonal issues, medications, it's an on-going medical condition. It's so much fun. Now, this scene is Audri filling a gymnasium with period blood. It's a gymnasium because, well, what girl doesn't have a horrible or hilarious memory of her period and gym class? Anyway, she's riding it out, but everybody else is dead. I really like this picture. It fulfils that desire I had as a teenager: the desire to kill everybody when I got my period.

for limbs. I had to sew his clothes around the spikes so they wouldn't be sharp. I had such an affinity for the image of my son with Burn Boy. It was so strange and innocent, it was sweet. I think there are echoes of Burn Boy in my art, I draw and make a lot of burnt creatures and things. Audri is one of my burnt things.

A friend of mine sculpted a little burnt head for his *Forrest Gump* figure and I was reminded of all my burnt people and newly inspired. So I drew a little sketch of a Burn Girl, but it was Audri. My friend who'd done the Forrest Gump sculpture said to me, "She looks like an Audri." And he was right. That was the very first sketch of Audri. She was a companion piece to burnt Forrest at the time, but also grew to be so much more. She was just so affecting and sweet. She had a blue dress and pink tufts of hair. I don't see her as a literal burn victim, but the feral incarnation of what everybody has inside of them, like inner instincts, like true selves.

Audri is always changing. I play with her form, the size of her head, the shape of her body, hair or no hair, nails, teeth. I play with it all in a fun way and also in a technical way. I think I realized it doesn't matter how an image turns out because it's always Audri in the spirit of her character. She is consistently, stylistically loose. That's Audri. For her scenes, I think I draw a little from *Calvin and Hobbes*. Audri is like Calvin in that she has this child's point of view. The childlike sense of wonder in everything that, as an adult, can be so hard to see, but once seen, is fun to explore. If an adult were to look up at the sky, at the universe, they may not even see the stars. I remember picking my son up from school and looking at all the art and thinking it was amazing. I took a picture of one particular drawing, because I loved it so much; it was kind of a terrifying butterfly monster. I loved it. I went back later in the evening and I saw the little girl that had drawn it, and I watched her mum's reaction to it: she wasn't into it. It made me sad that the mother didn't like it, didn't support it. I think that's why I love children's art and why my art went from technical and careful, to sometimes looking like children's scribbles.

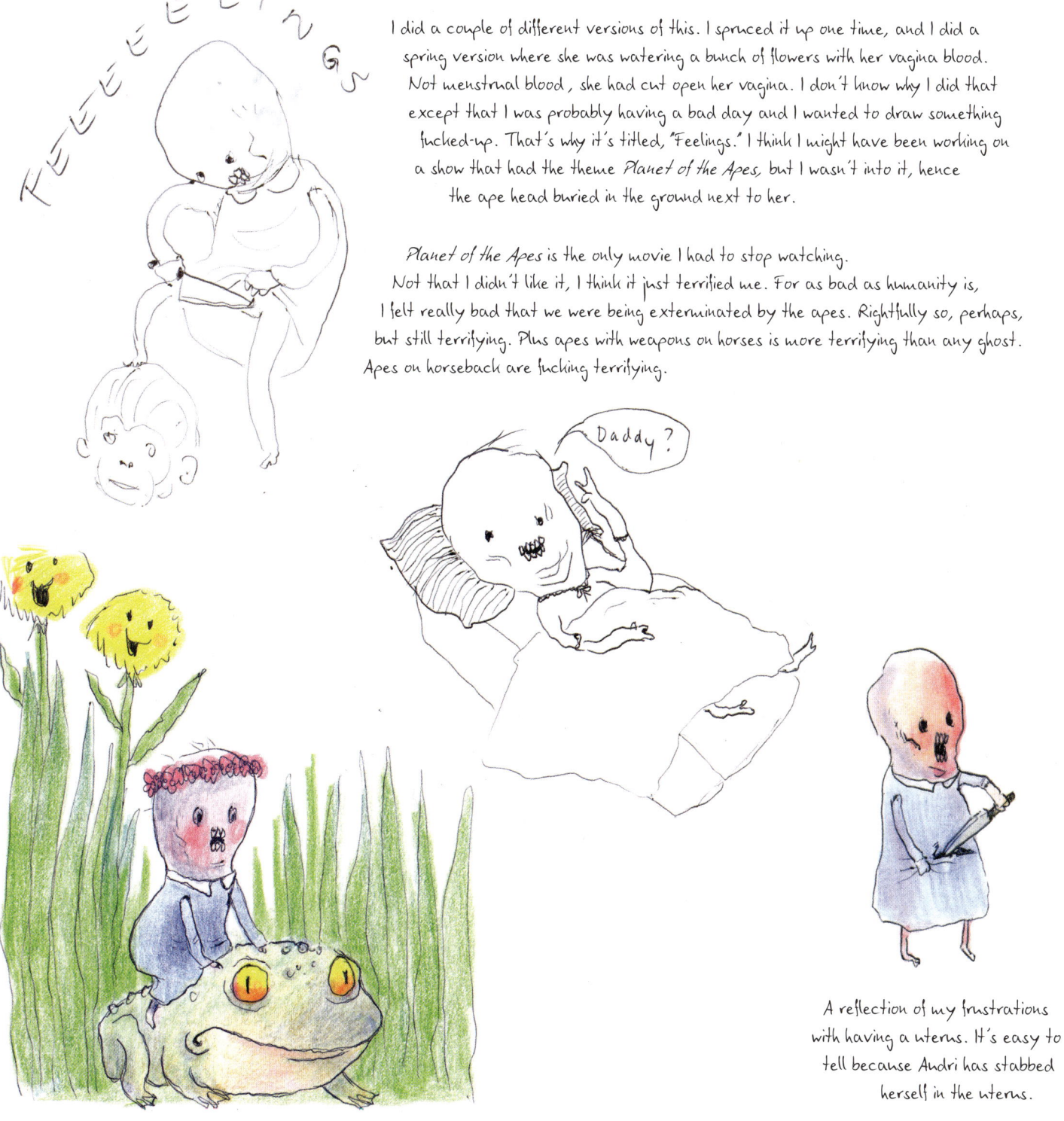

FEEEEELINGS

I did a couple of different versions of this. I spruced it up one time, and I did a
spring version where she was watering a bunch of flowers with her vagina blood.
Not menstrual blood, she had cut open her vagina. I don't know why I did that
except that I was probably having a bad day and I wanted to draw something
fucked-up. That's why it's titled, "Feelings." I think I might have been working on
a show that had the theme *Planet of the Apes*, but I wasn't into it, hence
the ape head buried in the ground next to her.

Planet of the Apes is the only movie I had to stop watching.
Not that I didn't like it, I think it just terrified me. For as bad as humanity is,
I felt really bad that we were being exterminated by the apes. Rightfully so, perhaps,
but still terrifying. Plus apes with weapons on horses is more terrifying than any ghost.
Apes on horseback are fucking terrifying.

Daddy?

A reflection of my frustrations
with having a uterus. It's easy to
tell because Audri has stabbed
herself in the uterus.

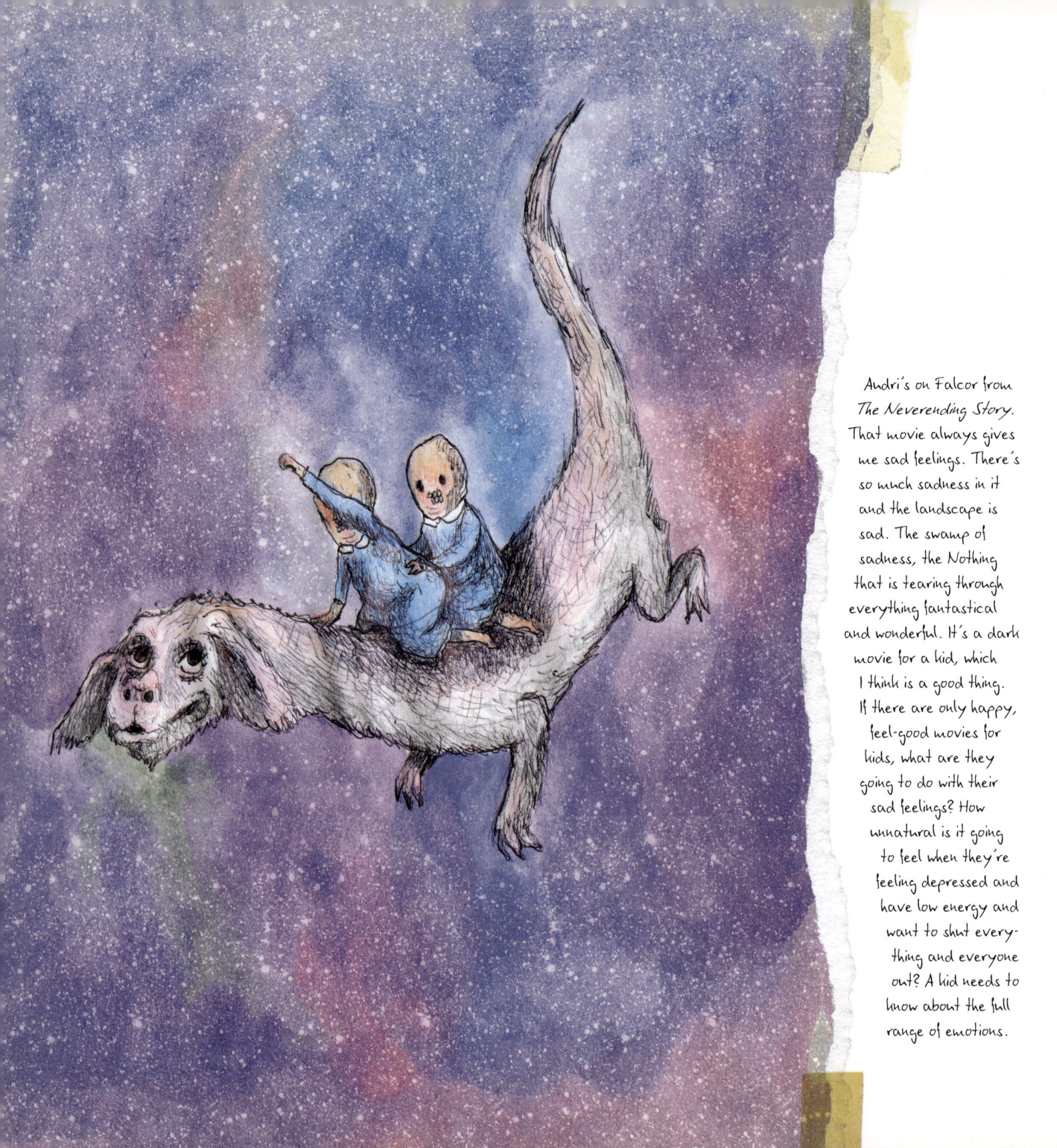

Andri's on Falcor from *The Neverending Story*. That movie always gives me sad feelings. There's so much sadness in it and the landscape is sad. The swamp of sadness, the Nothing that is tearing through everything fantastical and wonderful. It's a dark movie for a kid, which I think is a good thing. If there are only happy, feel-good movies for kids, what are they going to do with their sad feelings? How unnatural is it going to feel when they're feeling depressed and have low energy and want to shut everything and everyone out? A kid needs to know about the full range of emotions.

Audri is generally me playing out scenes from childhood, but with thoughts and insigh from adult me. For instance, there's this one crystal clear memory I have that I know Audri plays out. When I was little I used to go to the park alone. It was summertime and we didn't have money for a summer camp, so I had to entertain myself. I was alone outside by the park at Lake Ontario, and I found a message in a bottle. It was just floating there at the shore. I remember all the thoughts running through my kid-mind. Excitement. Anticipation. I mean, I was thrilled, I remember thinking, "Oh my God, it's magic!" I opened it and took out the note, and there was a map, and I think I thought I was going to have my own summer adventure, following the treasure map or a map to a murdered corpse or something. Then, out of nowhere a teen comes and says, "Could you put that back in the water?" He was a camp counsellor. The message in the bottle was for the summer camp. The summer camp I couldn't go to, the summer adventure I couldn't have. I wasn't allowed to participate in the magic. It was a crushing moment at the time but looking back it was also sweet and funny. Audri gets to really live it. She gets to find a real map in a bottle. She gets real magic.

Everyone has their own little Audri. She can be giant, I have an Audri head that I'm working on but it's too big, so I stopped for now. She can be sick, but she usually has a little helper-creature friend to make her better. She can be dancing with ghosts, she can be a doll, she can be sitting on a puppy because she doesn't know how to take care of it so, ride it, obviously. I know that I have an Audri swinging from the nipples of a giant woman monster and one braiding a giant woman's pubic hair. She shows up in my Christmas cards, with dead Santa or playing some sort of anti-Christmas prank. Audri isn't just special to me, she's supposed to resonate with everyone. I draw Audri for friends when they are feeling blue; I draw her on a lot of thank you letters and thank

Find the Nest. Destroy the Queen!

This is where one of the Audris has to be destroyed because she's too powerful and she's the Queen of an Audri nest that's gotten out of control. A horror movie throwback for sure.

you envelopes; I draw her in response to global events. I make her reference her own existence as a piece of art in her own world. Like breaking the fourth wall. I have one where she enters into a den of evil Audris and she destroys the egg. I have Audri in fan art, like *Neverending Story* images with Audri riding on Falcor, and I think that reaches a huge audience. My love of drawing children riding on things probably began with the *Neverending Story*, which is one of my favourite movies. There's also a large snail in that film, and now that I think about it, the whole fantasy universe is devoured by the Nothing, which is a sort of a wolf creature. All of creativity is metaphorically thrown in the garbage. That whole movie is my art in a nutshell.

I used to go fishing with my dad all the time, so I made an Audri fishing scene. I think she's pulling out an eel. My dad had this thing where he continuously fished eels out of Lake Ontario. He thought it was funny to swing the eel toward me to make me fall over in order to avoid being eel-slapped. He used to try and convince me it was a fish, but I'd argue that it was obviously a snake. It was always an eel. I love the way eels look, but I don't want to be slapped by one.

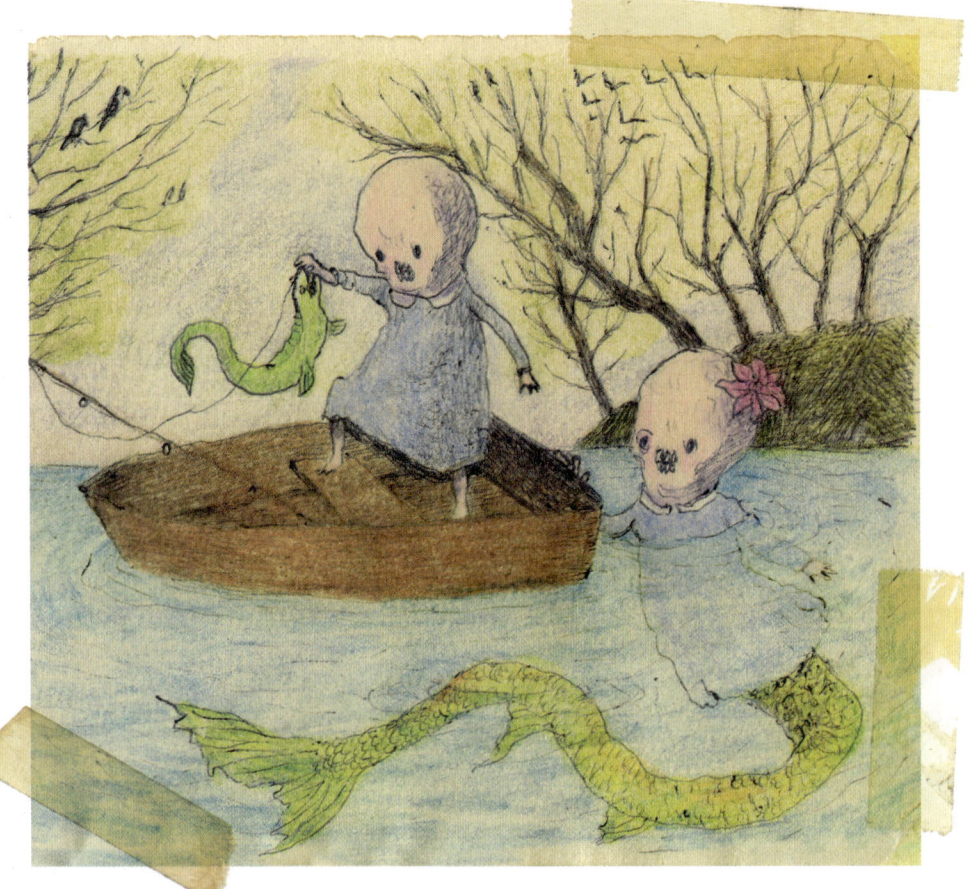

AUDRI'S GUIDE TO BEING OPEN

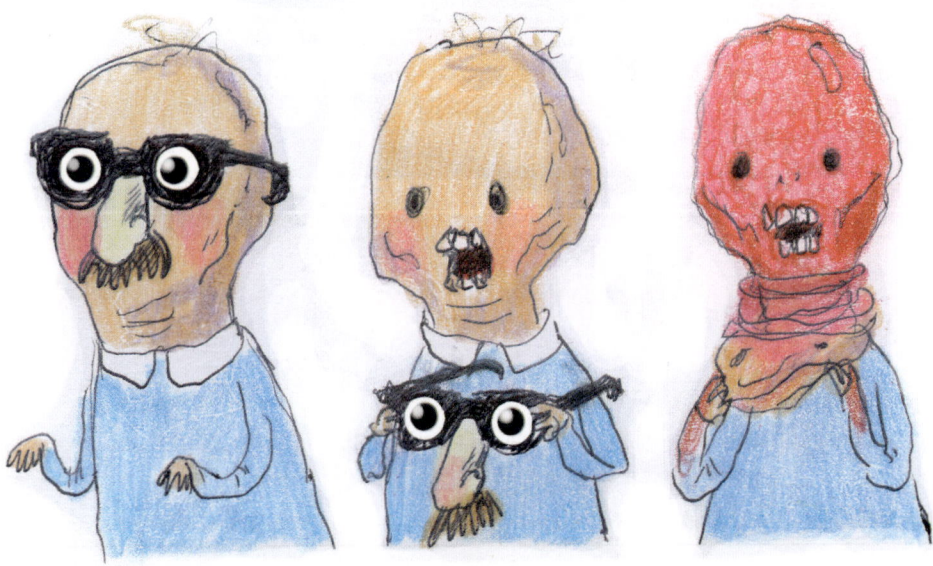

It's really hard to be open with people and it can feel unnatural. Audri has her own way of dealing with it, as demonstrated in the image, but I think this is one of many "Audri-isms" that have come up as I've explored her character. She has this child's-eye clarity, I guess. People seem to understand her too, without any explanation, people can understand an Audri image.

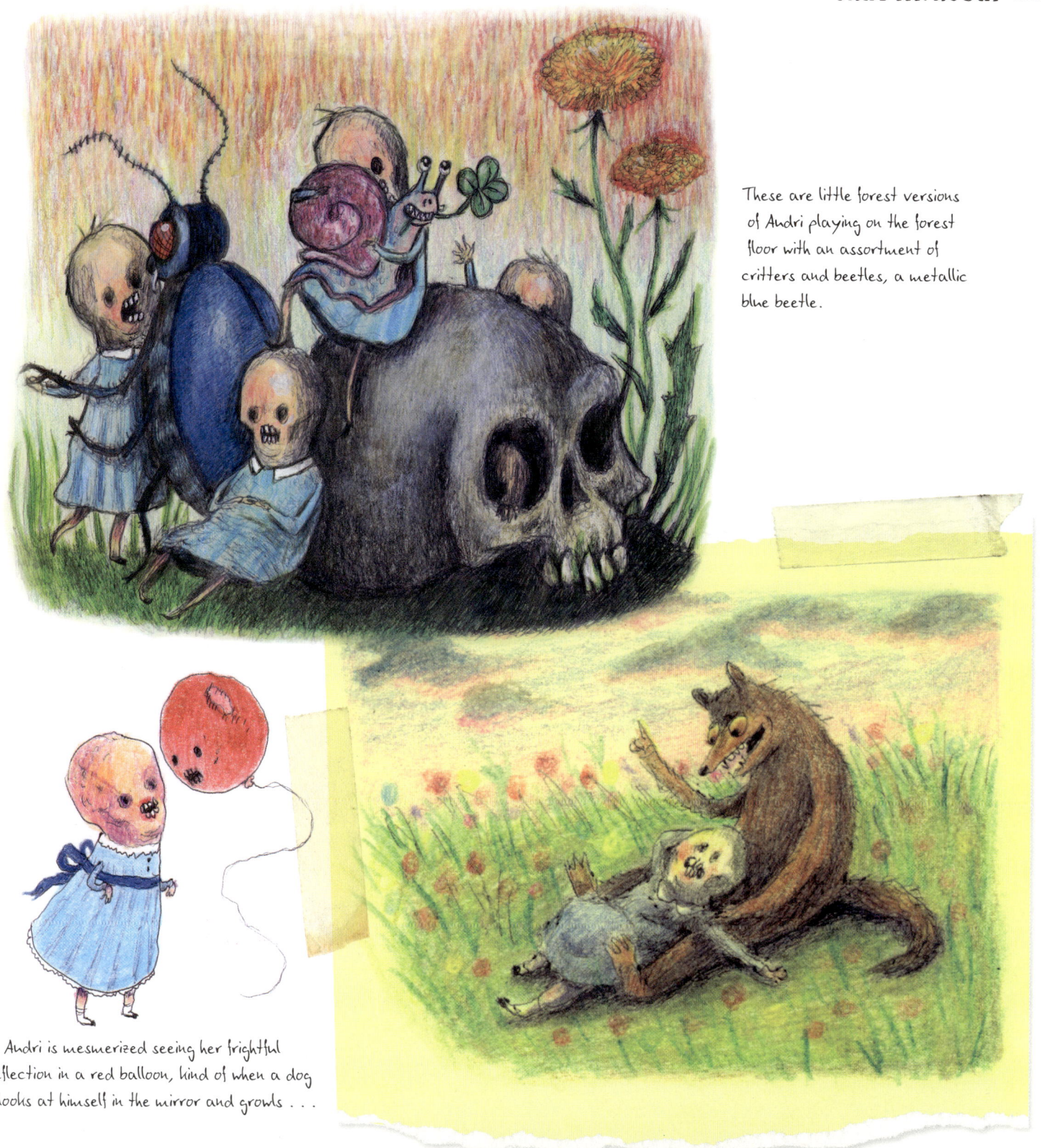

These are little forest versions of Audri playing on the forest floor with an assortment of critters and beetles, a metallic blue beetle.

Audri is mesmerized seeing her frightful reflection in a red balloon, kind of when a dog looks at himself in the mirror and growls . . .

The scene is that three of Audri's dead relatives come to visit her on her deathbed. There's a Satanic element too because Audri is kind of satanic, she's the Devil born in each of us, it's just part of her, part of us. I don't know if her sweetness is connected to that idea, but she's really lovable.

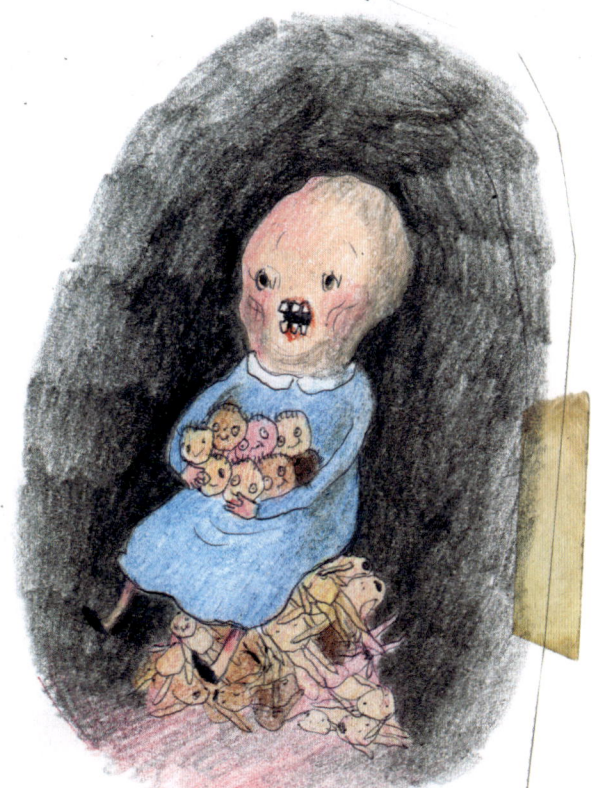

Audri collects the heads off all her dolls. I don't know what her plan is.

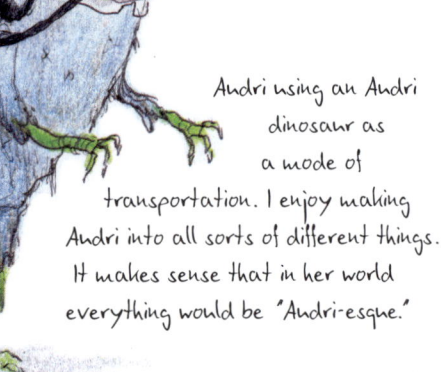

Audri using an Audri dinosaur as a mode of transportation. I enjoy making Audri into all sorts of different things. It makes sense that in her world everything would be 'Audri-esque.'

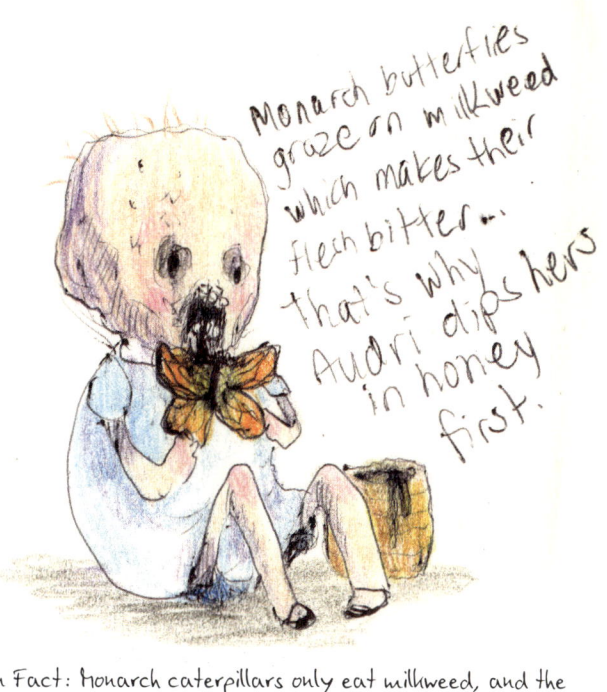

Monarch butterflies graze on milkweed which makes their flesh bitter... that's why Audri dips hers in honey first.

Fun Fact: Monarch caterpillars only eat milkweed, and the butterflies prefer milkweed nectar to any other flower. This makes them taste bitter, and actually toxic, to predators. So this is educational art! I thought it'd be fun to have Audri dipping her butterflies in honey before she eats them. She's this little monster but she wants to be sweet, so I try to bring some reality into it, because that always makes things a little bit more fun.

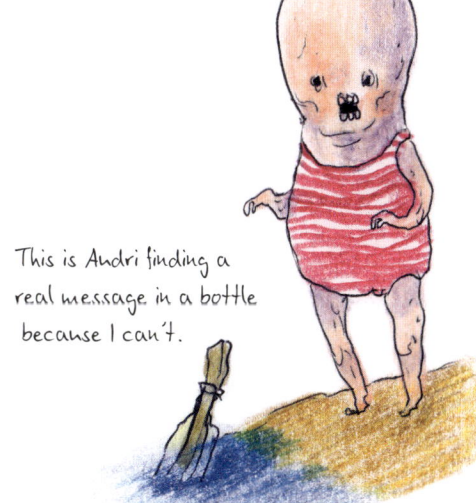

This is Audri finding a real message in a bottle because I can't.

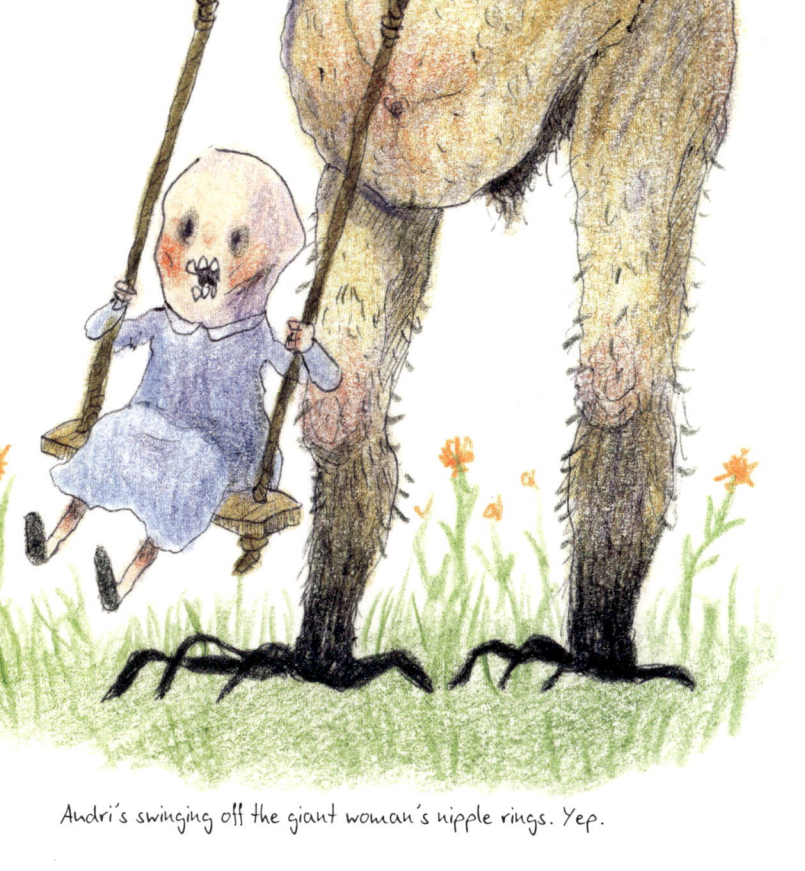

Audri's swinging off the giant woman's nipple rings. Yep.

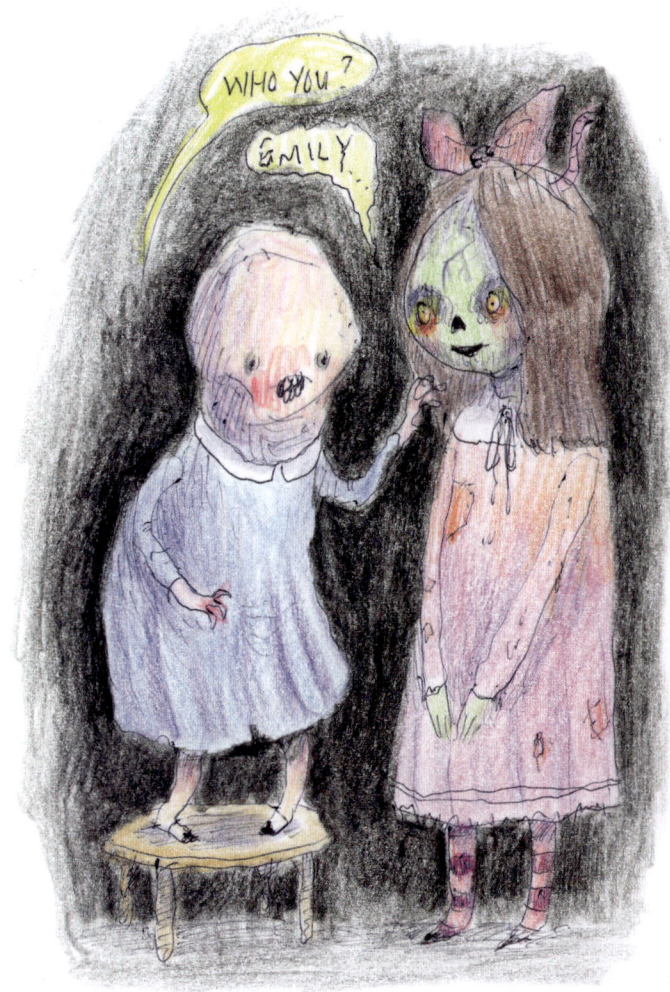

WHO YOU?

EMILY...

Andri's sick. And she's getting treated by an eyeless rat.

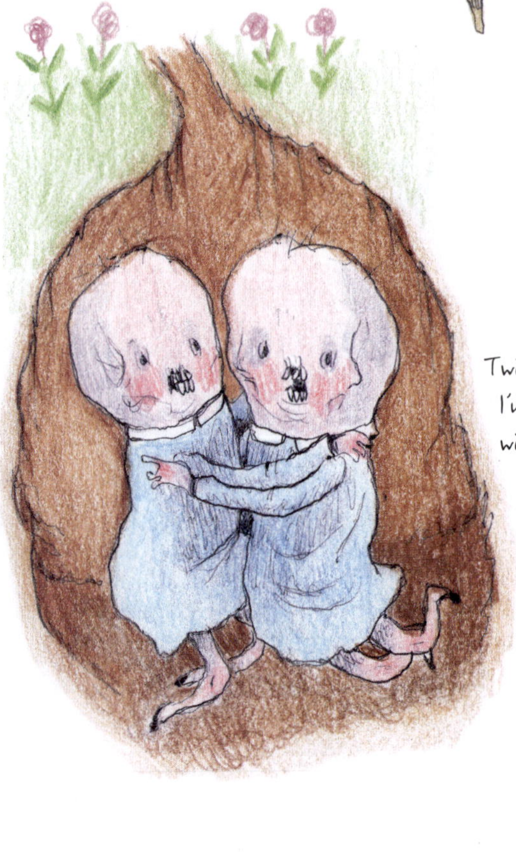

I think that this was the inkling of a story, but it never went anywhere. It's still on the back burner. I'm always thinking about what Andri meeting different characters would look like, and what would it be like for her to explore garbage world?

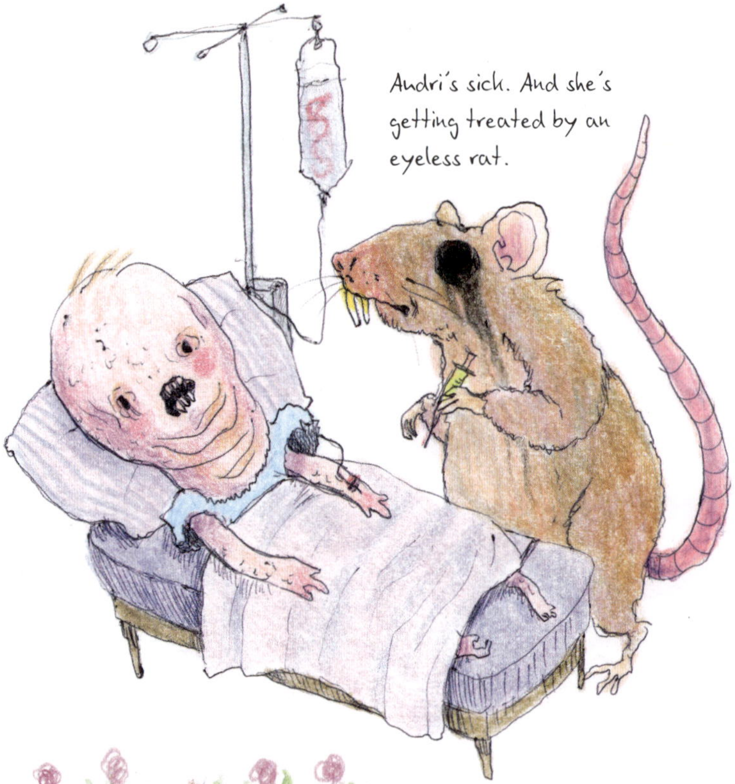

Twin Andris. I'm combining her with my concept of going underground to feel safe.

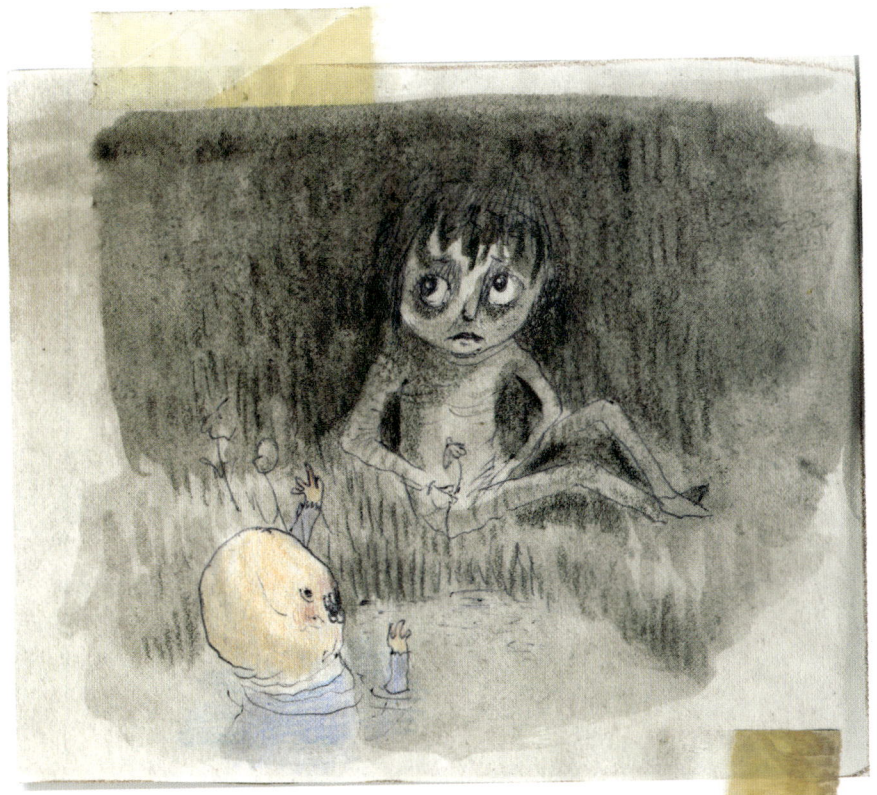

I did this for a sculptor friend of mine, Sandra Arteaga. She does a lot of dolls, and I've known her for years. She and I made art dolls around the same time, and she'd just started drawing. She drew this boy and it really struck me. I knew she was feeling sad, so I drew this picture to cheer her up. It was like the sad boy was her, and Audri was visiting her. I sent it to her.

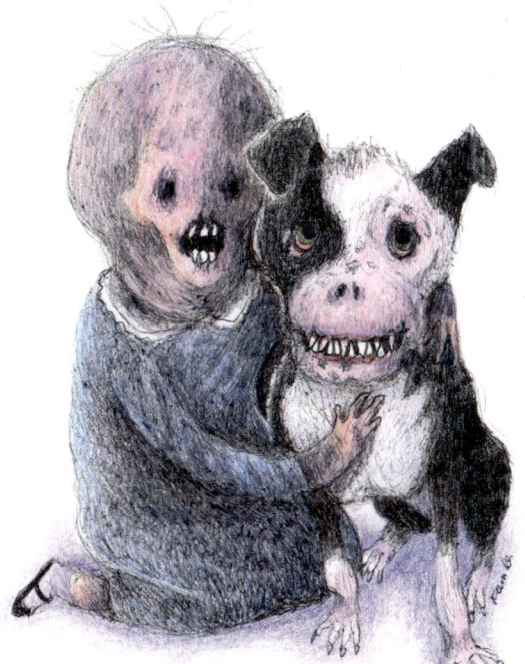

In Audri's world she has a dog equal.
This was a little bit of fanart for an internet-famous dog called Phoenix.

RELEASE THE PIGS!

A reference to
Jesus Christ Superstar, which I'm obsessed with.

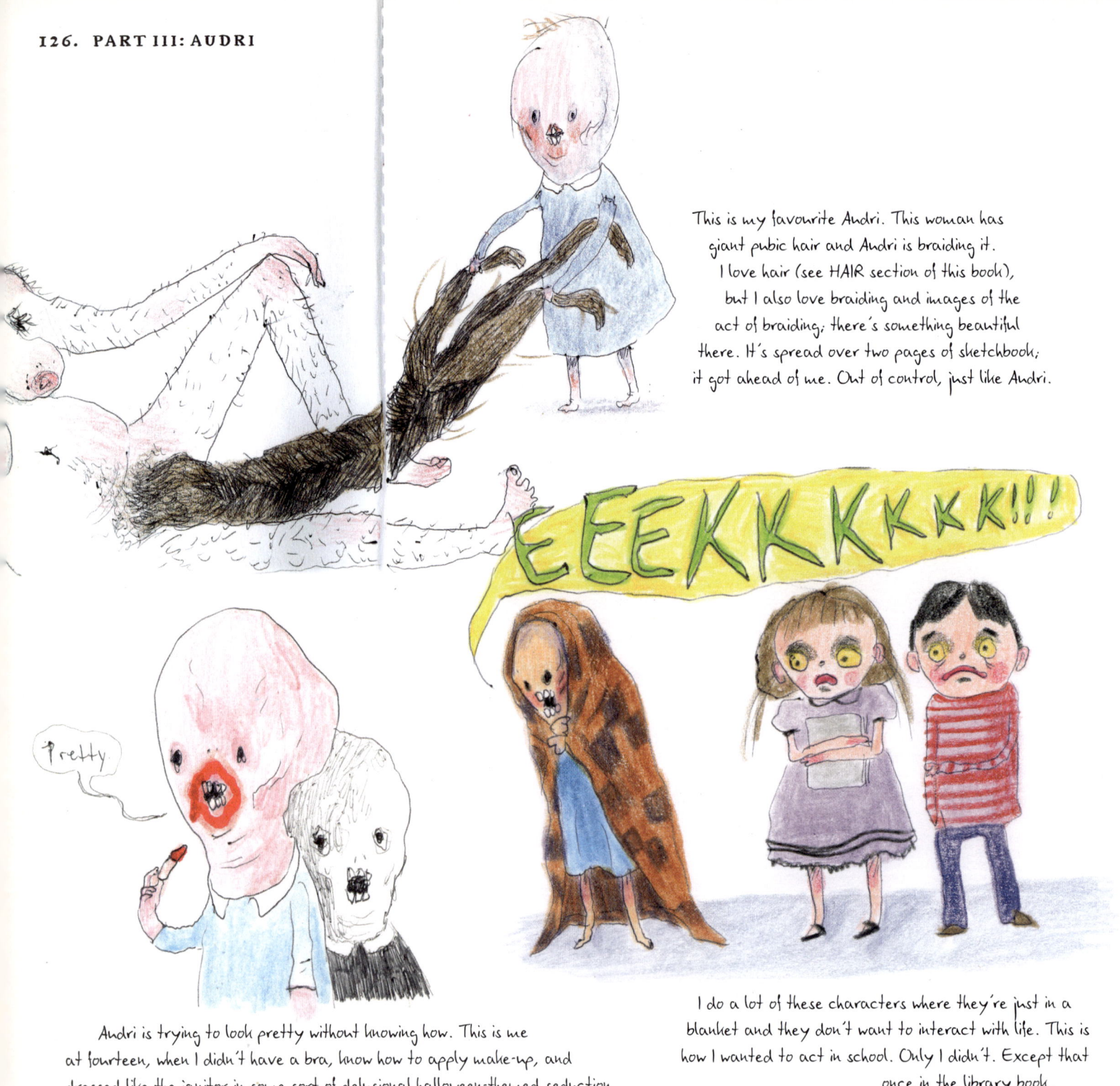

This is my favourite Audri. This woman has giant pubic hair and Audri is braiding it. I love hair (see HAIR section of this book), but I also love braiding and images of the act of braiding; there's something beautiful there. It's spread over two pages of sketchbook; it got ahead of me. Out of control, just like Audri.

EEEKKKKKK!!!

Pretty

Audri is trying to look pretty without knowing how. This is me at fourteen, when I didn't have a bra, know how to apply make-up, and dressed like the janitor in some sort of delusional halloween-themed seduction gambit. Audri is me and it's obvious that she doesn't know how to do anything, and that she really doesn't care. It's okay.

I do a lot of these characters where they're just in a blanket and they don't want to interact with life. This is how I wanted to act in school. Only I didn't. Except that once in the library book.

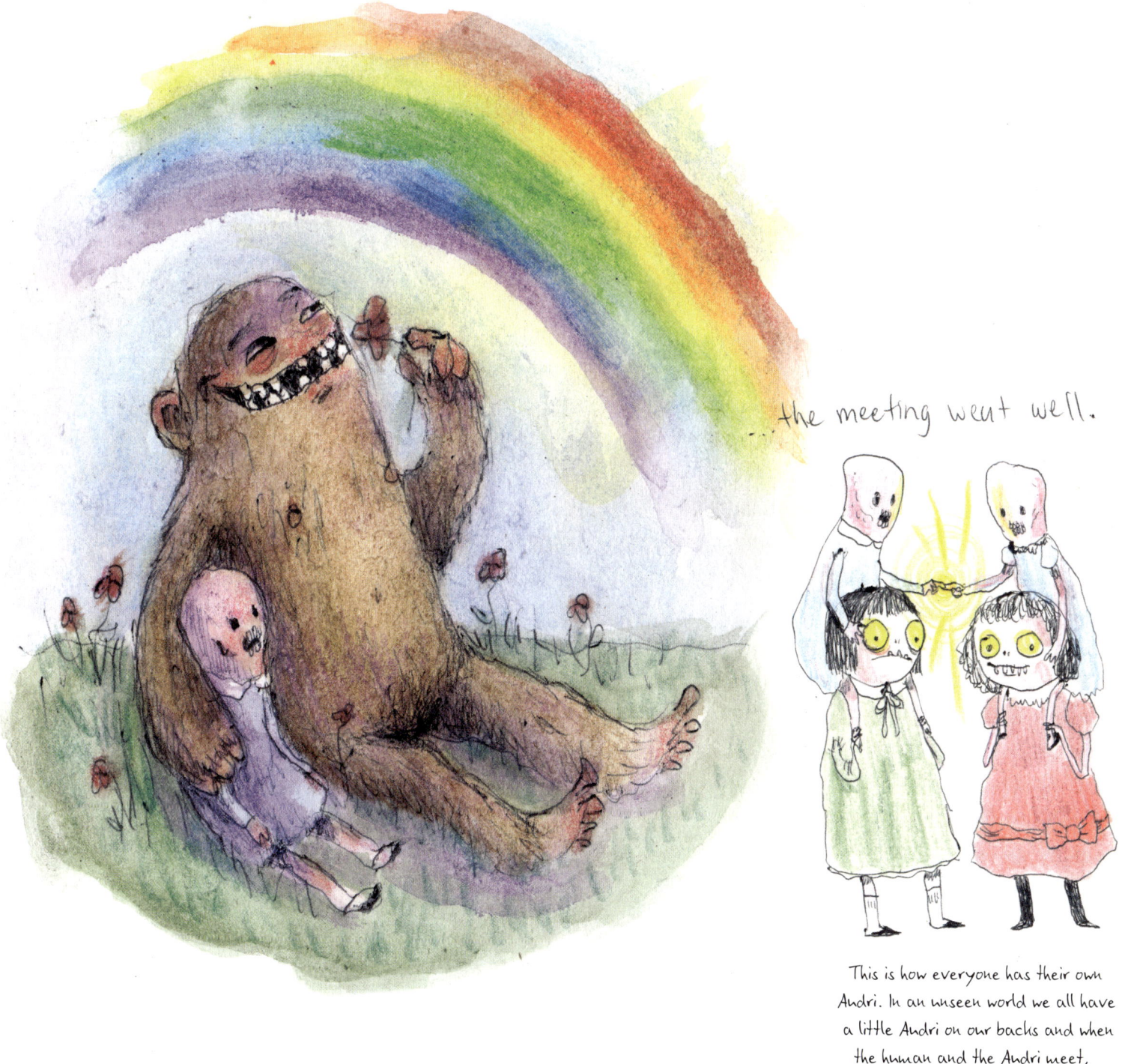

...the meeting went well.

This is how everyone has their own Audri. In an unseen world we all have a little Audri on our backs and when the human and the Audri meet, they touch fingers. Like in E.T.

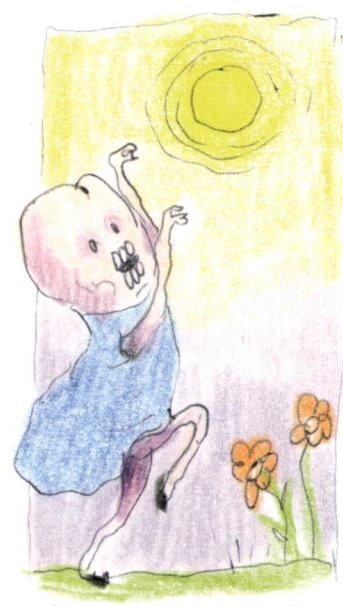

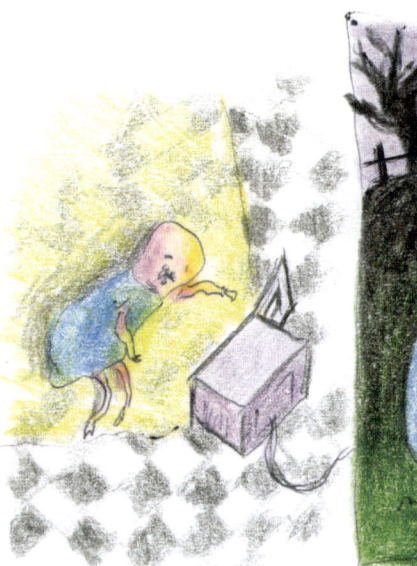

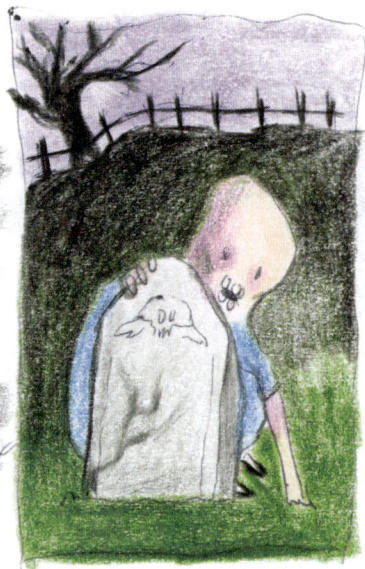

I've started doing these three panel comics, and that works well with Audri. This is about where Audri feels the safest which is in a dark kitchen with the microwave open. Obviously. The light of the microwave is the perfect brightness, the perfect lighting.

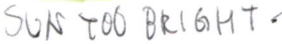

SUN TOO BRIGHT.   PERFECT.   NIGHT TOO SCARY.

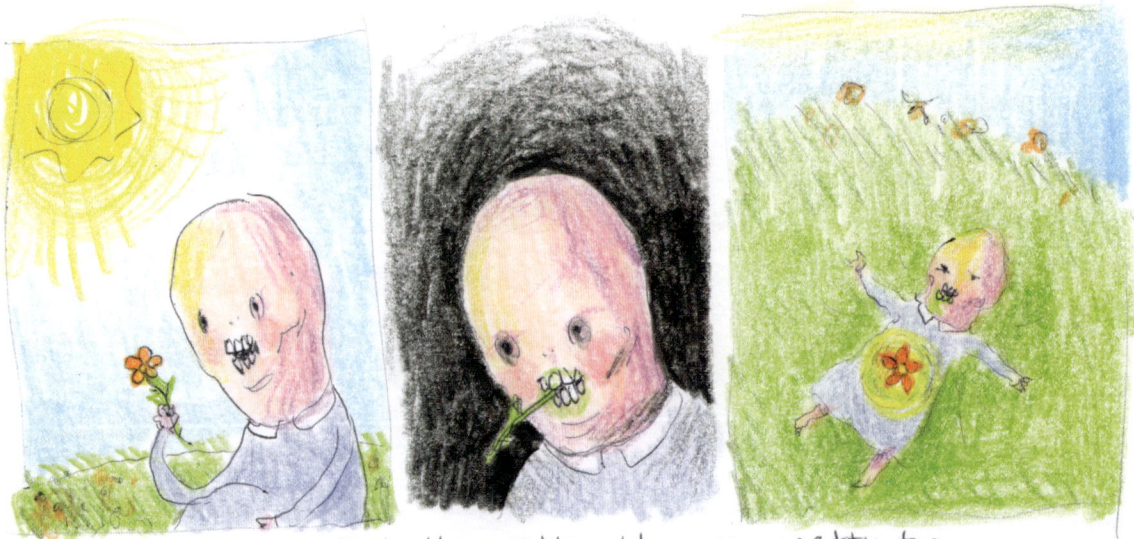

Pretty flower. Eat the pretty. Now am pretty too.

This is one of the first Audri cartoons I ever made. It's simple and silly and I didn't really notice that it was a comic at the time. People really liked it, so I thought maybe there's something there. But to me, this is Audri having simple childlike logic: "Pretty flower, eat the pretty flower. Now I'm pretty too." It's such a childish way of understanding what beauty is and how to obtain it. Audri logic.

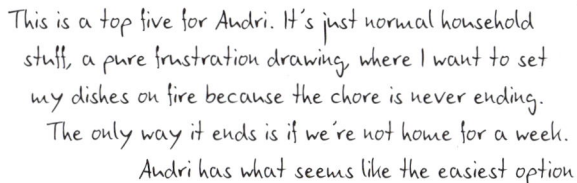

This is a top five for Audri. It's just normal household stuff, a pure frustration drawing, where I want to set my dishes on fire because the chore is never ending. The only way it ends is if we're not home for a week. Audri has what seems like the easiest option.

An expanded version of my sink on fire. Everything is on fire. "Audri is fireproof." So she's not on fire. Also, fun fact, I'm pretty sure this setting is the same as Roseanne Barr's house from *Roseanne*. I used to watch that a lot. Her house is burned into my memory, and now Audri is burning in it too.

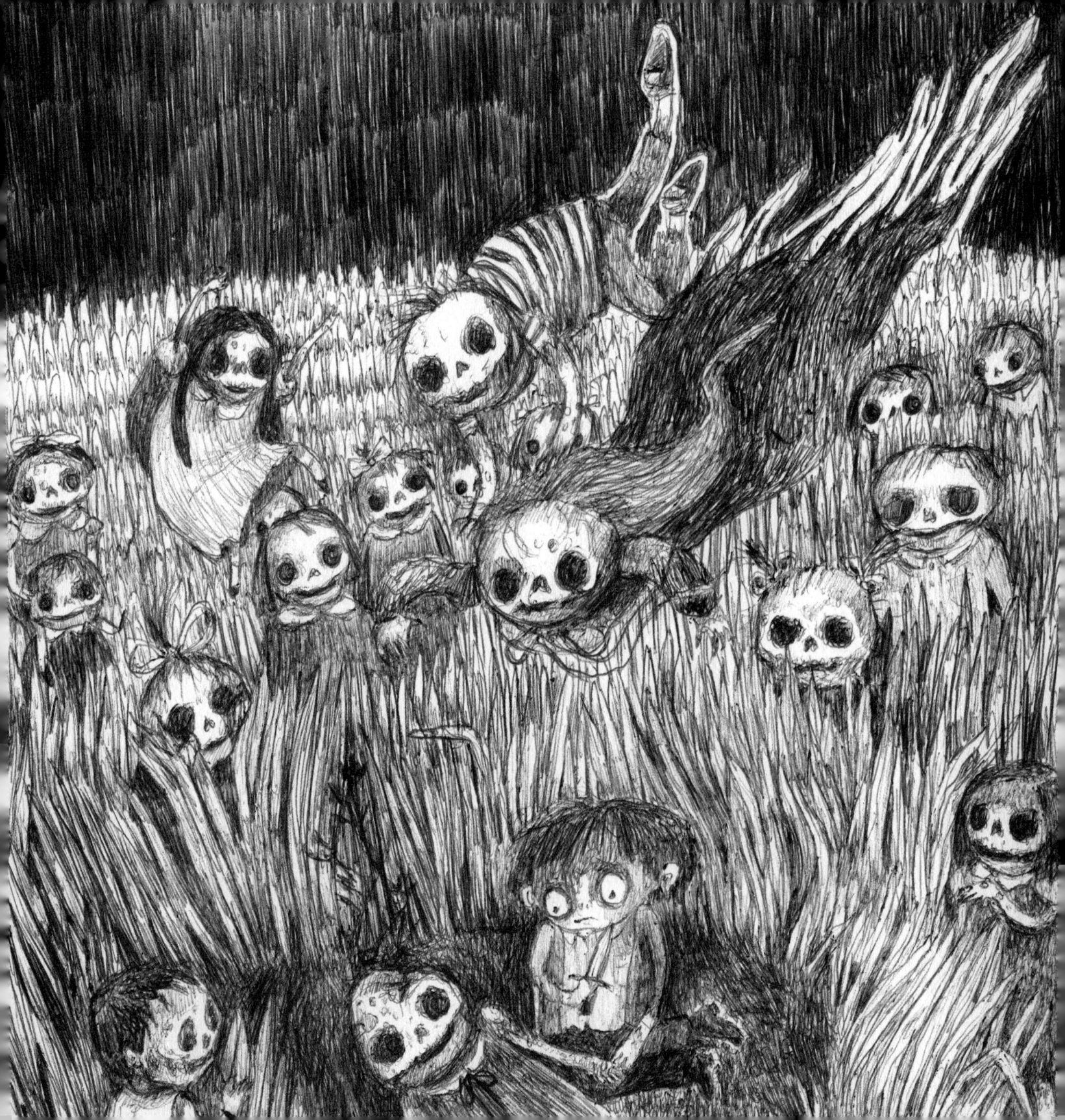

PART IV:

KISS *my* COLD, DEAD BODY

Worst case scenarios bring me the most comfort, a cathartic little drawing about how whatever problem I'm experiencing isn't as bad as a bear trap, probably.

MY OWN PROBLEMS RARELY MEASURE UP TO babies being eaten by a cannibal. Whenever I go through a tough time in life, whether it be death in the family, low-self-esteem, or simply the everyday battles of being human, I draw all the worst, horrible, honest things I can think of so that I can laugh at them. It lightens the mood. It makes me feel better. I feel worthy and useful after I create something and share it because other people's reactions (which are hopefully cheerful) show that I'm right, that happy-little-babies-being-eaten give everyone a little perspective, and a little joy because of the irreverence. Everyone is miserable

sometimes. It's comforting to see other people's misery or depictions of misery; it lets us know we aren't alone, and it lets us see how silly some of our own unhappiness is. I can get on with life.

These drawings came at the tail end of my re-learning how to draw phase. I relaxed and had a more absurd style. I started doing more personal work and more cartoonish work, weird, dramatic, mental health stuff. Hair, snails, poop, all of that stuff was bordering on the personal, where I drew from everyday life or I was allowing myself to draw in order to cope and then post

One of the things I do when I sink into a depression is watch really depressing television, reality or otherwise. I was watching *My 600-lb Life* on T.V. and also *The World's Heaviest Man* which is a documentary. I feel at once saddened but also somehow at home watching these people put their struggles out into the world. Like me, they are trying to help themselves and others, I think.

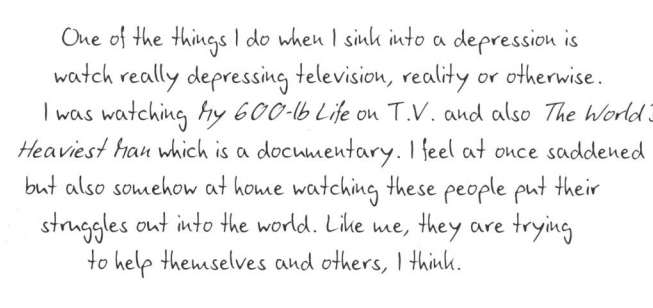

the world has nothing to do with us anymore...

A lot of these drawings have text in them, which is a recent development. The characters were empty, a lot of practice and play, but not a lot of substance. This is heading down the storytelling path, where I want the image to have a message. Sometimes I'll leave a drawing as something open, but when I get into the really dark and personal stuff, I feel like I need to explain. Some of them are little sad stories, personal reflections, that need an explanation. This one, "The world has nothing to do with us anymore." This is feeling isolated. Not only loneliness, but also boredom with my surroundings; my town is not exciting. Motherhood can also be very isolating. Organizing playdates is always difficult or awkward and I avoid going out with people, which means they start to treat me like a stranger after a while. The world has nothing to do with me, or maybe I'm just not really part of the world anymore.

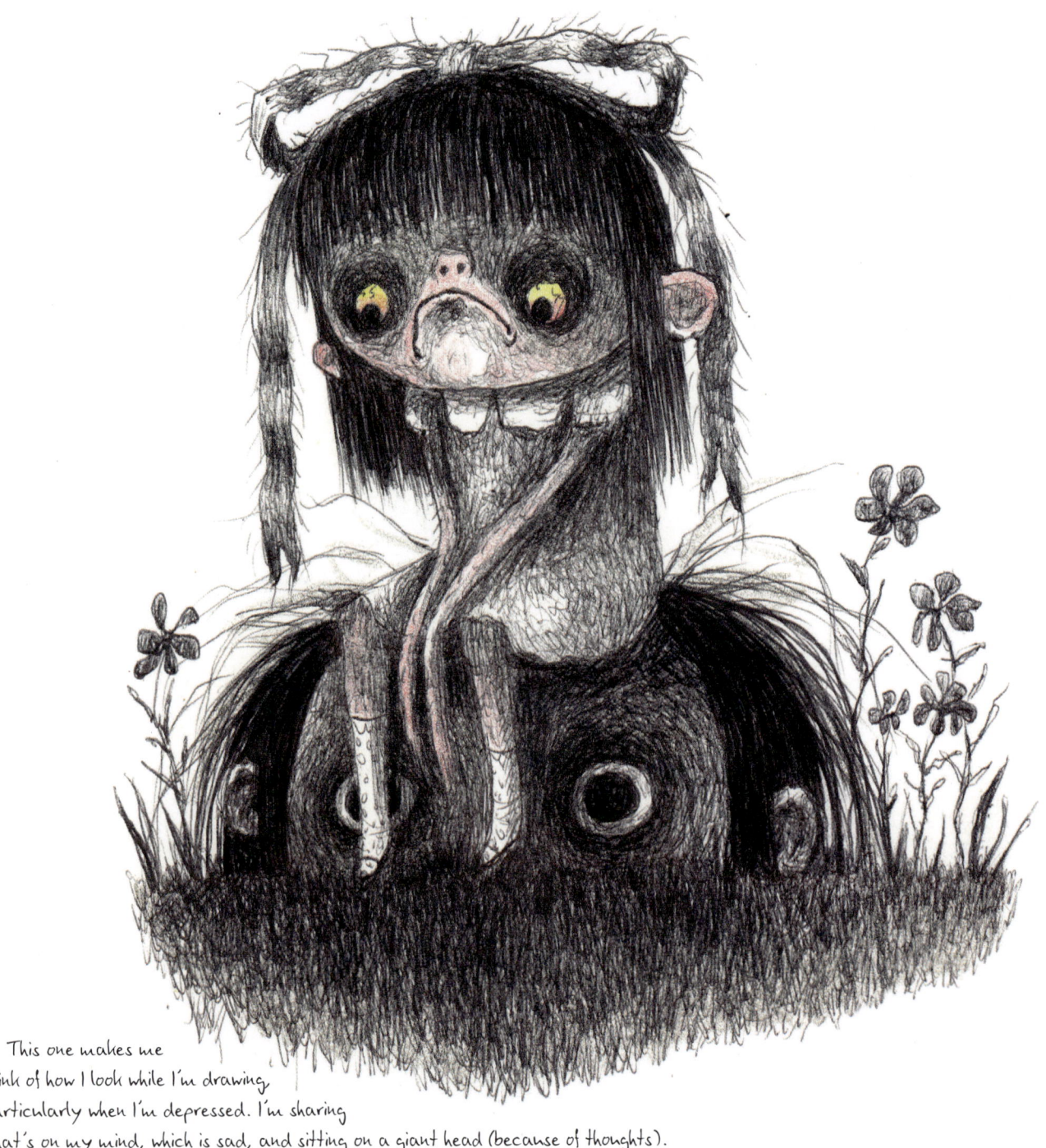

This one makes me
think of how I look while I'm drawing
particularly when I'm depressed. I'm sharing
what's on my mind, which is sad, and sitting on a giant head (because of thoughts).

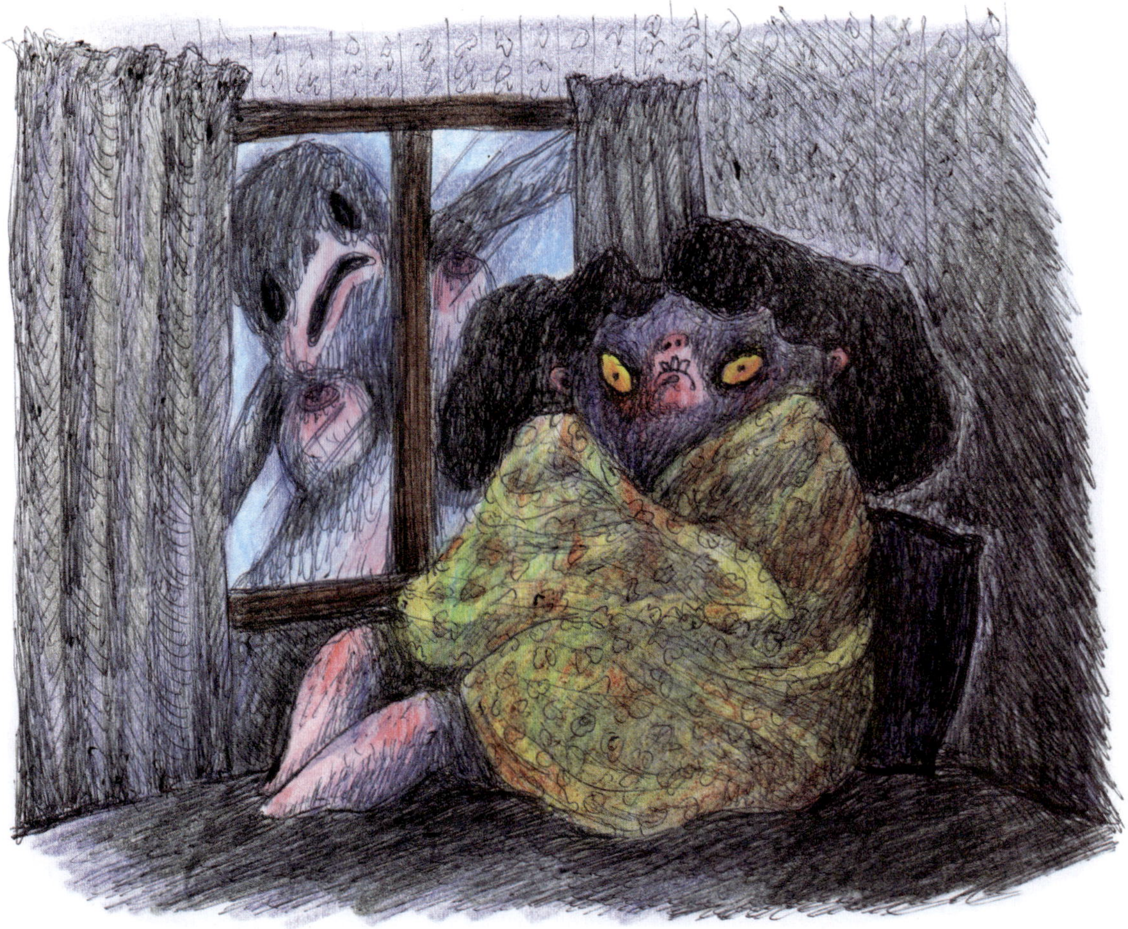

This is me not wanting to leave the house even though cool things are happening outside. Someone's rubbing their boobs on the window, that's the coolest thing I could think of, I guess. But I still don't want to leave and join the fun.

it online. It was a slow progression to characters which were much freer and more reflective of my own life. Once I progressed to full-blown scenes, the floodgates were open, and I was just drawing about me. It's still horror, because that's how I communicate, but it was all my own experiences. Once I didn't have to worry about the actual drawing anymore, it could be all about me, because it didn't have to be about me learning how to do the technical stuff anymore. There are still pieces where I'm practicing one skill or another but they are much easier and more purposeful.

At first, everything I drew was just corny or over-the-top. At least in my mind. It was hard to get over that.

So, I began infusing my personal stuff with horror so that the true meaning of the picture would be masked or softened by the absurd, morbid, gory, horrific details. Nothing I did in art school was personal, and nothing I did in art school was any good. It was all trash. The art dolls were personal to me in that they were my own creations, my own way of doing art (FINALLY!), but I don't think they were personal in that they reflected my inner turmoil. In the end I felt like I was making commodities that people wanted instead of art for expression. I was selling my soul, but I wasn't sharing the meaning of it. If I go back to making art dolls, I would want them to be different than before. I would want them to tell a story.

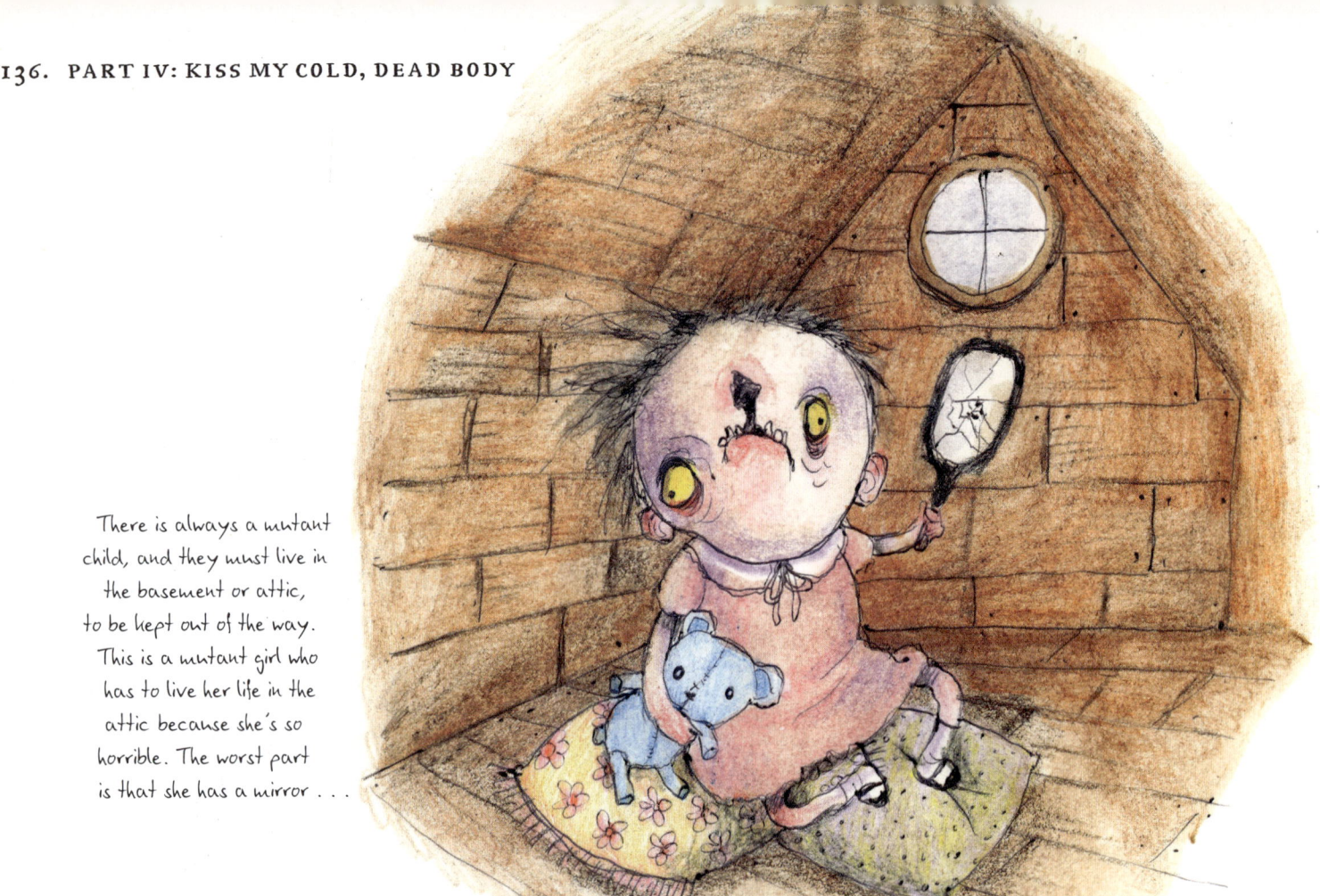

There is always a mutant
child, and they must live in
the basement or attic,
to be kept out of the way.
This is a mutant girl who
has to live her life in the
attic because she's so
horrible. The worst part
is that she has a mirror . . .

I think a turning point for me was when a friend of mine died. I dealt with it by drawing a lot, and I began drawing large-scale murals. A lot of really personal stuff came out that I wasn't even aware of until I looked back at the drawings. Horror was evident, of course. I dealt with being an adult and a parent, dealing with my parents as a parent, a lot of memories. I deal with daily issues and funny, random reflections. I deal with longstanding issues like depression or motherhood, and I also delve into my personal history from Poland or with my grandmother or being lonely as a child. If any of these images makes people laugh, then that cheers me up. I like to take something that's horrible, that's difficult to talk about, and turn it on its head or make it cute or push it to the edge, dress it in horror. Then if I talk about the drawing, it's a lot easier than talking about the horrible feelings or experiences the drawing represents.

I have a really morbid sense of humour; I probably always have. I should never go to funerals. I'm like a child. Bringing a child to a funeral is definitely asking for embarrassment. A kid is bound to say the most obvious, horrifying thing, like, "Granny smells bad."

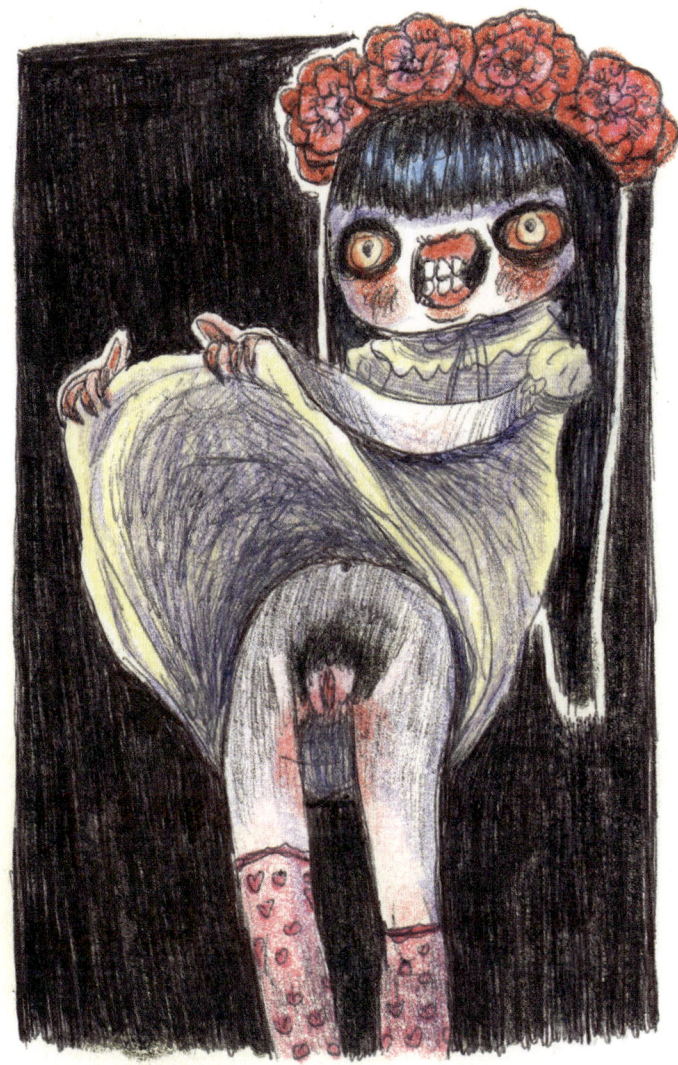

I find this image very appealing because it feels like I drew it without inhibitions. It also showcases how low my humour is: I think flashing is hilarious.

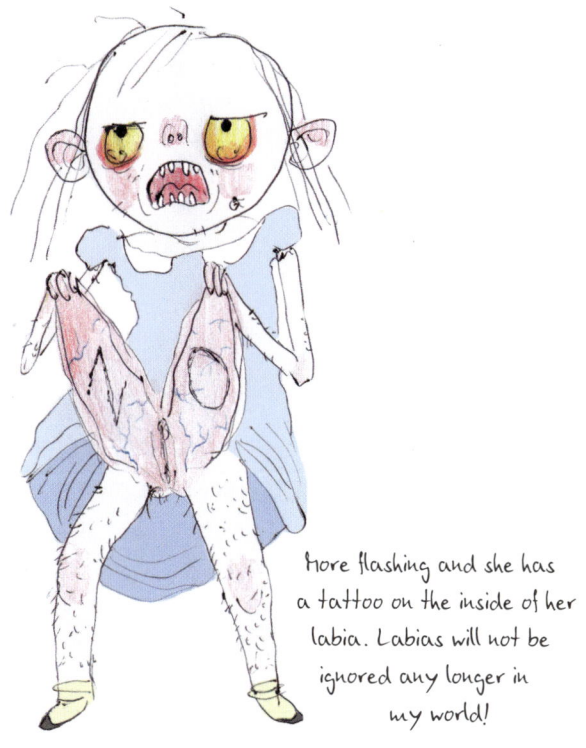

More flashing and she has a tattoo on the inside of her labia. Labias will not be ignored any longer in my world!

while the entire family is right there crying in front of the corpse. I'm going to say some inappropriate shit for sure, like, "I pity the fool who dies next." Not intentionally cruel or heartless, but to cope and as an attempt to make people laugh. A child, though, a child is so innocent and sweet, they can't be blamed. I had to go to a bunch of funerals when I was a kid. And I had to kiss the corpse. I think I had to kiss two corpses, actually. In Poland most people have open caskets, I have no idea why. I also don't worry if I can't make it to the funeral back in Poland because people take pictures of the corpse and of themselves with the corpse, like it's a tourist experience or something. So I can always look at pictures of dead relatives surrounded by flowers. I love that as a memento mori. It's sort of violent and innocent; the dead corpse surrounded by flowers is a sweet and sad image. So now I want an open casket funeral for myself. People should have to see me too, and kiss me too, surround me with flowers and remember me as a corpse. Take pictures of me and with me. I'll be a beautiful, violent-innocent corpse. My own little mother horror story. I feel like I'd be missing out if I didn't make my funeral totally depressing and morbid. I think my son will understand. I think it will give him a good backstory for the rest of his life.

There are two kinds of horror movies, good ones and cheesy ones. I think good horror movies are not actually that scary. They're not horror movies, they're intense realizations and stories about human emotion, and then there's usually a monster to make the plotline better and strengthen the symbolism. I think, when I talk about horror in my own drawings, that's what I'm trying to channel. The raw human emotion. I use horror elements to underline the intense human stuff going on in my head. Cheesy horror movies are self-explanatory. They are monster-of-the-week stuff, non-memorable, teen slasher films. If I finish a horror movie and I'm numb inside, then it was a good one that I'll be thinking about for weeks. *Hereditary,* for instance, hasn't left me yet. It was a family drama that was twisted into a horror movie and in such a brilliant way. It's the most horrifying thing that could happen. I'm into that.

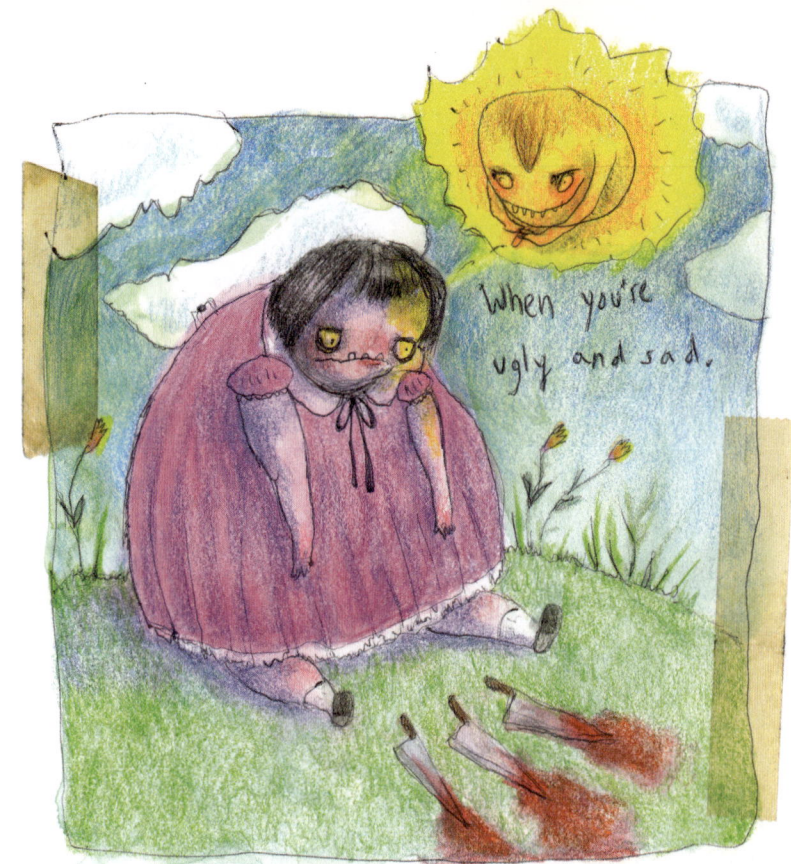

When you're ugly and sad.

This is clearly a bad day. I have an ongoing 'When you're ugly and sad . . .' theme that I use as a basis for some of my favourite self-portraits. It's absurd. It's melodramatic and when I draw it out it always puts a smile on my face. Bastard Sun pissing on me is that final cherry on top. Did I kill my enemies? Did I use a separate knife for each? I'm getting pretty darn smart since I watch twenty-four hours of murder docs a day. Now to bury them very deep, underneath an animal carcass or in a graveyard ideally. In reality, things aren't that bad. At least there's no piss in my hair, blood on my hands, and I'm probably not even that ugly anyways, probably.

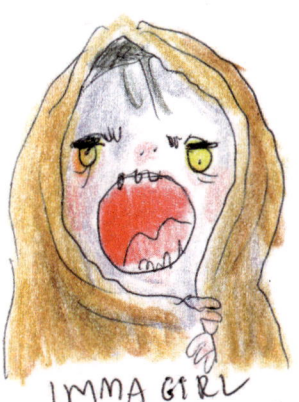

IMMA GIRL WIT A SECRET.

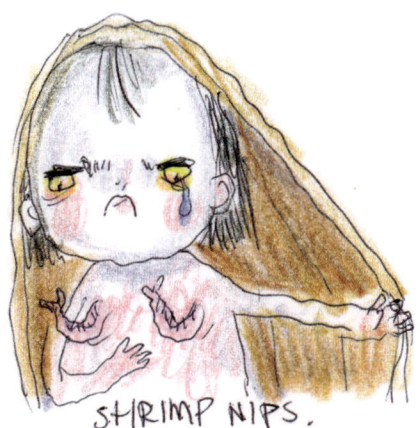

SHRIMP NIPS.

Shrimp nips. I have normal nipples. I just want to say that.
But I have an affinity for putting weird shrimps in my drawings. I've done shrimp eyes.
She has shrimp nips. I like the way that rolls off the tongue, and it's her big secret.
Her weird body is her own weird secret.

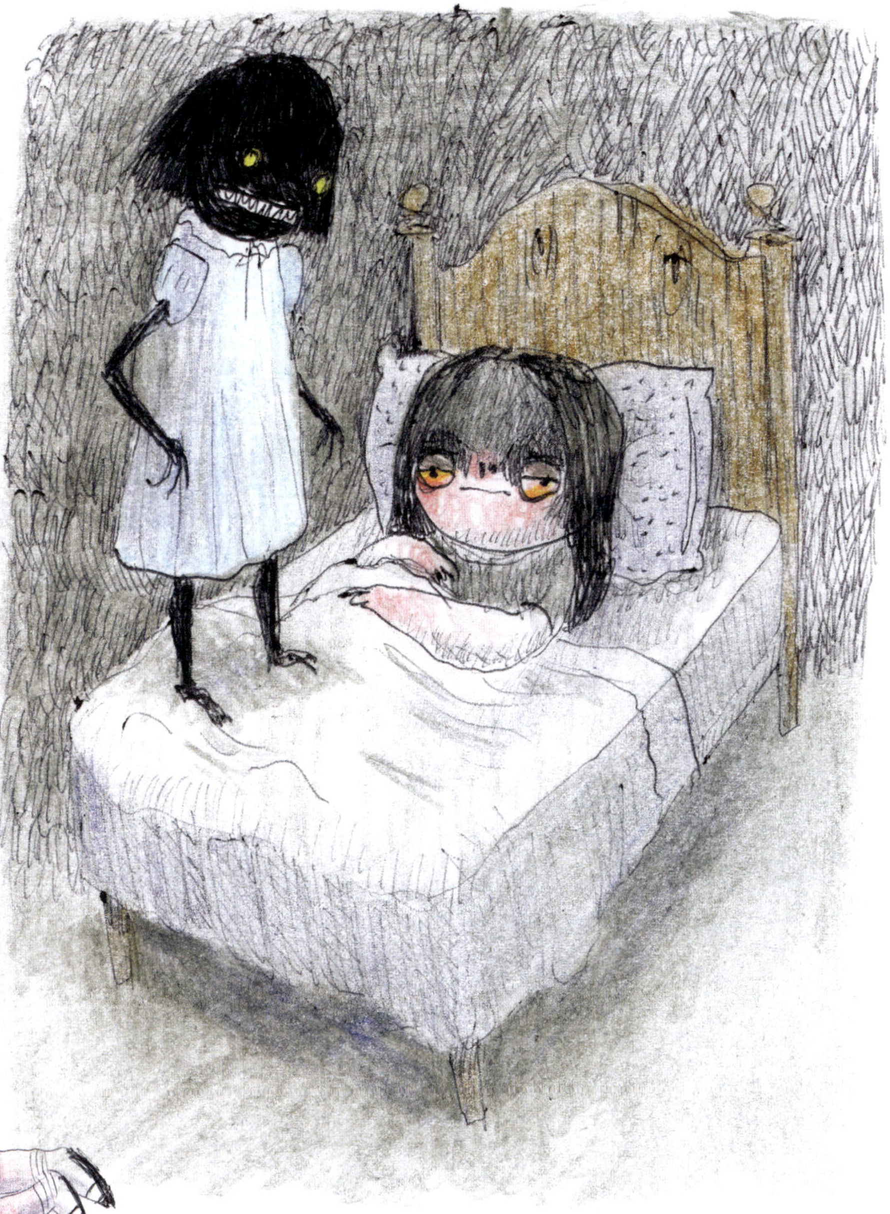

I think I was having trouble sleeping. Of course I turn insomnia into a ghoul standing on top of me as I'm trying to sleep.

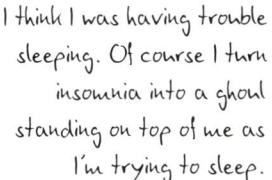

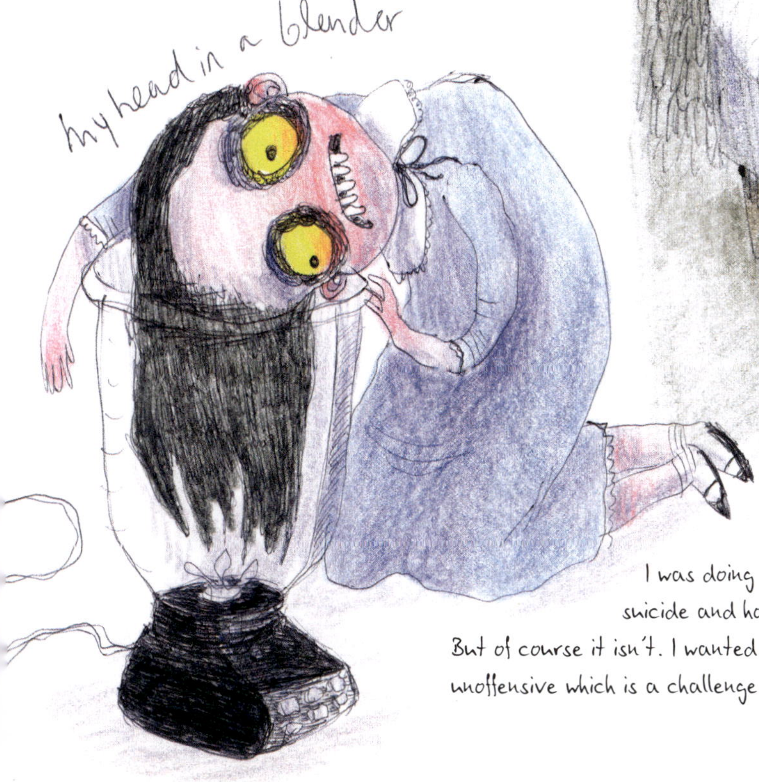

my head in a blender

I was doing a lot of suicidal pictures. I wanted to tackle suicide and how sometimes death feels like a great choice. But of course it isn't. I wanted to make it comical and simultaneously unoffensive which is a challenge. I had just gotten a new blender.
I think I succeeded.

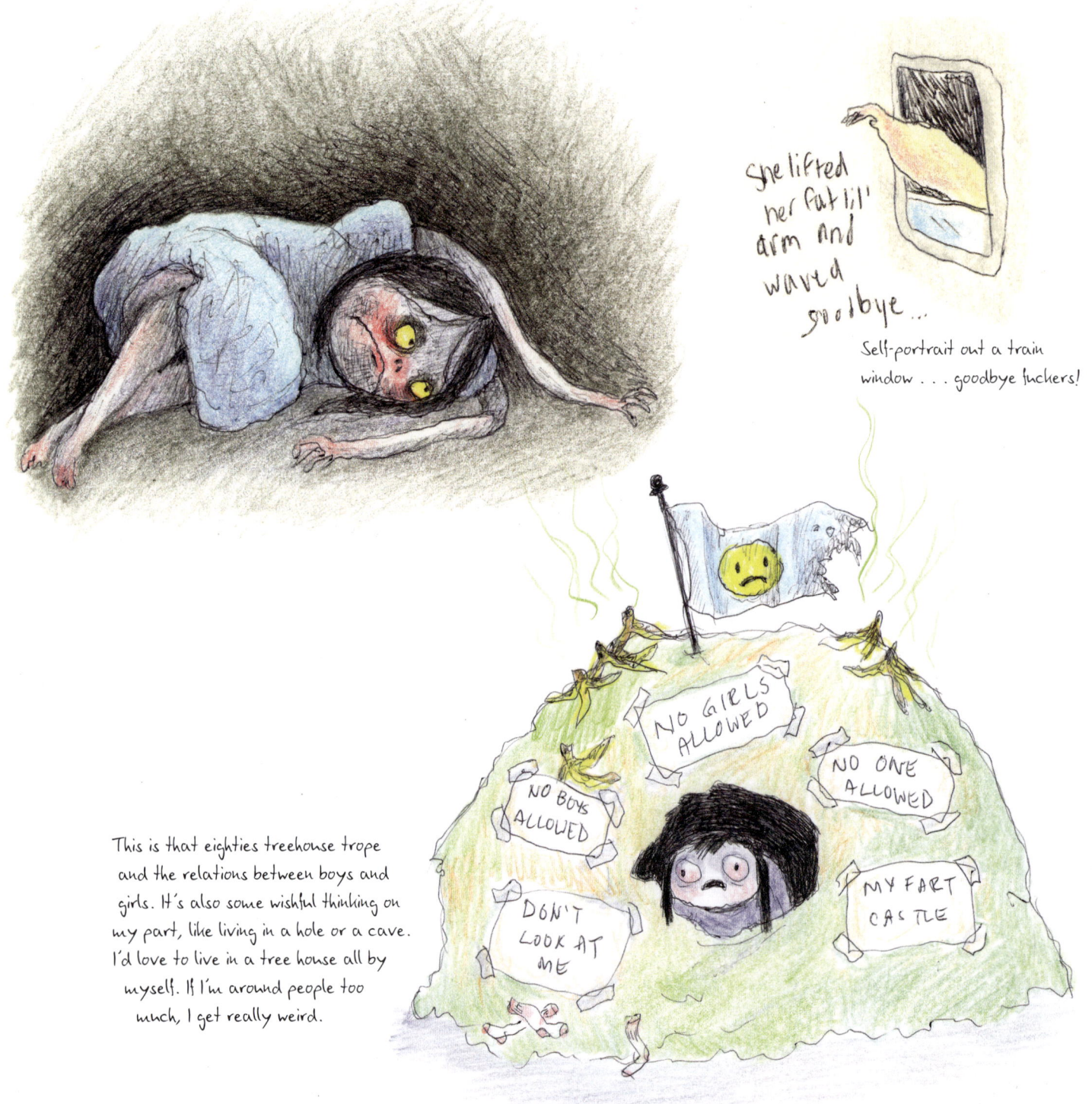

She lifted her fat lil' arm and waved goodbye...

Self-portrait out a train window . . . goodbye fuckers!

NO GIRLS ALLOWED

NO BOYS ALLOWED

NO ONE ALLOWED

DON'T LOOK AT ME

MY FART CASTLE

This is that eighties treehouse trope and the relations between boys and girls. It's also some wishful thinking on my part, like living in a hole or a cave. I'd love to live in a tree house all by myself. If I'm around people too much, I get really weird.

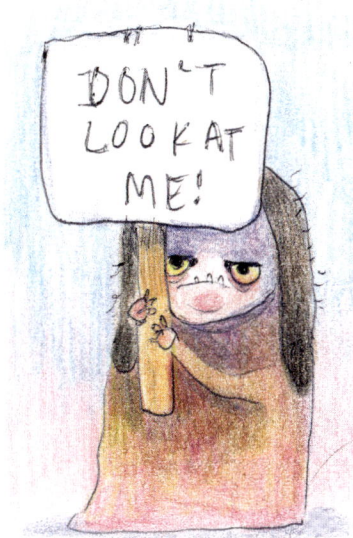

I do a lot of these, "Don't look at me," images. One time my partner told me that I have a set of catchphrases and he made a list of these horrible, depressing things that I say. It wasn't mean-spirited, it was fun, and true. At the top of the list was: "Don't look at me." Followed by, "Look at me." And, "Why are you looking at me?"

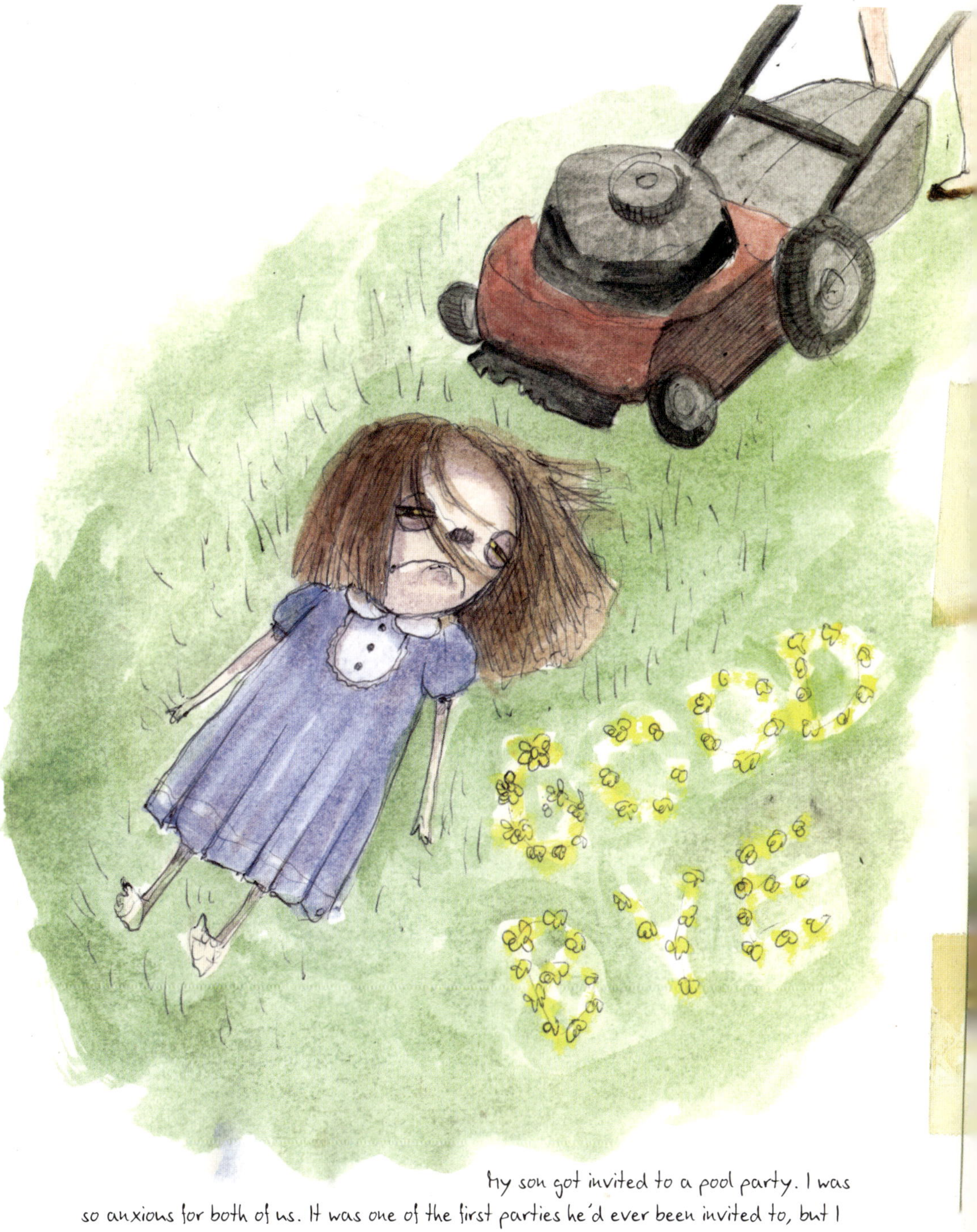

My son got invited to a pool party. I was so anxious for both of us. It was one of the first parties he'd ever been invited to, but I felt like we would both have a hard time and I dreaded the parent small talk. I scribbled this drawing down frantically right as I was leaving. It's wild how hard and fast inspiration can strike, especially at times of extreme stress. But it was a happy ending. He had a wonderful time and I didn't even have to stay. Yay!

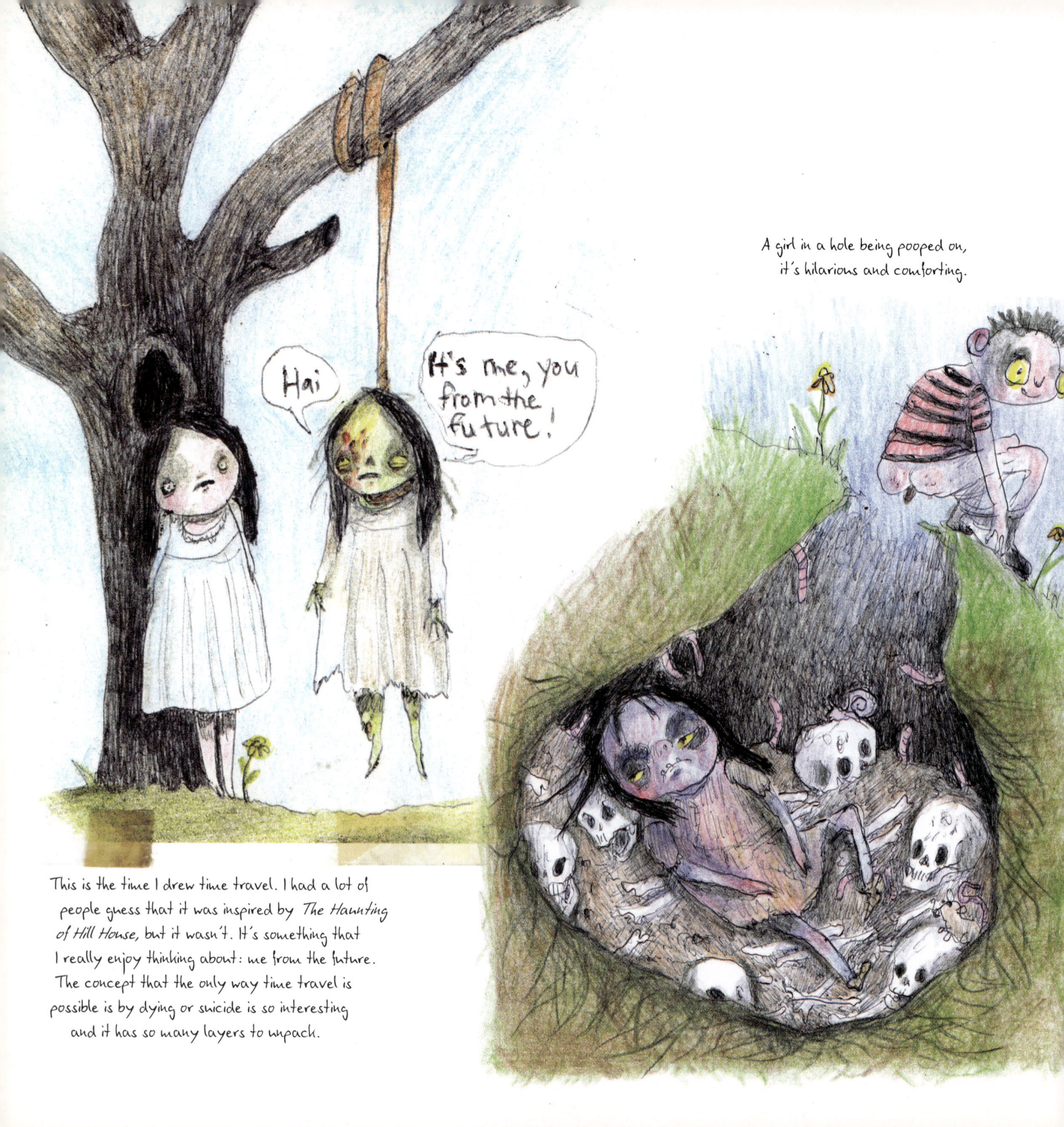

A girl in a hole being pooped on, it's hilarious and comforting.

> Hai

> It's me, you from the future!

This is the time I drew time travel. I had a lot of people guess that it was inspired by *The Haunting of Hill House*, but it wasn't. It's something that I really enjoy thinking about: me from the future. The concept that the only way time travel is possible is by dying or suicide is so interesting and it has so many layers to unpack.

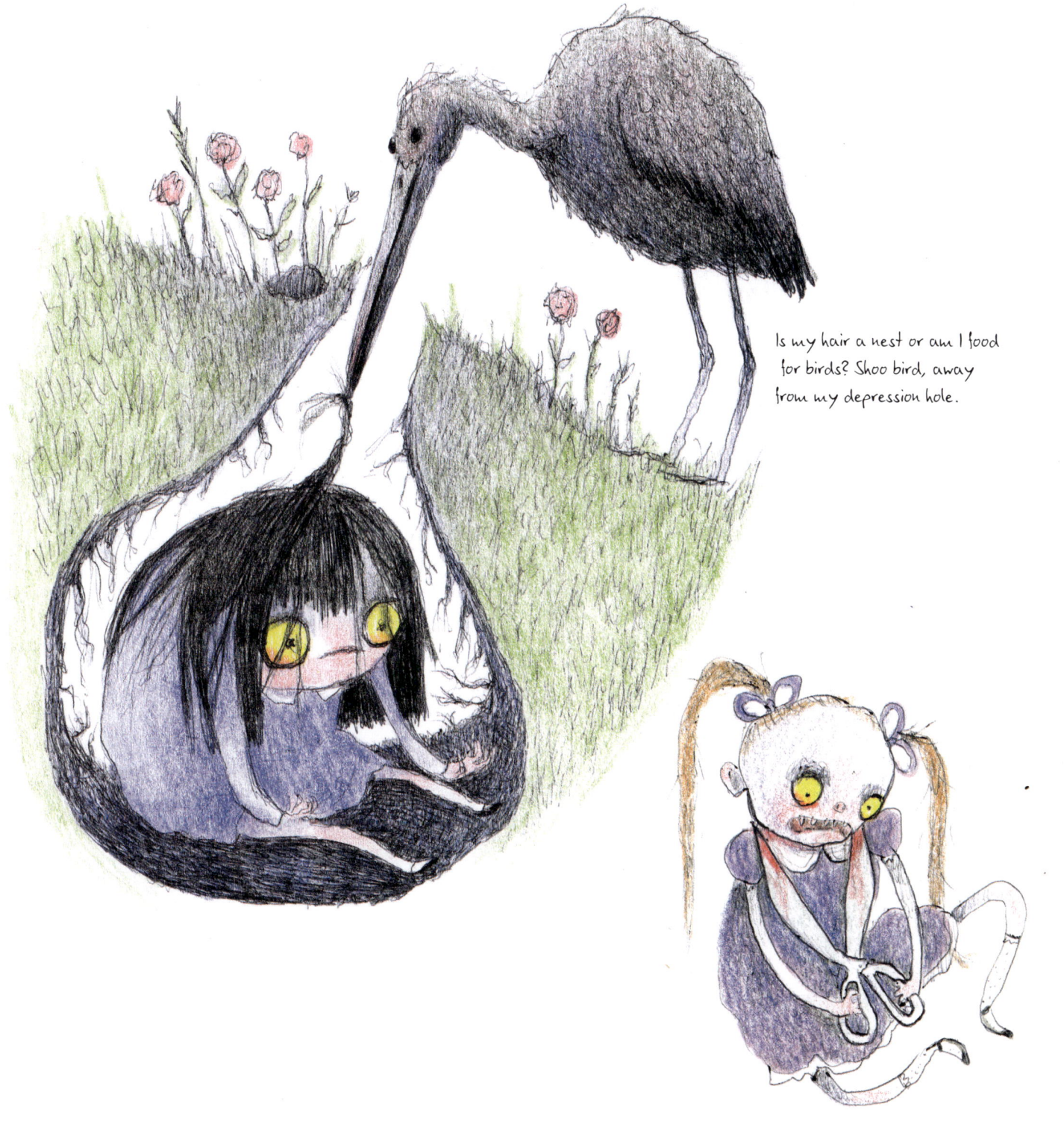

Is my hair a nest or am I food
for birds? Shoo bird, away
from my depression hole.

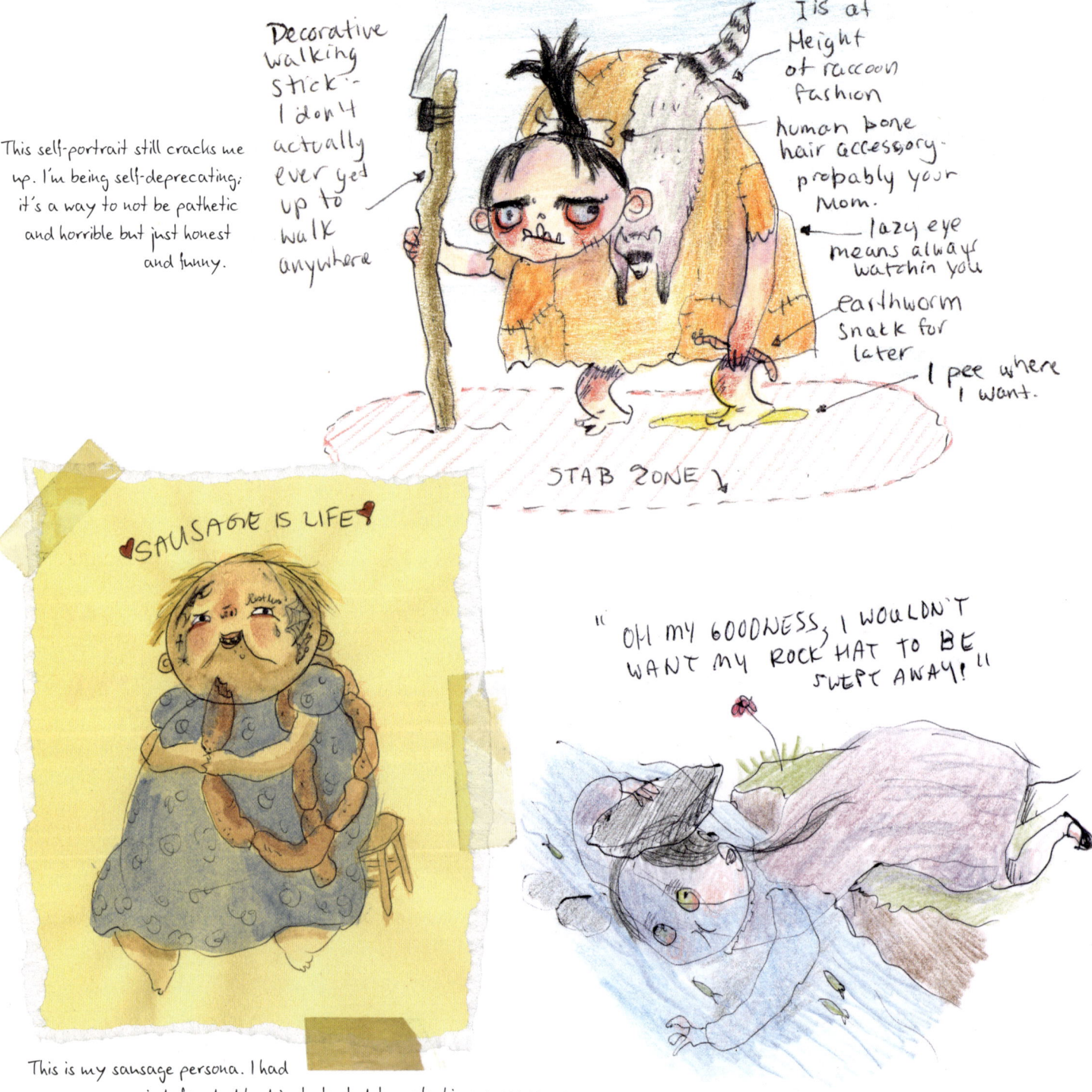

This self-portrait still cracks me up. I'm being self-deprecating; it's a way to not be pathetic and horrible but just honest and funny.

Decorative walking stick - I don't actually ever get up to walk anywhere

I is at Height of raccoon fashion

human bone hair accessory. probably your Mom.

lazy eye means always watchin you

earthworm snack for later

I pee where I want.

STAB ZONE

♥ SAUSAGE IS LIFE ♥

" OH MY GOODNESS, I WOULDN'T WANT MY ROCK HAT TO BE SWEPT AWAY! "

This is my sausage persona. I had sausage on my mind. My dad had just started to make his own sausages. Guess it's sad that somebody would eat this much sausage . . .

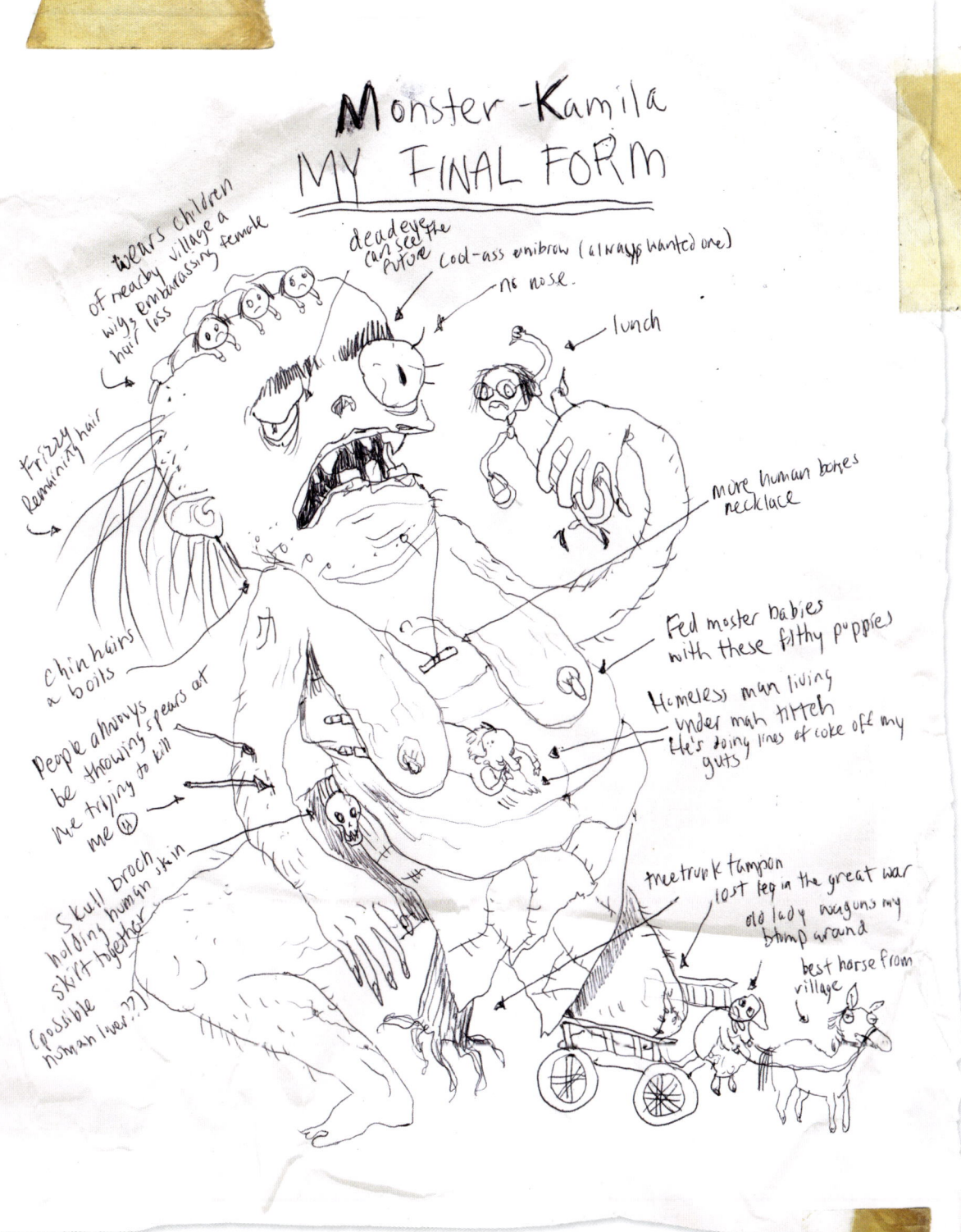

Sometimes it isn't enough to draw the worst thing imaginable. Sometimes I have to one-up myself and draw ridiculous things. This is me in my monster form. I lost a leg in the Great War and an old horse and cart drags my stump around. This is the best horse from the village, and there's a tree trunk tampon that I use. This is a homeless man living under my titty. He's doing lines of coke off my gut. I feed my monster babies with these filthy puppies. Human bone necklace. My lunch is a sacrificial girl. Chin hairs, of course.

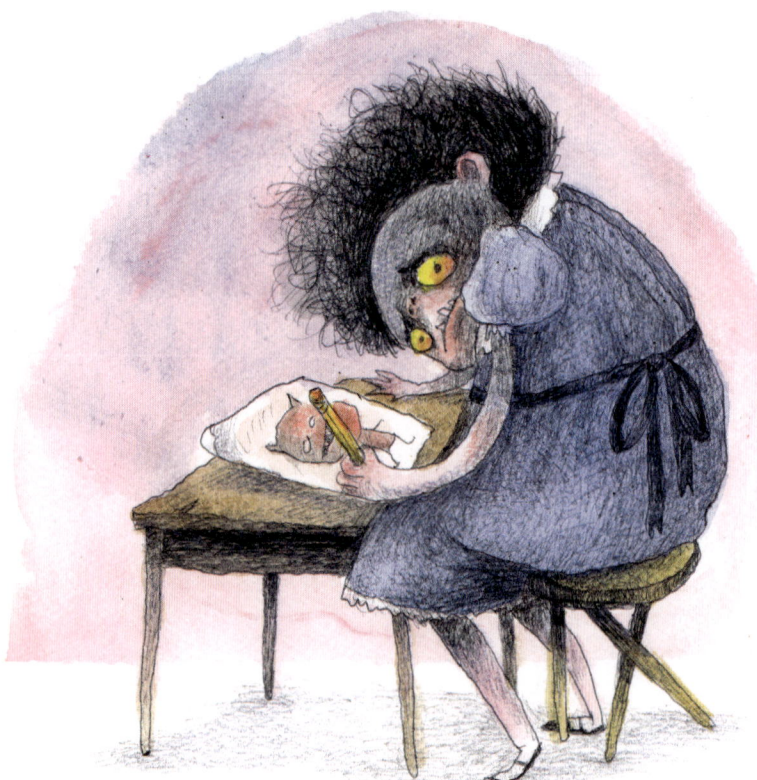

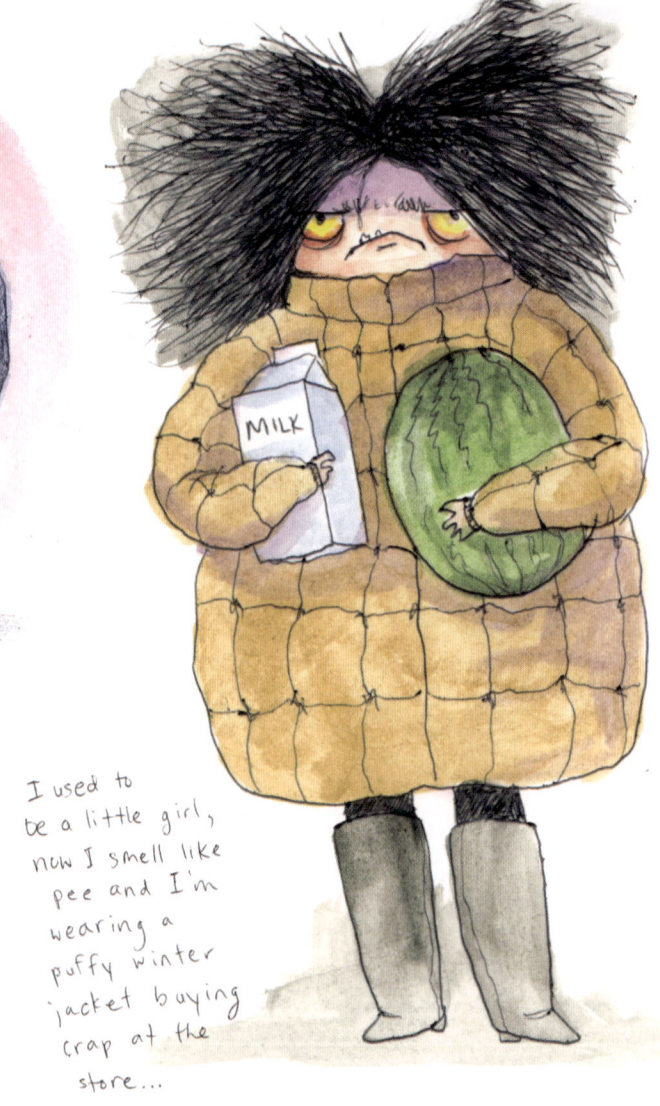

Again, this is a self-portrait.

I actually have a picture that this was based on.

When we first came to Canada, I was living at my great aunt's house with my Dad; my mom was in Chicago and joined us later. It was an old lady's house. There was T.V., but they were only watching *Wheel of Fortune* all the time. There were books, and one bookshelf filled with *The Far Side* and *Garfield*. Aside from that, I was just drawing. I had a little chair in the living room that I would draw in, and I remember the day my mum was supposed to come back. I was drawing. Everything was punctuated by me drawing quietly at my table. She was going to come back that afternoon and I remember thinking, "I'm going to kiss every part of her. I'm so excited to see her." I was only four years old or something, but then when I saw her, I froze. It had been over a year, and she seemed like a stranger to me, but I loved her so much. I just drew.

I used to be a little girl, now I smell like pee and I'm wearing a puffy winter jacket buying crap at the store...

I was miserable. I had just gotten a puffy winter jacket, because even though they are hideous, they are honestly warm. But I hate it. I had told myself I was too cool to ever have a puffy winter jacket, having it made me feel like a mom, like I had no other identity but "mom in a puffy jacket." I went to the store to buy milk and a watermelon and it was horrible. I was no one, just a miserable mom in puffy mom-jacket.

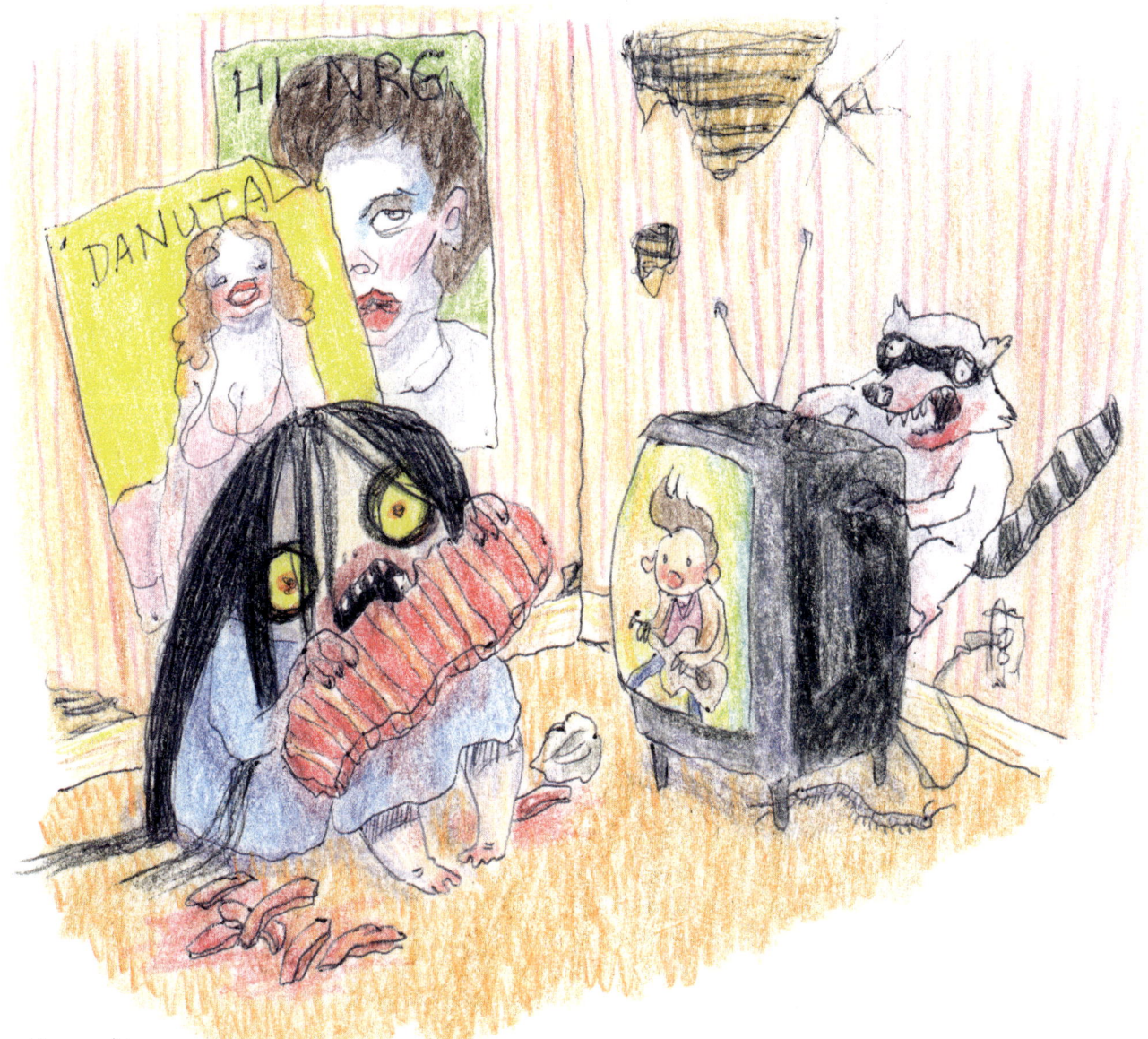

I have a thing
    for really bad
  eighties music. It's what I want playing at my open-casket, flower-filled, funeral. So again, I had a bad day, and I was really
  hungry for ribs because my taste buds had changed and all I was craving was meat. I'm beginning to exist only in the universe
    of my drawings. I just want to hunt and eat meat-things. This is me watching videos on an old eighties T.V. set. I'm trying
      to recapture my childhood, watching the 'High Energy' music video by Evelyn Thomas, "Boys, Boys, Boys" by Sabrina, or
      anything Danuta, who's originally Polish. So much hair and make-up, and so incredibly exposed. It's delightful to watch these
        really bad videos; they make me laugh. They're gold.

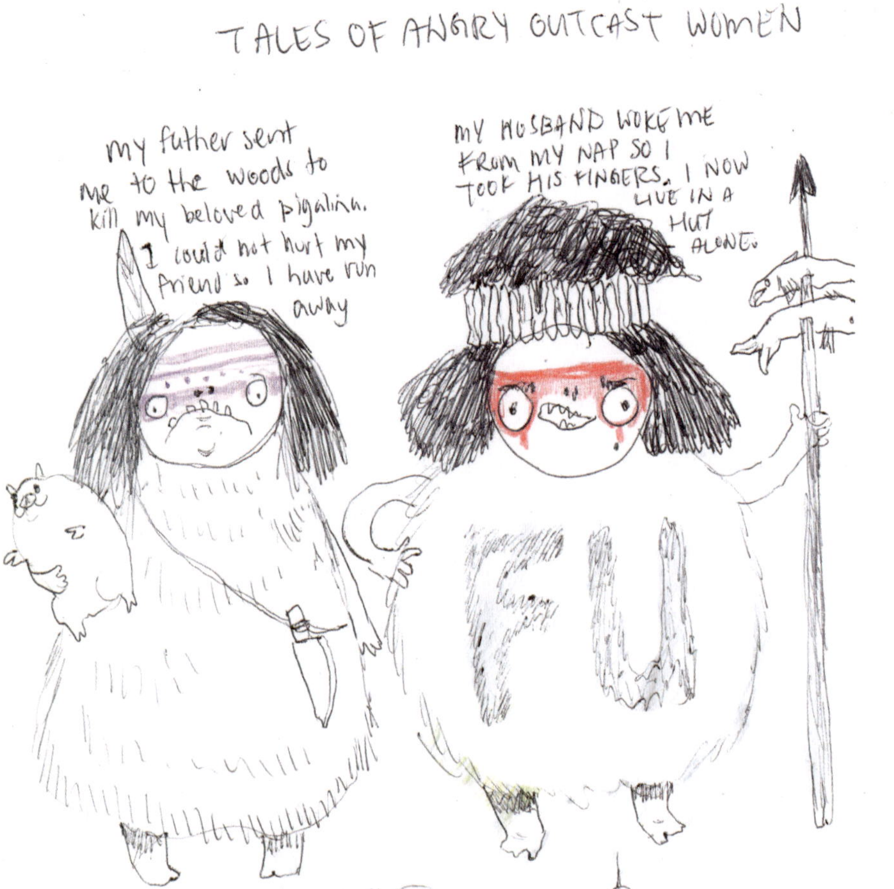

TALES OF ANGRY OUTCAST WOMEN

my father sent me to the woods to kill my beloved pigalinn. I could not hurt my friend so I have run away

MY HUSBAND WOKE ME FROM MY NAP SO I TOOK HIS FINGERS. I NOW LIVE IN A HUT ALONE.

FU

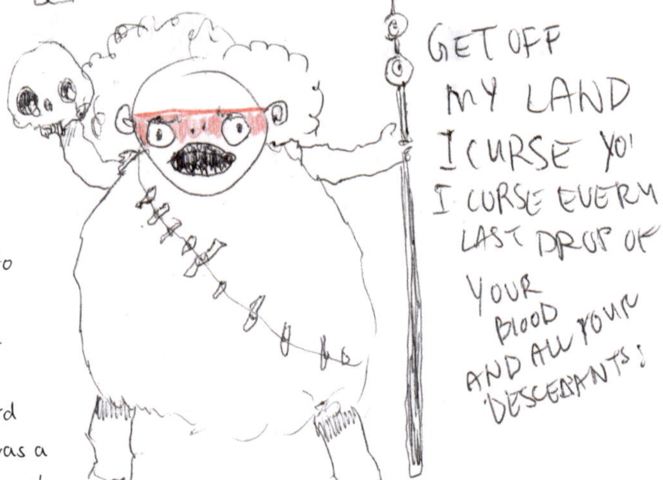

This is one of my 'wild women.' These are women who've gone off into the forest to drink themselves into a stupor. They've decided to abandon society and hunt animals and be weird by themselves. It was a fantasy of mine, even when I was a kid, to live like a hermit in the forest. Of course, I don't actually want to be bitten by mosquitoes and do anything for myself, but it's a nice daydream. This is a bunch of little characters that were tribeswomen of the same tribe of angry women.

GET OFF MY LAND I CURSE YO! I CURSE EVERY LAST DROP OF YOUR BLOOD AND ALL YOUR DESCENDANTS!

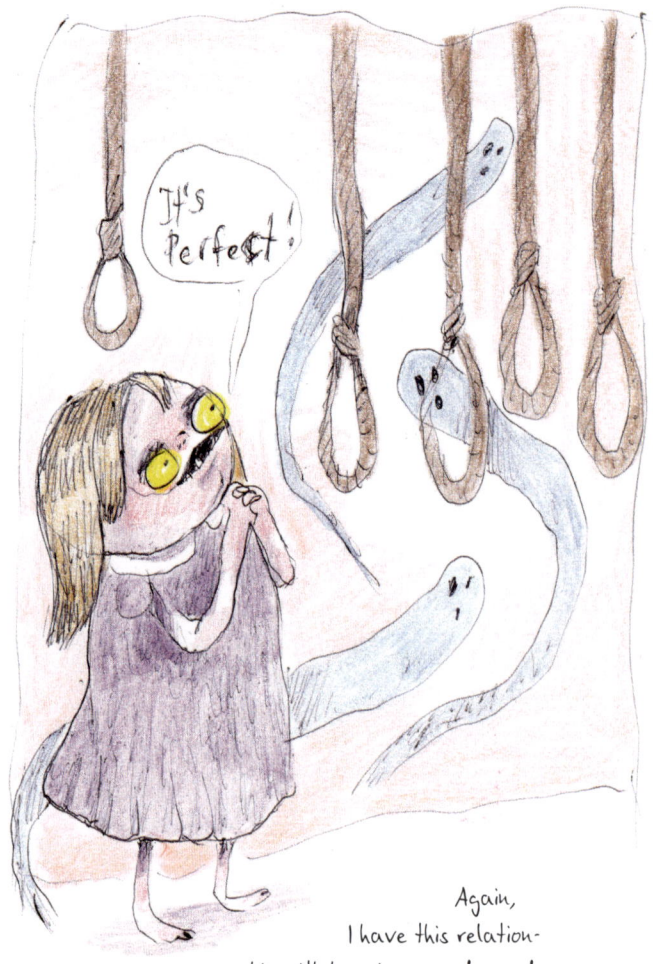

It's Perfect!

Again, I have this relationship with hanging as a form of suicide. A fixation for nooses. It's such an effective form of suicide and a lot of people choose it when they really, actually, want to die. I know that it's very dark of me to be researching this as my subject, but for me it's a kind of release. We never ever talk about the suicides that have happened in my family, which were by hanging. We never talk about suicidal thoughts. We barely talk about emotions at all. I'm not grieving, exactly. It's like there's a part of myself that's still a very curious child about it all and since I can't discuss it in a safe space, I draw it out in the open.

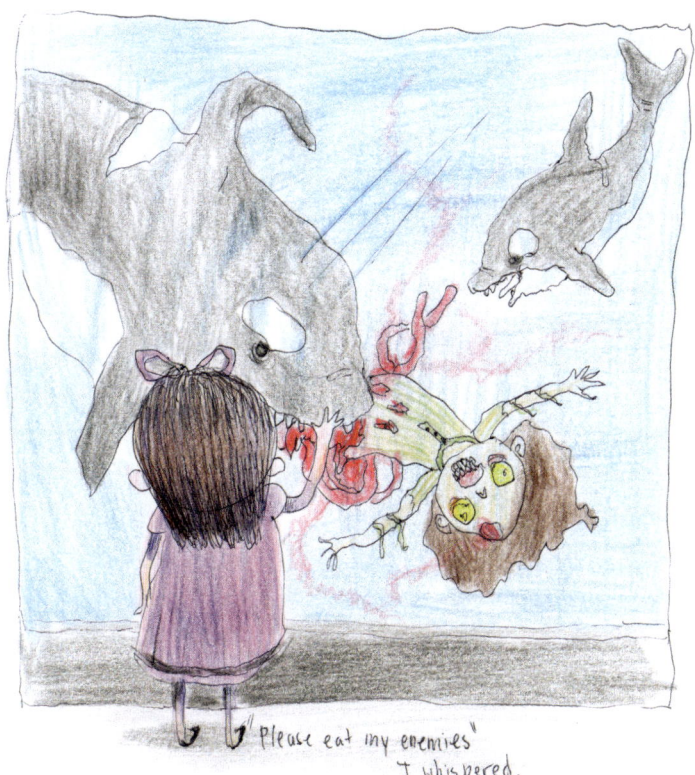

"Please eat my enemies"
I whispered.

This is that moment when the estrangement between the self and the rest of society is obvious. I looked up old friends on social media and saw that they were normal and happy, and that threw me into a funk. I hated everyone. And then I thought, 'What's a fun way to kill your friends, where it doesn't look like you're really disturbed to the public?' It's a realizing of impotent rage.

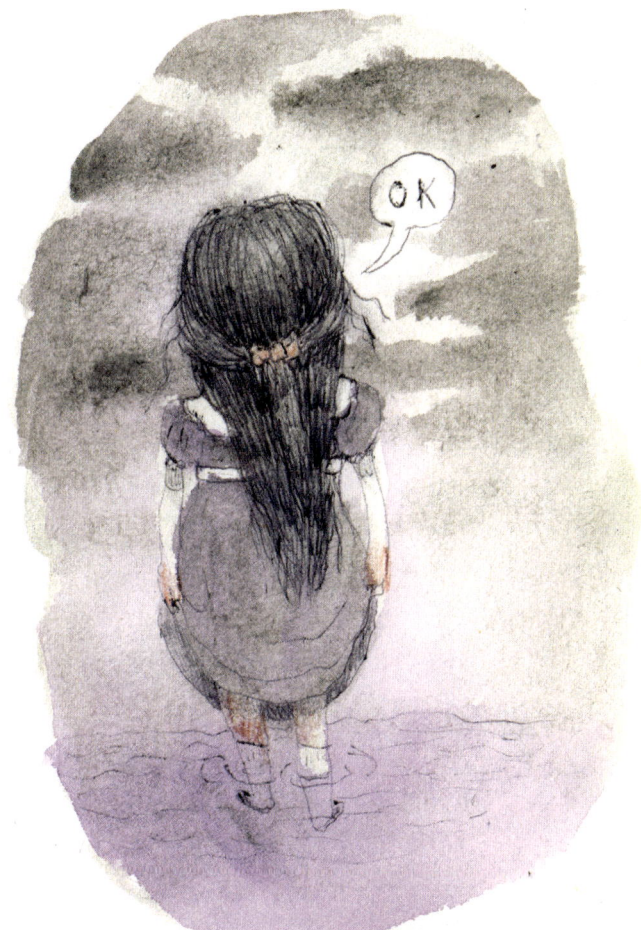

OK

I'm very tired. I have a full time job hating myself

I was annoyed at myself because I had a fight with someone, and the last thing I said was, "Okay." I didn't solve the issue, I gave in, and walked away. I hate that feeling.

Momentary sad feelings coupled with imposter syndrome. I think the biggest secret in the arts is that everyone feels like they're just copying everyone else. When an artist that I admire likes my work, at first, I'm flattered, and then I get really scared and think, "Oh my God, am I pulling something over on them? Are they confused? Why do they like my work?" I start to feel guilty that I have somehow tricked all the normal people. I think I was also thinking about all the normal people and wondering if I should get a normal job instead of being a weird, depressive artist that overshares.

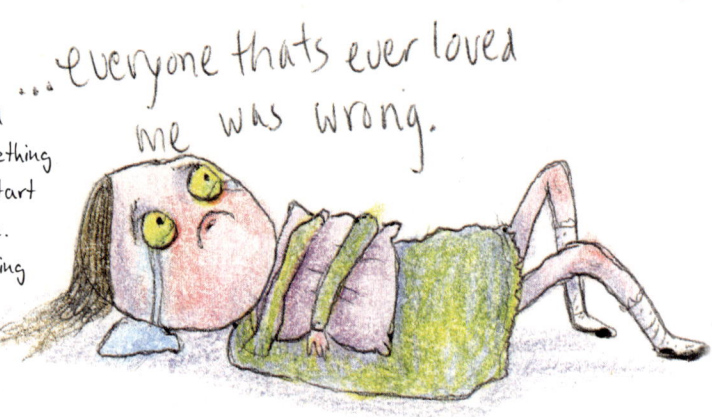

...everyone thats ever loved me was wrong.

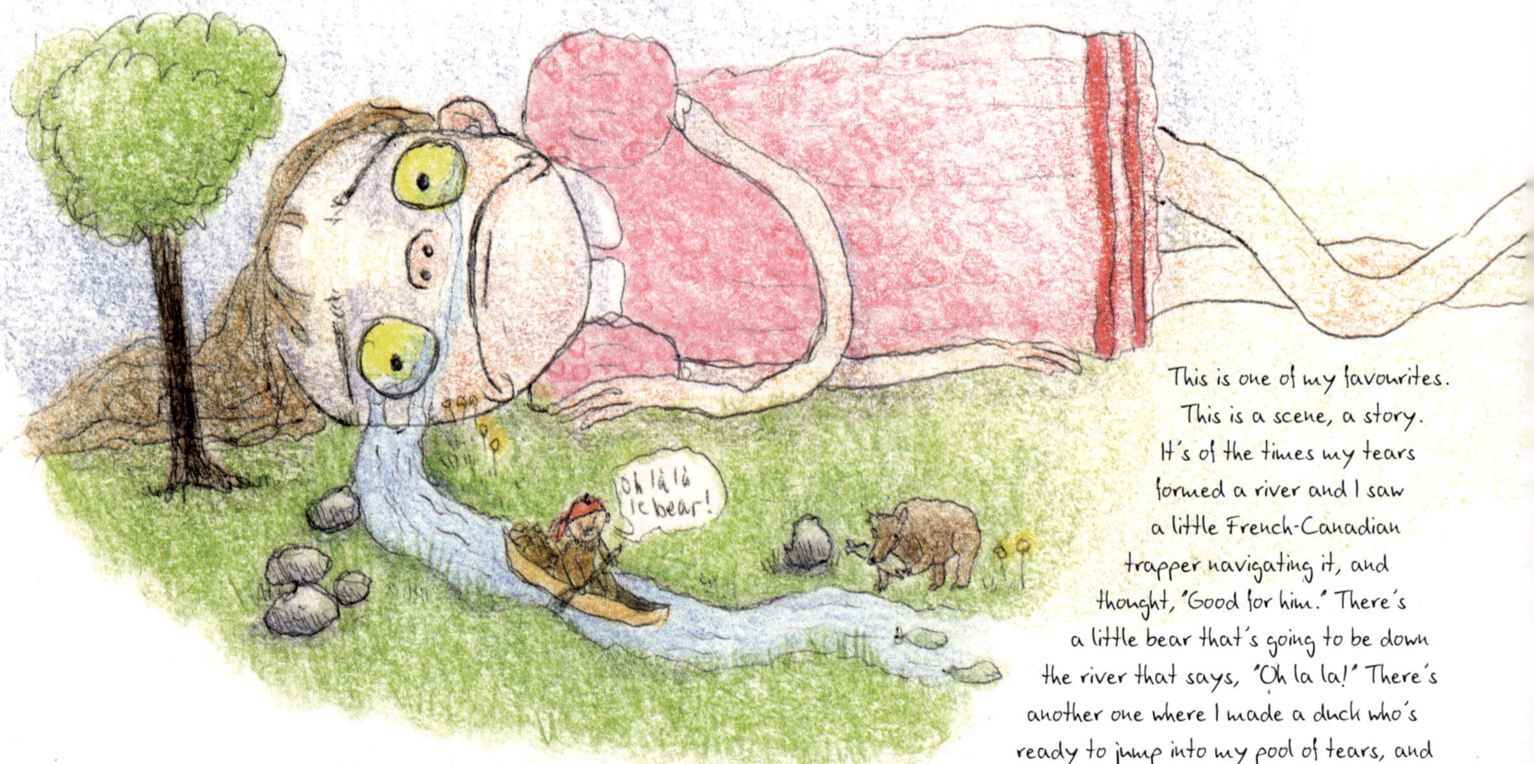

Oh là là le bear!

This is one of my favourites. This is a scene, a story. It's of the times my tears formed a river and I saw a little French-Canadian trapper navigating it, and thought, "Good for him." There's a little bear that's going to be down the river that says, "Oh la la!" There's another one where I made a duck who's ready to jump into my pool of tears, and it's saying, "Always be making habitats."

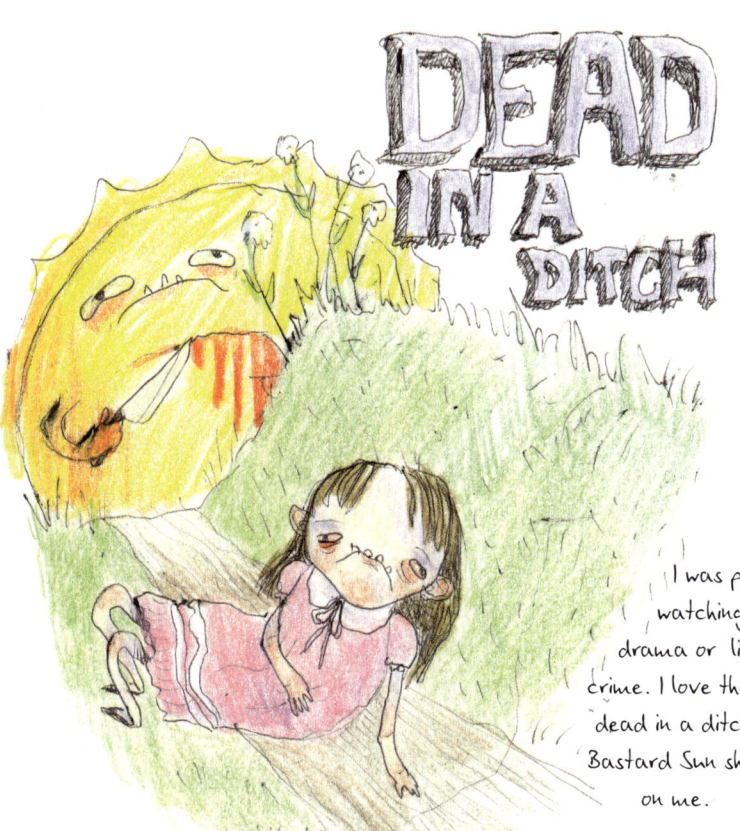

I was probably watching a crime drama or listening to true crime. I love that stuff. I'm dead in a ditch with that Bastard Sun shining down on me.

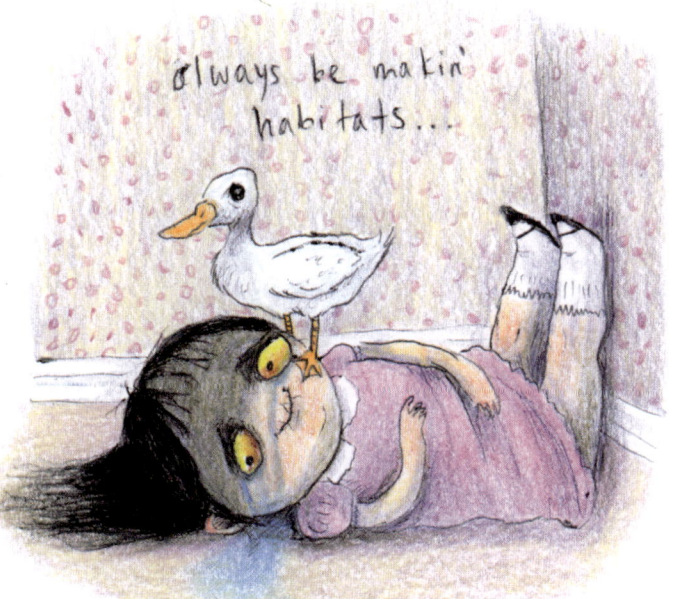

always be makin' habitats...

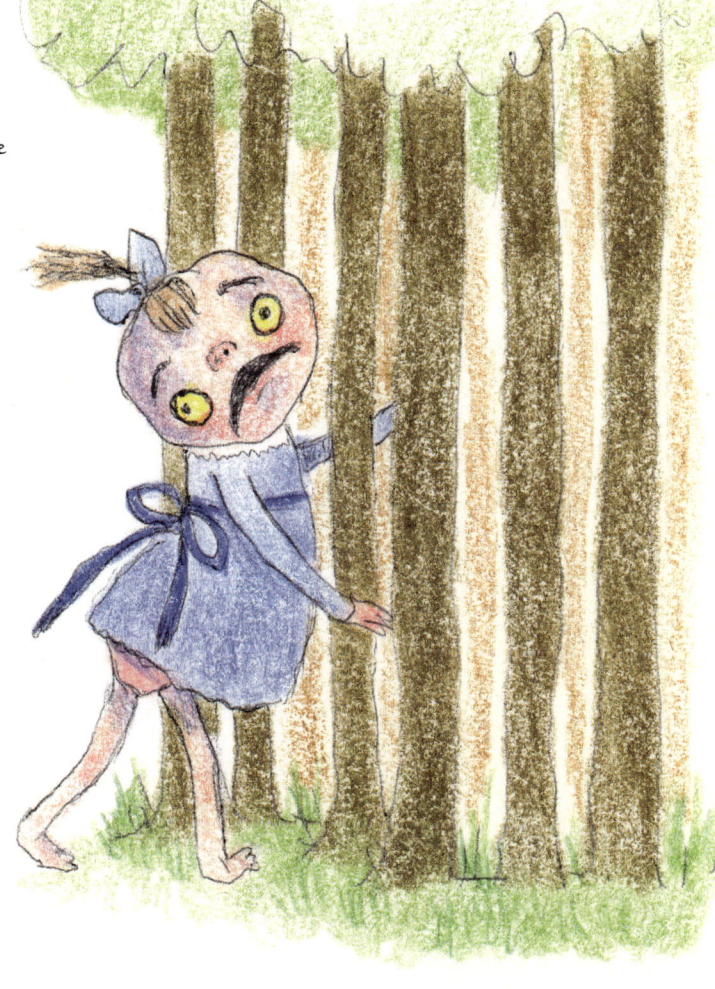

Oh hey... I didn't see you there. I have to go into the woods and die now...

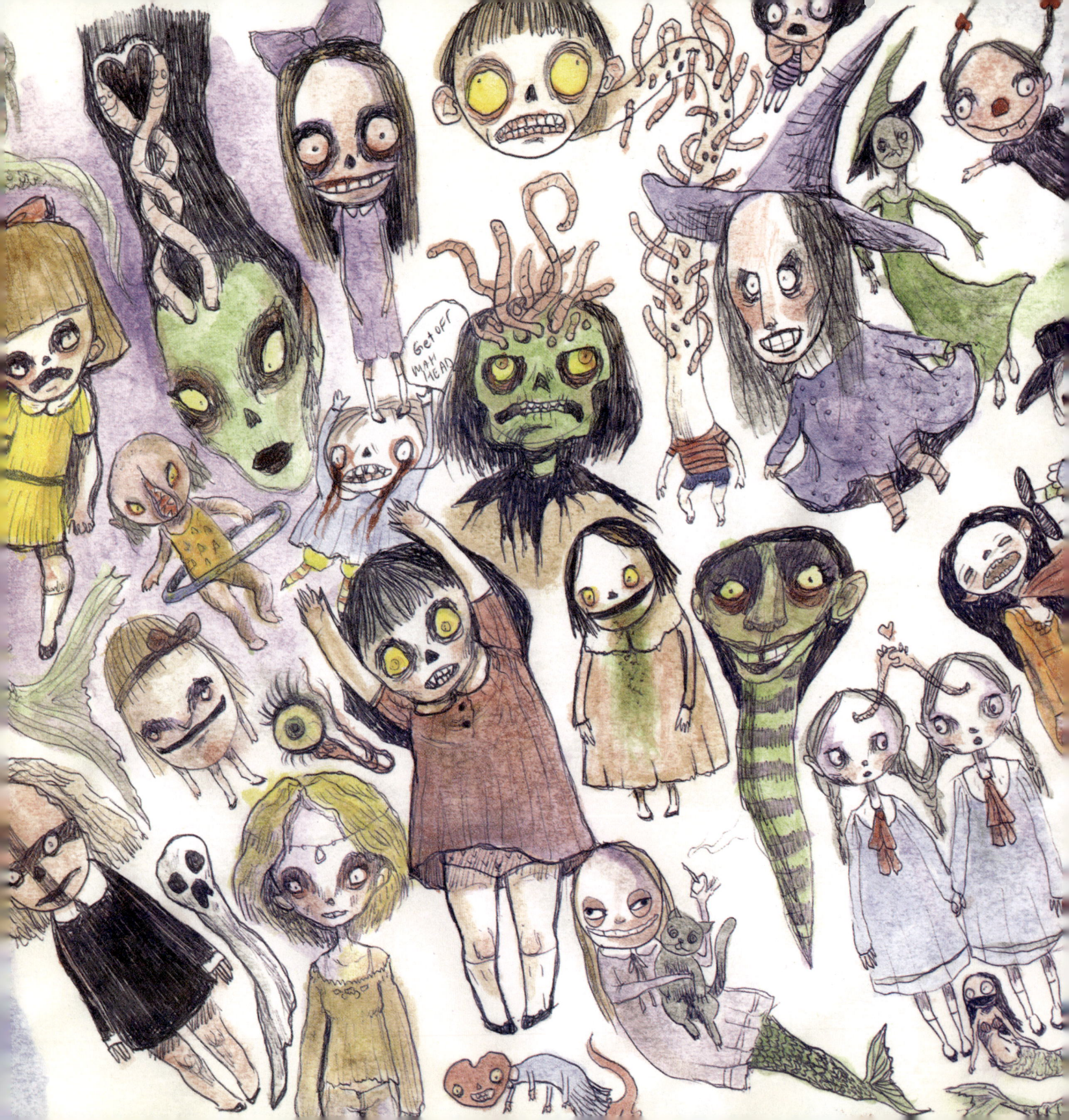

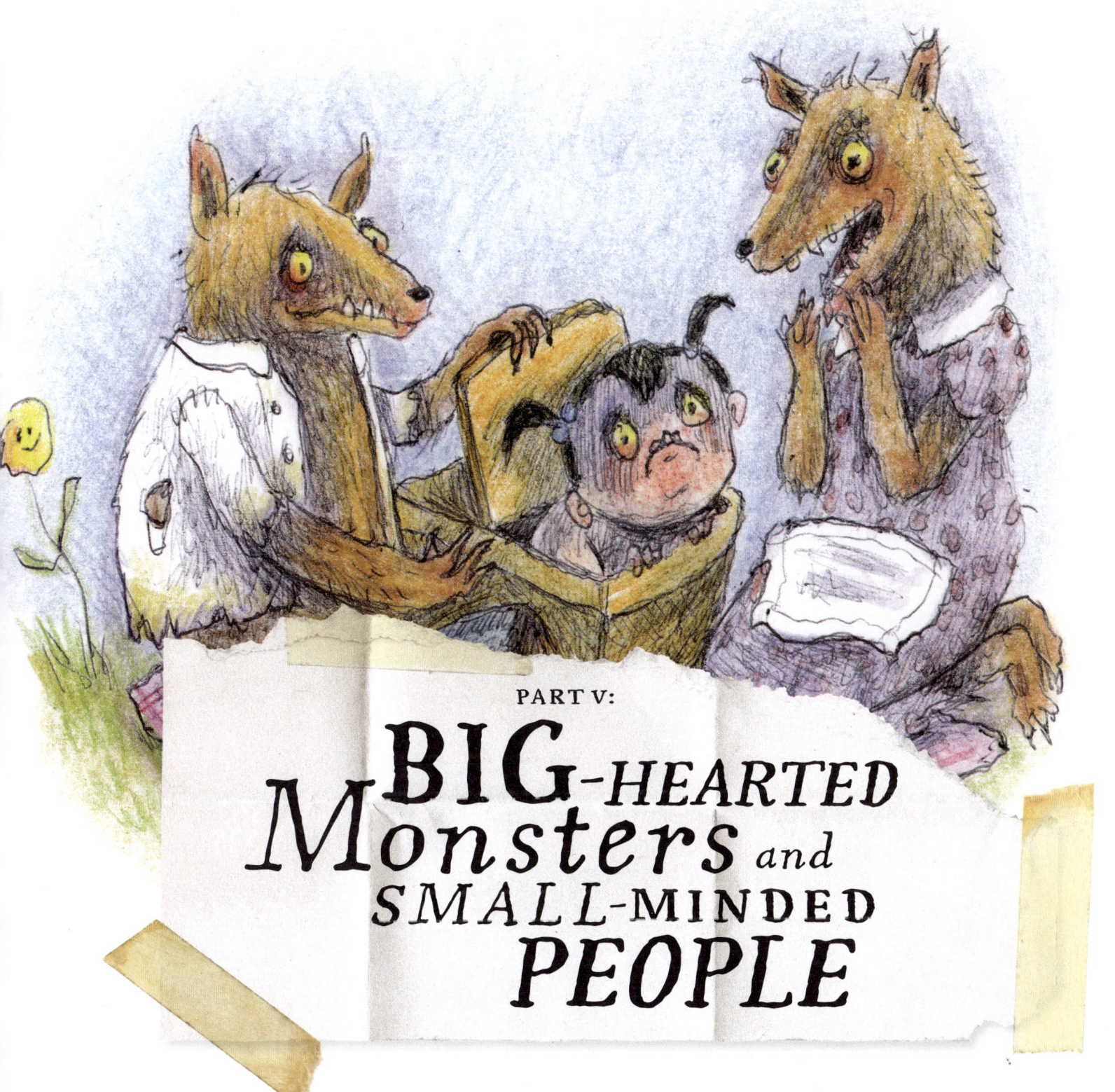

PART V:

BIG-HEARTED Monsters and SMALL-MINDED PEOPLE

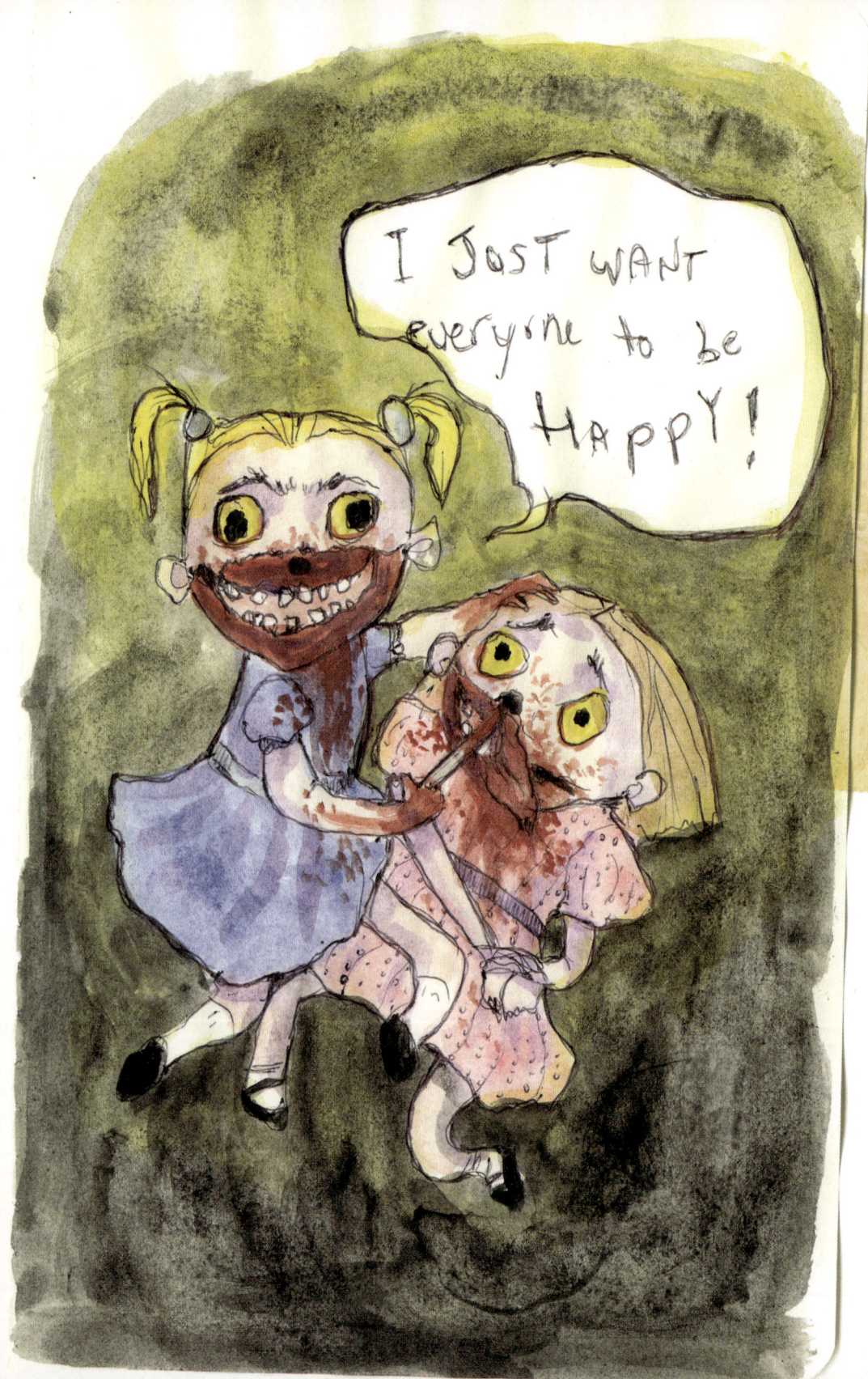

'We're all smiling under our skin.'
This phrase cheers me up, just
knowing that by pure biology we're
always smiling. I drew this murderous
girl, who carved the skin off the lower
half of her face. She does it to
everybody, to make them happy.
She thinks she's doing good. She is
violent-innocence. She has a sweet
misunderstanding and then some
violence and horror comes about
  because of it.

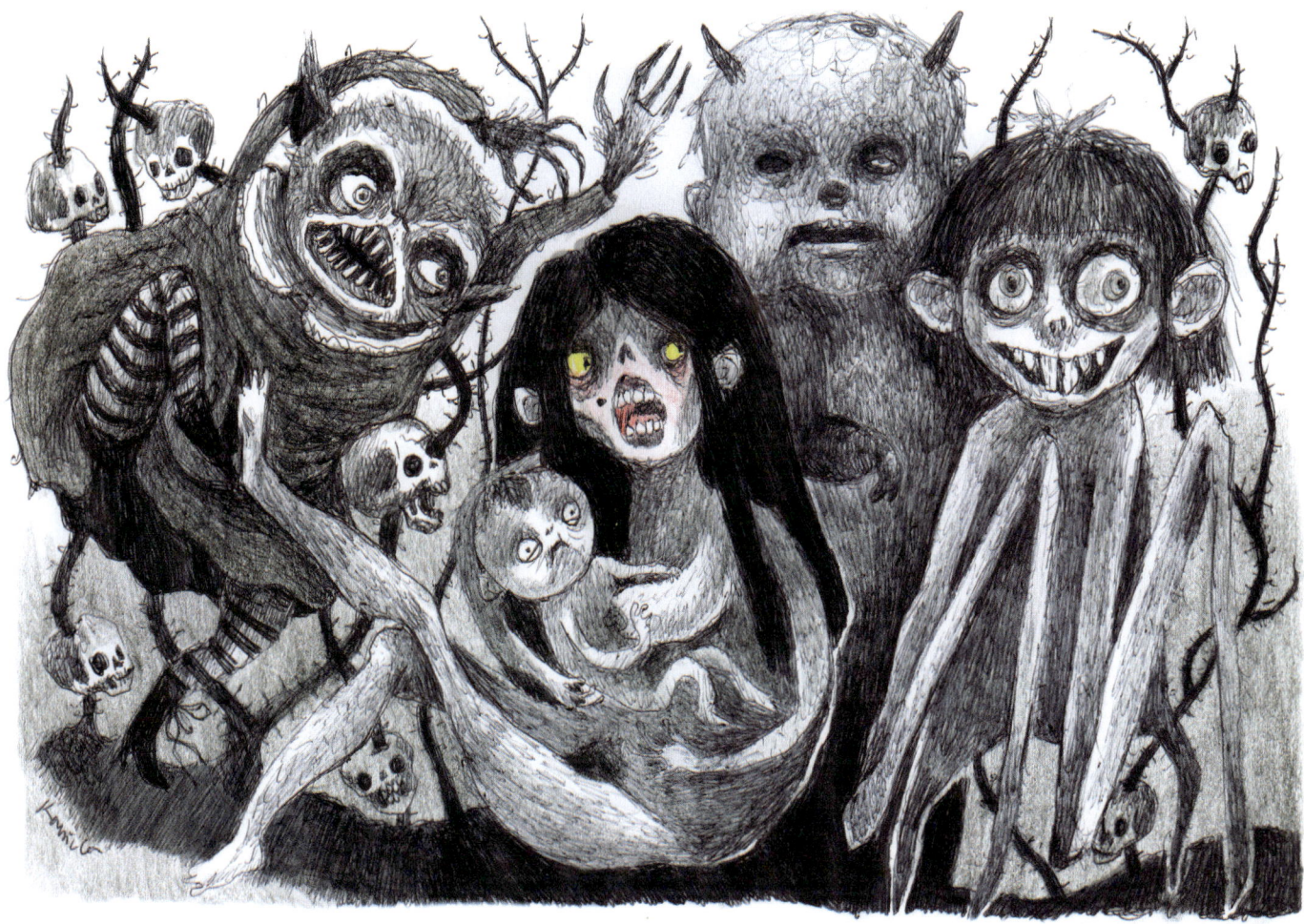

WHEN I STARTED DRAWING AGAIN, I HAD THIS bad habit of either drawing collages or one-off characters. I wasn't making sense or telling stories. These drawings are more evolved. They are stylized takes on the themes, preoccupations, and characters from the earlier drawings. There are gentle beasts, babies being eaten, mother child love, creatures and people covered in hair, and little helper-creatures like moths and snails and spiders. There is a theme of violent-innocence for sure, because all of the violence being done in these scenes is seemingly innocent, not necessarily ill-intentioned, and sort of absurd. It's my mischief and my way of portraying everything in a sentimental light. It's all very playful.

There are three different worlds that have started to take shape in my mind and on the paper over time: underground, garbage people land, and Audri world. I think these worlds were distinct for a long time, but the aesthetic of them all is starting to bleed together. I recently put Audri into the garbage world, she found a dumpster, and started crawling down into it and found a little girl buried there. I think I'm exploring and building a whole universe. The underground people

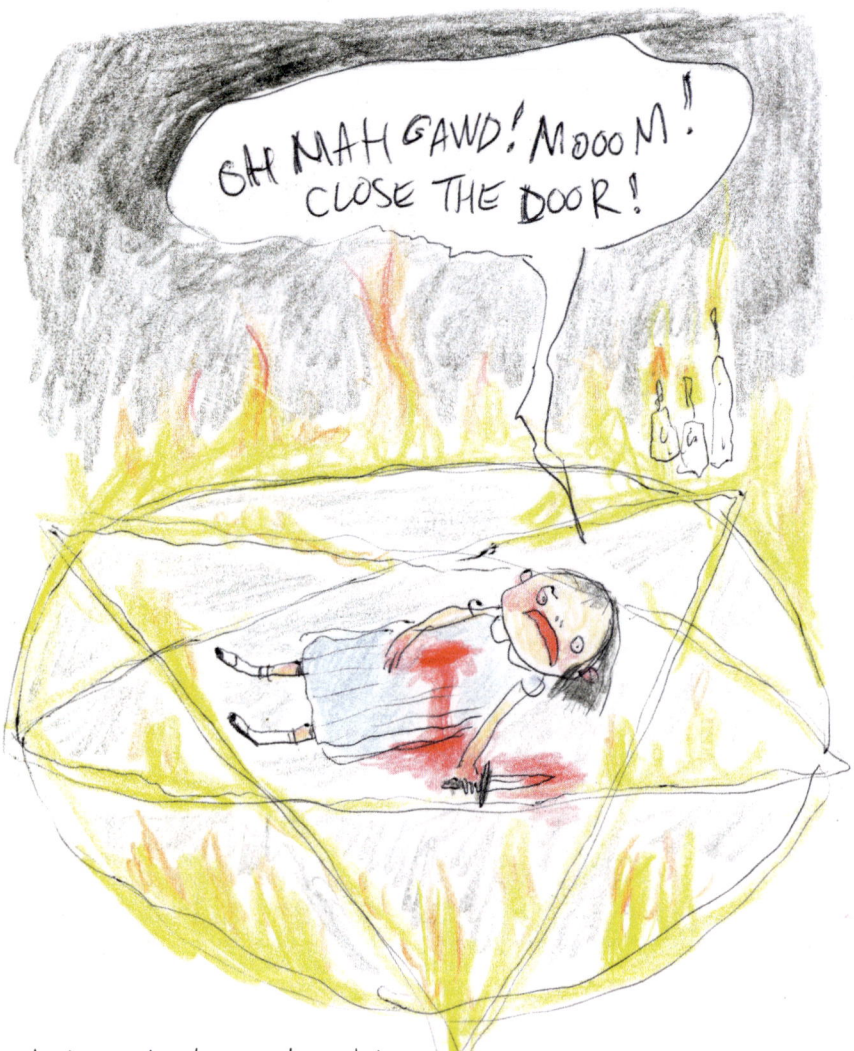

I enjoy movies where people are being sacrificed in the middle of a pentagram. Except I thought it would be funny if she was sacrificing herself, and then her mum walked in on her. I didn't have privacy as a child, there was no knocking, my mom would just walk in and whatever I was doing was judged and interrupted. It's funny, looking back on it, but I'm sure it might have been traumatic.

don't begin in the underground. They are placed there by mothers or climb down into it by choice. They survive on worms and have creature comforts like pee bottles, pillows, and worm friends, and they are generally happy underground children. Garbage people land is a little sketchier and scarier, my alternate, sideways *Sesame Street* characters lurk around every corner and there are more murderous possibilities above ground. The garbage kids have their own belongings too, like rags, boxes, dumpsters. Audri's world is the wackiest because she appears everywhere doing nearly anything, but I think there is a spawning place for Audris and a realm for all the Audris but they are freer, they are the ones breaking the boundaries between the worlds.

There is an evolved version of my helper-creatures in the scenes too, a darker version. After I researched the suicide forest in Japan, *Aokigahara*, I started drawing a lot of suicidal images because I was inspired by that history and place, the sentiment of it, and characters that would be drawn there. But I began getting asked by fans and the online moderators if I needed psychological help—I needed to find a way to make the drawings a little less "suicidal." So I put in the helper-creatures. These are the final form of the helpful poops, snails, and even the sentimental ghosts. They aren't quite fairies, but very dark sprites that can be helpful, mischievous, or downright sadistic. I did a whole series of dying or murdered girls featuring these sprites in them as the anti-murder message because they look sad, they are mourning the girls. They help me show an aspect of the image that is hard to express. I'm not promoting murder or suicide or anything horrible, but I do want to express myself through death, gore, and horror-esque images—it's dark art. I think my little sprites help.

I went through a phase where I was really annoyed that I couldn't draw butterflies. Every -one was wearing beautiful and cute butter- flies, but I couldn't draw a good one. I wanted my butterflies to be murderous and threat- ening. I thought that was very funny, and they would kidnap girls and eat their heads or take them away to a lair. There's an Edward Gorey story where an insect would pull up in a hansom cab, a praying mantis I think, and a girl was approaching the car. Typical Gorey, ominous, and not really violent. I love that and I'm practising drawing little pieces of things I love or my own version of things I didn't like. The more I draw, the more easily my worlds form. I think it takes years to develop that skill and develop that entire world and language. I have so many recurring characters now, like Bastard Sun, and Audri, and Sewer Boy, the specific way I draw dandelions, the worms, and all my little helper-creatures. It's a whole universe.

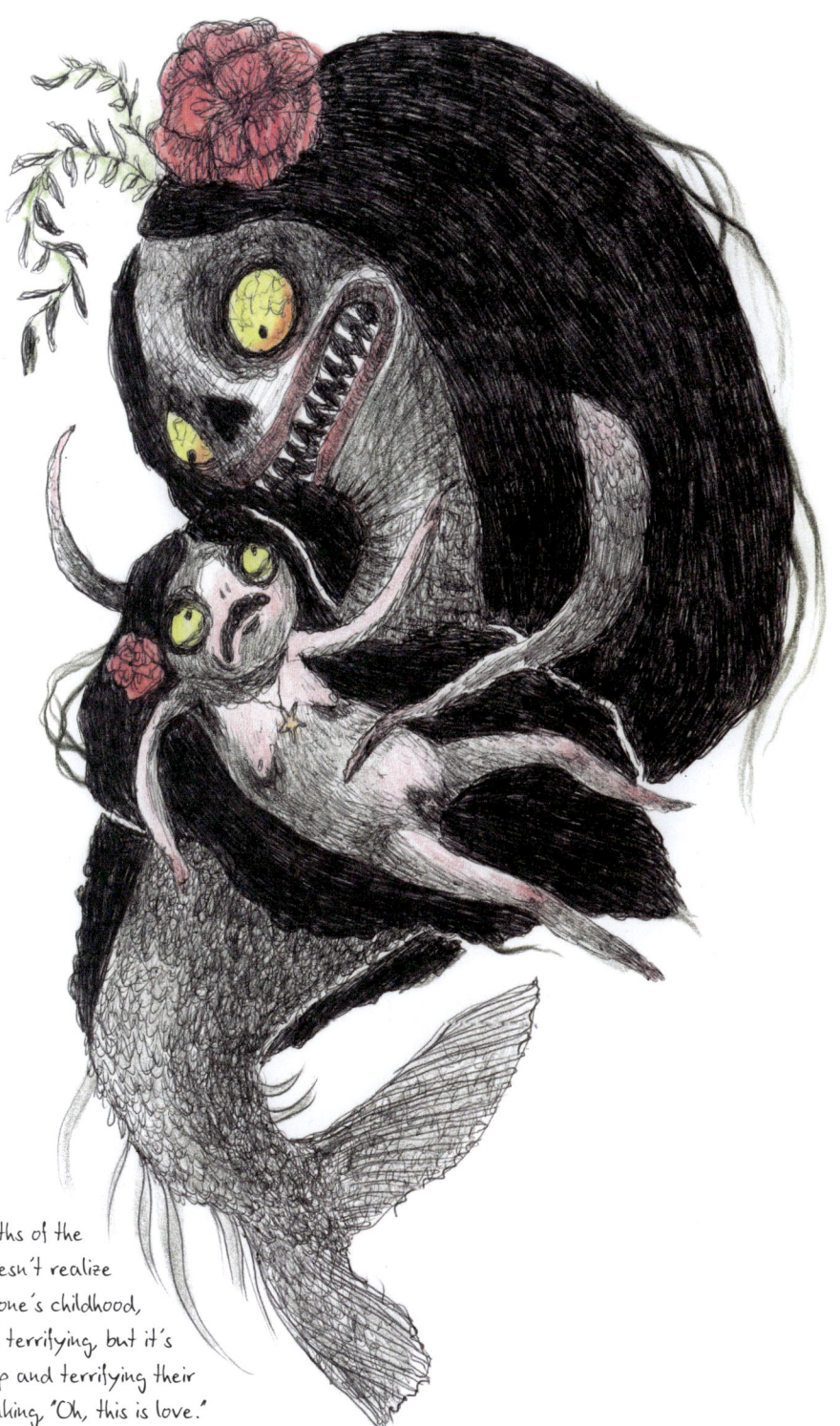

A mermaid monster. She's loving it in the depths of the ocean. The child looks terrified because she doesn't realize she's getting love, which is the story of everyone's childhood, right? Everything is terrifying and parents are terrifying, but it's love. Then one day, the child is grown up and terrifying their own children thinking, 'Oh, this is love.'

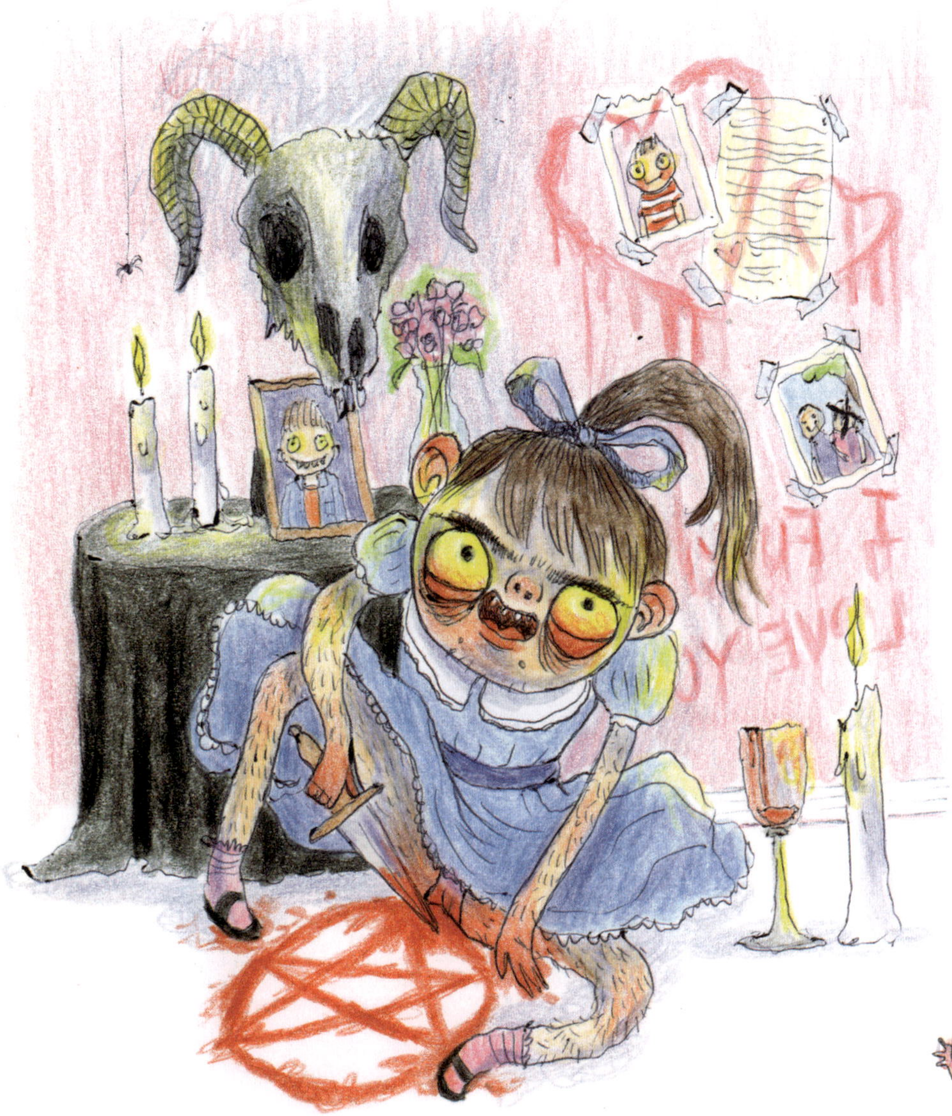

This one's a little more violent than innocent, but she's having fun. I watched *Let the Right One In*, a Swedish romantic horror film, around the same time. I liked the protagonist in it; she wasn't quite a child, she was a vampire and had lived a long time, but she maintained the child-like guise and a sense of innocence about love. I also adored her feral, monstrous side, which I draw a lot of.

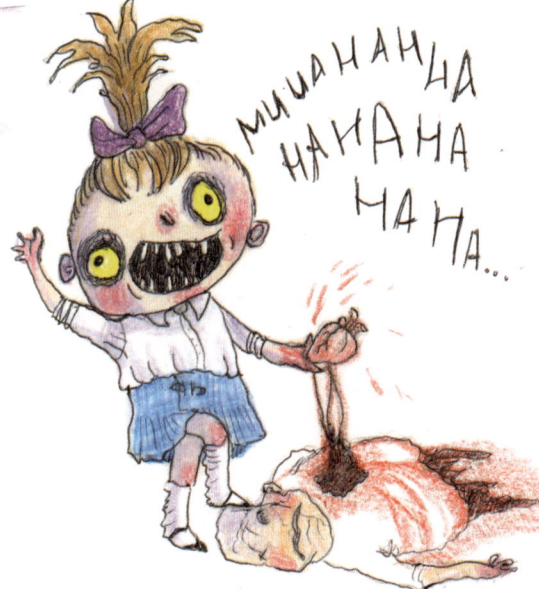

MUUAHAHHA HAHAHA HA HA...

Guess what asshole, you just drank mah menstrual blood. You're mine!

People weren't as weirded out by this one as I thought they might be. There's this cliche that a woman can make a spell to make a man fall in love, but in this version the man has to drink the woman's period blood first. I like the stalker background and the added touch of the pentagram.

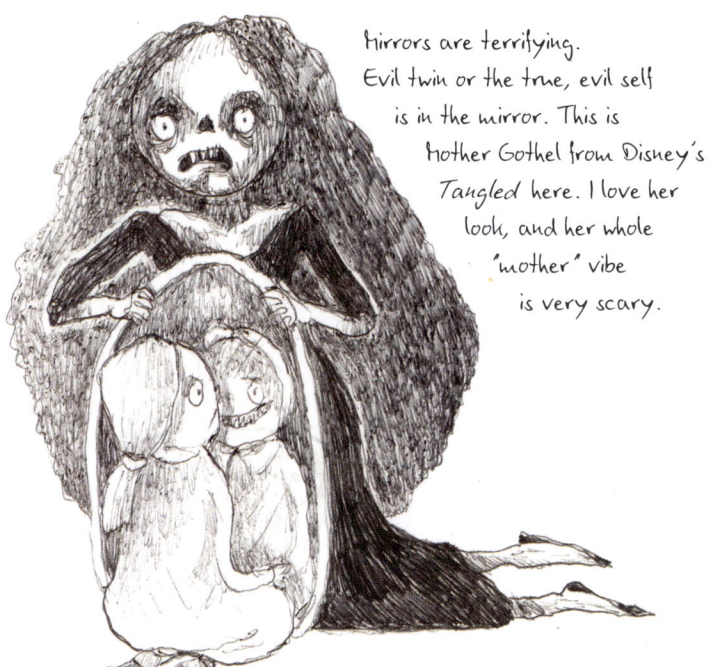

Mirrors are terrifying.
Evil twin or the true, evil self
is in the mirror. This is
Mother Gothel from Disney's
Tangled here. I love her
look, and her whole
"mother" vibe
is very scary.

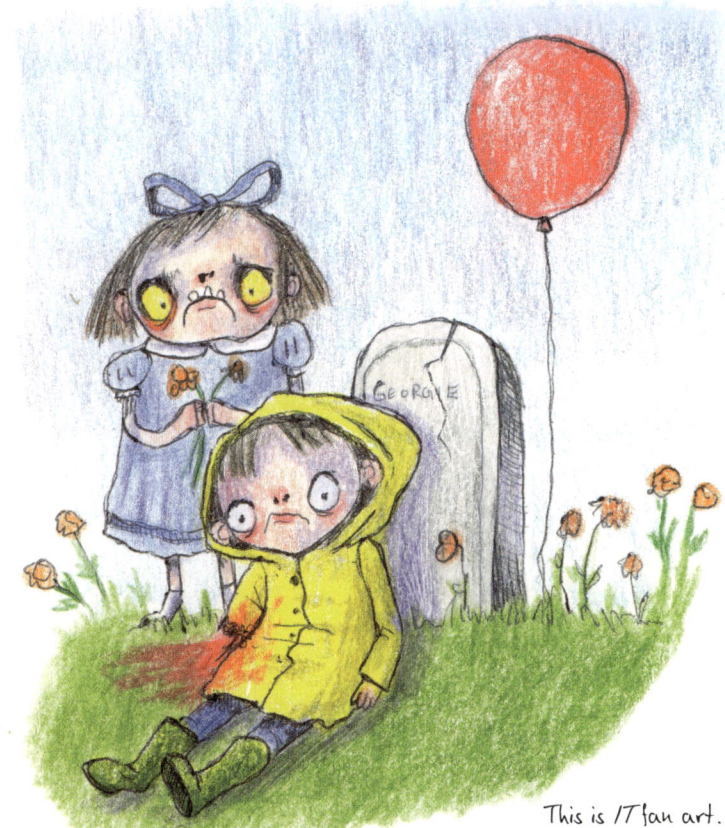

This is *IT* fan art.
I really like Georgie. Little
boys in danger or that die are my kryptonite; I can't watch
them usually. But *IT* is from my childhood, so it's okay.
Georgie has to die for everything to happen. I put myself in
the picture because I'm sad about him so I'm going to put
flowers on his grave and maybe I'll kiss his corpse.

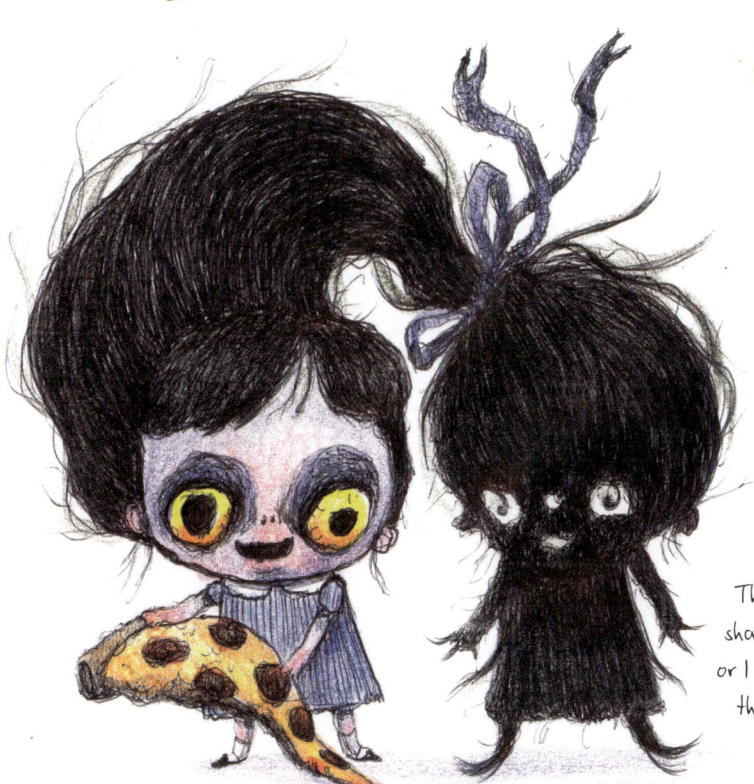

This is a girl making an imaginary friend out of her hair and
sharing a pizza slice. I never had an imaginary friend as a child,
or I don't think I did. I really like the concept, like this hair friend or
that ghosts are actually imaginary friends (or vice versa?).
Maybe I just wish I were haunted.

This is my version of *The Creature from The Black Lagoon.* I like the creature backstory and design.

I like to counter
my garbage children,
who live above ground and have things like garbage bags
and pieces of wood, with my underground children.
They are in the woods and they live in holes and are
also feral and isolated. They have their underground
environment filled with necessities like worms and
bottles of pee. It's a place where I would want to
curl up and sleep.

This is a monster with a gentle
heart that has run off into the
wilderness. Of course, he's being hunted
down because the message is: everyone but
the monster is monstrous.

Whenever I draw the creature, I always draw him as an accidental murderer. The monster has the same mindset of a violent-innocent child. Like, Frankenstein or Lenny from *Of Mice and Men*, I draw the monster in a state of realizing his mistake, that moment of awful awareness.

TAKE ME TO HELL!

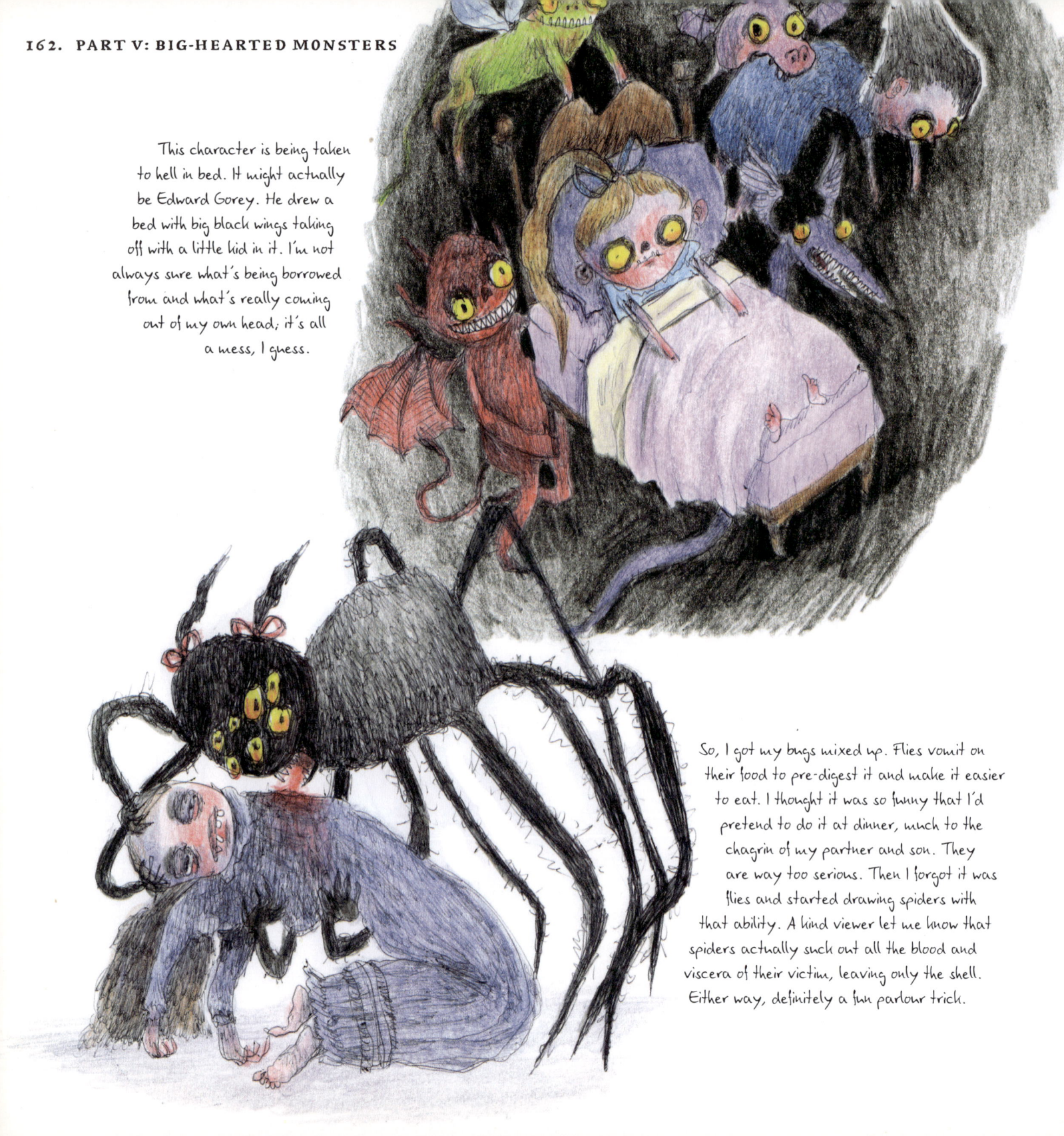

This character is being taken to hell in bed. It might actually be Edward Gorey. He drew a bed with big black wings taking off with a little kid in it. I'm not always sure what's being borrowed from and what's really coming out of my own head; it's all a mess, I guess.

So, I got my bugs mixed up. Flies vomit on their food to pre-digest it and make it easier to eat. I thought it was so funny that I'd pretend to do it at dinner, much to the chagrin of my partner and son. They are way too serious. Then I forgot it was flies and started drawing spiders with that ability. A kind viewer let me know that spiders actually suck out all the blood and viscera of their victim, leaving only the shell. Either way, definitely a fun parlour trick.

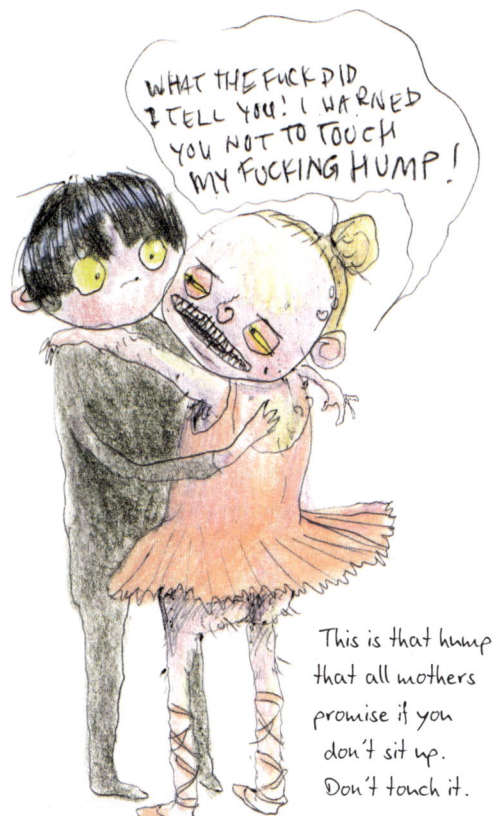

WHAT THE FUCK DID I TELL YOU! I WARNED YOU NOT TO TOUCH MY FUCKING HUMP!

This is that hump that all mothers promise if you don't sit up. Don't touch it.

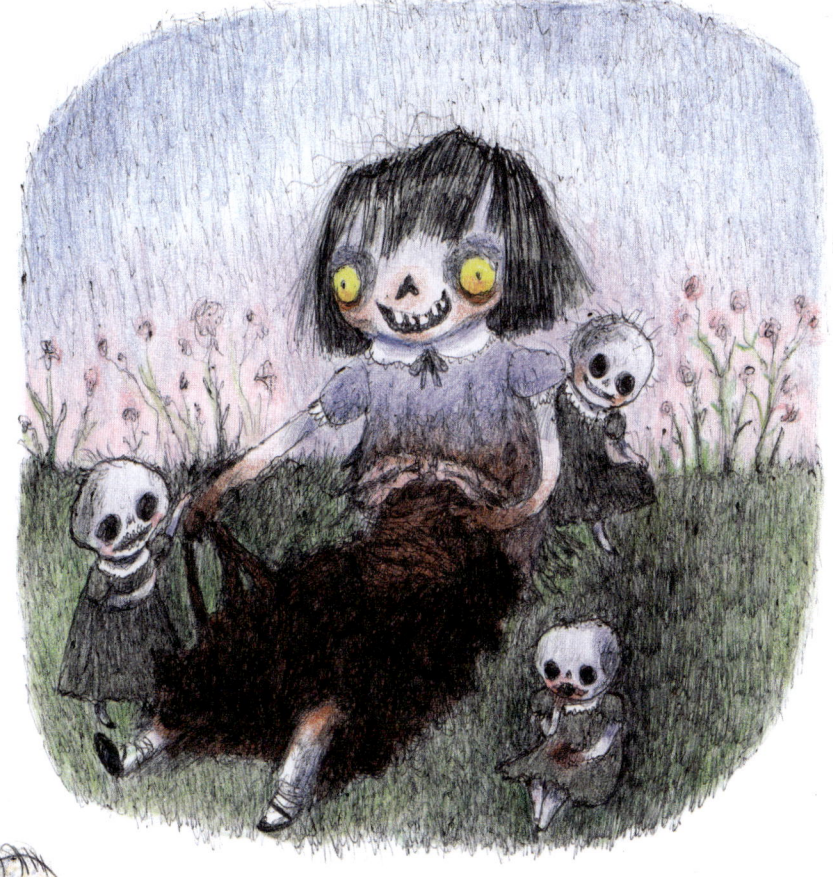

THERE HAD BEEN A TERRIBLE ACCIDENT...

More children of violence. This was inspired by my sister, who had accidentally cut her friend's hand with my dad's hunting knife while they were playing in the tree house. I'm ten years older than my sister, so I never really played in the tree house. It was hers. My dad certainly never went there because it was a small space, a child's space. The little friend, who I didn't really care for anyway, came out running and screaming with blood streaming from her hand. It wasn't serious or anything and, in the end, everyone was alright, and no one was in too much trouble.
It was all just violent and bloody but in an innocent way.
I think I loved my sister more that day.

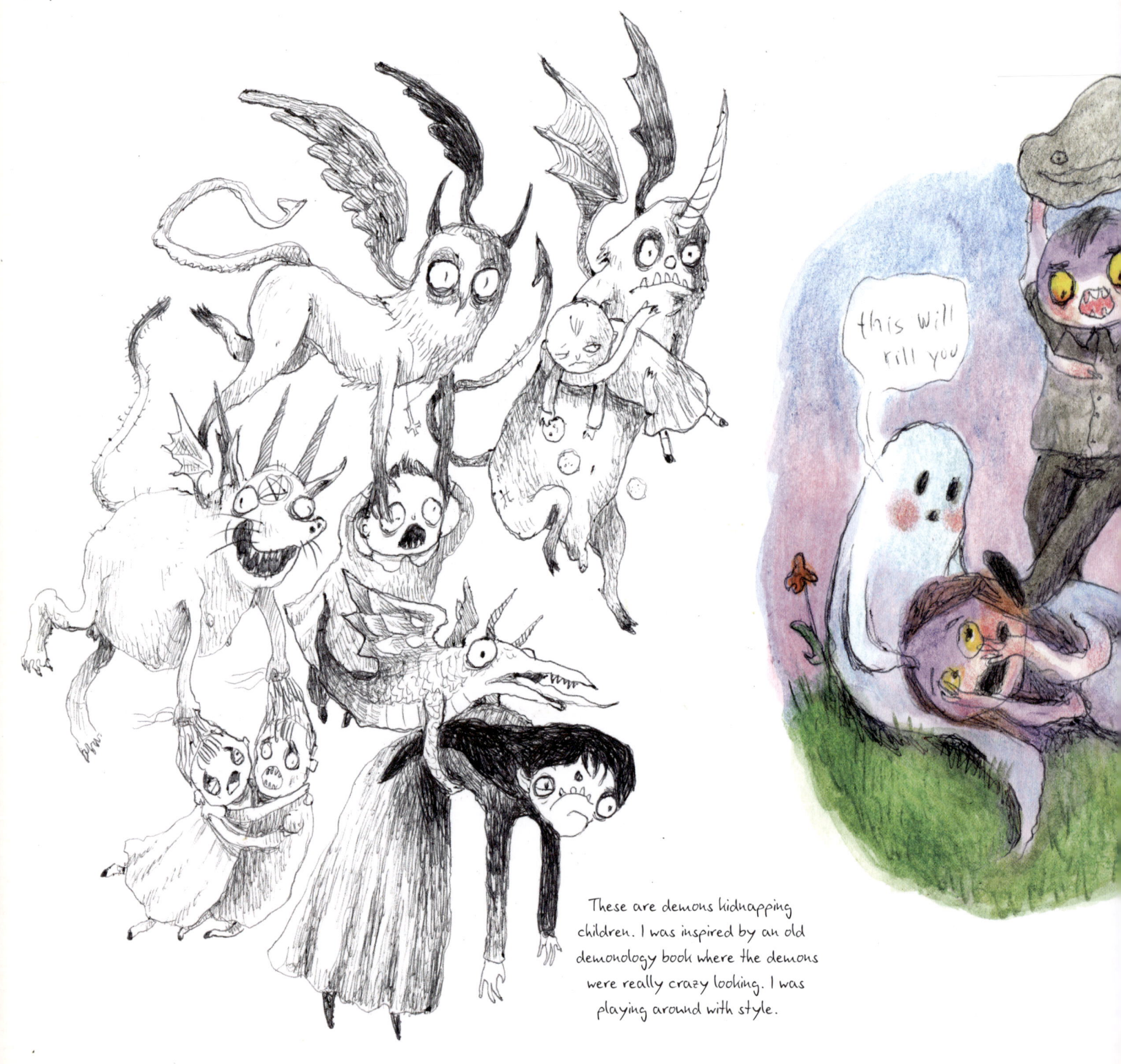

These are demons kidnapping children. I was inspired by an old demonology book where the demons were really crazy looking. I was playing around with style.

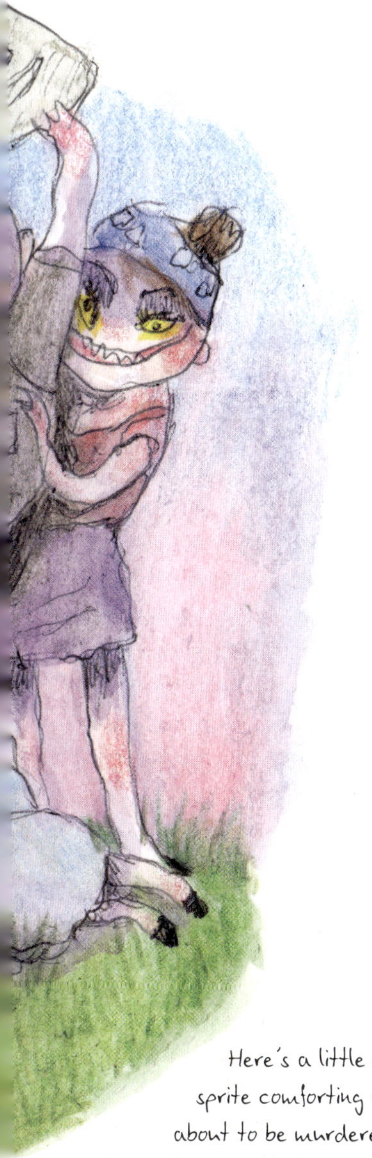

Here's a little ghost sprite comforting a girl about to be murdered. I often have dreams of being murdered but no sprite shows up for me. Sad.

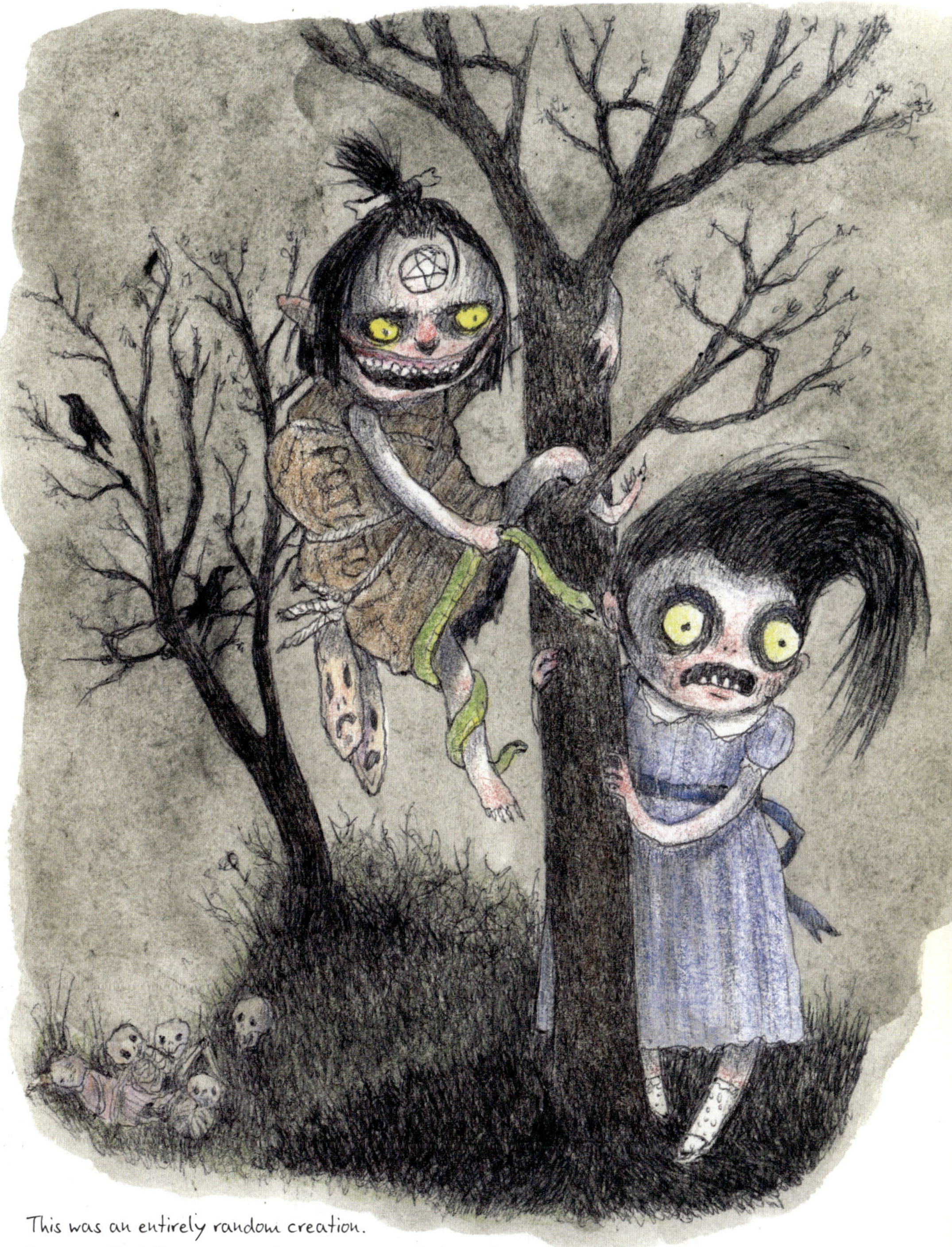

This was an entirely random creation.
I really enjoy that the demon girl is wearing a potato sack and
collects faces. It feels like my own demented version of Adam and Eve,
but it's just a creepy girl and her snake and a bunch of dead kids in a pile in the background.

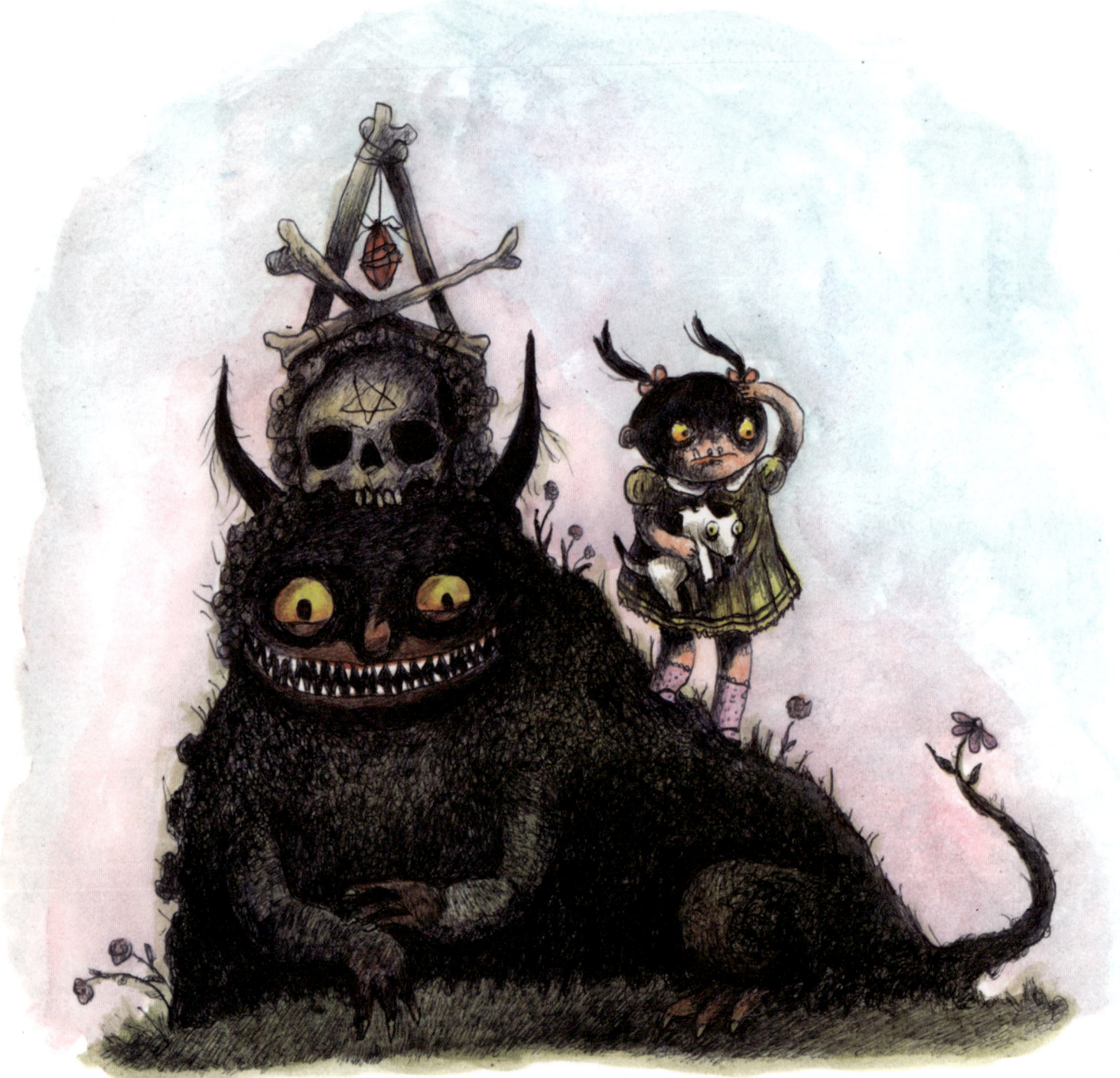

This is the middle of a story where this girl is on a sacrificial hill,
but we don't know the beginning or end of the story.

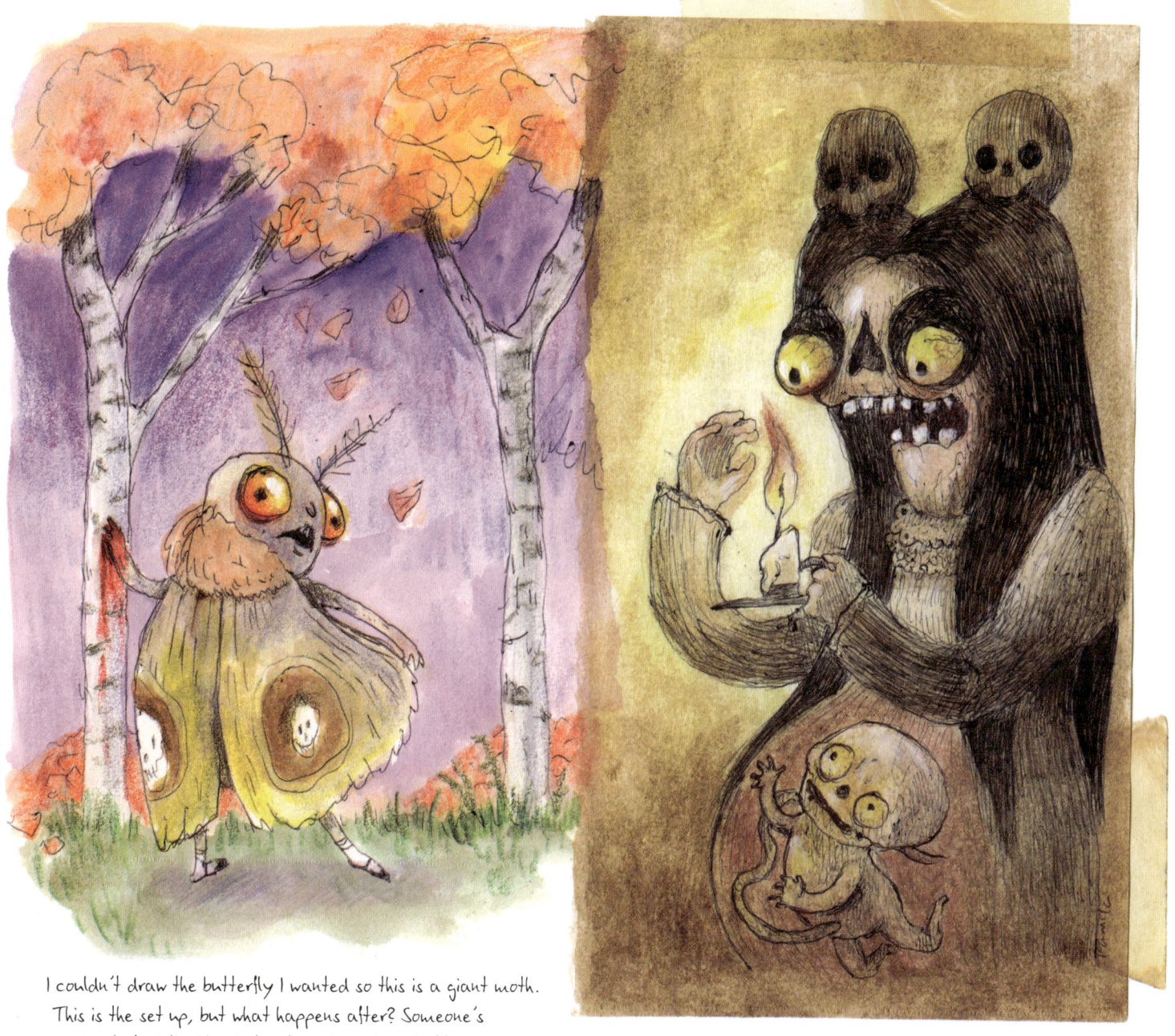

I couldn't draw the butterfly I wanted so this is a giant moth. This is the set up, but what happens after? Someone's going to find the blood streak and wonder what's going on. The giant moth did it, I think.

This is *Crimson Peak* inspired because of the colouring and the outfit and hair. I was also going through a phase where I enjoyed drawing pregnant people. I can't really push the limit with pregnancy, it's a personal line that's nearly unbearable to cross. It can be too real sometimes. I like when it's kind of absurd.

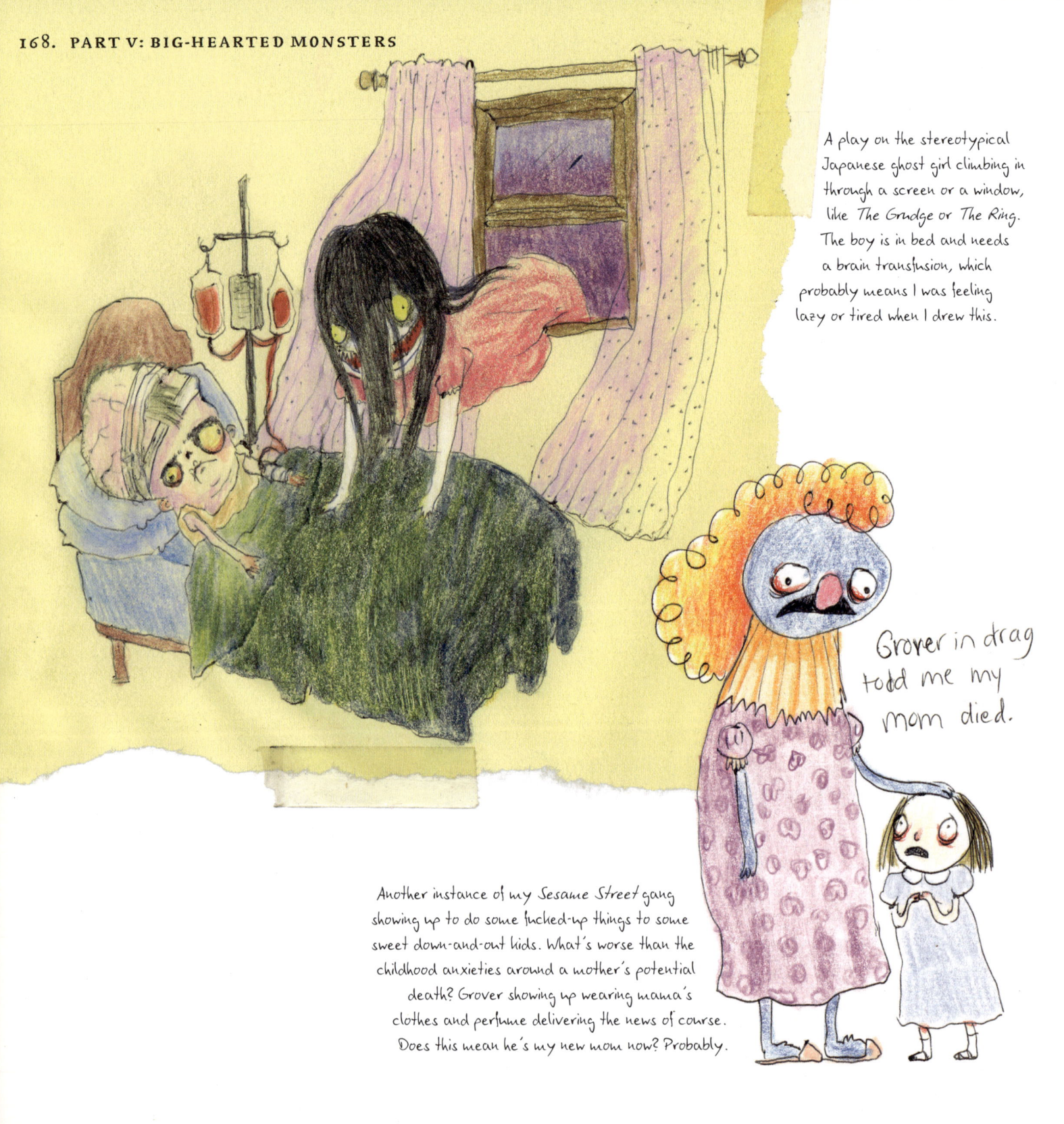

A play on the stereotypical Japanese ghost girl climbing in through a screen or a window, like *The Grudge* or *The Ring*. The boy is in bed and needs a brain transfusion, which probably means I was feeling lazy or tired when I drew this.

Grover in drag told me my mom died.

Another instance of my *Sesame Street* gang showing up to do some fucked-up things to some sweet down-and-out kids. What's worse than the childhood anxieties around a mother's potential death? Grover showing up wearing mama's clothes and perfume delivering the news of course. Does this mean he's my new mom now? Probably.

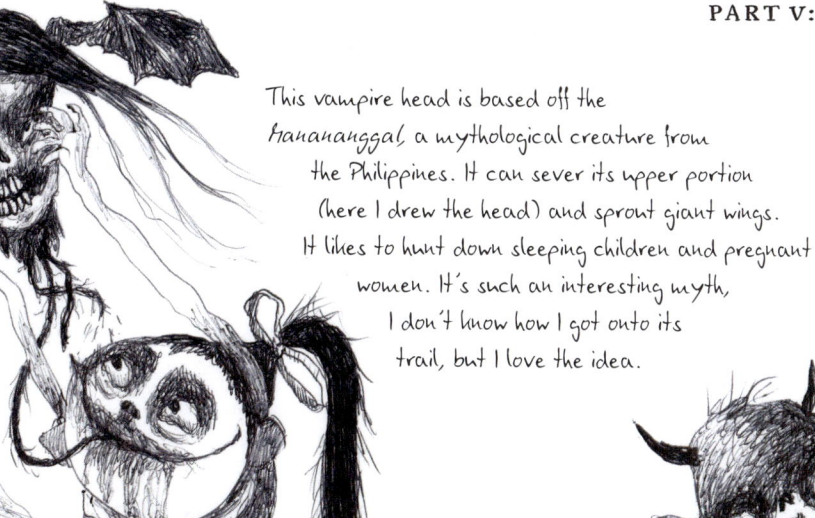

This vampire head is based off the
hananangal, a mythological creature from
the Philippines. It can sever its upper portion
(here I drew the head) and sprout giant wings.
It likes to hunt down sleeping children and pregnant
women. It's such an interesting myth,
I don't know how I got onto its
trail, but I love the idea.

There's a Polish phrase,
hustajac diabetica
which means, "Oh, you're
swinging the Devil."
Imagine a child sitting
and swinging their feet,
because they can't reach
the floor. Now imagine
the Devil sitting on top
of their feet, swinging
and having fun.

Please
baptize me
I don't want
to go
to hell

I have this ongoing thought stream
about baptism. I have at least two
unbaptized baby art dolls that I did.
I find it ridiculous that people actually
think an unbaptized baby will go to hell.
That's such an incredible suspension
of disbelief in the name of religion,
and I like to poke fun at logic holes
like that, particularly in anything
dogmatically believed in.

When a kid does that, that's
what they say. I remember always thinking
my retort was, "Oh the Devil's my friend."
So when I draw the Devil, he's always
hanging out with someone. This was half
exploring that theme, and the other
half was playing with technique, drawing
the elongated torso and dripping eyeballs.

what to do if you got clones of yourself.

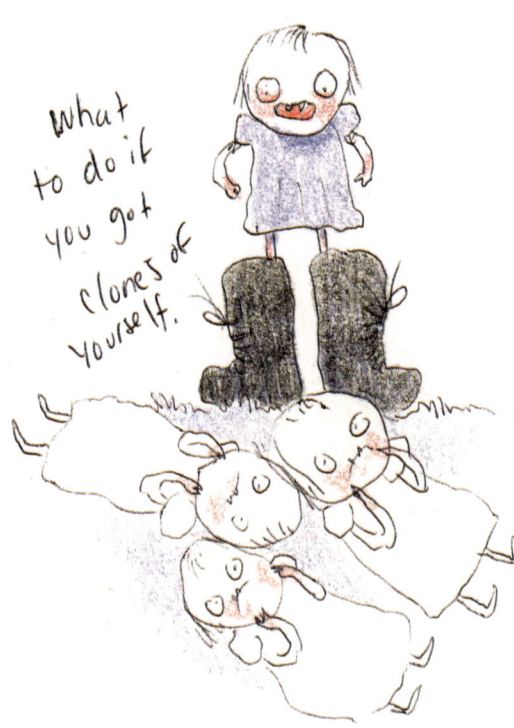

These are the little helpful forest sprites. I also started to do a lot of giant women. This one has retractable breasts and the little sprites are trying to steal them, but they aren't going to get very far. It's a playful scene, weird more than sexual, like an ancient goddess portrait.

There ain't no cure for havin' shrimps for eyes.

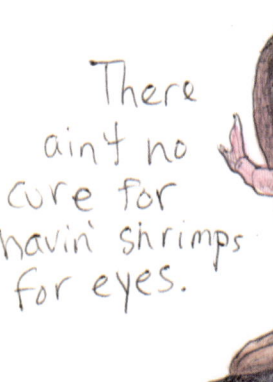

This is such a simple and stupid drawing. "There ain't no cure for shrimp eyes." Which might be true . . . if shrimp eyes were really a thing. So stupid. The little sick boy in a wheelchair who has shrimps for eyes. Absurd.

MINE. FRIEND.

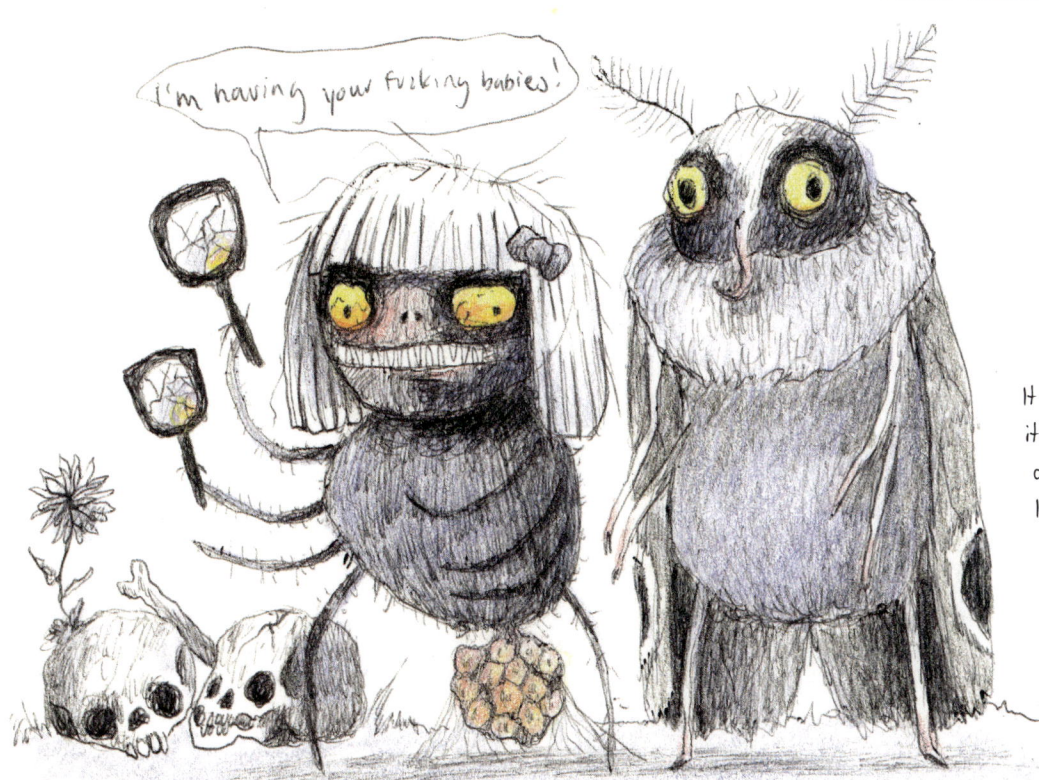

It's a spider woman who made it with a moth, and she's acting annoyed, but she's excited about it. I think I might want more babies. I love them so much.

her head had gone bad... like an old pumpkin

I had been watching a pumpkin rot all through October, and I thought it'd be really funny if a girl's head was rotting the same way, so . . . here's that.

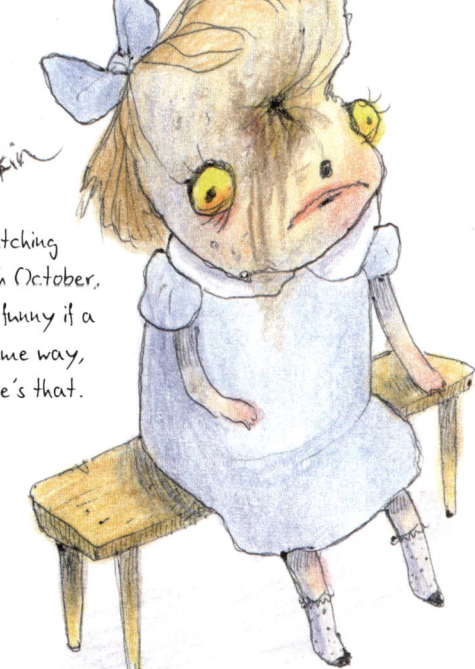

Monster Girl tries to make friends. She might be a sprite. Anyway, she makes friends with whoever or whatever doesn't run away from her, in this case, a bird skull.

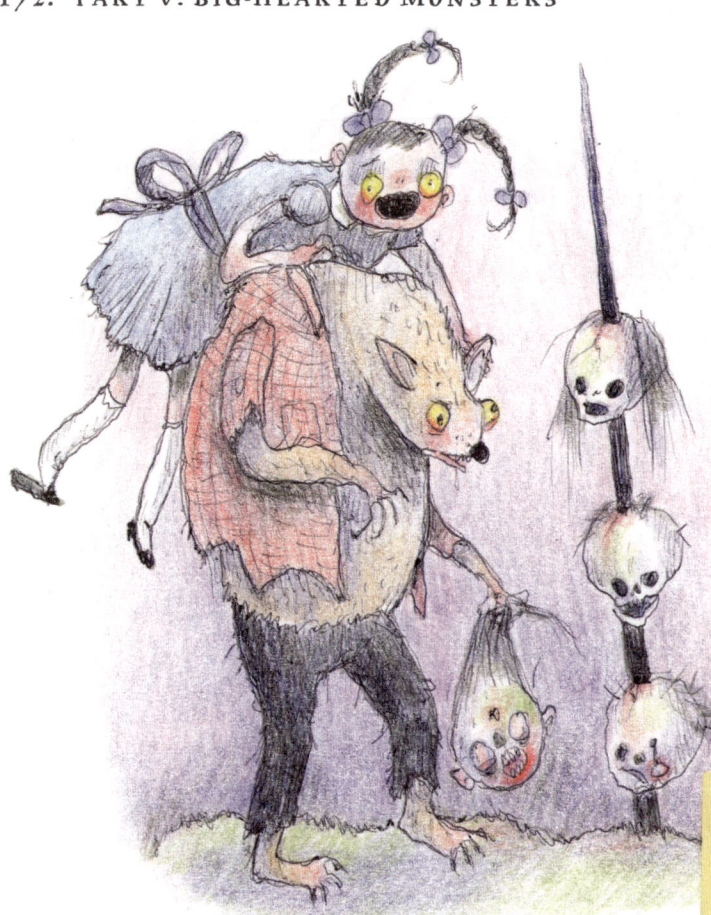

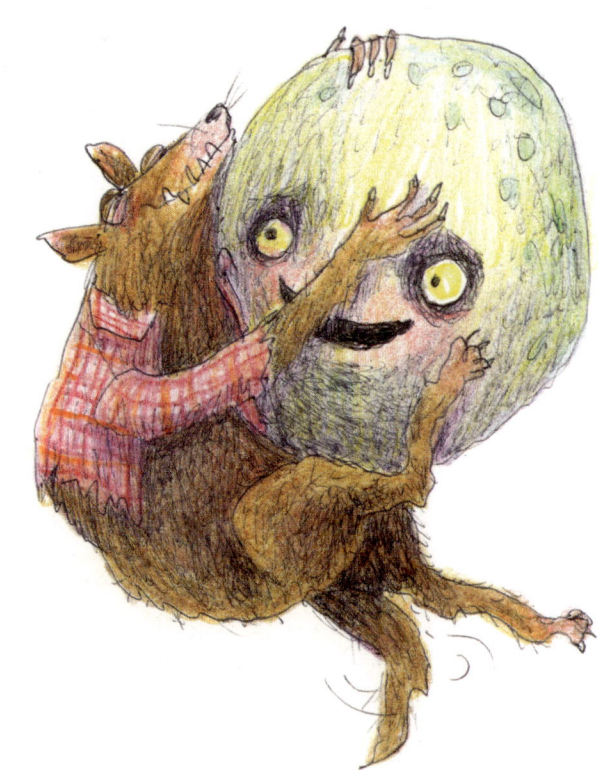

For some reason,
   with werewolves I like to draw heads on spikes.
      That's me on his back.

One of my favourite werewolf drawings.
This werewolf is in love with the moon, but they can
never be together because one is earthbound and one
is in the sky, and she has to go away every day.
They're saying goodbye. Werewolf stuff can be so tragic.
He's always being given a little girl as a sacrifice, but
she's sweet, he doesn't want to eat her. But he does.

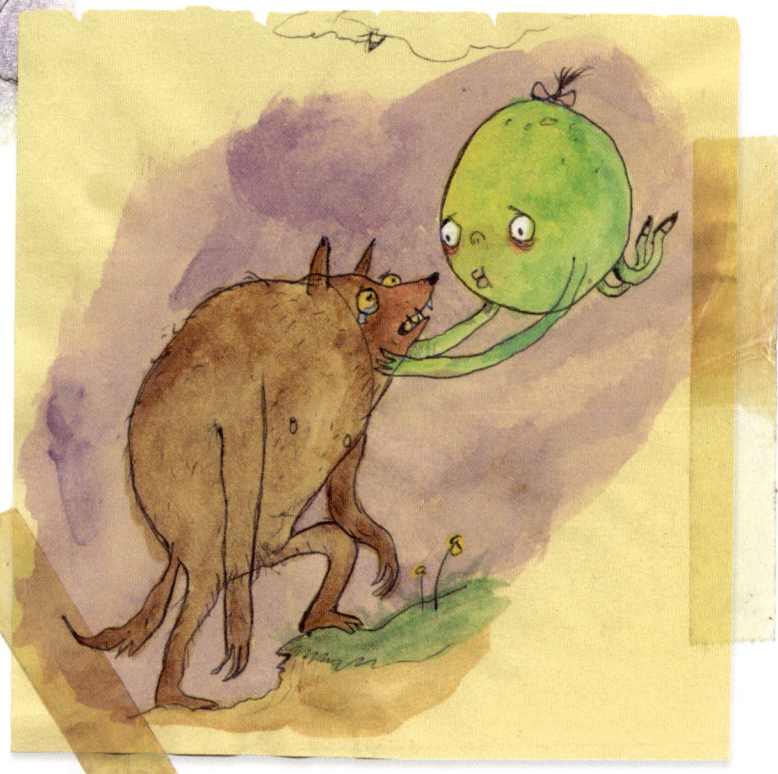

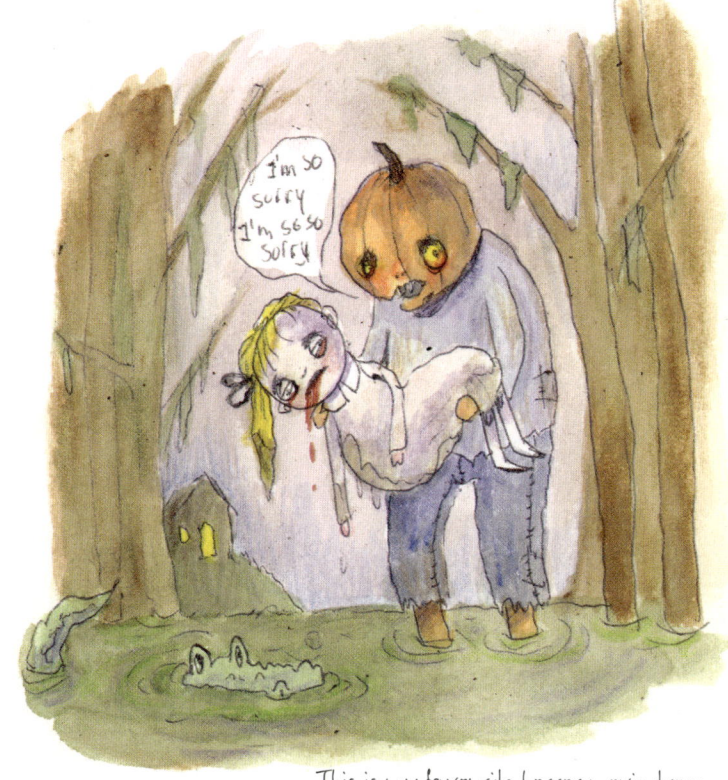

This is my favourite horror movie trope.
The creature is secluded and estranged
and then he accidentally commits murder
because he doesn't know his
own strength.

This is the birthday werewolf.
He's just about to kill these three girls,
and he says, "I hate surprises," because
it's a birthday and he's the surprise.

Here's a werewolf wrestling with
himself because the little girl sacrifice
is giving him a little wreath and it's
so cute, but he's hungry.
But she's so sweet and
stupid. He's trying to figure
out what he wants to do and
what he should do. He's confused.

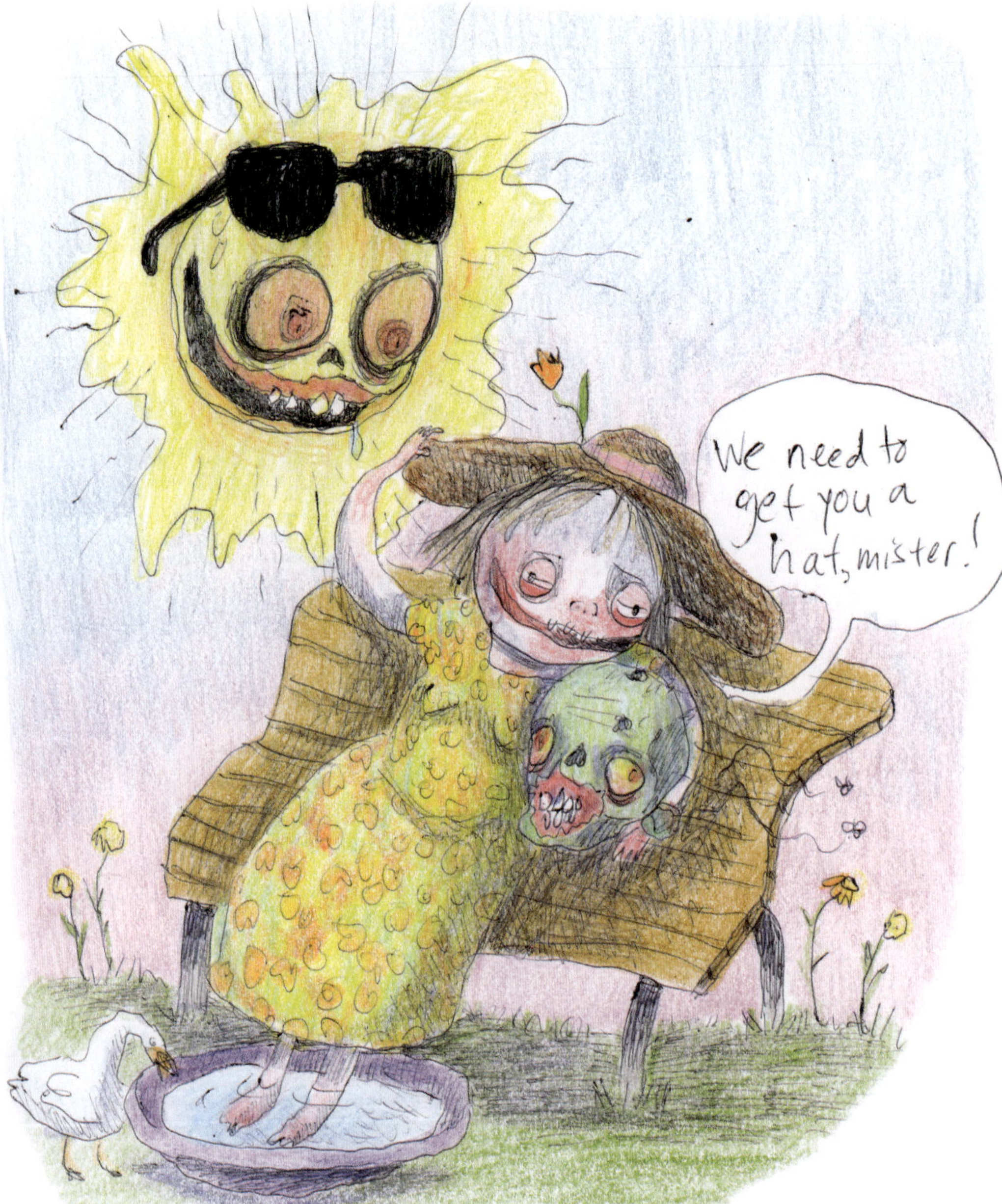

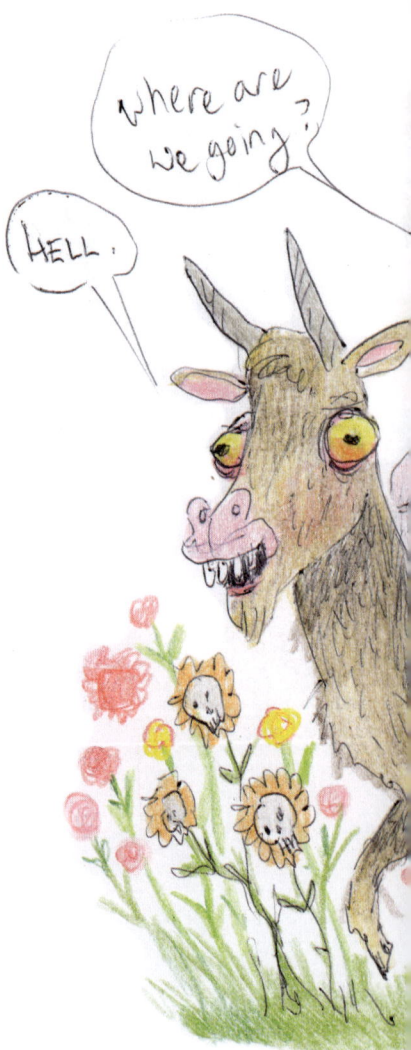

I was doing research about men who dug up corpses just to be around someone.
This is a female version of that. She's dug up or found this head that she hangs out
with. In my mind, it's an old Polish woman, maybe a babcia because she's lonely
and she's soaking her feet, and she forgot that she needed to care for him and
bring a hat and sunscreen.

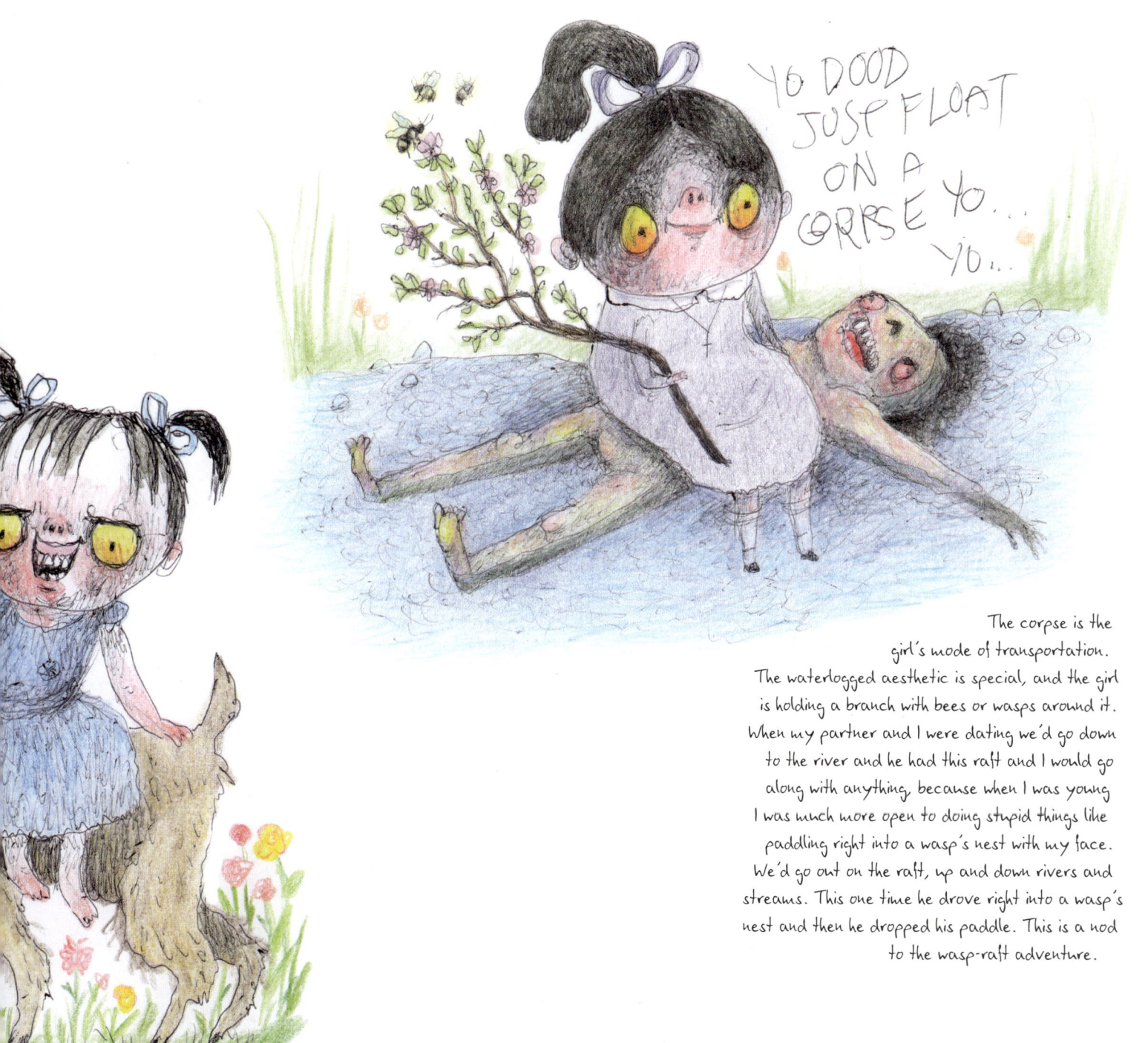

YO DOOD
JUSF FLOAT
ON A
CORPSE YO...
YO...

The corpse is the
girl's mode of transportation.
The waterlogged aesthetic is special, and the girl
is holding a branch with bees or wasps around it.
When my partner and I were dating we'd go down
to the river and he had this raft and I would go
along with anything, because when I was young
I was much more open to doing stupid things like
paddling right into a wasp's nest with my face.
We'd go out on the raft, up and down rivers and
streams. This one time he drove right into a wasp's
nest and then he dropped his paddle. This is a nod
to the wasp-raft adventure.

Another happy
trip down to hell.

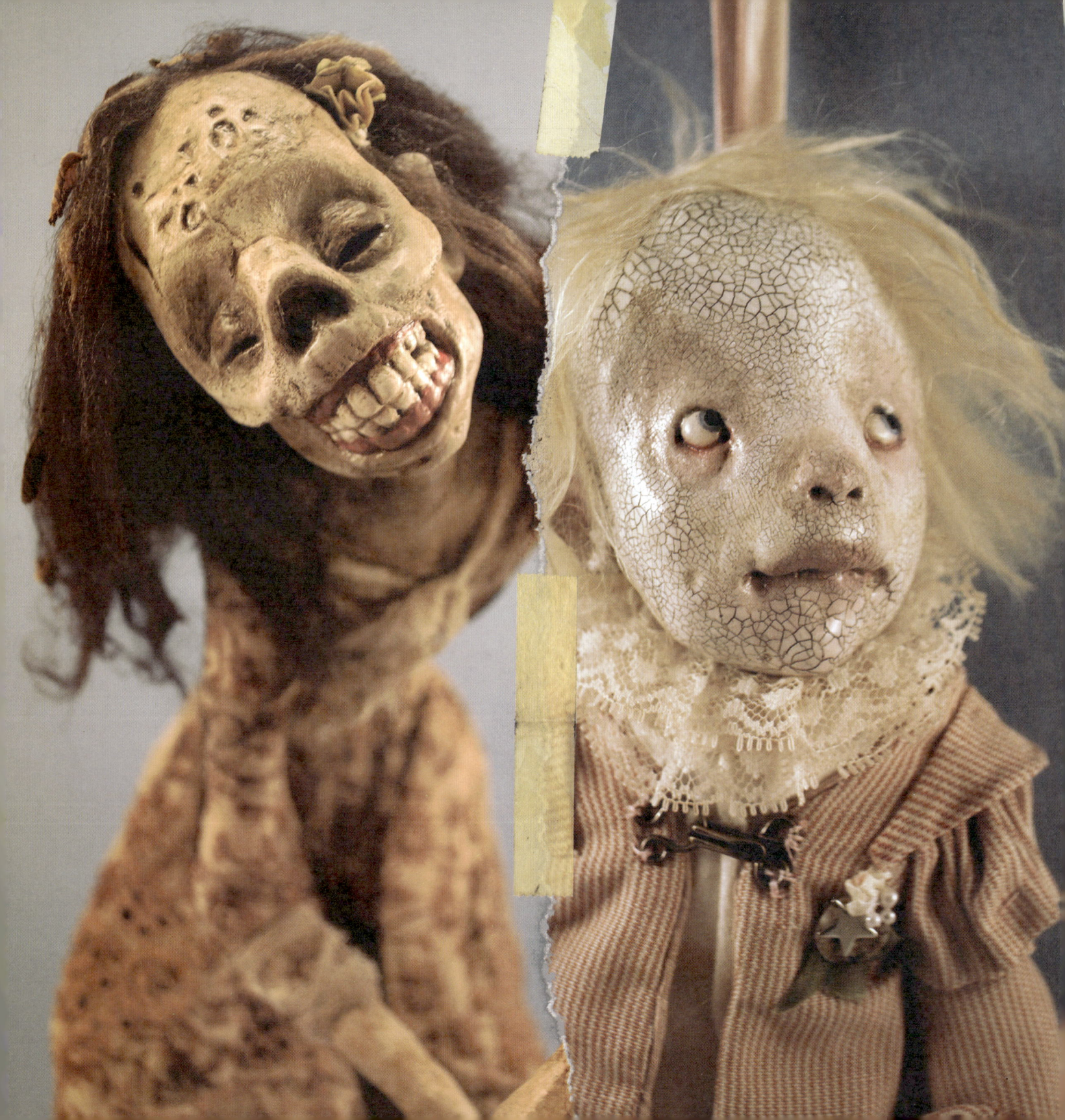

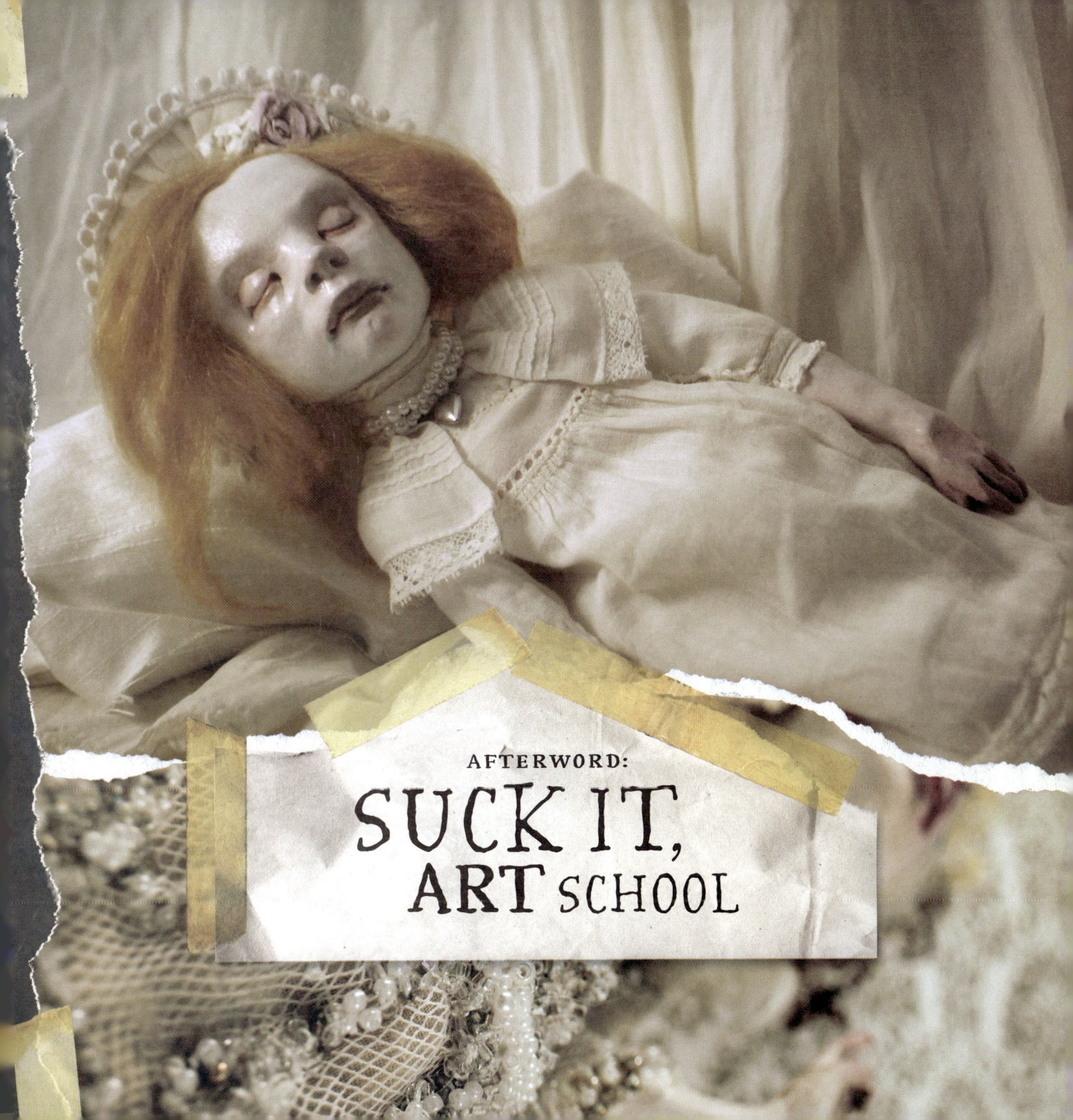

AFTERWORD:

SUCK IT, ART SCHOOL

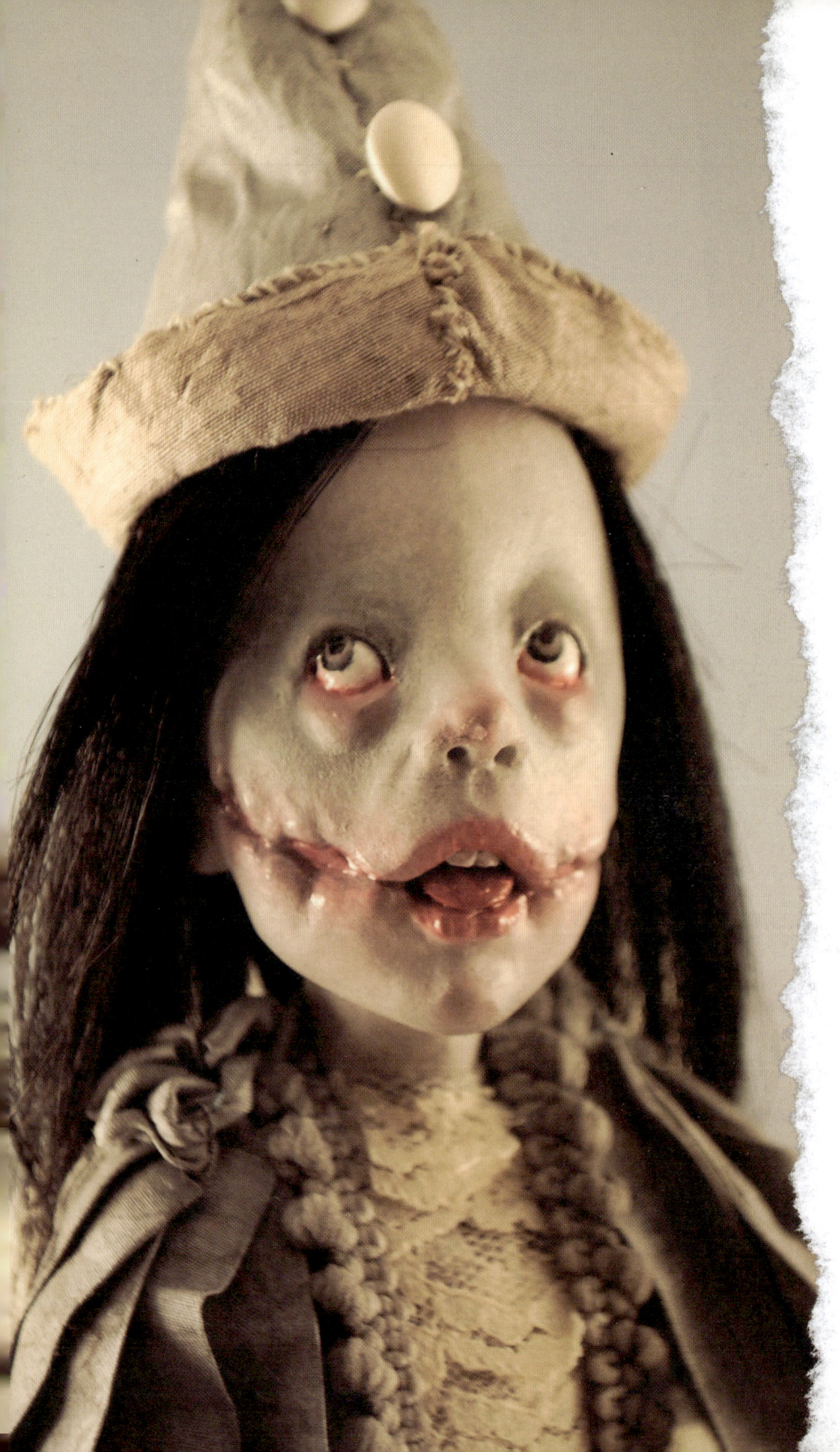

ART DOLLS WERE MY FIRST rebellion. I couldn't take it. After art school, I did nothing, no art. I call those the "dark years." When I slowly started again, it was painful. I made a comeback with my art dolls. Nothing I learned in art school is present in the dolls. Can you ever imagine that having other people judge your most precious, internal creations is a good and healthy way to learn and grow? No. That's fucked-up. When I started making art dolls, I was trying to make "legitimately nice art," or whatever art professors are looking for when they grade. And then I thought, "I'm just doing what I did in art school, I'm trying to meet expectations." So I forced myself to actually listen to myself, and that's where these creepy, wonderful dolls came from. I was stunned, honestly, that when people really saw them they understood that the dolls weren't just gratuitous gore, but beautiful and sweet. After that, I continued to push myself away from everything I learned in art school, and down the path of horror. If it just wasn't done, then fuck it, I'd do it! It rocked.

Learning how to create art dolls is what made me an artist. I experimented with materials, I would order these old baby baptism dresses and use them with the dolls, and I'd find ancient lace that was already discoloured and frayed and delicate and

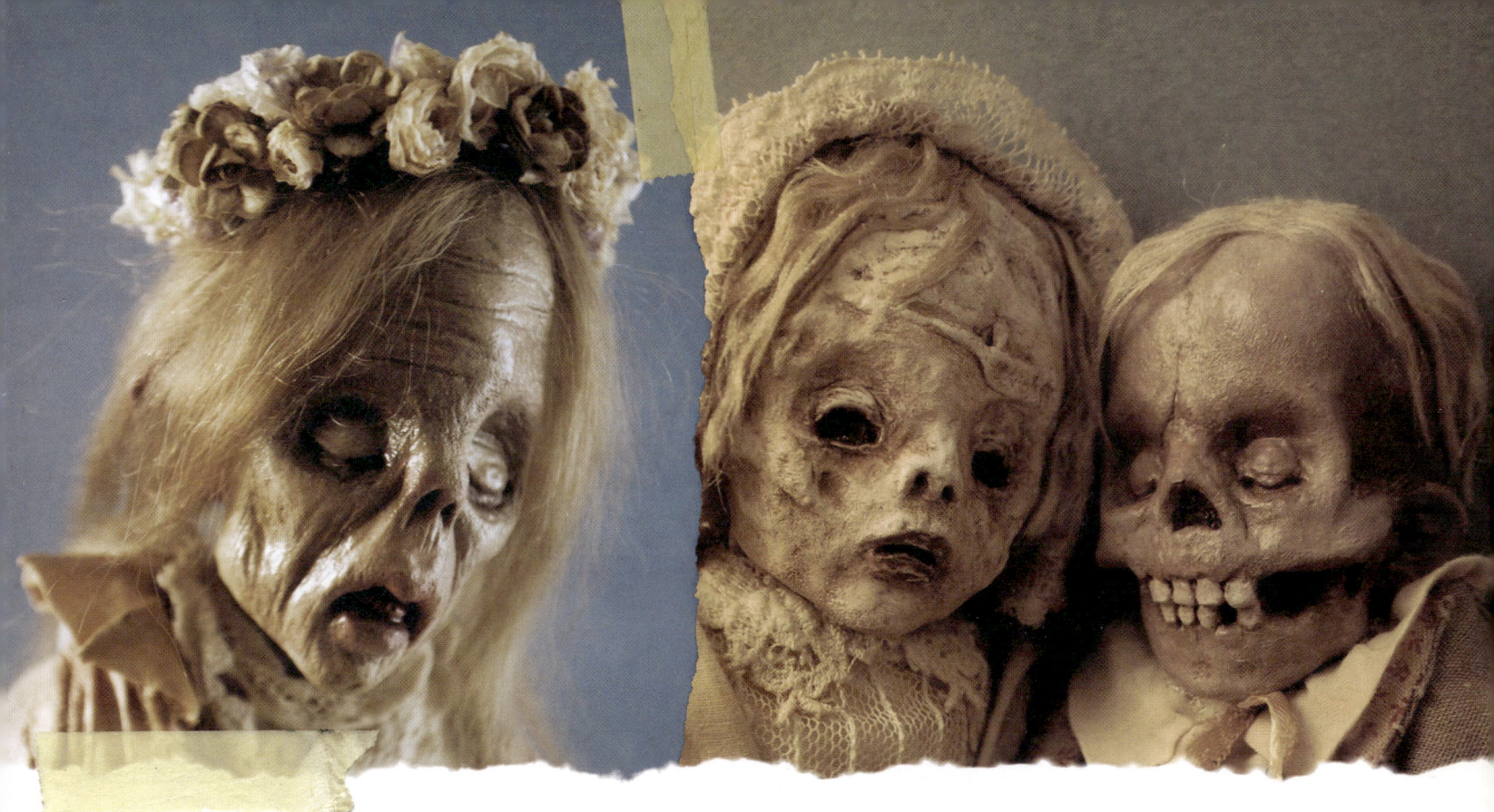

I played with that. I explored technique, style, and design elements. I enhanced the distress of a fabric or played with eye (dis)colouration or fiddled with the bandage wrappings on mummy dolls. They helped me learn a lot about the meaning of art, which comes down to this: it's all subjective. What matters is what I think. So it was awesome that I could hold something I'd created and that I actually liked. That had never happened at school.

The moral of the story? Don't go to just any school for art if you like art. In hindsight, I did just that. I went to school for an art degree because I loved art in a general way. I figured I wanted to be an illustrator. They stuck me in the design "stream," and I took a bunch of classes that were horribly rigid. There was just no room for fucking-up. No space for experimentation. All I really wanted to do was just go batshit in a room and paint in swathes of colour and pour out onto a canvas. So, as you can imagine, school was horrible for me, it was soul deadening. I wished I'd gone for nursing or garbage truck driver or something practical. Whether in school or in an artist's own mind, there must be a safe space to fuck up.

And, let me tell you, I'm a master at fucking-up. There have been so many times I've ruined a piece of art because I was in love with something, an inspiration or a technique or an idea. I might have known that what

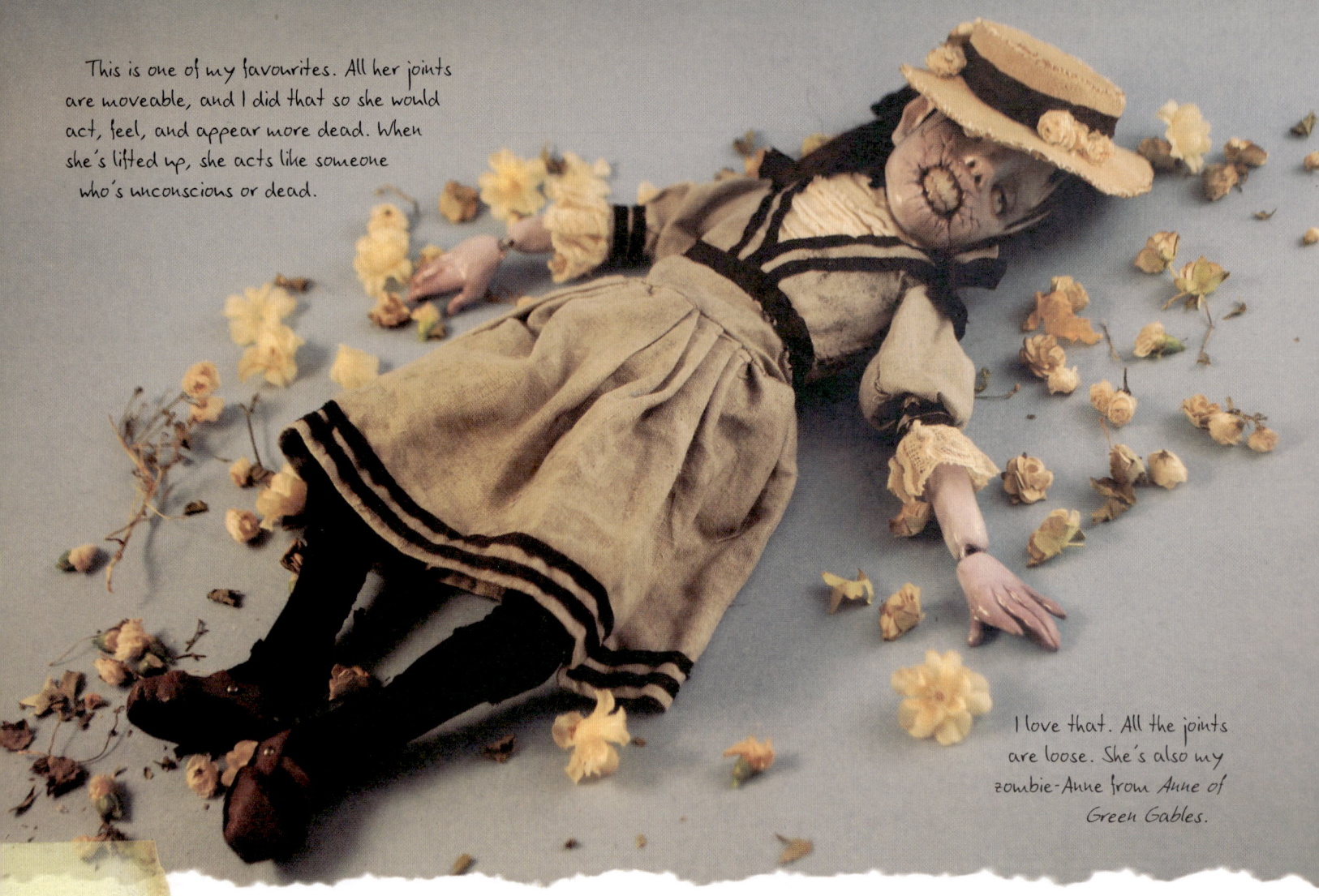

This is one of my favourites. All her joints are moveable, and I did that so she would act, feel, and appear more dead. When she's lifted up, she acts like someone who's unconscious or dead.

I love that. All the joints are loose. She's also my zombie-Anne from *Anne of Green Gables*.

I was doing wasn't working, or I might not have, but I couldn't kill it. That's a skill an artist can only learn through practice: to recognize what isn't working and to kill it. Kill your babies. Kill them all! That's part of the reason why it's weird to be eighteen or nineteen and go to art school. At that point, an artist is just a kid who doesn't even know themself yet, they haven't fucked-up enough yet.

After making art dolls for a few years, I plateaued.

I was done with dolls. I wasn't able to express myself enough, or effectively, through art dolls anymore. I was a sell-out with them. So instead of planning the art dolls, I started drawing these horrible, morbid things and that totally made me happy. I found catharsis. Drawing helped me in a way art dolls didn't. By drawing the darkest, most horrible stuff possible, I began creeping (pun intended?) out of my funk. I don't want to make stuff just because other people will like it, that's what art school encourages, and I refuse that idea. Not me, no way.

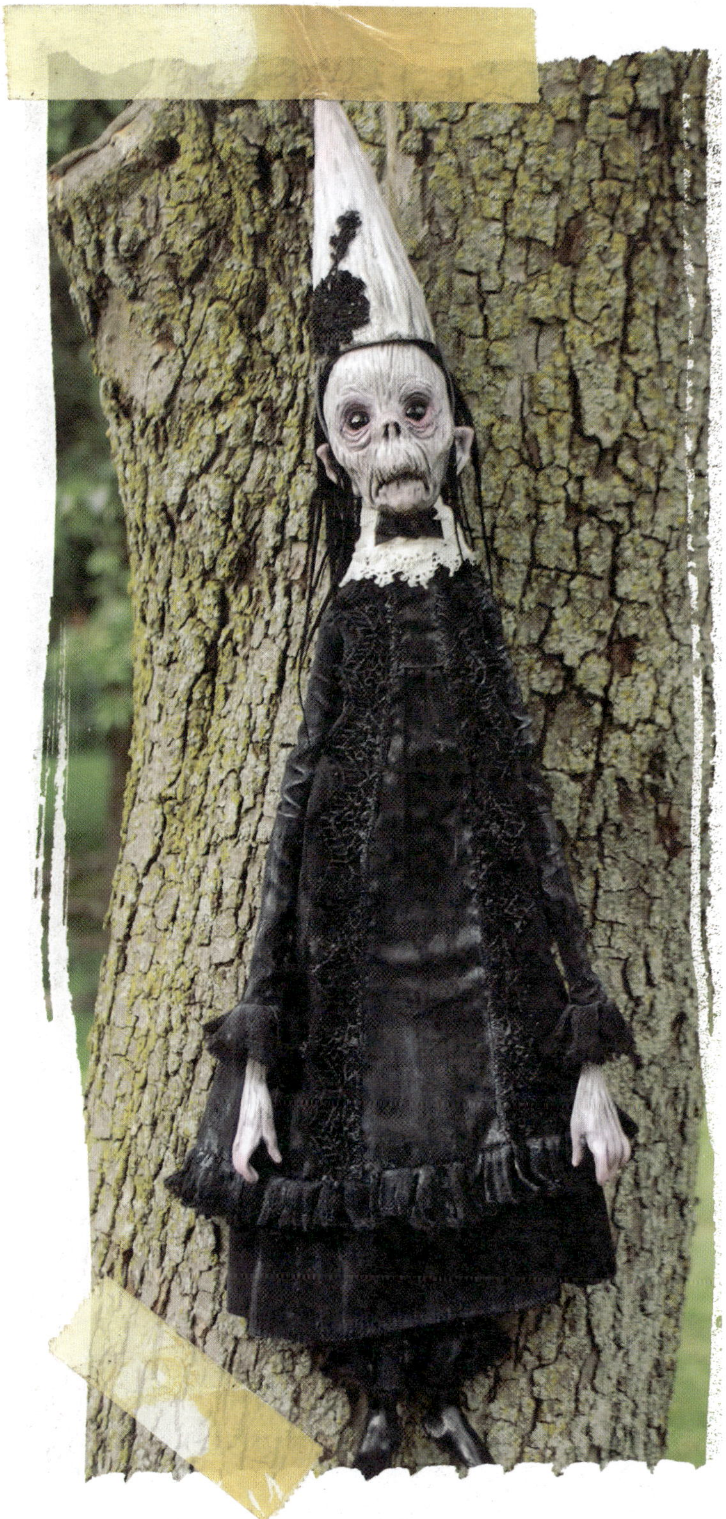

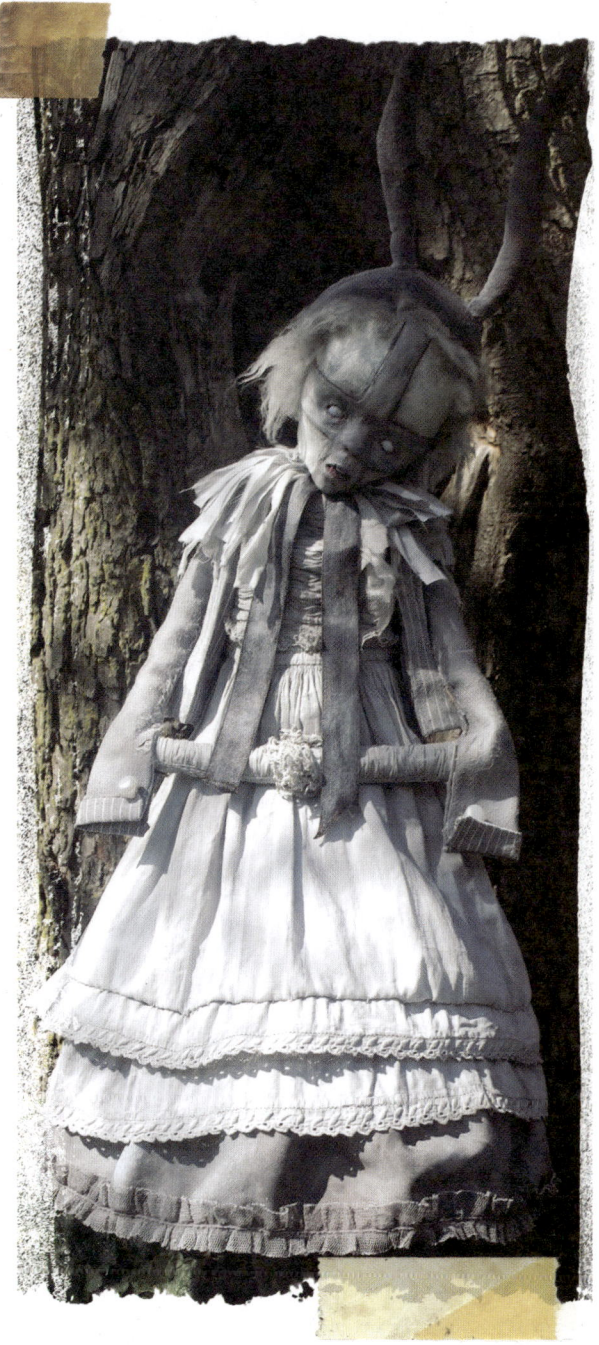

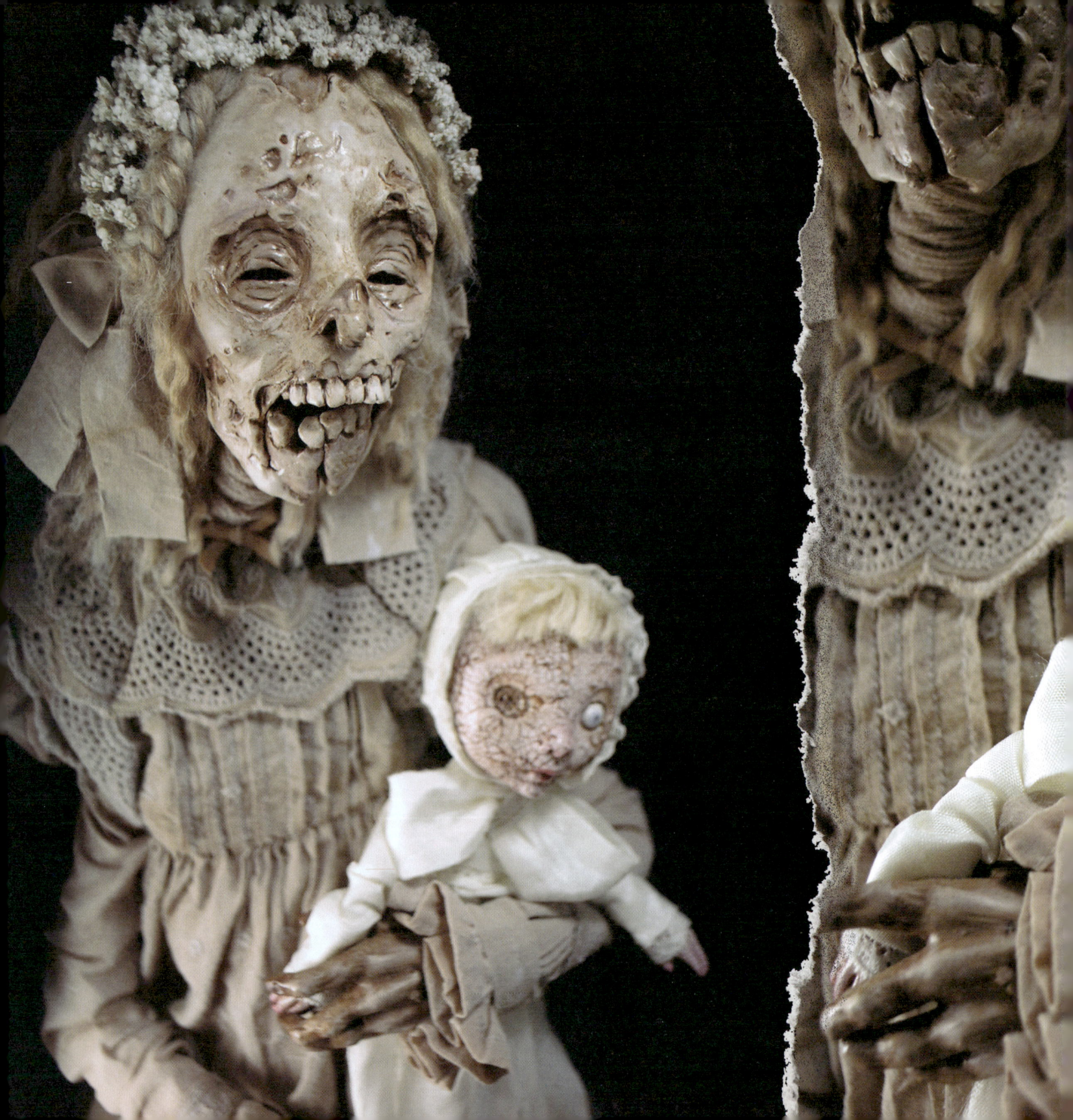

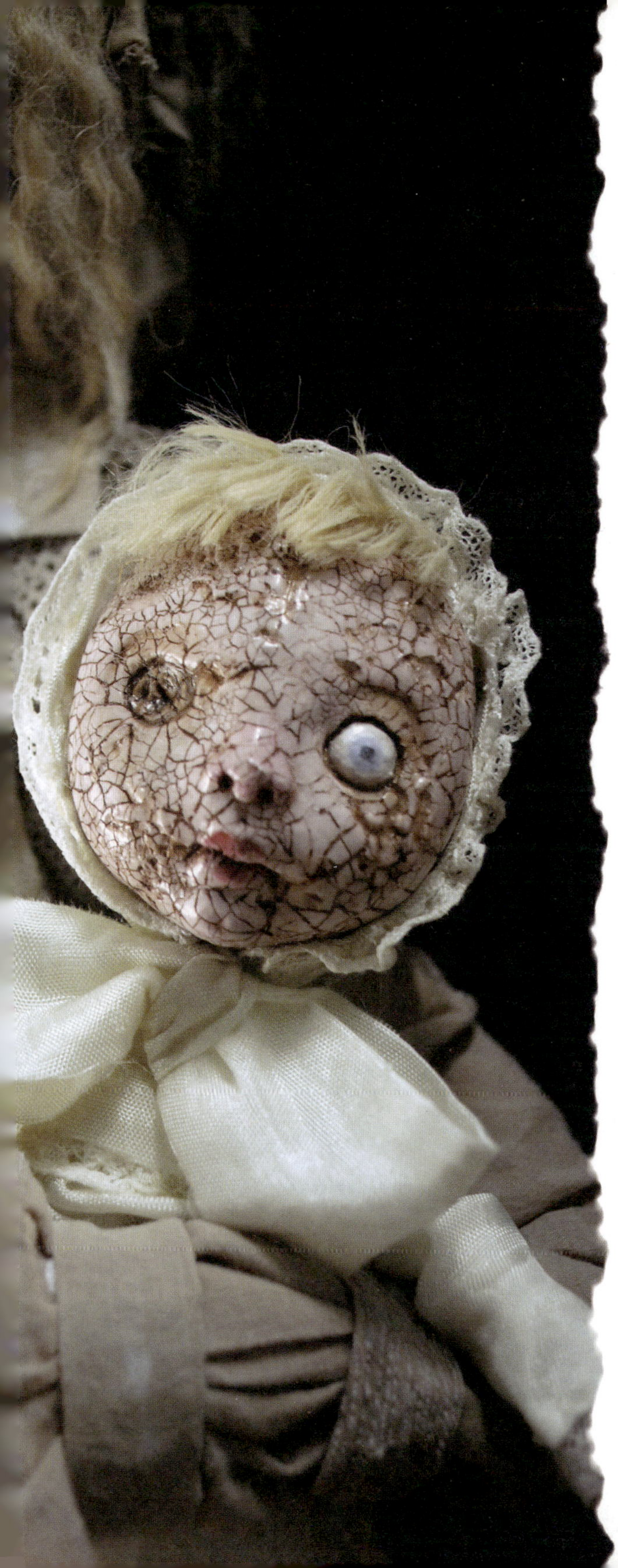

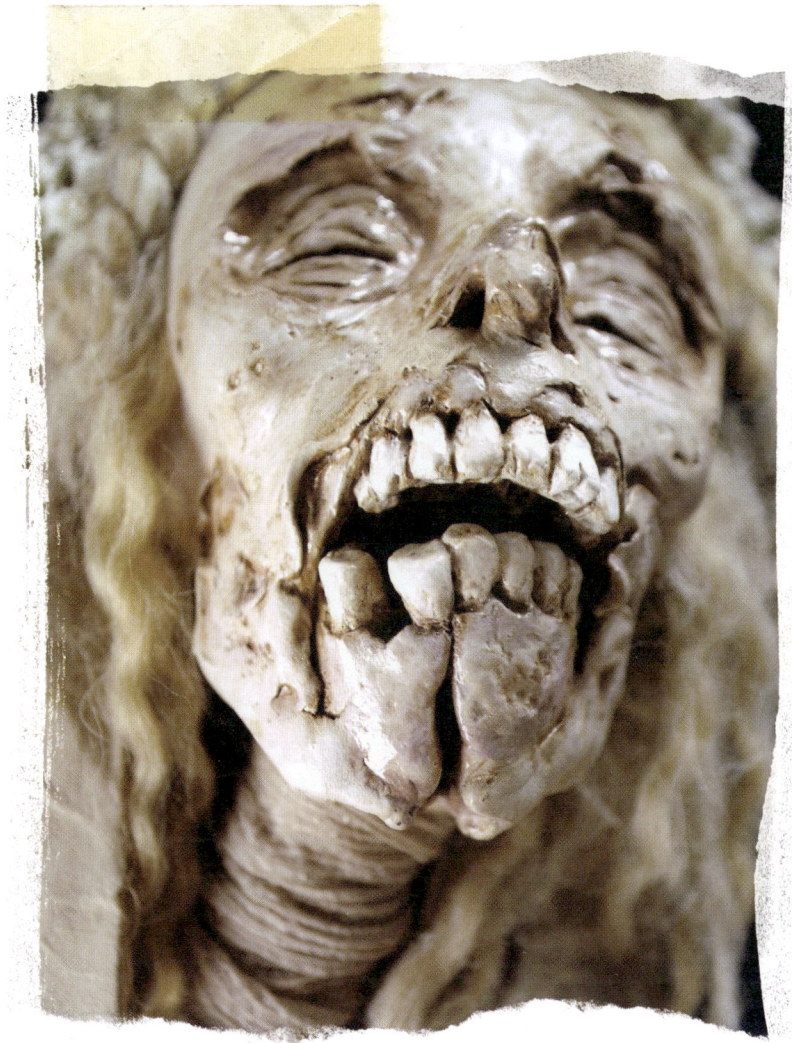

This is based on a mummified girl found in a crypt
in Krakow, Poland. She's holding her shattered doll. The story
of the original mummy was that she'd gotten married but was
killed by her family, poisoned, because the person she loved
wasn't high-class enough. So the father and mother and who
knows who else this girl had grown up with and trusted and
loved, they all just killed her rather than let her be married
and happy. Horrible stuff, and turning it into art releases it,
the horror of it. This is one of my last dolls, and probably one
of the best ones, technically.

This one is very small,
maybe four or five inches. This is
one of the few times I used glass
eyes because they didn't feel as
natural as painted ones to me even
as perfect as the glass eyes can look.
But for this little one I think it worked
out really well, makes her look like
a little demon.

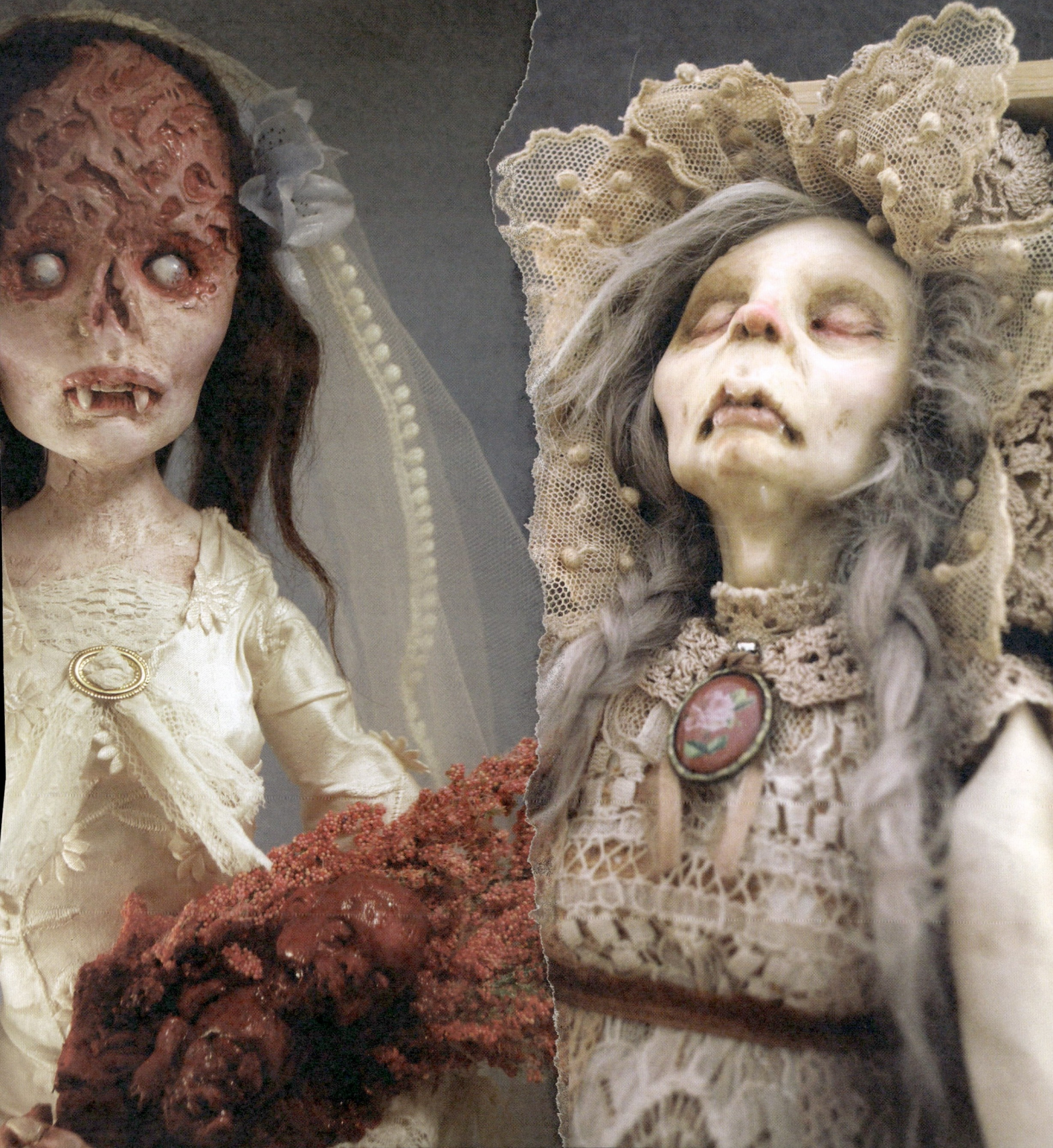

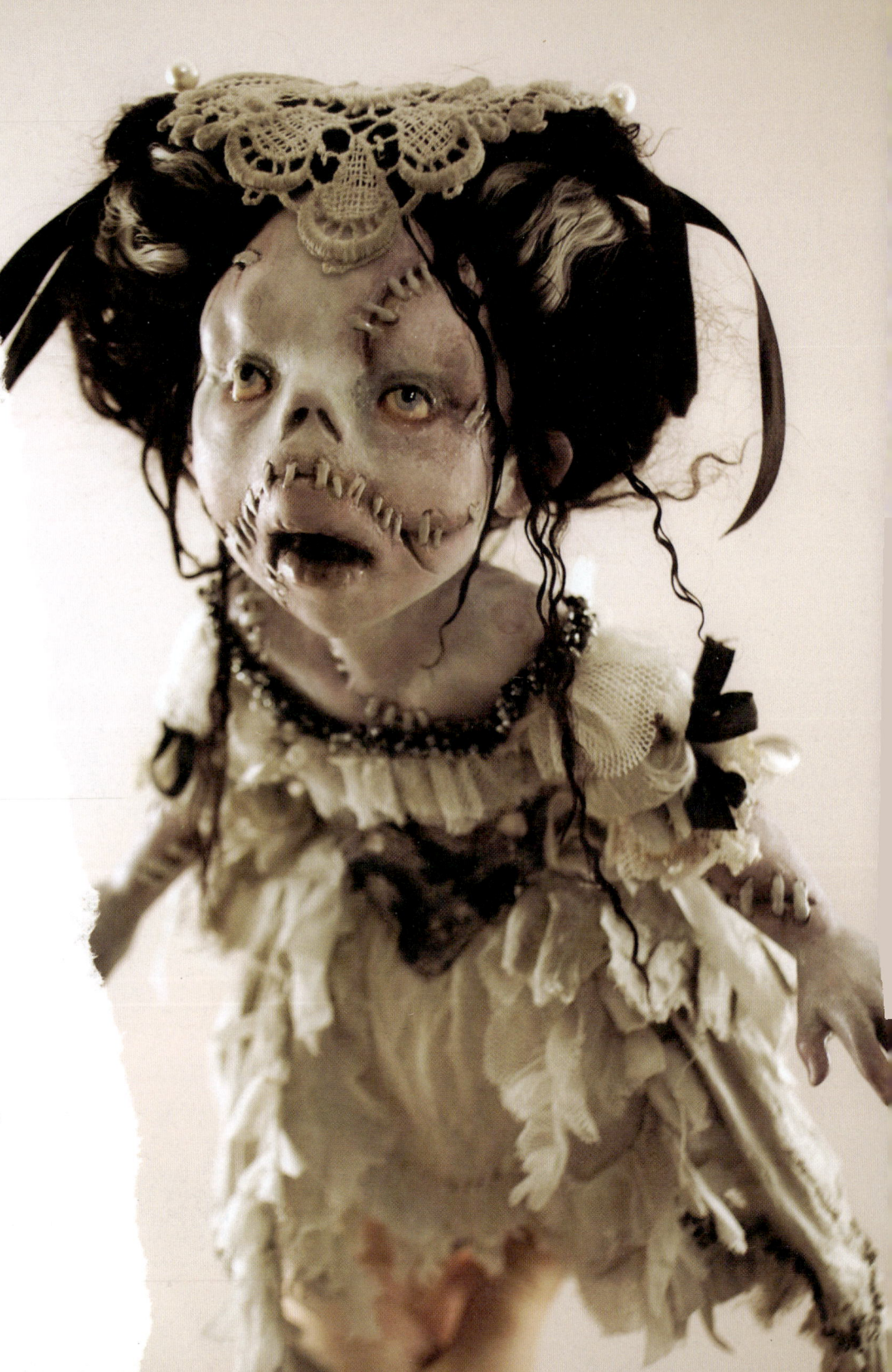

She's called "Child of Frankenstein,"
and again, she's one of my favourites.
She was so fun to make. I used all
these antique fabrics and silks, which
I had aged with tea and also sand
treated so that it would be more
delicate and wispier, and I had to be
incredibly careful. Her whole outfit was
so delicate that if ruffled the wrong
way, it would fall apart. I like that,
it's part of the experience. It was an
amazingly fun piece to make, and
I learned a lot from making her.

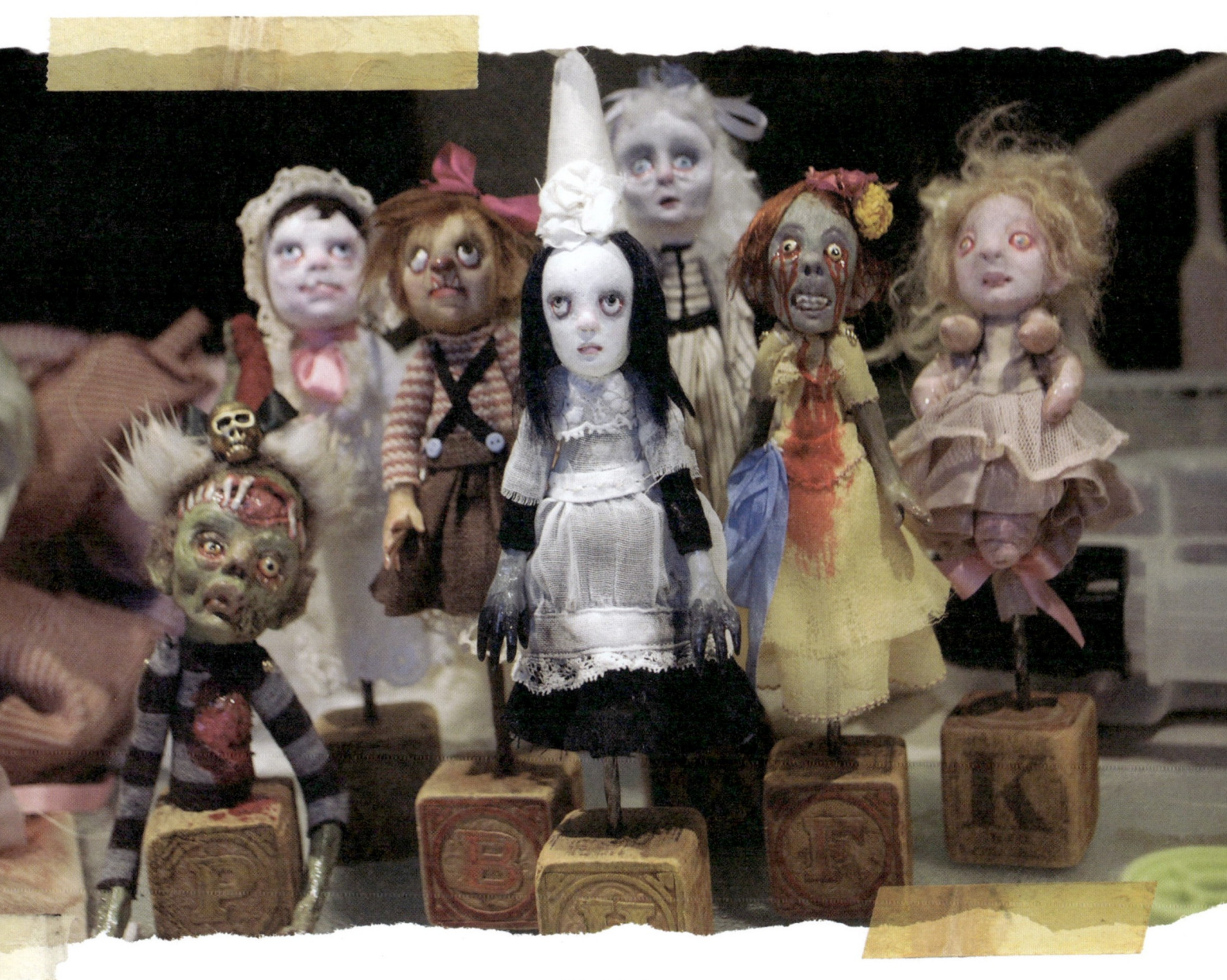

The End.

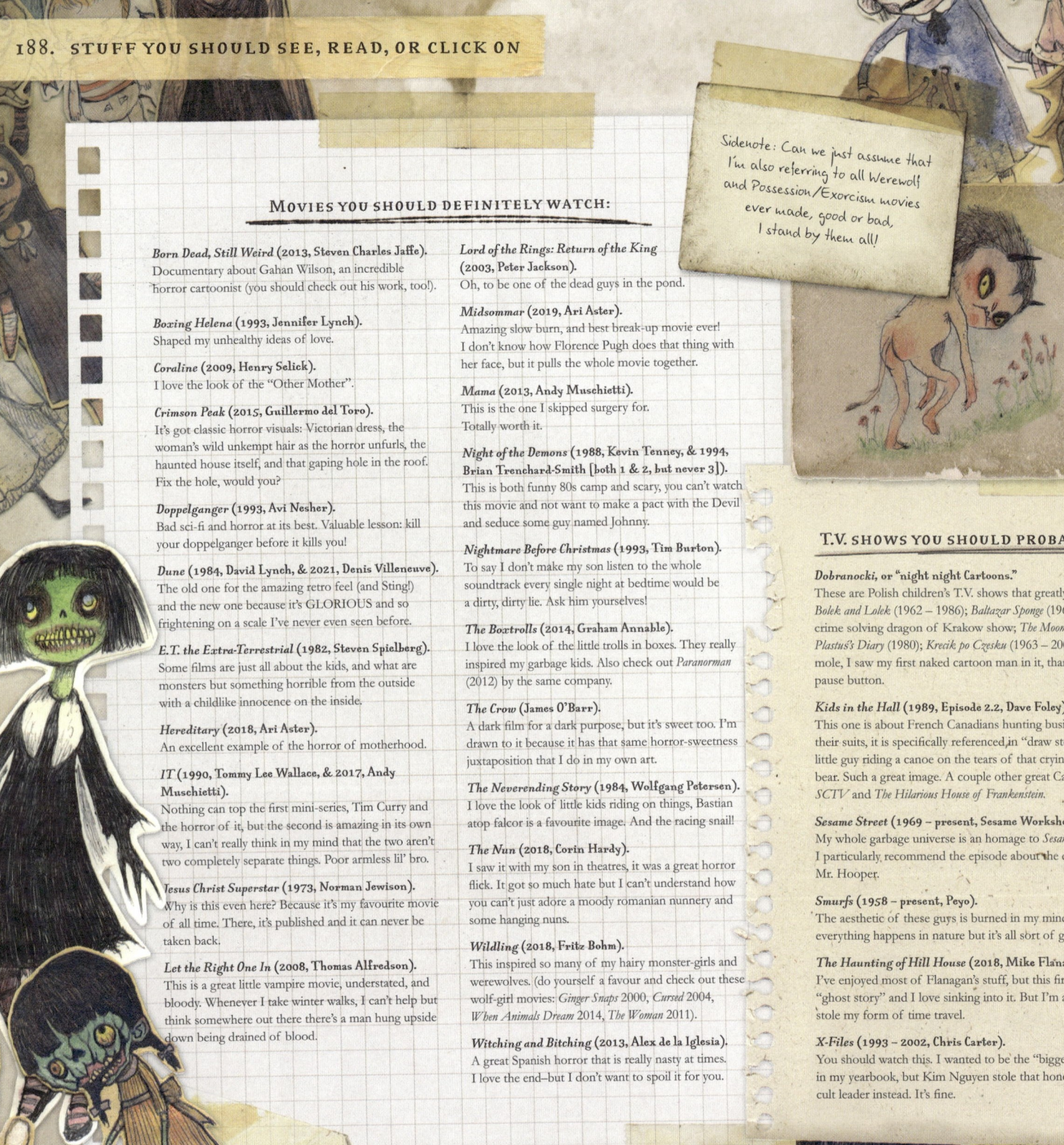

Sidenote: Can we just assume that I'm also referring to all Werewolf and Possession/Exorcism movies ever made, good or bad, I stand by them all!

MOVIES YOU SHOULD DEFINITELY WATCH:

Born Dead, Still Weird (2013, Steven Charles Jaffe).
Documentary about Gahan Wilson, an incredible horror cartoonist (you should check out his work, too!).

Boxing Helena (1993, Jennifer Lynch).
Shaped my unhealthy ideas of love.

Coraline (2009, Henry Selick).
I love the look of the "Other Mother".

Crimson Peak (2015, Guillermo del Toro).
It's got classic horror visuals: Victorian dress, the woman's wild unkempt hair as the horror unfurls, the haunted house itself, and that gaping hole in the roof. Fix the hole, would you?

Doppelganger (1993, Avi Nesher).
Bad sci-fi and horror at its best. Valuable lesson: kill your doppelganger before it kills you!

Dune (1984, David Lynch, & 2021, Denis Villeneuve).
The old one for the amazing retro feel (and Sting!) and the new one because it's GLORIOUS and so frightening on a scale I've never even seen before.

E.T. the Extra-Terrestrial (1982, Steven Spielberg).
Some films are just all about the kids, and what are monsters but something horrible from the outside with a childlike innocence on the inside.

Hereditary (2018, Ari Aster).
An excellent example of the horror of motherhood.

IT (1990, Tommy Lee Wallace, & 2017, Andy Muschietti).
Nothing can top the first mini-series, Tim Curry and the horror of it, but the second is amazing in its own way, I can't really think in my mind that the two aren't two completely separate things. Poor armless lil' bro.

Jesus Christ Superstar (1973, Norman Jewison).
Why is this even here? Because it's my favourite movie of all time. There, it's published and it can never be taken back.

Let the Right One In (2008, Thomas Alfredson).
This is a great little vampire movie, understated, and bloody. Whenever I take winter walks, I can't help but think somewhere out there there's a man hung upside down being drained of blood.

Lord of the Rings: Return of the King (2003, Peter Jackson).
Oh, to be one of the dead guys in the pond.

Midsommar (2019, Ari Aster).
Amazing slow burn, and best break-up movie ever! I don't know how Florence Pugh does that thing with her face, but it pulls the whole movie together.

Mama (2013, Andy Muschietti).
This is the one I skipped surgery for. Totally worth it.

Night of the Demons (1988, Kevin Tenney, & 1994, Brian Trenchard-Smith [both 1 & 2, but never 3]).
This is both funny 80s camp and scary, you can't watch this movie and not want to make a pact with the Devil and seduce some guy named Johnny.

Nightmare Before Christmas (1993, Tim Burton).
To say I don't make my son listen to the whole soundtrack every single night at bedtime would be a dirty, dirty lie. Ask him yourselves!

The Boxtrolls (2014, Graham Annable).
I love the look of the little trolls in boxes. They really inspired my garbage kids. Also check out *Paranorman* (2012) by the same company.

The Crow (James O'Barr).
A dark film for a dark purpose, but it's sweet too. I'm drawn to it because it has that same horror-sweetness juxtaposition that I do in my own art.

The Neverending Story (1984, Wolfgang Petersen).
I love the look of little kids riding on things, Bastian atop falcor is a favourite image. And the racing snail!

The Nun (2018, Corin Hardy).
I saw it with my son in theatres, it was a great horror flick. It got so much hate but I can't understand how you can't just adore a moody romanian nunnery and some hanging nuns.

Wildling (2018, Fritz Bohm).
This inspired so many of my hairy monster-girls and werewolves. (do yourself a favour and check out these wolf-girl movies: *Ginger Snaps* 2000, *Cursed* 2004, *When Animals Dream* 2014, *The Woman* 2011).

Witching and Bitching (2013, Alex de la Iglesia).
A great Spanish horror that is really nasty at times. I love the end—but I don't want to spoil it for you.

T.V. SHOWS YOU SHOULD PROBABLY KN

Dobranocki, or "night night Cartoons."
These are Polish children's T.V. shows that greatly inspired me *Bolek and Lolek* (1962 – 1986); *Baltazar Sponge* (1969 – 1970) crime solving dragon of Krakow show; *The Moomins* (1990); *Plastuś's Diary* (1980); *Krecik po Czesku* (1963 – 2002) a show a mole, I saw my first naked cartoon man in it, thank god for th pause button.

Kids in the Hall (1989, Episode 2.2, Dave Foley).
This one is about French Canadians hunting businessmen for their suits, it is specifically referenced in "draw stoopid" with little guy riding a canoe on the tears of that crying girl with th bear. Such a great image. A couple other great Canadian creat *SCTV* and *The Hilarious House of Frankenstein*.

Sesame Street (1969 – present, Sesame Workshop).
My whole garbage universe is an homage to *Sesame Street*. I particularly recommend the episode about the death of Mr. Hooper.

Smurfs (1958 – present, Peyo).
The aesthetic of these guys is burned in my mind, where everything happens in nature but it's all sort of grungy.

The Haunting of Hill House (2018, Mike Flanagan).
I've enjoyed most of Flanagan's stuff, but this first series is a "ghost story" and I love sinking into it. But I'm a little salty t stole my form of time travel.

X-Files (1993 – 2002, Chris Carter).
You should watch this. I wanted to be the "biggest *X-Files* fa in my yearbook, but Kim Nguyen stole that honour. I was vo cult leader instead. It's fine.

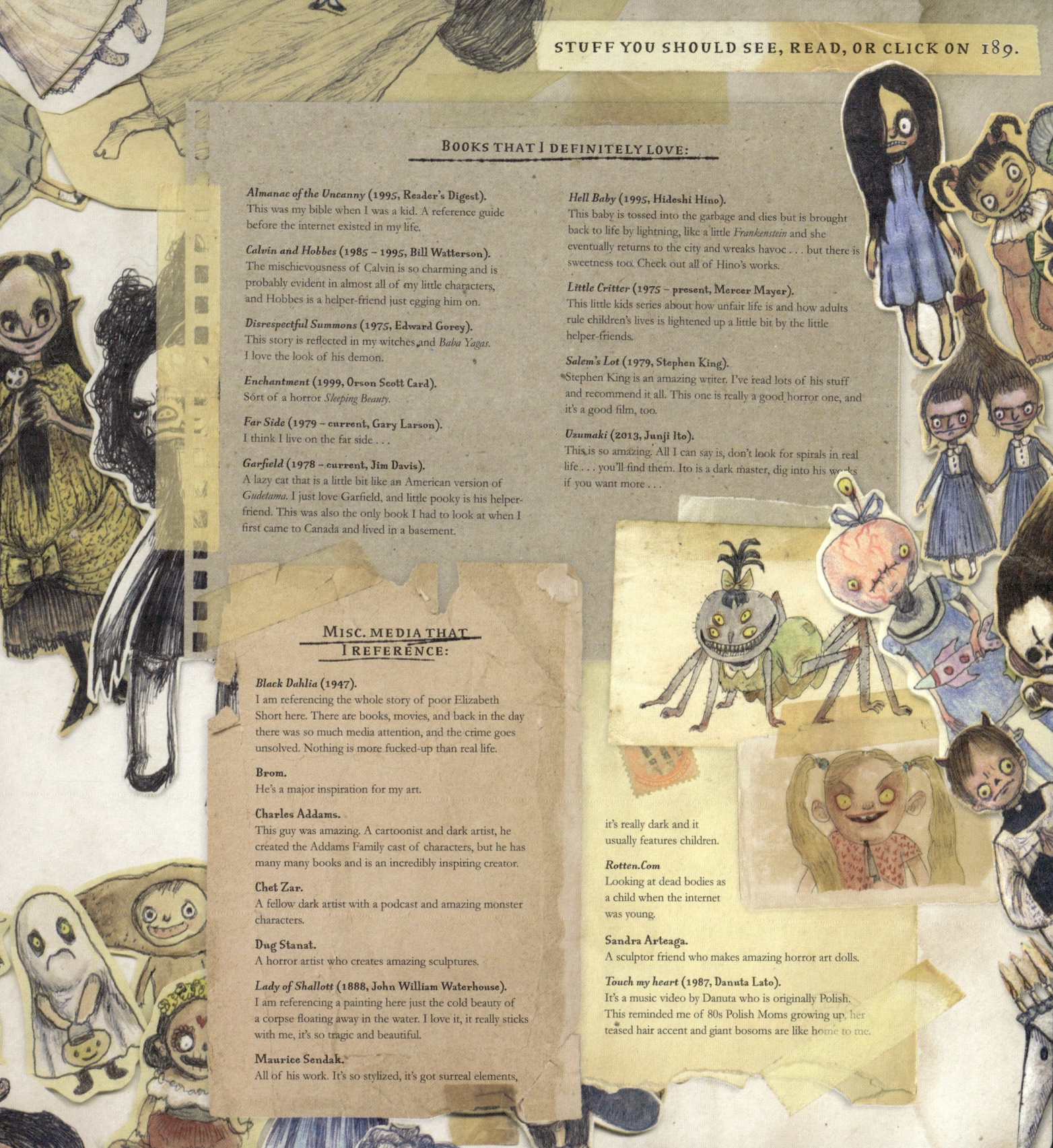

BOOKS THAT I DEFINITELY LOVE:

Almanac of the Uncanny (1995, Reader's Digest).
This was my bible when I was a kid. A reference guide before the internet existed in my life.

Calvin and Hobbes (1985 – 1995, Bill Watterson).
The mischievousness of Calvin is so charming and is probably evident in almost all of my little characters, and Hobbes is a helper-friend just egging him on.

Disrespectful Summons (1975, Edward Gorey).
This story is reflected in my witches and *Baba Yagas*. I love the look of his demon.

Enchantment (1999, Orson Scott Card).
Sort of a horror *Sleeping Beauty*.

Far Side (1979 – current, Gary Larson).
I think I live on the far side . . .

Garfield (1978 – current, Jim Davis).
A lazy cat that is a little bit like an American version of *Gudetama*. I just love Garfield, and little pooky is his helper-friend. This was also the only book I had to look at when I first came to Canada and lived in a basement.

Hell Baby (1995, Hideshi Hino).
This baby is tossed into the garbage and dies but is brought back to life by lightning, like a little *Frankenstein* and she eventually returns to the city and wreaks havoc . . . but there is sweetness too. Check out all of Hino's works.

Little Critter (1975 – present, Mercer Mayer).
This little kids series about how unfair life is and how adults rule children's lives is lightened up a little bit by the little helper-friends.

Salem's Lot (1979, Stephen King).
Stephen King is an amazing writer. I've read lots of his stuff and recommend it all. This one is really a good horror one, and it's a good film, too.

Uzumaki (2013, Junji Ito).
This is so amazing. All I can say is, don't look for spirals in real life . . . you'll find them. Ito is a dark master, dig into his works if you want more . . .

MISC. MEDIA THAT I REFERENCE:

Black Dahlia (1947).
I am referencing the whole story of poor Elizabeth Short here. There are books, movies, and back in the day there was so much media attention, and the crime goes unsolved. Nothing is more fucked-up than real life.

Brom.
He's a major inspiration for my art.

Charles Addams.
This guy was amazing. A cartoonist and dark artist, he created the Addams Family cast of characters, but he has many many books and is an incredibly inspiring creator.

Chet Zar.
A fellow dark artist with a podcast and amazing monster characters.

Dug Stanat.
A horror artist who creates amazing sculptures.

Lady of Shallott (1888, John William Waterhouse).
I am referencing a painting here just the cold beauty of a corpse floating away in the water. I love it, it really sticks with me, it's so tragic and beautiful.

Maurice Sendak.
All of his work. It's so stylized, it's got surreal elements, it's really dark and it usually features children.

Rotten.Com
Looking at dead bodies as a child when the internet was young.

Sandra Arteaga.
A sculptor friend who makes amazing horror art dolls.

Touch my heart (1987, Danuta Lato).
It's a music video by Danuta who is originally Polish. This reminded me of 80s Polish Moms growing up, her teased hair accent and giant bosoms are like home to me.

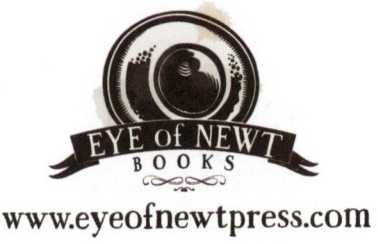

www.eyeofnewtpress.com

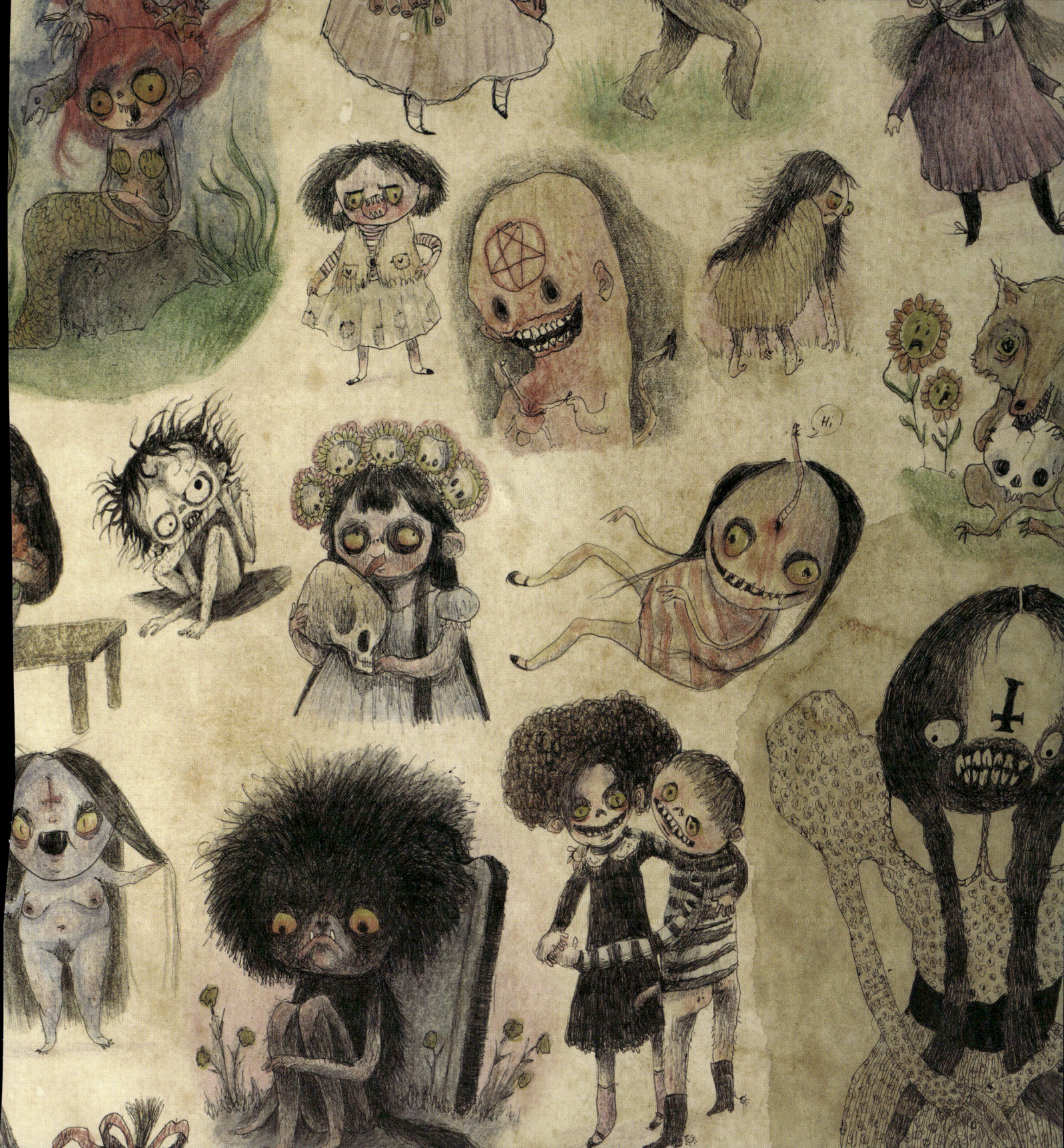

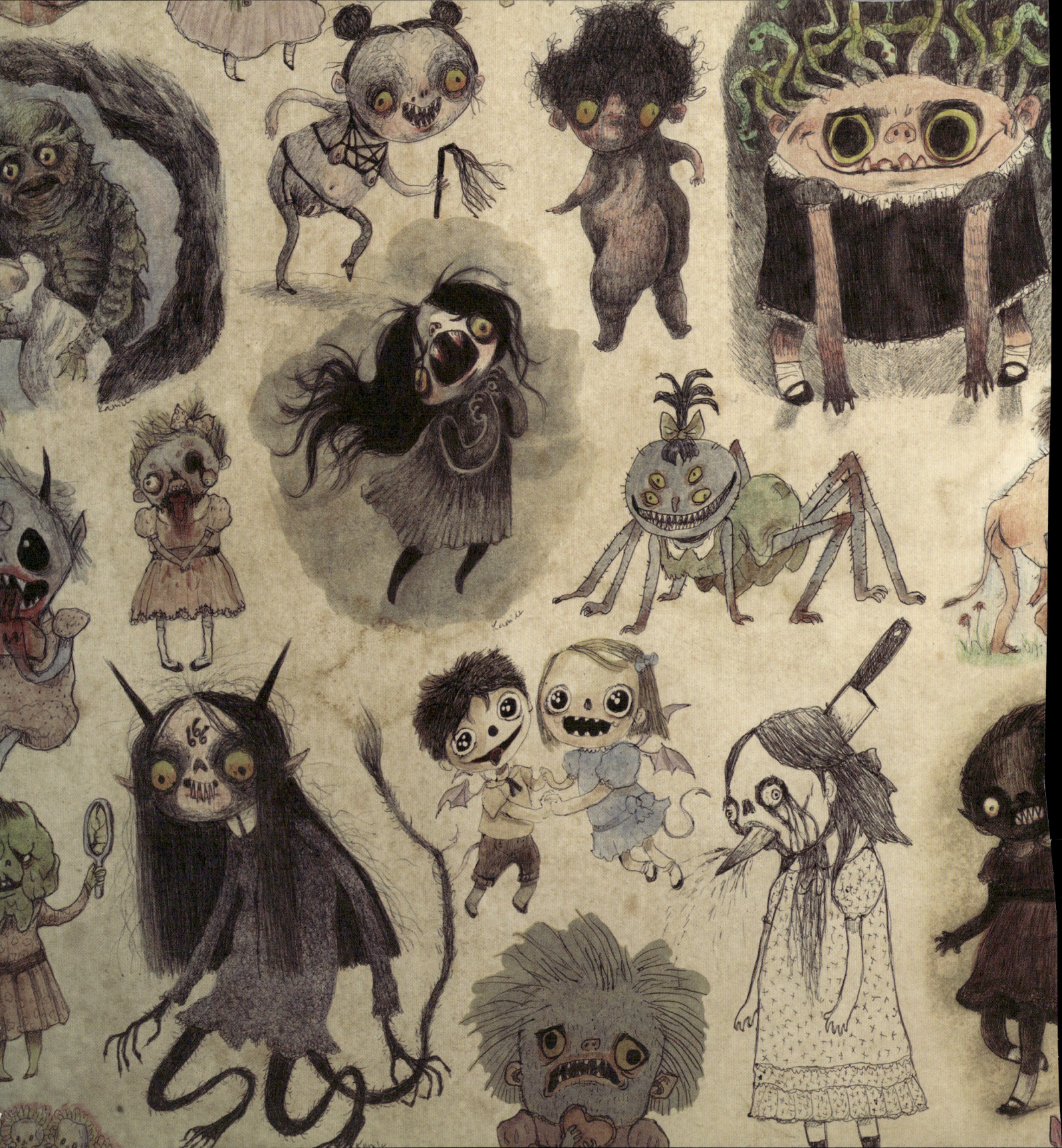